Alternative Educational Systems

Edward Ignas
DePaul University School of Education, and
Human Resources Center for Research, Education and Training,
University of Chicago

Raymond J. Corsini
Adjunct Professor, University of Hawaii

F. E. PEACOCK PUBLISHERS, INC.
ITASCA, ILLINOIS 60143

CONTENTS

Foreword

The word "alternative," when applied to schools and educational systems, has a wide range of meanings. Most commonly, perhaps, it means a break with an array of practices perceived to characterize bureaucratized state and national systems of schooling. These practices grew up not necessarily because they are sound educationally but because they make possible some minimum essentials of learning for large numbers of students in reasonably orderly, efficient ways. In recent years, the word sometimes has been used to convey not a departure from the traditional but a return to it—from new ways of schooling perceived to be overly progressive or innovative.

In general, the authors of what follows seek to describe a genuine alternative to conventional schooling. For the most part, however, they are less concerned with the concept of "alternative" than they are with a set of concepts to guide practice at each decision-making point. School practice involves decisions about subject matter, grouping, instruction, materials, inter-personal relations, and so forth, regardless of one's philosophical position. Each of these matters is a commonplace of schooling. If each commonplace is approached from three different philosophical perspectives and results in three different sets of decisions about a series of commonplaces, three alternative systems of schooling emerge. In subsequent chapters, the authors come with differing perspectives and come out with differing systems.

I refrain from the temptation of analyzing and comparing the alternatives presented. This is the reader's task and opportunity, made particularly challenging by the fact that the authors, while addressing some of the same commonplaces, do not address a common set. I have chosen, instead, to examine the idea of alternatives in education and schooling.

At the adult level, our educational system abounds with alternatives made available by university extension, community college "outreach" programs, dozens of specialized "schools," job-oriented improvement classes, and television (particularly with the advent of videotapes). How far we should go with the development of options for children and youth depends in large part on our conceptions of education and the role, if any, of the common school. My views of both lead me to the conclusion that whatever can be convincingly justified under the rubric "alternative" belongs in the education of the young and the common school.

This is not the place to define education and to argue the role of the common school. I have done both elsewhere.* But a brief exposition is desirable. Education is a relatively sustained process through which one's understandings, skills, values and sensibilities are refined and developed. It is not just a process of attaining social, vocational, and personal goals. Education is more a process of growth through which one perceives new possibilities and sets goals which would not have been perceived before. If schools have any purpose, surely it is to assure such growth experiences.

What bothers me about almost all the rhetoric surrounding alternative *schools* is the appeal to some special interest or talent of the young or of some concentration—on the arts, a vocational pursuit, or a method of instruction. This may be the sort of thing *all* children and youth should be able to select from—perhaps with a handful of vouchers to assure satisfaction of personal interests far beyond what schools can provide. But it is not the kind of education likely to stimulate interest in *alternative* subject matter, modes of thought, and personal possibilities. What is labeled "alternative" may be even more limiting than the traditional schooling for which new ways are supposed to be a desirable substitute. The education most likely to prepare for and lead to alternatives carries an old label; it is *liberal* education.

One of the most useful examples of non-liberal education is that alternative schooling seeking to go back from perceived modern excesses (largely non-events, however). The only stated educational goal pertains to the basic skills and the methods are more training than educational. The other goals have more to do with adherence to rules and strict obedience to teachers and parents. Grade standards for promotion are sharply observed; the methods of instruction are limited in variety; students play a relatively passive role.

The problem with such education is its alternative character— alternative to what we know about learning and education as a growth process. Unfortunately, other alternatives, however enticing their descriptive language and however different from the one just sum- marized, can be almost equally limiting. Consequently, I can get more excited about common schools in which all students pursue an array of defensible alternatives than I can about schools offering *an* alternative.

What is particularly interesting to me about most of what follows is that the authors propose not schools specializing in an alternative mode or subject-orientation but entire *systems* of schooling within which most commonplaces are perceived and acted upon differently than in what they perceive to the traditional system. (The book would be more correctly entitled *Alternative Systems of Schooling,* since only a very few chapters—notably the concluding one—take us beyond schools.) The common emphases in most are for a more active role for the individual in his or her education and greater assurance that development of individual potential will be uppermost in the process. Psychotherapeutic and behavioristic approaches could be (and many times are) argued as complete systems but I would prefer to argue for them as part of a comprehensive educational system providing experience with several modes of learning and developing.

We appear to be at a time when support for the public, common school is at a low ebb. Many reformers have given up on it. The present system is in danger of being replaced by a comprehensive voucher system designed in part to encourage alternative schools. Consequently, a voucher plan would be likely to gain support from a strange assortment of groups: those who think it will cost less, those who simply want to dismantle the present system, those who think education should be largely in the hands of parents, some of those who think that an exciting era of experimentation leading to better schools for all would be ushered in. There is little likelihood that all of these interests would be satisfied simultaneously; I doubt that any one would be satisfied adequately.

Nonetheless, the public, common system of schooling seems unable to change its traditional ways rapidly enough to prevent its own demise. The infusion of alternative ways of doing what schools traditionally have tried to do and what new knowledge and a global age now suggest they do is imperative. If we did not have a system of schooling, I believe it would be necessary to create one. Would it be a system of relatively discrete alternatives; one of those described in subsequent chapters; some combination of several; or selected elements from most? What I hope it would not be is a government-regulated collection of alternative schools, each catering to the special interests of the parent-clients providing for its support. How best to provide simultaneously for both the general education and special educational interests of all children and youth is one of the most important and difficult challenges facing our society. We must approach it more seriously and with greater understanding of its complexity than we have done in the past. How much of what follows describes the shape and substance of what is likely to come—or, better, what we would like to see come?

John I. Goodlad
University of California, Los Angeles
        and
Institute for Development of
Educational Activities, Inc.

*John I. Goodlad, *What Schools Are For*. Bloomington, Indiana: Phi Delta Kappa Educational Foundation, 1979.

Preface

This book is presented as a survey of modern educational thinking. The first chapter, which reviews the components of the traditional educational system in the United States, provides a summary of past developments. Chapters 2 through 9 describe ten different alternative school systems currently in use. The final chapter considers factors that will have impact in the evolution of educational systems.

This survey is intended to provide educators, especially those preparing the teachers of the future, with a broad overview of:

—the success and failures of past and current sytems;

—the theoretical bases for various alternative systems of education;

—descriptions of how these alternative systems are implemented;

—a comprehensive view of the major challenges which face educators of today in the future.

No one engaged in education today is unaware of the difficulty of the educational task. Scholars and philosophers have long struggled to clarify what is meant by education, what its goals are, and upon what theoretical foundations it may best be accomplished.

Concurrent with these theoretical issues are very concrete challenges facing the teacher, parent, administrator and all who take responsibility for the educational process. The growing complexities of the modern world add up to an awesome tally of strikes against our schools: economics, politics, ethics, commerce, science—every aspect of human enterprise today seems to add to the burdens of the school systems. Commonplace issues such as inflation, changing racial patterns, the evolving needs of business and labor, changes in the moral tone of our culture, and various combinations of public ire and/or public apathy all affect what happens in our classrooms which in turn affects society once again.

In a spirit of ongoing inquiry and experimentation and sometimes in hot debates, various educators naturally question the traditional approaches to education, and challenge both its philosophical base and its results.

There have been a variety of approaches to this critical process, approaches that generally fall into two categories: diagnostic—describing what is wrong—and curative—prescribing what to do about it. The diagnostic approaches generally conclude that much is wrong with the system of education itself. This means there are serious disorders in the formal relationships between four classes of people: school administrators (principals and their staffs), faculty (teachers, counselors, etc.), children and parents.

The diagnostic approaches tend to question many features of our traditional educational system, such as grades, homework, compulsory education, etc., which many people in the field of education assume to be natural and normal, and which most parents accept as part of how education operates.

Taking the second, the curative approach, involves not only questioning present practices, but developing alternatives. This book serves as a forum for the examination of a number of alternative systems. Each of these approaches is based on some theoretical model of humans and of society, sometimes made implicitly and sometimes explicitly. Each of these alternative systems is also essentially critical of the present system and has proposed itself as an alternative to the current one.

In selecting alternative systems for inclusion, we were guided by a number of principles. First, we wanted to avoid, if possible, systems that were more-or-less identical. Consequently, the contents of this book consist of different approaches based on different theories and concepts. Second, we wanted to pay due attention to well-established and successful systems, such as the Montessori system and Individualized Guided Education, and so we have included them. Third, we were concerned with systems based on well-established psychological schools of thought and have included five points of view: Behavior Modification, Individual Psychology, Rational-Emotive Theory, Reality Theory and Person-Centered Theory. Fourth, we wanted to give the reader exposure to several somewhat different and unusual systems such as Education by Appointment.

Our general purpose is to alert those in education, especially the faculty of schools of education, to the strong and developing movement towards the reform of education. While each proponent of an alternative essentially says, "My system is best" and suggests its adoption, the perceptive reader should be able to extract from the contents of this book a variety of ideas that the alternative systems have in common.

Our aim, of course, is to contribute to the ongoing process of innovation by presenting what is the best thinking in this field and providing the information in a convenient manner. To this end, we have asked the various authors to prepare their chapters—except for the first and last chapters—according to a uniform plan. Every one of our substantive chapters follows the same outline. This means that the reader who is concerned with comparisons between the systems can read this book "horizontally" rather than in the usual chapter-by-chapter approach. That is to say, one can read "across" from section to section. This process, used in two other books so far, has proved to be quite useful as a learning device. We would recommend for those seriously interested in educational innovations to read the book first in the traditional fashion, and then read various sections "across" the book.

We, the editors, have had considerable cooperation from many individuals in a wide variety of ways.

First, we wish to gratefully acknowledge our wives, Helen and Kleo, who were supportive and tolerant of the hours and days we spent on this project, which took much more time and energy than had been anticipated.

Next, we wish to acknowledge the following individuals who were most helpful and supportive. Listing them alphabetically, they are: Robert K. Burns, Rita A. Cashman, Don Dinkmeyer, Austin Flynn, Robert R. Freeman, George M. Gazda, Wallace G. Lonergan, John and Dorothy Mendoza, Paul F. Munger, Edmund R. Parpart, Jennette S. Rader, Robert E. Saltmarsh, Dan N. Simon, Edgar E. Swanson, Pearline Thigpen, Thomas E. Van Dam, and William O. Webb.

We also wish to thank Thomas R. LaMarre of the F. E. Peacock Publishers, Inc., who was most gracious and helpful in a number of ways.

Finally, our thanks and appreciation are extended above all to the authors of the chapters, all busy professionals involved with their own affairs, who were willing not only to write chapters, but to follow a highly restrictive format, and who graciously accepted our editorial suggestions.

Edward Ignas
Raymond J. Corsini

CHAPTER 1

Introduction

EDWARD IGNAS

The creation of new educational systems is an endless process. Throughout the history of civilization, new concepts and new practices have appeared, had their day or their year or their century, and then have disappeared. There is almost a Darwinian struggle when an old educational system no longer seems to meet the needs of individuals or groups or societies, grand battles take place, the defenders of the traditional system struggling to keep the old system alive, and the modernists or revisionists or radicals attempting to displace it with a new policy or procedure. And, when the new system succeeds, it too has its day, and then eventually it, too, is superseded.

Modern educational philosophy and theory can be probably best considered beginning with the early 16th century, when John Colet started the first public school, St. Paul's Grammar School, in 1510. His contemporary, Thomas More, in his famous *Utopia*, published in 1516, argued for a total school that would combine social, political and educational aspects. In Germany, Martin Luther, not content with only reforming the church, also attempted to reform education, wishing to establish universal schooling financed by the citizenry. In 1500 he published a paper with the intriguing title, "Discourse on the duty of sending children to school." Among other sixteenth century educational reformers were Philip Melanchthon, who developed a new secondary school system, Johannes Sturm who developed a very strict and formalistic school system devoted to training children through the classics, and Valentin Friedland, who took exactly the opposite tack, attempting to make schools happy places.

The sixteenth century reforms in education may have contributed to the end of the Renaissance, in that the seventeenth century saw the beginning of a period of enlightenment, with schools being made more available, books becoming more popular and the middle classes of society receiving formal education. The notion that the world could be improved through education grew; and political concepts of equality began to surface. Science began to develop and the old concepts of the Middle Ages began to lose their importance. But the greater reforms waited for the 18th century, with emphasis on teaching in languages other than Latin, an emphasis on science instead of the old classical curriculum, and variations in teaching methods.

Even during the early period of formal mass education there were a variety of theories to which we can barely allude here: some thought of children as needing a great deal of discipline (read punishment) and others saw children as requiring the opening of their minds through gentle instruction. There were debates about the importance of education to maintain the welfare of the state, or the importance of education as a means of maintaining morality, of advancing science for the love of learning, of developing the total individual, and so on. Even today there are constant differences among educational reformers relative to the true purpose of education—whether it be to learn the basics, or become disciplined, to seek truth, to develop the self, and so on.

But whatever the objectives, the various educational innovators disagreed with one another on how to achieve the objectives, even when they agreed on the same objectives; and naturally, if they disagreed over objectives, they argued all the more over how to achieve them.

The Twentieth Century

At the present time the traditional educational system has been in effect in this country for about two hundred years. Below are some of the general features of this system:

—Children attend schools up to legal age.
—Children attend schools in their geographic area.
—Children assigned to classes in terms of their ages.
—Children under the hegemony of a teacher assigned to the class.
—Children not to leave classes without permission.
—Content of learning is mostly "academic" based on words, spoken and read.
—Children assigned homework and out-of-school projects.
—Misbehavior punished.
—Success measured mostly by remembering material read and spoken.
—Report cards sent to parents.
—Parent-teacher conferences.
—Honors given to students who do well academically.
—A pre-established curriculum presented to all in a rigid sequence.

—Evaluations mostly subjective: teachers' opinions.

As can be imagined, innumerable minor variations of the so-called traditional system have been made by principals and teachers. Some major modifications were also attempted, but none succeeded. Three that took place this century were:

1. *The Dalton Plan*

This system developed principally by Helen Parkhurst in Dalton, Massachusetts was a reaction to the conventional system which paid no attention to individual variables in learning. The curriculum was divided into monthly segments. A pupil could not start a module until he finished a prior one. Children were to set their own work schedules. This system had a number of "contracts" between children and their advisers. The concept of contracts and units still exists.

2. *The Winnetka Plan*

Developed by Carleton Washbourne, a school principal in Illinois, pupils were directed to goals. It was up to the child to achieve the goal, such as "write a friendly letter." After the child felt that he was ready, he was asked to take a test to see if he had, indeed, achieved his goal: if so, then he went on to a new "goal."

3. *The Gary Plan*

This system was more ambitious in intent than the prior two, in that it represented an attempt at a totalistic education in which children learned to play, to socialize, to study and to work. Developed by William A. Wirt the school ranged from kindergarten through high school, and consisted of a complex of buildings in which a wide variety of activities took place 12 months a year.

None of these three systems found general favor, and were steamrollered out of existence by the traditional system.

THE TRADITIONAL SYSTEM

In view of the unsuccessful attack of alternative systems and the hardihood of the traditional educational system, the latter might appear to be viable and essentially a good system. However, this does not appear to be the case at all. Almost without exception, educational theorists and practical students of education have condemned the present traditional system as ineffective and inefficient. It just does not do what it is supposed to and it is very expensive; this is the common conclusion of such individuals as James Conant (1977), Rudolf Dreikurs (1957), John Holt (1964), Nathaniel Hentoff (1967), Ivan Illich (1970), R. D. Laing (1969), Hyman

Rickover (1963), T. W. Schultz (1963) and Charles Silberman (1970)—to name only a few who have written strictures against the educational system found in almost every public elementary and high school today.

Indeed, the current educational system finds almost no defenders in print. Nevertheless, as we have seen, it has fended off all sorts of rivals, and maintains itself despite criticisms by those experts on education and by criticisms of the press, parents, students, teachers, principals and superintendents. To understand why this should be so may be of some interest and value, especially in terms of the general purpose of this book: to improve education; and in terms of the more specific purpose of this book to make known a variety of educational systems that compete with the traditional system.

Resistance to Change

In psychotherapy, this phenomenon is well known. People who come voluntarily for psychotherapy nevertheless do all sorts of things to prevent changing. These various escape methods are known generally as "resistance." People do not want to change even when they say they do, and even when they pay to have some one help them change. Probably much the same is true in education: the very people who are unhappy about the schools are those who keep the present system in force, sometimes even preventing experimentation with model, alternative schools. It may be worthwhile attempting to understand this paradoxical situation.

The reader

The typical reader of this book is most likely a forward-looking, openminded, concerned student of education, whether he or she is a university student preparing for an educational career, a teacher interested in the latest developments, a principal eager to have a better school and put into it features of proven value, or a superintendent looking for an innovative school system to establish in his territory. Nevertheless, as shall be shown, it is entirely possible that these very people will be opposed to educational innovations, even though it may be quite obvious to them that the present school system is terrible and needs fundamental change.

The resistance to alternative schools probably comes out of a deep sense of loyalty to the educational system one has suffered in. This paradoxical statement is the heart of a concept in psychology known as *cognitive dissonance.* We love what we suffer for. Therefore, one reason why some readers may have an almost visceral reaction against educational experimentation is this irrational loyalty.

A second important reason for resistance has to do with the probable fact that the typical reader is a success in the present system. The reader most likely enjoys being educated and educating others. If the present system has provided you with an education and the chance to educate others, you may be expected to feel loyalty and gratitude to that system, and perhaps even to have feelings of superiority over the others who didn't "make it."

As Vernon Smith discusses in the next chapter, about one-third of all students are successful in the schools as they are. This one-third tends to be the best educated, the most advanced, the leaders, and because of these factors, they tend to be cautious and suspicious of anything different. Maybe in another type of school they might not have done so well!

In any event, one—probably major—reason for resistance has to do with the attitudes of earnest, progressive, well-meaning educators who deep down have affection and loyalty to the system. This writer has some experience in introducing new educational systems in school districts, and has found that even when the school board, the superintendent and the principal decide on a radical educational change, and operate with volunteer faculty who have been briefed on the new system, the faculty frequently operates as though guilty of disloyalty to the old system, showing a variety of behaviors such as anxiety, insecurity, feelings of estrangement from other teachers who are still using the old system, etc.

The point here is that even when cognitively all are satisfied that the traditional system is not working and some other system seems to be more desirable; when changes are actually made, frequently the faculty and others concerned with the school suffer some degree of emotional stress, which in turn may make returning to the traditional system more comfortable.

THE CHANGE PROCESS

Nothing, according to the Greek philosopher Heraclitus, ever remains constant: everything is in perpetual flux. This is true of schools. They change constantly, sometimes slowly, evolving various forms, and sometimes rapidly, changing drastically. Since this book which discusses a variety of educational systems is concerned with the possible movement of schools from the traditional system to other systems, the general change process should be discussed.

There are two opposing tendencies in people, within them and between them, relative to any particular educational system. On the one hand there is a general desire to remain constant, faithful to tradition; and on the other hand there is a desire to change and experiment, to try something new. Now, to introduce a new system generally calls for the combined approval of all parties, since if even one party to the system objects, the likelihood is that no change will take place. Parties include the school board, the superintendent, the principals, the faculty, and the parents. If one or more parties want a change in a particular direction, they are likely to be opposed successfully by some other party, since change ordinarily happens in schools only when the change is unopposed.

Some summaries of the relevant literature about educational change may be of value. Agnew and Hsu (1960) state that in the American culture, there is a constant readiness to oppose change, if the change is imposed by "outsiders." Consequently, if an "outside" group, say the school board, suggests a change, an "inside" group, such as the faculty, is likely to resist the change. Abbot (1965) remarks that individuals in an educational system tend to look upwards for changes. If changes are suggested by a party on a lower rung of the hierarchical ladder, as when the faculty asks to experiment, those "above," such as the superintendent, are likely to oppose change as a matter of principle. The higher up one goes, the more conservative the individuals. In many schools, teachers are seen as having obligations while the administration has rights. Abbot believes that a new conceptualization is called for in education, a horizontal leveling of responsibilities and privileges. But no hierarchical system will voluntarily permit such democratization.

Timothy W. Costello, former deputy mayor of New York City (1968) points out that there are significant differences between the private sector and the public sector in regard to making changes. The "bottom line" in business is profits. Accountants can readily determine the profitability of a business, and having this information, decisions can be made about the advisability of any change. But the success of a public institution, such as a school, is not so easily assessed. In addition, while there is a clear-cut division of responsibilities and privileges in business, for example, the owners can do whatever they want within the limits of the law, the constituency of a governmental agency is more heterogeneous, and power is diffused. Personnel in government, Costello points out, ordinarily do not feel they have the power to make changes as readily as do businessmen. Consequently, changes in government are usually cosmetic, window dressing. Sometimes the leadership goes, but the bureaucracy remains intact. This solid group near the top usually struggles to maintain the status quo.

The bureaucracy's opposition to change need not always be considered illogical or harmful. They provide stability and protection from unwarranted change. Not all changes are desirable. However, Pincus (1974) points out that generally schools have self-perpetuating bureaucracies with captive populations. The natural tendency for these people who have the power to make changes is to keep the status quo, and to perpetuate the old system, since any changes can threaten them. If innovations are made, Pincus suggests, they are such as to enhance the image of those involved. If changes are suggested from the "top"—we now find opposition from the "bottom"—as it were. Four reasons are suggested: (1) those affected by changes will feel that they are not given sufficient guidance to put changes into effect properly; (2) faculty itself, especially older members, resist changes which call for them to behave differently; (3) some personnel, high and low, are more interested in appearing to do things differently than actually doing things in new ways; and (4) frequently, the administrators who are faced with contending positions attempt to satisfy both parties by saying they are making changes to satisfy the parties that press for change; and then they do nothing, thereby satisfying those who don't want changes.

Change Strategies

It is evident that some school systems do introduce variations, and do permit innovations in the way of alternative systems, and that despite the problems of change as suggested by Costello, Abbott and Pincus, some variations are found. In other words, despite the generally conservative attitudes in the schools, in some cases some changes are made. The question we shall concern ourselves with here is, what do the various experts say about the proper way to attempt to make changes?

Howard (1967) makes six suggestions:

1. All individuals affected should have a clear picture of the whole philosophy of the new system, stated in specific terms. Everyone affected should have a clear picture of whatever is going to happen and why.

2. The new programs should be built inductively: specific details of operations should be made clear.

3. The innovators should engender an experimental attitude in all those involved, establishing a concomitant evaluative attitude—"We're all in it together and let's see how it will work."

4. The pace should be steady: not too fast, not too slow. There should be consistent monitoring of efforts and direction by those in charge.

5. Organize, organize, organize. The administrator must always be alert to make sure changes move along pre-established schedules.

6. Maintain high standards. While there should be some degree of flexibility, nevertheless the administrator must make certain that things are done right and in the proper direction, keeping in mind the tendency for people to revert to old ways.

Griffiths (1964) makes seven points regarding to the strategy of change in educational institutions.

1. Ordinarily, the major impetus for change comes from the outside. An organization, like a living organism, protects itself from outside forces, tends to homeostatic parity, and repels efforts of outside forces. This means that a kind of power

struggle results when changes are suggested. For the efforts to succeed, strong forces must be applied, otherwise the educational bureaucracy will defeat the efforts of the invaders.

2. Change is a function of amount of force applied. The more fundamental the change, the greater the force required.

3. The organization responds to force in three stages: (a) resistance, (b) over-compensation (active reaction shown by hostility, and (c) collapse.

4. Changes are more readily made with new administrators. Administrators up from the ranks are likely to be loyal to the old system. Occasionally it is necessary to put in a new administrator to effect a real change.

5. The number of innovations is inversely proportionate to the length of time that an administrator has been in power. The older the administrator and the longer he has been in authority, the fewer and the weaker the innovations.

6. Changes come from the top down, not the bottom up.

7. The more interaction between the sub-systems in a school, the less possibility for change.

It may be evident to the reader by now that there is a remarkable consistency between these two points of view. They also give theoretical explanation for the educational phenomena already discussed:

1. There is a strong tendency for schools to go on as they have been going on.

2. There is a strong general dissatisfaction with the present educational system.

3. Changes are resisted even though the resisters may know that the traditional system is not successful.

4. Some amount of educational change has taken place.

Evaluation of Schools

In discussing schools we hear of "good" schools and "bad" schools. Parents are generally eager that their children go to a "good" school, but they are vague about what this means. Usually they mean a school with a good reputation. For the purpose of this book, it is important for us to have more precise definitions of good and bad schools. We can pursue these definitions by asking three questions:

1. What is it that the school *attempts* to do? In short, what are its goals?

2. The next point is how *effective* is it? How well does it meet the goals it has established?

3. The final point—one rarely considered, incidentally—is how *efficient* is it? How much time and energy is spent in achieving the stated goals?

All three criteria must be considered in evaluating any school in terms of its "goodness-badness." Thus, we may say School A has good goals, but is ineffective and inefficient; and we may say School B has poor goals, but it achieves these goals effectively but inefficiently. If we consider each criterion separately, we can have nine "types" of schools. Thus school 1 can be labeled Good-Good-Good if it is considered good in terms of its goals, its effectiveness and its efficiency, while school 9 might be Bad-Bad-Bad if it has poor goals, is ineffective in achieving its goals, and is also inefficient. Naturally, we all aim at schools that are Good-Good-Good.

Let us now examine these three criteria. The first one, concerning the goals of the school, is difficult to settle, since different people have different concepts of what a school should be about. Two extreme positions are: (a) the school should concentrate exclusively on the "academic basics"—language arts, mathematics, science and social science; and (b) the school should develop the "whole child"—mentally, morally, physically, socially, etc. We see immediately that in terms of the school's goals, people will differ. Between those who take the 3 r's approach and those who take a global approach there really can be no rapprochement.

So, *what* should a school teach? What is an ideal school in terms of goals? Where can one obtain some sort of yardstick to evaluate the systems in this book? Unless we can offer some means of measuring the value of a school, the compilation of systems will really not lead anywhere.

The solution, it seems to us, comes from the efforts of committees of the National Education Association, which have met several times over a more than fifty-year span to discuss the objectives of education. The reader will find a summary of the seven principles of education discussed by Harold Shane on page 395. We suggest that the reader go to these pages at this point since they will give you a more complete frame of reference in terms of our further discussion. The seven points summarized are (a) health information, (b) command of fundamental processes (such as the 3 r's), (c) home membership, (d) vocational efficiency, (e) citizenship, (f) worthy use of leisure, and (g) ethical character.

We see these objectives as an example of training the "whole child"—and our bias steers us away from the highly constrictive position of only the 3 r's. We suggest that these seven objectives be used as the standard against which to judge the goals of the various systems of education found in this book.

This leads us to the next questions: How can one rate effectiveness and efficiency, and what do these mean?

Effectiveness

The concept here is simple enough: if a school does, in fact, achieve what it says it does, then it is effective. Let us suppose the purpose of a school is to have highly disciplined children, children who will do just what they are told, unquestioningly. If a school based on a military model achieves just this, then it is effective in terms of its own goals. But if our standards are the seven principles listed above, and if the school's only achievement is to mold disciplined children, then it is an ineffective school, since this kind of discipline is not in the NEA standards.

In short, we can view effectiveness three ways: we can see schools as always effective in terms of what they actually accomplish, because all of them do accomplish some things well (even though these may be highly undesirable outcomes); as being effective or not in terms of what they want to accomplish; or as effective or not in terms of the NEA principles. To illustrate this point: if school X happens to achieve a high degree of academic competence, we would say that it is effective in terms of the second NEA principle. But if it accomplishes nothing in the way of health education, then it is ineffective in terms of the second goal. However, if this goal is considered unimportant by all in the school, then this is a "good" school, since it accomplishes what it considers good even though the NEA standard was not met.

Efficiency

In our judgment, this is really the most important aspect of this whole issue of evaluation of schools. We should not only ask what a school is trying to teach and how well it is teaching it, but we should also ask—how efficiently (that is, in how much time, and how much cost) is the school doing what it does?

Let us illustrate. Two schools, M and N, both aim for a high degree of academic learning, which both achieve to exactly the same degree. In short, they are both equally effective. Now, let us say that school M expends X amount of time/energy and that school N expends 2 X amount of time/energy. We now see that school M is twice as efficient as school N, since it uses only half as much time/energy.

To be more specific: let us say that in the curriculum of school M children get 20 minutes a week of spelling, and that in school N children get 40 minutes. If at the end of a year—four years, etc., it turns out that the children in both schools do equally well, then it is evident that as far as spelling is concerned school M is twice as efficient.

It is our belief that the essential measure of a good school is *not* its program and is *not* its effectiveness, but is really its efficiency! We make this assertion because in reality, these days, practically all schools *say* that they try to teach the whole child. Only a few schools openly admit that their intention is less than that. While a school may emphasize one aspect, such as the "academic basics," all modern schools attempt—or at least will say they attempt—to train the "whole child." So, from where we stand, a proper evaluation of a school can be put on a mathematical basis in a relatively simple formula, based on the seven NEA objectives:

Goodness = %a+%b+%c+%d+%e+%f+%g

If school Q achieves each of the seven goals to perfection, it is a perfectly good school; while if school R achieves none of the seven goals it is a perfectly awful school. Some people might see school P as better than school K if each had these proportions:

P = 100%a+0%b+0%c+0%d+0%e+0%f+100%g—this school achieves academic learning and character.

K = 75%a+40%b+50%c+100%d+80%e+90%f+80%g —this is a balanced school.

We suggest that the reader may evaluate a school system by determining, on the basis of information given in the several chapters of this book the degree of probable achievement of each of the seven goals of the NEA.

Now, these need not be the only goals. For example, in this writer's opinion, the NEA left out a most important goal: *love of learning for the sake of learning.* Other people might consider other aspects important. My co-editor believes that possibly the single most important way of measuring the goodness of a school is simply measuring the happiness of the people in it. If the faculty is happy, if the students are happy and if the parents are happy, then it must be achieving its purposes, and therefore must be a good school. If there is violence and vandalism in a school, it is an unhappy and consequently not a good school.

We must note that there is no way at the present time to measure adequately some of these NEA goals, such as ethical character. In our judgment it is a terrible indictment of the whole school community that no efforts have been made to measure these factors, since we will always operate on the basis of guesses until we have exact measures. In industry cost benefit effectiveness is used to evaluate programs: something of this kind is needed for education.

IMPLEMENTING AN ALTERNATIVE SCHOOL

It is hoped that readers will find in the substantive part of the book at least one system that really *seems* to make sense. Say that the decision is made to implement this model, that is establish this new system in place of another system. Perhaps the relatively modest aim is to put in one school of this new type. What are the most effective steps one can take?

In this section, briefly, a model of implementation will be described which will help prepare the initiator for real life consequences. This section may be considered as a kind of game simulation to clarify the innovator's thinking and operations. We shall discuss this process in terms of phases.

Phase 1—Conceptualization of the Process

In considering intruding on a present system and putting in innovations, one must accept three premises:

Choice.
Individuality.
Motivation.

What this means essentially is that an innovator must operate in such a manner as to respect individuals' *choice,* realizing that only if they make decisions on their own will they willingly go in the direction desired. Second, the *uniqueness* of each individual must be respected. Third, one must consider the person's *value structure,* what is important for that person. Now, if a change agent sees a change as important and is sure that certain proposals are good, this is just not enough. The change agent must consider others' psychological position. Otherwise, a power contest will evolve with each party asserting statements and counter-statements. Understanding others is a prerequisite for successfully initiating change.

Phase 2—Establishing Catalytic Relationships

To actually succeed in making changes, relationships with others must be established to make them want to do what you want to do. This means that one must have the trust and support of others. Whether you are a consultant hired to do a job, the superintendent who wishes to install a system, or a principal who wants to put a new system in, it is necessary to establish harmonious relations "above," "below" and at "par" with all who are a party to the change.

We shall not attempt to discuss in detail any of these points, leaving this to another publication, but here are some sub-phases of this first phase:

—training staff members
—examining alternative systems
—discussions leading to decisions
—establishing a game plan for implementation
—obtaining of relevant data
—taking a position of helpfulness

Essentially, the goal here is to generate a relationship of trust creating a climate for working together successfully. This catalytic relationship is of primary importance.

Phase 3—Purposive Responding

Let us say now that we have attained an attitude of interest and cooperation in terms of a particular goal. But such enthusiasm may fade away unless the change agent shows strength and support, and this is the aim of this third phase. To operate successfully, a knowledge of human psychology is called for, including understanding the special goals of individuals within the system with whom one works with and a knowledge of the present school system, including the history of the school and its strengths and deficits. Drawing on knowledge of human nature, one can see each person moving towards personal goals in reference to one's family, one's work, and one's society. Realizing this, the change agent will be careful to avoid any conflicts with these goals and indeed should attempt to show how personal goals will be assisted by the change.

Understanding the school, especially if one is an outsider, calls for a deep historical understanding of the school and of all involved in it, including as discussed earlier, the loyalty people have to a school system. In short, even though the intent is to eliminate the old system, care must be taken not to attack it, since people may react emotionally to any criticism of what they have believed in.

We now must also consider the various power groups in any school. In one school, parents are well organized and strong while the school board may be weak and passive; in another school, there may be a highly assertive and powerful superintendent; in another school, the principals may be the key people. The change agent must be able to assess the "political" situation and be able to deal with the powers that be. To make incorrect assessments means wasting time, and possibly generating unsuccessful power contests. Consequently, while cooperation is needed on all sides, what is absolutely necessary is a correct evaluation of who has the power.

This refers to efficiency, proper use of time and energy. The change agent must be careful to avoid conflicts, to avoid wasting time with people who have no power, and to avoid getting into situations that will generate hostility. This calls for comprehending a system of individuals, subgroups and groups. It means taking into consideration emotional, cognitive and motivational aspects.

Phase 4—Developing Awareness

Before a school system can begin planned activities for implementing a new alternative system, it must accept the fact that it has problems, develop insight into the problems, sincerely want to change, and seek help from within or without the school district. Developing the awareness of existing problems, and then making the decision to implement an alternative school system are the two essential elements of phase four.

Our experience in working with schools throughout the country indicates that it is unrealistic to assume that most districts have the necessary resources to implement new viable educational systems, especially when it comes to this phase. Generally, there is a need for the services of a competent change agent or consultant. During this process of developing awareness, clients are never told what to do, but are helped to look at the purposes of their behavior and at where the school system is in relation to where they would like it to be. Staff members then are left to draw their own conclusions.

This communication process is characterized by high degrees of understanding, respect, authenticity, and creativeness, and is a prerequisite if an individual is to understand and change his own behavior or the basic structure of his school system. As the awareness process continues, possible solutions to the problems are suggested and discussed, and strategies for improvement are explored. During the course of discussion and training sessions, members of the group become committed to doing something about their school problems. Hence, at the awareness stage, staff members translate their interpretations of the problems into definite commitments to change and examine alternative school systems and prospective means of action.

The emotional commitment necessary for making recommendations for change involves:

The full acknowledgement of the problem.
Willingness to accept help.
Willing to lose their pessimism.
Believing things can change.
Cooperation and work together.
Taking action, the first step.

Field trips are a great aid in developing awareness. Through carefully planned field visitations, a consultant can enable individuals to look in on and experience a new alternative school system. This observation often becomes highly motivational and instills confidence in the staff that they, too, can create this alternative system within their own district.

Phase 5—Establishing a Plan of Action (Identifying Focal Units of Change)

The success of any attempt to change a total school system is measured by the way in which plans and intentions are transformed into actual achievements through integrating plans of action and monitoring the system. During the time the changes are being made, reactions from individuals within the system and the community are obtained and plans are evaluated and upgraded. Research consistently affirms the importance of climate in implementing change. Personnel who work in an environment of trust, who are made to feel an integral and important part of the organization, are managed according to relevant objectives, are involved in decision making and problem solving, and are rewarded for their contributions to their own development and to the organization, have high levels of creativity and productivity. Furthermore, such an organization is better able to find solutions to problems and to adapt to changing conditions.

This phase of the process involves the following through of objectives determined by the work groups and approved by the school administration. It is at this point that the plan of action must be formulated and implemented or the long and tedious process of reaching the decision may have been in vain. A plan of action is a simple, step-by-step method for achieving objectives. Small, achievable, and schedulable steps are established so that success will be possible. Success at each step is in itself a motivation to try another step that will ultimately lead to implementing the new school system.

The thirteen key steps for results most commonly identified in successful plans of action for establishing alternative schools are:

1. Gain staff support.
2. Develop a communication system within the system and community.
3. Determine management plan and systems.
4. Select administration and teaching staff.
5. Identify student selection procedures.
6. Determine inservice training activities.
7. Identify student objectives.
8. Complete cross referencing system.
9. Assign curriculum committees, roles and responsibilities.
10. Furnish materials and supplies.
11. Identify facilities needed and make room assignments.
12. Complete monitoring and feedback system.
13. Develop a cost effectiveness program.

In our research, investigation and development activities, these thirteen key areas have been found to be critical for successful implementation of a new alternative school. Identifying these individual key areas and developing corresponding plans of action, can, under the direction of a committed professional staff and consultant, greatly reduce the time, effort and resources expended effectively implementing a new system.

Phase 6—Entry Renewal

In essence, the entry renewal phase is the initial refinement of the new school system, a process which enables the school system to be more relevant to the needs of students in the community. During this phase, emphasis is on helping a new system assess problems, learn from experiences and move toward greater organizational maturity.

The entry renewal phase of this proposed change model consists of three steps:

1. Implementing the new system.
2. Diagnosing problems.
3. Making refinements, continuing operations and monitoring process.

1. Implementing the new system

At this phase of introducing the new alternative system, the application must involve the total system's modification and not an atomistic modification. There must be a shift from one coordinated system to a new one, incorporating all the while the integrity of the new system and its component parts. For example, a school moving from system X to system Y should modify all its operating procedures: leadership, decision making, communications, evaluation, supervision, compensation, organizational structure, curriculum, motivation, discipline, etc. The change should commence by altering first the most influential, causal variables, such as policies, goals, philosophy, and values. There should be systematic plans to make adjustments in coordinated steps all of the operating procedures which now anchor the educational structure into its present administrative position. If this is done, a well integrated system of management will emerge.

Equally important during the entry renewal phase to staff development activities, is to apply the new system's principles. In-service training to promote cognitive, affective and select skill development must be consistent with the school system's new philosophy, goals and administrative structure.

2. Diagnosing problems

Throughout the entry renewal phase, schools are in a state of continuous change, and there is a never ending requirement for diagnosis and concomitant decisions. The primary purpose of diagnosis during this phase of implementation is to provide the administration and teaching staffs with information to help them guide their own decisions and behavior. The obtained data further assists the members within the system to accomplish the specific goals they have set for the school system. It is important to emphasize that the diagnosis is not done in a punitive manner. Efforts are made to encourage the support of all staff members while collecting data in ways that will result in accurate measurements.

The measurements and diagnosis of organizational problems for school systems involved in the entry renewal phase of implementation are complex. Well qualified and trained professionals should view the measurement of causal and intervening variables. Accurate information correctly interpreted can be too valuable to a school district, and faulty data too costly, to permit the work to be done by a person lacking the basic scientific and technical competencies.

3. Refining, continuing operations and monitoring

The ultimate aim of this stage of entry renewal is to make the newly implemented alternative system a viable and self renewing educational organization within a short period of time.

The training provided during this process of entry renewal is normally organized in three stages: *Upgrading communication skills.* Change agents may provide specialized training to build increased openness and ease of interpersonal communication. *Modifying norms.* New norms are developed which support helpfulness among staff and introduce of conflict resolution methods for problem solving and decision making purposes. *Planned change.* New functions, roles, procedures and policies are built to establish new structures for sustaining the renewal process.

Phase 7—Renewal

The basic purpose of the renewal phase is to continue the process of helping the alternative school system to adapt to the new system, to effectively respond to problems, to remain effective in meeting identified goals, to grow and develop from experiences, and to move toward higher system efficiency. There are a number of basic elements on which our renewal model places major emphasis. These elements constitute an excellent checklist by means of which the school system can monitor its performance.

The important elements are:

Quality of communications.
Internal structure of system—fluid or adaptive.
Opportunities in situations for self criticism.
Program to recruit and develop talented manpower.
Environmental factors that encourage motivation and individualities.
Capability of system to cope with procedural build up.
System's ability to cope with change.
The climate of the system, e.g. trust.
Sub group working relationships.
The clarity of systems, philosophy, goals and decision making processes.
The frequency and willingness to evaluate the system's philosophy, goals and decision making processes.
The quality of the staff development program.
The degree of the administrative, staff and community support.

During the renewal phase, most of the training interventions are focused on three areas: improving communications skills, identifying and implementing norms and values which emphasize humanistic qualities, and implementing structural changes which are concerned with new functions, procedures, roles and policies. Outside change agents are frequently employed to conduct renewal training with key school systems people and related groups. In addition to addressing the three areas mentioned above, in-service training also addresses the need for increasing the collaboration and lessening the amount of competitiveness of district personnel members.

Phase 8—Institutionalization

Institutionalization is the process of planning recycling strategies to implement the newly established alternative school system in other schools or throughout the entire district. Essentially, the same phases of this change model will be followed throughout the institutionalization process. This stage of development will be most likely to succeed if the superintendent and top policy making group are committed to the change in the early stages of the relationship. The leadership, however, for institutionalization should come from the principal, staff and outside change agent who provided the original courage, work and support necessary to implement the first alternative school system. These people now have an opportunity to share a new school system that may afford significantly more opportunities for the growth and development of children of the entire district.

SUMMARY

In view of the unhappy state of traditional educational systems in this country and elsewhere, on considering the deep resistance to change which exists for reasons we have discussed, there is already a need not only for information about new, alternative systems of education, but also for a model of change implementation based on a theory of change. The various phases of this model attempt to help professional educators see clearly the kind of behavior commonly manifested as individuals attempt to implement new alternative schools in educational settings. The logical sequence and simplicity of this model are designed to create motivation for change on the part of teachers and other educational leaders. Hopefully, this model will be a means of assisting educational leaders of providing a wider range of helpful alternatives as they embark upon initiating new systems.

REFERENCES

Abbot, M. Hierarchical impediments to innovation in educational organizations. In M. C. Abbot and J. T. Lowell (Eds.), *Change perspectives in educational adminis-*

tration. Auburn, Alabama: Auburn University, 1965.

Agnew, P. C. & Hsu, F. L. K. Introducing change in a mental hospital. *Human Organization,* 1960, *19,* 195–198.

Cawelti, G. Innovative practice in high schools. Who does what—and why—and how. *Nations Schools,* 1967, *79,* 56–88.

Conant, J. B. *The citadel of learning.* Westport, Connecticut: Greenwood Press, 1977.

Costello, T. W. Change in municipal government: A view from inside. Paper presented at the American Psychological Association, California, September 1968.

Dreikurs, R. *Psychology in the classroom.* New York: Harper, 1957.

Griffiths, D. E. Administrative theory and change in organizations. In M. B. Miles (Ed.), *Innovations in education.* New York: Bureau of Publications, Teachers College, Columbia University, 1964, 425–436.

Hentoff, N. A. *Our children are dying.* New York: Viking, 1967.

Holt, J. *How children fail.* New York: Pitman, 1964.

Howard, E. How to be serious about innovating. *Nation's Schools,* April, 1967, *79,* 89–90, 130.

Illich, I. *Deschooling society.* New York: Harper & Row, 1970.

Laing, R. D. *Divided self.* Westminister, Maryland: Pantheon, 1969.

Pincus, J. Incentives for innovation in the public school. *Review of Educational Research,* 1974, *44,* 113–144.

Rickover, H. *American education, a national failure.* New York: Dutton, 1963.

Schultz, T. W. *Economic value of education.* New York: Columbia University Press, 1963.

Silberman, C. *Crisis in the classroom.* New York: Random House, 1970.

CHAPTER 2

Traditional
Education

VERNON SMITH

DEFINITION

The traditional educational system has been the dominant form for elementary and secondary education since the last half of the Nineteenth Century, and it represents the culmination of an eclectic search for the "one best system."

Some major characteristics of the traditional system include: (1) children are usually assigned to a school within a geographical district; (2) children then are assigned to classrooms, usually based on their ages; (3) children enter at specified ages; (4) they then move annually from grade to grade; (5) schools are authoritarian in principle, with students expected to conform to preestablished behavioral standards; (6) the teacher has the responsibility for instruction, following a pre-established curriculum; (7) the major portion of instruction is teacher-directed and print-oriented; (8) promotion is based on teacher judgment; (9) the curriculum centers on academic subjects; and (10) the most common curriculum instructional materials are textbooks.

The traditional educational system is based on some generally accepted but unvalidated assumptions, such as: (1) there is an important body of knowledge and skills that children should learn; (2) that a major proportion of children can learn these elements best in schools; and (3) that children learn best in age-graded classrooms.

INTRODUCTION

Objectives of Education

It is difficult to consider the objectives of education without considering their social context. To a great extent the objectives of education grow out of a society's expectations for its schools. In Colonial America, religion, morality, and the schools were perceived as closely related. Society wanted literate, moral citizens who could read and interpret the Bible. The religious influence was reflected in the colonial schools' instructional materials. Later the new nation recognized an educated electorate as the basis for a constitutional democracy, and the nationalistic influence gradually replaced the religious influence. As the nation moved from an agrarian age to an industrial age, society needed a trained work force. Immigrants were a primary labor source, and the schools were assigned the task of "Americanizing" immigrant children and youth. In general the schools responded effectively to each of these society-imposed tasks.

Since World War II our society, perhaps overconfident in its schools, has expected them to take on several major tasks within a relatively short time: mass secondary education, and even mass college education, to prepare a highly educated work force for an advanced technological age, the racial integration of society through the racial integration of the schools, and the elimination of poverty and inequality through equal educational opportunity.

With society's demands upon the schools changing dramatically, the objectives of education might be expected to reflect these changing demands. This has not been the case. There have been a few noteworthy attempts to spell out the goals of education at the national level. The first comprehensive goal statement that was widely accepted and quoted was the *Cardinal Principles of Secondary Education* by the Commission on the Reorganization of Secondary Education in 1918. These seven principles or goals were (1) health, (2) command of fundamental processes, (3) worthy home membership, (4) vocation, (5) citizenship, (6) worthy use of leisure time, and (7) ethical character.

In 1938, twenty years later, the Educational Policies Commission of the National Education Association developed objectives of education in four areas: (1) self realization, (2) human relationship, (3) economic efficiency, and (4) civic responsibility.

In 1961 the Educational Policies Commission of NEA reaffirmed these two earlier goal statements and added one additional goal: "The purpose which runs through and strengthens all other educational purposes—the common thread of education—is the development of the ability to think." That this goal had not appeared in any earlier widely circulated goal statements is worth noting.

The NEA Bicentennial Commission nominated an International Panel to reframe the seven cardinal principles and to develop educational guidelines for the 21st century. Shane (1977) reported that ". . . the seven goals [the cardinal principles] have retained their usefulness and their importance even after the passage of nearly 60 years." On the basis of interviews with the 46 international experts on the panel, Shane reinterpreted the seven cardinal principles in anticipation of the 21st century and adds 28 Cardinal Premises for 21st Century Education.

With the notable exception of the 1961 Educational Policies Commission's addition of thinking, the widely accepted objectives of education have changed little in this century. When the incredible changes that have taken place in the world in this century are considered, the stability of educational goals should be a matter of grave concern.

Paul Woodring wrote in 1957, "Today we are engaged in a great national debate over the aims and purposes of education . . . " He was referring to a debate among the critics of the schools. Today, twenty-plus years later, it is obvious that the American public and the mainstream of the education profession have never entered this debate.

In 1787 Thomas Jefferson wrote to James Madison: "I think our governments will remain virtuous for many centuries; as long as they are chiefly agricultural; and this will be as long as there shall be vacant lands in any part of America. When they get piled upon one another in large cities, as in Europe, they will become corrupt as in Europe. Above all things I hope the education of the common people will be attended to; convinced that on their good sense we may rely with the most security for the preservation of a due degree of liberty." (Hechinger and Hechinger, 1975)

Jefferson was right and wrong. It did not take "many centuries" for the vacant lands to fill, and for agriculture to assume a minor role. If, as Jefferson said many times in many ways, the fate of a democracy rests on the education of its citizenry, the public and the profession must come to grips with critical questions about the objectives of education, such as: Are the schools preparing an electorate capable of charting the course of the country into the 21st century? Do the schools prepare all citizens to assess the effects of government, business, the media, and the educational system on the quality of life now and in the future? If the democratic experiment fails, will it be because the political concept was wrong or because the educational process was ineffective?

Reasons for Traditional Education

The traditional educational system has served the country well. Americans of all races have greater access to schooling and go further in school than the citizens of any other country, ancient or modern. When comparative studies are made, the top academic students in the U.S. compare favorably with their counterparts in other developed nations.

Evidence based on achievement tests and other measures suggests that today's children and youth learn more in traditional schools than their parents and grandparents did. Historically, Americans have taken great pride in, and have held high expectations for, the traditional educational system. Parents generally expect that their children will go further in school than they themselves did. Today the vast majority of white and blue collar workers expect their children to attend college.

The continued success of the traditional system has increased the public's demands and expectations. This is both a problem and a paradox. As soon as the schools began to achieve the goal of mass elementary education in the early part of this century, the public began to expect mass secondary education. This proved to be a more difficult task, but long before it was completed, the public's expectations had moved to mass college education.

In 1900 fewer than ten percent of the youth in this country graduated from high school. Today almost 75 percent do. This remarkable increase has been accomplished in spite of continued increase in the secondary-school-age population which has doubled in almost every decade in this century until this one.

The paradoxical result of the traditional system's successful mass education is that today the schools are being attacked as never before. The schools are being attacked by the conservatives for straying too far from the basic skills. They are concerned about declines in some standardized test scores, and they call for a "back-to-basics" movement. Some liberals, on the other hand, criticize the schools for their failure to solve society's major problems: integration, equality, and poverty. They call for the schools to invest more efforts in social reform.

The traditional system which has so successfully responded to public and societal demands in the past is in serious trouble today. While it still performs its traditional role as effectively as ever, it appears to be unable to respond to these new and conflicting demands.

The compelling reason for the traditional educational system has to be consumer satisfaction. While the recent annual Gallup Polls of the Public's Attitudes Toward Public Education indicate some decline in the public's attitudes toward the schools, the majority of parents with children and youth in the public schools continue to be satisfied with the schools' performance. (Smith and Gallup, 1977) In a recent poll 82 percent of the parents responding were satisfied with what their children were learning in school, and 85 percent reported that their children liked to go to school.

HISTORY

Beginnings

The roots of traditional education in America extend back more than 300 years—before our constitutional government, before the abolition of slavery, before the birth of psychology, before women's suffrage, and long before the notion of educational research. The traditional educational system which dominates elementary and secondary schooling has evolved from what Cremin (1970) described as "a fascinating kaleidoscope of endless diversity and change" in colonial times to a system that is basically monolithic and highly resistant to change.

Gradually over the two-hundred-plus-year history of the nation the traditional system of schooling has transformed from schooling as luxury to schooling as necessity, from incidental schooling to intensive schooling, from majority non-public schools to majority public schools, from voluntary schooling to compulsory schooling, from the one-room schoolhouse to the age-graded, multi-room school, from the single village school to the large bureaucractic school system, from elitism and the intentional elimination of the majority of youth to the responsibility for the custody of all children and youth of school age.

Schools were not very important to early Americans. The typical colonists had probably never attended a school and did not expect their children to do so. Children and youth were a vital part of the colonial family economy. As soon as they were old enough, they were expected to work side-by-side with their parents for the family livelihood. For those families who sent their children to school at all, it was for a few weeks in the winter when there was little work to be done in the home or fields.

By 1800 each individual in the population had attended on the average 82 days of school (Cubberly, 1909), or less than half a year by today's standards. By 1900 this figure had reached 998 days or over five of today's academic years.

The traditional educational system had no founder. Schools of many varieties, but mostly parochial, were transplanted here by the early colonists. The first step toward public education was probably the Massachusetts law of 1647 which required every town of 100 families or more to provide a school. The earlier Act of 1642 had made parents responsible for their children's literacy. These laws were rarely enforced and probably had little effect, for it was over 200 years later in 1852 that Massachusetts became the first state to pass a compulsory attendance law requiring all children from eight to fourteen to attend school for twelve weeks a year.

Thomas Jefferson, who did consider schooling important, sponsored an unsuccessful bill in the Virginia Legislature in 1779 that would have provided three years of schooling without charge for every free child in the state. A similar bill was also defeated in 1814 indicating that the majority of Virginia legislators still disagreed with Jefferson 35 years later (Smith, Barr, Burke, 1976). Jefferson's bill did not mention compulsory schooling. He apparently felt that most parents would take advantage of schooling if it were provided by the state.

The age-graded classroom originated in Quincy, Massachusetts in 1848, long before there was a psychology of learning. It may have been the most sweeping innovation in the history of American education, for it eventually brought about the demise of the one-room school, which was the principal vehicle for schooling for well over 200 years.

By the time of the first compulsory schooling law, the principle of the common or public elementary school was generally accepted. Other states soon followed Massachusetts, and by 1890, 27 states had similar compulsory schooling laws. Mississippi in 1918 was the last state to enact compulsory schooling legislation.

Acceptance of universal secondary schooling was much more recent. While the first public high school was established in Boston in 1821, it wasn't until 1872 that the Kalamazoo Decision confirmed the legality of publicly supported secondary schools. Well into this century most parents expected their children to find full-time jobs by age twelve or soon after. By 1900 more than 10 percent of the fourteen-to-seventeen-old population were attending school, but only a minor portion of these were graduating. Not until about 1940 were a majority of youth enrolled in high schools with about 40 percent of those enrolled graduating. Today, mass secondary education is a reality with almost 90 percent of youth enrolled and with nearly 75 percent graduating.

Current Status

During the third quarter of this century (1951–1975), a number of developments have taken place which are affecting the status of traditional education today. Due to the successful efforts to implement mass secondary education, over a fourth of our population is enrolled in school today from pre-school through graduate school. Education is the nation's largest business with an annual budget of well over a hundred billion dollars, considerably larger than the country's military-defense budget. Schooling is big business. At the same time its primary source of funding is the local property tax, a system developed in previous centuries to support the village one-room school.

Increasing enrollments in the schools caused increases in school budgets. During this same period (1951–75) spending for education increased proportionately more than in other areas. Expenditures for public education increased 50 percent faster than the increase in the GNP (gross national product) during the 1960s.

Public interest in education in general, and in public schools in particular, also grew. This was partly due to the growing needs of a technological society and partly to growing competition in world politics and the world economy.

Educational criticism became an established vocation, and the media made the critics more accessible to the public. Criticisms of the schools with dramatic titles—*Why Johnny Can't Read, Compulsory Miseducation, Why Children Fail, Death at an Early Age, Our Children Are Dying, Crisis in the Classroom, School Is Dead*—became best sellers and influenced the popular view of the effectiveness or ineffectiveness of the traditional educational system.

After the Russians launched Sputnik, the first space satellite, in 1957, Congress responded with the National Defense Education Act of 1958. With this first large-scale expenditure of federal funds in elementary and secondary education, Congress acknowledged the necessity of educational reform in our competition for world power. As a result, the late 50s and early 60s were characterized by national curricular reform efforts.

The Supreme Court decision in Brown vs. Topeka in 1954 was to have long term effects on the nation's public schools. Twenty years later desegregation had still not been accomplished in many of the country's major cities.

In the late 60s federal interest switched to efforts to improve schooling for the poor through the Elementary and Secondary Education Act, which was part of the "war on poverty." Whether the schools can play a significant role in this area is controversial.

The major efforts to change the traditional educational system in the 1960s were not generally successful. Paul Nachtigal of the Ford Foundation, who had been involved in various school reform efforts during this period, summed up his conclusions from a field study of attempted innovations this way in 1972, "I am not sure we have any real clues at the present time on how to reform the [traditional] educational system."

In spite of general parental satisfaction with the traditional school system, there are disturbing indications that the schools are not responding effectively to today's educational needs. Absenteeism, truancy, suspensions, and dropouts are major problems. Since the 1950s over one million youth have dropped out of school each year. When school enrollments were increasing the percentage of dropouts was declining. Now that enrollments are declining the proportion of dropouts is on the increase.

Violence and vandalism in the schools are at an all time high. A U.S. Senate Subcommittee reported that the schools spend more on vandalism than on textbooks, nearly 600 million dollars per year (Bayh, 1977).

The schools' failure to respond to the needs of the poor and the culturally different, particularly the black, the Mexican American, and the Native American, is well documented. But go to any predominantly white, middle class school, and you will find some children and youth not doing well. One estimate is that one-third of all white, middle-class children and youth are not succeeding in the schools.

Some test scores are declining. The Scholastic Aptitude Test of the College Entrance Examination Board has shown a gradual decline for the last 15 years. The National Assessment of Educational Progress has indicated declines over the last five years in science, mathematics, and social studies. Only in reading has there been a general improvement. Studies of American adults indicate that the typical adult has not mastered the skills necessary to live intelligently in today's world.

Partly as a result of these concerns, there have been more than a dozen major national reports on the traditional educational system since 1970. All of these reports are critical of the schools, and all suggest that major reforms are needed. While the reports do not agree on solutions to these problems, there are some common recommendations. One such recommendation is to diversify the present monolithic system so that it will be more responsive to the needs of more children and youth. The 1973 report of the National Commission on the Reform of Secondary Education urges that: "Each district should provide a broad range of alternative schools and programs so that every student will have a meaningful educational option available to him."

Alternative education within public school systems is the most agreed-on response to the schools' serious problems. Action learning programs are designed to get children and youth outside the schools for learning experiences in the community—"the real world." The 1974 Coleman report, *Youth: Transition to Adulthood* is highly critical of the schools for isolating youth from the real world outside the school.

Partly as a result of these reports, and partly because of the demands of some parents within individual communities, there has been a movement for alternative schools and alternative programs within the traditional school system since 1970. A variety of optional alternative public schools are in operation today in about one-third of the nation's public school systems. At least two-thirds of the large school systems have alternative schools. In 1971 Neil Postman predicted, "All of the reforms that will take place in education in the next decade will have their origin in the alternative school movement." He was probably right.

In the last few years (1975–1978), much attention has been paid to magnet schools—optional public schools that would attract students from all over a city—in those cities where court-mandated desegregation is underway. Magnet schools are currently part of desegregation strategies in Boston, Chicago, Cincinnati, Dallas, Detroit, Houston, Indianapolis, New Orleans, Pasadena, San Diego, Seattle, and quite a few others.

Another development has been the parental demand in some communities for the fundamental back-to-basics school. In 1975 there were probably no more than a dozen of these fundamental schools throughout the country. By 1977–78 there were at least two hundred with many more being planned.

Another recent response to the curricular concerns has been the development of competency-based programs and competency-based tests. To date, more than half of the states have legislated some form of competency-based testing requirements. As yet, these efforts have not had nearly as much grass-roots support as the alternative education movement.

It is difficult to judge the significance of current educational developments, but it seems obvious that alternative education and competency-based programs will be part of the traditional educational system for some time to come. Certainly the two are compatible. Many alternative public schools have been in the forefront in developing competency-based programs. The St. Paul Open School, a public school for kindergarten through grade 12, has developed a comprehensive competency-based program with competency-based graduation requirements.

THEORY

*1. While the traditional educational system
dominates elementary and secondary schooling, there
are few "pure" traditional schools in existence*

A recent analysis of the elementary schools in a large midwestern city school system revealed the following: About 3 percent of the schools were classed as open schools by the principal and staff. About 12 percent were classed as continuous progress schools, and about 18 percent were classed as traditional schools. No school was classified as fundamental, Montessori, free, IGE (individually guided education), micro-society, or other. Two-thirds of the schools were not classified by their staffs under any describable existing model. This situation would probably be found with varying proportions of various types in most, if not all, public school systems. The typical contemporary school does not well fit any of the models of school types described in educational literature.

The typical contemporary school is an eclectic blend of tradition and innovation which may include elements from different and conflicting theories of learning and teaching. Contemporary schools within a school system may assume a common pattern, or they may each be an eclectic, idiosyncratic unit based on their own peculiar history, community, and professional staff. Most contemporary schools defy a generalized description. For illustration, one contemporary elementary school might have non-graded open classrooms in grades K-2, team-teaching with flexible grouping in grades 3 and 4, and a departmentalized organization in grades 5 and 6. Another contemporary elementary school might have an open classroom kindergarten, self-contained classrooms in grades 1 and 2, and Individually Guided Education in grades 3 through 6.

Learning

1. There is no coherent stated theory of learning
underlying the traditional educational system

This should not be surprising, but it should be a matter of concern to parents as well as educators. The traditional system of education is several hundred years older than the psychology of learning. The basic structure of the classroom was determined before Columbus deluded himself that he had discovered a new world. The classrooms of William Shakespeare, Thomas Jefferson, Abraham Lincoln, and John Kennedy had more similarities than differences. Anyone who had ever been in a classroom in colonial times could walk into a traditional classroom today, and recognize it as such at once.

Thus thirty desks, more or fewer, facing the front of a room, provide an operational definition or theory of learning. Thirty identical sets of instructional materials, whether they be the horn books of colonial times, the McGuffy readers, or today's colorfully illustrated textbooks, confirm the position that the thirty students sitting in the thirty desks with thirty identical textbooks should be doing the same thing. This might be termed the lock-step theory of learning. While many educators would deny it, this lock-step approach is still a mainstay of the traditional classroom today, in spite of the evidence that it is contrary to our knowledge of the learning process.

As principles of learning have been conceived and accepted they have been incorporated into this structure by some school systems, some schools, and some individual classroom teachers. Thus the theory that governs the traditional system could be termed eclectic, and frequently is, even though its structure and its parts are frequently incompatible. This may be why the theory underlying traditional education has never been stated.

2. Motivation is based on punishment, reward, and
competition

Because competition, punishment, and reward are such ingrained factors in our society, in the family, and in the school, many teachers use them constantly without realizing it. Teachers frequently deny that they use punishment though some of their students may feel punished frequently and regularly. It would certainly be rare today for a teacher to use corporal punishment on a student because he has failed to learn or as motivation for further learning. However, corporal punishment is used in many traditional classrooms for misbehavior and other forms of inattention.

The punishment in general use is more subtle and more symbolic. Common forms of punishment employed in connection with classroom learning would include teacher disapproval, peer disapproval, grading, and designating "losers." Similarly forms of reward could include extrinsic rewards, praise, teacher approval, peer approval, grading and designating "winners."

A teacher conveys her approval or disapproval of a student by words, by tone of voice, by a look, by a facial expression, or by other body movements. Students learn these same behaviors from their teachers and their parents. A stranger in a classroom could guess with some accuracy whether a student called upon by the teacher is a good student or a poor one, is popular with his peers or unpopular, before the student has had a chance to respond.

Grading is the obvious way that teachers reward and punish their pupils. While teachers usually take care to make grading appear to be an objective process, there is considerable evidence to suggest that it is more subjective than objective, based on the value system of the teacher.

Competition is so American that it seems subversive to question it. Among other virtues, competition is supposed to produce the rugged individualism so essential to a democratic society. Competition as used here, means all the ways that there are to determine winners and losers in the classroom, including reward and punishment in all their forms: grading, testing, spelling bees, games, teams, attendance prizes, scholarship recognition, other honors, the assignment of responsibilities to selected students, and so forth.

Since society expects all children to learn and to complete both elementary and secondary schooling, the role of competition in the traditional system is controversial. The benefits of competition in the learning process are unspecified and unclear. Two things are clear and both are detrimental to the learning process. Through competition winners and losers are identified at an early age. They are then labeled with terms such as bright, dull, achiever, non-achiever, advantaged, disadvantaged. Many children are labeled "losers" and are doomed to twelve years of losing.

The heavy stress on competition destroys the potential for learning and teaching cooperation. "Do your own work" implies that there is something wrong with helping a friend do hers. Only a few learning tasks are approached cooperatively in the traditional classroom and these are usually the tasks perceived by the teacher and students to be relatively unimportant. They are rarely "graded."

3. Rote learning and the recall of information are stressed in the traditional educational system

The traditional educational system is based on the assumption that there is a body of knowledge to be passed on to each new generation. Learners are expected to absorb information from their textbooks and teachers and to recall this information upon request. Study after study indicates that teacher classroom questions and teacher-made tests emphasize recall. This does not mean that the other cognitive skills are neglected entirely, but it does mean that recall is stressed to the detriment of the development of higher level thinking skills.

In Wisconsin vs. Yoder the U.S. Supreme Court decided that compulsory education laws did not apply to Amish youth at the secondary school level. In that decision the Court said that Amish society stressed "wisdom rather than technical knowledge." Many parents other than the Amish would prefer wisdom to technical knowledge.

Higher education has always had a strong influence on elementary and secondary schools. Since college courses stress recall and since college preparation is a major focus of secondary education, the emphasis on recall is partly a reflection of the college curriculum and the college professors' behavior.

A common criticism of the traditional system is that this overemphasis on recall doesn't prepare people for a world of rapidly expanding knowledge. Students today need to develop the higher level cognitive skills, the learning-how-to-learn skills.

4. Behavioral psychology has had a definite influence on the traditional educational system

Behavioral psychology in general and B. F. Skinner in particular have had a great influence on the traditional system. In this century behavioral psychology and its stimulus-response theory have dominated educational psychology. Skinner's philosophy of engineering human behavior, although rarely acknowledged, underlies the methods that the schools use to direct and modify the learners' behaviors.

Behavior modification which is used in some schools and some classrooms would be an extreme example of this. From the moment the learner enters the school or classroom his behavior is conditioned by a system of reward or reward and punishment. While the majority of traditional schools do not employ a total behavior modification system, they do attempt to control and modify learners' behaviors.

5. *Cognitive psychology has not had a strong influence on the traditional educational system*

The cognitive psychology of Jerome Bruner and others was instrumental in bringing about the curricular reform attempts of the 1960s. Bruner (1960) suggested that the structure of a discipline (an academic subject area such as physics) determined the heuristics of the teaching-learning experience. Students at any age could be put into situations where they could make the same discoveries as an experienced physicist.

The "spiral curriculum" suggested by Bruner would be based on discovery and development of the perceptual and cognitive skills, and concept formation. The curricular and instructional emphasis would be on the process rather than on the knowledge.

Bruner's ideas were the foundation for the major curriculum development projects of the 1960s. The New Math was an example. But the intent of the curriculum developers was rarely realized at the classroom level. Teachers and schools were unwilling and unable to move from the established knowledge-based curriculum to the process-based curriculum. While there is considerable lip service to cognitive psychology among traditional educators, the influence of cognitive psychology on classroom practices has been slight to date.

6. *The hidden curriculum plays a key role in the lives of learners*

Every school has a stated curriculum. In every school a great deal of learning takes place that is not part of this planned curriculum. The hidden curriculum refers to the incidental learning that takes place in schools. (Overly, 1970). This incidental learning may affect the learners permanently. For example, some children learn to cheat in response to the academic demands of a teacher. Surveys of youth shows that over 90 percent have cheated in a school situation while in secondary school.

Children learn quickly who they are. They learn what social class they belong to and in what esteem teachers and peers hold that social class. They learn about race and racism. They learn about the moral values and the moral behavior that teachers expect, usually the moral values of the white, middle-class society.

Much of this incidental learning has to do with the learning process. In most traditional schools learners are dependent rather than independent. They are not expected to take the responsibility for their own learning. They soon learn that learning is something someone else is responsible for.

The hidden curriculum of all schools needs more exploration and analysis, for it may have more effect on the futures of learners than the overt curriculum.

Teaching Theory

7. In general the teaching process in the traditional educational system has not been guided by a theory of instruction

Most educators would agree that a complete theory of instruction has not been formulated to date. Early metaphors for the teaching process pictured the child as a vessel to be filled with annual layers of knowledge, as a blank tablet to be written upon, or as a flower whose growth could be either natural or cultivated.

Historically, in the traditional school, teaching was perceived as something that one did to someone else. Teachers are expected to be responsible for their classrooms and for their students.

Teaching is guided more by tradition and by the expectations of professionals and parents than it is by any theory of instruction. Studies indicate that most teachers teach as they themselves were taught.

8. Teacher talk is the dominant mode of instruction

Studies of traditional classrooms at both elementary and secondary levels indicate that when there is any form of verbal interaction in the classroom, the teacher talks from 60 to 90 percent of the time. This holds true whether the teacher is involved in what he perceives as lecture, discussion, or recitation and whether he is involved with a whole class, a small group, or an individual student.

9. The traditional educational system has various ways of grouping students for instruction

While some schools do not group at all, that is, students are assigned to classes at random or by a voluntary sign-up plan, most traditional schools group students in various ways. Some grouping procedures are administrative; some are counseling; some are classroom; and some are incidental.

Ability grouping has been widely used in the traditional educational system. Students are assigned to classes on the basis of some previous performance: a score on an intelligence test, achievement test scores, grades in previous school work, teacher recommendations, or a combination of these. The purpose of ability grouping is to make classes more homogeneous so that instruction can be geared to the "class level." In practice this rarely works out because there are probably more individual differences than similarities within any group, no matter how well the initial grouping criteria were applied.

The objections to ability grouping are that it creates an academic caste system with a halo on the high groups and a stigma on the low groups, that students in the lower groups don't have good peer models for learning, and that even when students are grouped by ability, teachers don't vary their instructional methods and materials to fit the groups.

Ability grouping may be illegal. In Hobson vs. Hansen a Federal District Court judge found that ability grouping in the Washington, D.C., public schools caused *de facto* segregation and declared it constitutionally illegal. Since this case was not appealed to the Supreme Court, many schools are still using ability grouping.

A common method of grouping students within the secondary school is by tracking or streaming. The school provides several different routes to the diploma: an honors track, a college prep track, a general track, a vocational track, a business track, etc. Students with their parents choose the appropriate track. Frequently the counselors recommend certain tracks for certain students on the basis of past performance. When students aren't doing well in their course work, another track is suggested.

Streaming or tracking could be considered a form of ability grouping and has the same drawbacks and advantages.

Classroom grouping procedures may be flexible or rigid. A teacher may group her students in two, three, or four groups for reading instruction on the basis of performance in reading. She may then regroup them in different groups for math on the basis of math performance. These groups might remain intact for the school year, or she may move students from group to group as their performance gets better or worse. Another teacher may sub-group within her classroom on the basis of overall performance for all subjects, and again these groups could be fixed or flexible. A team of teachers might sub-group students in the same ways.

This sub-grouping within a classroom or a multi-room unit allows teachers to adjust instruction to the needs of the various groups. In general, flexible grouping within the classroom is more effective than ability grouping or tracking. While some secondary school teachers sub-group within their classrooms, this is more common at the elementary level or within team teaching units at the secondary level.

Some grouping is incidental. For example, some middle-class parents may request a particular teacher because they feel that she is particularly effective. The secondary school schedule frequently results in grouping. For example, if the school offers one advanced science class and one advanced math class, students electing these two classes may tend to have common schedules for the rest of the day.

Within secondary schools student grouping is common; for example, friends may try to get classes together, band members may tend to have similar schedules, athletes may choose the same courses.

10. A few modes of instruction dominate the traditional educational system

At both elementary and secondary levels, teachers use a few modes of instruction most of the time: class discussion, recitation, and lecture, although teachers rarely admit to using lecture frequently. Demonstration is used more in some subjects such as science and home economics than in others. Modeling is also used in some subjects such as foreign language, and physical education. Student work at the blackboard is used in some subjects, particularly math. Supervised study is common at both elementary and secondary levels.

Individualized instruction is not common, but it most frequently occurs when individualized materials such as programmed materials or individual learning packets are provided. Individualized instruction usually means that students learn the same materials at different rates.

Tutoring and individual conferences, one teacher to one student, are rarely used during regular class time, probably because the teacher feels an obligation to the whole class.

Student presentations, student-led discussions, peer teaching, and peer tutoring are rarely used. In many traditional classrooms they are never used. This is unfortunate because there is considerable evidence that peer tutoring is a most effective technique for remedial reading and remedial math.

Overall teachers get much more practice in talking than their students. Some students get more practice in listening.

APPLICATIONS

Academic Curriculum

The academic curriculum of the traditional educational system has evolved over a period of more than two hundred years, changing gradually for the most part, but certainly rather suddenly when the demand called for it. Classical Greek and Latin were gradually replaced by modern foreign languages. American History was inserted at several grade levels, and English grammar was included in the secondary school curriculum because the schools were expected to "Americanize" the sons and daughters of our large immigrant population in the late 19th and early 20th centuries.

But for the most part, changes in the curriculum have consisted of adding new subjects as there was a demand for them; such as home economics, physical education, driver education, and sex education (in some communities).

Most people are familiar with the standard curriculum of elementary and secondary schools because the subjects offered are similar throughout the country. In fact, for all intents and purposes, there is a national curriculum in spite of lip service to local control of schools and in spite of locally developed curriculum guides. Since Webster's blue-back spellers and McGuffey's readers gained wide acceptance in the 19th century, textbooks have been the dominant influence on the traditional curriculum.

In the traditional system each student is usually provided a textbook in each academic area. Estimates vary, but most observers would agree that the textbook provided for each student determines the major portion of the course content. While there is usually some local flexibility in the selection and use of textbooks, the overall content of the textbooks is determined by the national textbook market and by a few, probably not more than a dozen, major publishers that dominate it.

About half of the states have state textbook adoptions today. In a typical adoption, a state committee selects several books at each grade level in an academic area such as English or mathematics that will be put on the state adopted list for a five-year period. Local school systems are usually required to buy basic textbooks from the state adopted list. Each school system determines how textbooks will be selected from those on the approved list. Some states require parent involvement as well as teacher involvement in the local selection process.

State textbook adoptions are highly competitive. As many as twenty or more publishers may be competing for a few slots on the state adopted list. When large states such as Texas and California have adoption years, publishers may bring out a revised edition in those years so that their book will appear to be the most up-to-date. When one publishing company is particularly successful in state adoptions in a particular area such as science or music, other companies will frequently imitate the attractive features so that in the long run textbooks become more similar.

State textbook adoptions in a few states have significant influence on the textbooks available all across the country. Suppose that the state textbook committee in a large state expressed objections to pictures of elephants in textbooks. Most publishers would revise their textbooks omitting all pictures of elephants for that state's next textbook adoption. Then that revised elephantless edition would be sold in all states. This is exactly what is happening today in various controversial issues in every area of the curriculum.

The same process works in reverse. If the textbook committee in a large state wants something not previously in the text inserted, the publishers will include it.

Thus for the schools using textbooks in each subject area of the curriculum, and almost all schools in the traditional system do, there is a national curriculum. Regardless of the prevalence of this national curriculum, the classroom teacher has considerable flexibility in how he chooses to use and not use the textbooks provided.

A second characteristic of the traditional curriculum is that it is structured by time. At both elementary and secondary levels the school day is divided into periods. The academic curricular subjects are then assigned to various periods. At the secondary level credit is given on the basis of time spent in a course, usually a semester or a year. Two students both receive credit for a year of French. Does this mean they speak French equally well? Of course not, but traditional schooling is nevertheless based on time spent. How much French have you had? Two years.

At the primary level (grades 1 to 3) children are usually placed in a self-contained classroom where all the academic subjects—reading, language arts, arithmetic, science, and social studies are taught by the teacher. Art, music and physical education may also be taught by this teacher or by specialists in those areas.

In the intermediate grades instruction may also be in the self-contained classroom, or it may be departmentalized with children moving as a group to a mathematics teacher, a language arts teacher, a social studies teacher, a science teacher, and others.

At the secondary level the curriculum is departmentalized. In some junior high schools and middle schools, the whole class of students moves from one teacher to another. In others and in almost all high schools, students are scheduled individually and move from class to class according to individual schedules.

Several current developments are affecting the traditional curriculum. Federally funded curriculum projects, particularly those sponsored by the National Science Foundation, have produced new curricula in various fields. The full impact of these is probably not felt in most classrooms until the new curricula are included in textbooks.

The growing interest in specific instructional objectives, sometimes referred to as behavioral objectives or performance objectives, has resulted in national objective exchanges and in similar looking sets of objectives in schools across the nation. Trivia in Palo Alto is similar to trivia in Hoboken.

Phase elective programs, short courses that secondary school students can choose among, have appeared in some schools in English, social studies, and science. Instead of a year-long course titled English IV, a student might elect four nine-week courses such as Creative Writing, Science Fiction, Shakespeare's Tragedies, and Generative Grammar.

In the last few years at least three-fourths of the states have legislated some form of competency testing requirements for the schools. Competency testing is sure to have a lasting effect on the traditional curriculum. And competency is probably about the same in Detroit, Michigan as it is in Lame Deer, Montana.

In spite of various influences to change the academic curriculum, the traditional schools are basically conservative, and the curriculum is resistant to change attempts. In spite of massive publicity on educational innovations in the last two decades, people who attended traditional schools in the period just after World War II would probably not find today's traditional school curriculum to be dramatically different.

Non-Academic Curriculum

The academic curriculum would normally include all of the subjects or fields that could be classified under the broad category of arts and sciences. The non-academic curriculum would then include everything else. Agreement on whether an area is academic or non-academic is far from perfect. Manual training, vocational training, general business programs, and the development of psychomotor skills would all be classed as parts of the non-academic curriculum. Physical education or journalism would be classed as academic by some and as non-academic by others.

Extracurricular or cocurricular activities such as athletics, clubs, student government, yearbook production, debate, and other such activities would be part of the non-academic curriculum of the traditional educational system.

Critical parts of the non-academic curriculum cannot be identified as either school subjects or as extracurricular activities. For example, the development of social skills is an important part of the non-academic curriculum. The development of attitudes and values is an extremely important part of the curriculum for each child. Attitudes toward learning and attitudes toward self and others will play a major part in school and in life outside of school.

Schools place great stress on competition. Children very early learn that there are winners and losers in the classroom. This is unfortunate because the child who perceives himself as a loser has little to look forward to in school but more losing. By its emphasis on grading, by grouping (the blue birds and the buzzards), by teacher behavior toward those who learn quickly and those who don't, the traditional educational system places too much emphasis on competition too early in the elementary school years for the optimal development of all children. The early and continuous stress on competition also results in a low value on cooperation. Most of us as adults find ourselves in at least as many situations that require cooperation as that require competition.

Another important aspect of the non-academic curriculum is the learning that the school provides in the community. Field trips, work-study programs, other community experiences all help to break down the barriers between school and community so that the students don't perceive the school as isolated from the real world. Several recent national reports have criticized the schools for isolating children and youth from the community.

Student Evaluation

Student evaluation in the traditional educational system is the responsibility of the individual classroom teacher. The teacher evaluates students achievement as measured by classroom tests and personal observation and judgment, and reports to parents. Report cards with letter grades are generally used.

Some elementary schools use parent-teacher conferences for reporting, particularly in the early grades. Other schools may use a combination of conferences and report cards. In the elementary schools the classroom teachers determine whether students should pass on to the next grade or be retained for another year in the same grade.

At the secondary level letter grades (A, B, C, D, F) are used almost exclusively, and students' grade-point average determines their rank in their graduating class.

In addition to grades for academic achievement, some elementary and secondary schools also give grades or reports on citizenship in the classroom. Citizenship usually includes classroom behavior, attitudes, and other subjective factors. In both academics and citizenship, many teachers would state that grades are based on objective evidence, but this would be hard to prove in many cases.

Most school systems have standardized testing programs. Standardized achievement tests are used regularly, sometimes annually, sometimes more frequently, but usually less frequently, to determine achievement gains or losses within the school system. Recently in many communities these test results have been made public, and comparisons among the scores of individual schools are possible.

Standardized test scores are not well understood by the public, nor are they easy to explain. Most standardized test scores are in the form of grade-level equivalents. For example, a standardized test of reading might be given to one thousand third graders. The average score for this sample of students would be called third-grade level. This is the point that half the students are below and half are above, except for those students whose scores fall exactly at this point. This is called a norm-referenced test because it is based on normal behavior for a population. It tells how a third grader compares with other third graders in reading, but it tells little about how well third graders read.

When the media report that one-half of the third graders in Anytown are reading below grade level, a natural result of the norm-referenced test, this is frequently interpreted as cause for alarm and as a deficit in the local schools.

Partly because of this problem, some school districts are moving to criterion-referenced tests. A criterion referenced test is usually based on a specific objective, for example, that all third graders should be able to read a news story on the front page of the local newspaper and answer questions about the factual content of the story. Thus a criterion-referenced test tells whether students can accomplish a specific task, but it doesn't allow comparisons with the national norm. We can't tell whether Anytown's third graders are reading better or worse than a neighboring town unless the neighboring town uses the same criterion-referenced test.

Some classroom teachers use criterion-referenced tests as a part of their regular student evaluations.

The results of standardized achievement tests can be used to determine how effective a school district is as compared to national norms or state norms, or how effective a school is when compared to national, state, or local norms. The results of standardized tests are not used to compare individual classrooms. Teachers may report standardized test results to parents, but these test results are usually not part of the teacher's evaluation of the student.

Standardized test results may be used to group students. Many traditional schools group students by ability. Students who score low on a reading achievement test may be assigned to a "low" reading group or to a remedial reading class. Students who score high may be assigned to a "high" group. Underachievers, students who have the capacity to learn to read well, as demonstrated by an intelligence test, but who score low on a reading achievement test, may be identified for special instruction or for further study.

Counseling

In the traditional educational system much counseling, both formal and informal, is done by classroom teachers and by principals. Professional counselors are generally employed at the secondary school level only. Teachers and principals counsel students on personal problems, family problems, social problems, educational problems and anything else that comes up.

In the secondary schools where a formal counseling program exists it usually has two facets: academic counseling regarding college selection and admission and vocational counseling regarding jobs and vocational schools. Usually vocational aptitude tests and vocational interest tests are part of the counseling program to help students make choices of possible college majors and possible vocations. Since counselors have all graduated from college, the college counseling is usually more effective than the vocational counseling.

Since schools usually have one counselor for several hundred students, individual counseling is relatively rare and may be restricted to students with particular problems. Many counselor functions are accomplished through group counseling. In some schools classroom teachers are an integral part of the group counseling program.

Counselors, teachers, and principals are also called upon to counsel parents on their children's schooling and on school-related problems. Part of parent counseling would include the interpretation of students' test scores to their parents.

Counselors' duties usually include setting up college and vocational programs for students and parents, administering the school's testing program, helping students with scheduling and scheduling problems, liaison with local colleges and employers, helping students find summer and part-time employment, making college and vocational information readily available to students, and other similar activities. Almost all counselors complain that there are too many students and too few counselors to do an effective job.

In some schools, perhaps a majority, counselors are required to assume responsibility for discipline in the school even though this is generally agreed on by counselors to be definitely not part of counseling and guidance. Counselors feel that heavy involvement in discipline interferes with their counseling role by putting them in an adversary role with those they are supposed to counsel.

In a few schools, particularly small schools, the counselors may be asked to perform administrative duties.

Counseling in traditional schools tends to be eclectic, that is it follows no single counseling theory. While individual counselors may be consistently directive or non-directive, most counselors would be directive at times and non-directive at other times.

Discipline

Each year in the annual Gallup Poll of the Public's Attitude Toward the Public Schools the public cites discipline as the number one problem facing the traditional educational system. School vandalism and school crime are at an all time high reportedly costing about $600,000,000 per year, more than is spent on textbooks and instructional materials. Truancy and absenteeism are also high. In a recent poll of secondary school principals, they reported that absenteeism was the number one problem in secondary schools.

Discipline problems, vandalism, and absenteeism are occurring in all types of schools in all types of communities today. Why? No one, inside or outside of education, seems to know. Some would blame the discipline problems on the traditional school system which they say has not kept up with the changes in society and the world. Others would contend that the schools and society are too permissive. And still others see the discipline problems in the schools as symptoms of unrest and distrust in society in general.

A few schools do have racial problems, and in some cases, these have been caused or magnified by court-enforced desegregation plans. But there is so much violence and vandalism in schools that are not involved in desegregation that this should not be considered a major cause of the problems.

Most traditional schools today have discipline codes or policies. Many of these policies may have been determined by the school board for all of the schools in the district. Many large schools, particularly secondary schools, have security forces. Some schools have elaborate alarm systems. Some traditional schools still have dress codes, but they are not enforced as strictly as they were in the 1960s.

Since the Supreme Court decided that students were entitled to due process, schools have explicit procedures for suspension and expulsion. A student must be notified of the reason for her suspension and given an opportunity to respond. Corporal punishment is still used widely except in a few states where it is outlawed. Recent court cases have upheld the use of corporal punishment in schools, and it is likely to be used in many schools for some time to come.

Many behavior problems originate in the classroom, and many feel that effective classroom management is the key to school discipline. Preservice and inservice training for teachers have not focused on discipline and classroom management.

There is considerable evidence that smaller schools have fewer discipline problems, less violence and vandalism, and less absence and truancy. This is true whether the schools are traditional or any other type.

ROLES

Roughly one third of the nation's population, over 70,000,000 people, are directly involved in schooling from pre-school through graduate school. This includes students, teachers, administrators, school board members, and service personnel. If educational textbook publishers, educational film

makers, educational television and radio personnel and all others indirectly involved in schooling were added in, the figure would be much higher.
If parents were included, over three-fourths of the population would be
involved in schooling. Schooling is the nation's largest business costing
well over one hundred billion dollars annually.

There are approximately 50,000,000 students enrolled in elementary and
secondary schools with almost 10 percent of these in non-public schools.
The majority of these, perhaps as high as 90 percent, are enrolled in
schools that would be classified as within the traditional educational
system. During this century the tendency has been to combine public
school districts so that there are fewer and larger school systems. In the
thirty plus years since World War II, over 100,000 school districts have
been consolidated into the about 15,000 in existence today.

In a few states separate elementary and secondary school systems exist
side by side with separate school boards and separate administrations. But
the typical school system is a large bureaucracy which includes both
elementary and secondary schools. A typical public school system is one
of the largest employers, if not the largest, within its community.

Each local school system is governed by a local board of education with
powers delegated by the state. School board members are local citizens
who are usually elected, but sometimes appointed, to the school board.
The school board is responsible for all of the public schools in its local
area. The school board makes local policies, hires the superintendent, and
monitors the school system to see that it operates within state laws and
that board policies are carried out.

School board members could be classified in two general types: those
with children in the local schools who are concerned about improving the
schools for their children and thereby all children; those without children
in the schools who are performing a "civic responsibility" and who may
be concerned about the cost of education within the local community.

Administration

The superintendent of schools is the chief administrative officer. He is
appointed by the school board to run the school system and to carry out
board policies. The superintendent has a staff, which may consist of a few
people in a small school district or of hundreds, or even thousands, of
people in a large school district. This central staff carries out the superintendent's instructions and performs various services for the elementary
and secondary schools within the system. Among the responsibilities of
the central staff would be curriculum and instructional services, research
services, personnel services, transportation services, business services,
food services, pupil accounting.

Each central staff has its own organizational pattern. In a very large district there might be an assistant superintendent in charge of each of the areas above. While all of these services are for the schools, the curriculum and instructional services are more directly related to the teaching-learning process in the schools. There would normally be a director, or an assistant superintendent, in charge of curriculum and instruction. There may also be a director in charge of secondary schools and another in charge of elementary schools. All three of these people would work directly with the school principals on matters of curriculum and instruction. This office would be responsible for curriculum planning and development and for inservice programs for teachers. Typically teachers would be involved in these activities, and occasionally parents are also involved.

In a very small school district of just a few schools the superintendent may take the central responsibility for curriculum and instruction. In larger districts there may be a curriculum and instruction staff of several hundred, including subject matter specialists (a supervisor or coordinator of social studies) who work directly with elementary and secondary teachers.

The central administrative staff, whether large or small, is organized and intended to be a resource of services for individual schools, for principals and teachers. But it is rarely perceived this way by the individual school faculties. To the individual teacher the bureaucratic hierarchy in the central office looks more like a bunch of bosses, each with more power and more to say about what goes on in the system than those at the school level.

In some large school districts the central administration (the above-school administration) is decentralized. Instead of one central administrative office, the school system is divided into geographic districts. Each district has an assistant or area superintendent for its chief officer, and each area superintendent has a staff such as that described earlier. The intent of decentralization is to put the central services closer to the schools when the total school district community is very large. Sometimes teachers and principals see this a more effective way to operate, and sometimes they don't.

Faculty

For most parents, most students, and teachers and principals the individual school and its faculty are the key element in the schooling process. Most parents and students never see the central administrative staff. Some would not even be aware of its existence.

The principal, of course, is the head of the school. In this capacity she has several different roles, including instructional leader, business manager, and parent and public relations director. In larger schools, particularly larger secondary schools, there may be one or more assistant principals who assist the principal in these roles. One of the inherent drawbacks of having three roles to perform is that a principal may spend more of her time on the roles she enjoys most and less on the other roles where more time should be spent for the good of the total school.

As business manager, the principal must see that supplies and equipment are ordered on time and received on time. She supervises the clerical and custodial staff. She monitors the food services, health services, and transportation although she may not control these directly. She is responsible for the total school facilities, buildings and grounds. She is responsible for the school budget although she may delegate some of the funds to others. She is responsible for the extracurricular activities programs, including any interscholastic activities such as athletics, debate, music, etc. The principal usually works a longer year than the teachers. She is responsible for closing up the building in the early summer (if it closes) and for reopening the building in the late summer. She is responsible for accounting for the schools funds, including any money collected from parents and students and any student funds.

In the area of parent, student, and public relations the principal represents the school in the community. She may be asked to attend and speak at various community affairs. She is probably the first faculty member that new families meet when they come to the school because she has the responsibility for assigning students to classrooms. If the school has a P.T.A. or P.T.O. she is automatically one of its officers and participates in its meetings. She may have one or more parent advisory groups to advise him on aspects of the school's program. She is expected to attend all school functions.

Since the main business of the traditional educational system is teaching and learning, the principal's most crucial role is that of instructional leader. In this capacity she is responsible for what will be taught and who will teach it. She schedules the classes and assigns the teachers and the students to them. She may have a voice in hiring the teachers, but whether she does or not, she is responsible for them once they are assigned to her school. She helps new faculty members adjust, and she evaluates their work as well as that of tenured teachers. She is responsible for the inservice program and for the continuing development of her faculty. She confers with teachers individually and as a faculty. She should be aware of their problems, of students' problems, and of parents' problems. She is usually involved in any serious discipline problems. She is responsible for the grading practices within the school, for the guidance and testing program, and for the total instructional program.

Since the principal is responsible for the evaluation of teachers, there is a natural adversarial relationship between the principal and the teachers. There is also an adversarial relationship between the school and the central administration. The principal is often caught in the middle. The group that she works with most closely is the teachers. The group that she feels the most in common with is her fellow principals, but she sees them rarely.

The teachers have a similar problem. They spend the bulk of their day in the classroom with students where there is a natural adversarial relationship. In the traditional educational system the teacher is responsible for teaching the students what the community, through its schools, say they should learn.

Most traditional classrooms are organized with thirty chairs facing the front where the teacher's desk is. It's fairly logical that if thirty students are facing the front, something ought to be going on up there. The traditional system puts the teacher in an authoritarian role. The authoritarian pattern was imported to the United States from western Europe and was well established before the American revolution. Some people think that the authoritarian system of schooling became obsolete when the United States became a constitutional democracy.

Some teachers try to assume a more democratic role, involving students in goal setting, choosing learning activities, and peer teaching and evaluation. This is difficult within the traditional school because the students and the faculty are used to the authoritarian system. When a teacher deviates significantly from the traditional role, other teachers perceive this as inferior teaching because it is different, or as a threat because it suggests that their way is not effective.

The traditional role of the teacher in the traditional school is self perpetuating. Most teachers teach as they were taught. This is natural because they probably made a decision to become teachers based on their experiences with teachers in traditional schools.

Since it is no easy task to keep thirty minds focused on anything for an hour or a day or 180 days, the traditional teacher is expected to be a strong disciplinarian. Some teachers are uncomfortable with this role.

Teachers in the traditional system use, and are expected to use, a narrow range of modes of instruction: lectures, teacher-led discussions, recitations, and supervised study are the primary ones. Student presentations, student-led discussions, individual conferences, and individualized assignments are used occasionally. At some point on their brief trip through a teacher preparation program, someone, usually a methods teacher, may have suggested that traditional schools were too authoritarian and that there were alternative ways to teach. This was probably meaningless because most of their college classes, possibly including their methods classes, were taught in a traditional authoritarian manner.

Students

The student's role in the traditional educational system is a relatively passive one. He is expected to attend school, to pay attention, to do what he is told, to work hard, and thereby to become a true scholar. Some students accept this role and are comfortable with it. Some students do not accept this role, and some accept it but are uncomfortable with it.

Some students wish to have more voice in their own learning. They want more responsibility for determining what they will learn and when they will learn it. Some of these students find responsibility in other school activities and spend more time and energy on those than on their classroom work.

Some students don't want to be scholars. Some perceive that they don't have the ability to become scholars. The traditional system of education has never worked well for all children and youth. Until very recently it was not expected to. Traditional schooling was supposed to eliminate students at various ages so that they could join the work force where they were needed. It did this very well. Even as late as 1900, more children of elementary school age were working on farms and in factories than were attending school. When we no longer needed child labor, mass elementary schooling became a reality.

After World War II the nation no longer needed teenage youths in the labor force, and there was a sincere national commitment to mass secondary education. Schools designed to eliminate some students were now charged to keep them all and to provide them all with secondary education. The fact that about a million students have dropped out of schools each year for the last fifteen years and the fact that some high school graduates are functionally illiterate indicate how difficult the transition to mass secondary education has been and will be.

The roles of students have been changing dramatically for the last twenty years; they are changing dramatically today; and they will change dramatically for some time to come. It's difficult to analyze contemporary trends, but here are some items for consideration.

Three recent studies suggest that the academic aspect of schooling, instruction and curriculum, have little impact on our students. Their experiences with their peers, their after-school-hours life, and even extracurricular activities are much more significant. (Cusick, 1973; Keyes, 1976; Medred and Wallechinsky, 1976)

As a nation, we are much less inclined to respect people in authority today. From our highest leaders to the local police and the classroom teacher, we are much more critical and sceptical of those in authority. Naturally this affects the classroom relationship of teachers and students.

Several years ago this writer read somewhere that scientific knowledge was being discovered so rapidly that every 40 minutes there was enough new knowledge to fill a twenty-four volume encyclopedia. At some point since 1950 students must have realized that their parents and teachers didn't know much more about the world than they did. For example, the student who watched Jacques Cousteau on television last night knows more about some aspects of marine biology than his biology teacher does unless the biology teacher also watched Cousteau last night. For at least 300 years the school was a major source of information in our society. This is no longer true today. This has to affect the roles of students and their teachers.

Children and youth today are spending more time watching television than they will ever spend in elementary and secondary schools. At some point since 1950 the schools received the first television generation, and teachers hardly realized it. If students watch TV more than twenty hours per week doesn't it change the way they look at the teacher at the front of the room?

There has also been a considerable change in the rights of students in schools. The courts have cut deeply into the authoritarianism of the school in such areas as dress code, due process, freedom of the student press, freedom of student speech, etc. Students in schools today have almost the same rights as other citizens.

Parents

The ideal parent in the traditional educational system is the one who stays away from the school but sends money frequently. Parents all know that the school has many ways to collect money. Someone estimated that if a student in a suburban high school participated in all the school activities that he was expected to, the total cost would be well over $1,500 per year.

Most schools have a number of superficial ways to involve parents: P.T.A., parent advisory groups, room mothers (particularly in elementary schools), attendance at various school events, parent-teacher conferences, etc.

But parents are not expected to take an active role in the schooling process. Many parents dread hearing from the school at all because they assume that all school news is bad, that a call from school means their child is in trouble. Most parents are not comfortable in coming to the school. Many schools, like other public buildings, are not friendly places.

Parents who do raise serious questions about the operation of schools are led to believe that what goes on in schools is based on some vast professional knowledge that cannot be interpreted to the man or woman in the street. The traditional school trains parents not to take an active role in their children's schooling. Most parents accept this and do what the school wants. A few do not.

SYSTEM IN ACTION

In the primary grades a child will be assigned to one classroom and one teacher for the school year and school day. In this self-contained classroom the teacher teaches all of the academic subjects, and she may also teach music, art, and physical education. The teacher probably likes children, and they in turn like, and love, her. (More men are becoming elementary teachers today, and a few do teach in the early grades.) The classroom will normally be orderly. The teacher achieves this order more by "nudging" students than by harsh words and punishment.

More instructional time will be spent on reading than on other subjects. Reading may take from one-third to one-half of the total instructional time with reading periods in the morning and in the afternoon. There are pupil textbooks for reading, mathematics, science, social studies, language arts, and spelling. There is usually a workbook for reading, and there may be workbooks for some of the other subjects.

In the early grades children will have little, if any, homework. Writing, other than penmanship, is rare. Drills and exercises, written and oral, are very common.

There is a morning recess, an afternoon recess, and a lunch period. In some elementary schools children go home for lunch. In others they remain at school. When children move around the school, they probably go as a class unit with their teacher. Even at recess the young children may stay in this class group so that the class unit is generally isolated from the rest of the school.

The classroom furniture may be flexible so that student desks can be pushed together to form tables. Chairs are frequently separate from the desks so that flexible seating arrangements are possible. Even when the furniture is flexible, the most common seating arrangements would have all students facing the teacher.

For reading instruction, and occasionally for other subjects, the children will probably be assigned to small groups. A class of thirty might be divided into two, three, four, or more reading groups, but three groups is very common. While the teacher works with one group in the front of the room, the other two groups are given specific "seat work" to do, usually in the reader or in the reading workbook.

The reading groups usually have names selected by the teacher, such as the bluebirds, the redbirds, and the blackbirds (or the buzzards). These names are used instead of words like *high, average,* and *low* to mask the groups. But the children and the teacher all know that the bluebirds are the better readers and that the buzzards are the slower readers. Most teachers at all grade levels feel strongly that ability grouping results in more effective instruction. They may be right, but there is little, if any, evidence to support this conclusion.

Since children spend a significant portion of their school day in these ability groups, they have a great influence on each child's present and future attitudes toward school and toward learning. There is evidence that ability grouping is not good for the buzzards. They don't have peer models of good reading within their group. When they are doing seat work, the only person they can turn to for help is another buzzard. (The redbirds and the bluebirds will have different assignments.) Needless to say, there is a stigma on the buzzards, and if they don't realize it, their parents will point it out to them. Ability grouping creates an academic caste system within the classroom. Elitism may not be very good for the bluebirds either. The use of ability grouping in the traditional system results in the early labeling of children and in emphasis on competition rather than on cooperation. Educators don't really know what effects early ability grouping may have on the self-concepts of children, on feelings about self, and on feelings about others.

There is evidence that small heterogeneous groups work better than ability groups. In such groups good readers can be assigned to help poor readers when the teacher is not available. But this system is rarely used in the traditional classroom where ability grouping and competition are well established.

As children move to the upper elementary grades, less time is spent on reading, but it still gets more time than any other subject, and ability grouping is still commonly used. Students in the upper elementary grades are likely to have some homework, but the amount varies considerably from school to school and from teacher to teacher.

Any form of written composition is rare in the elementary school. Writing is usually that required by textbook exercises: filling in blanks, copying words and sentences, and short answers to questions. Modest efforts are usually made to provide differentiated reading materials within the classroom. Instruction in the upper elementary grades may be in self-contained classrooms or in departmentalized classrooms, where the class has one teacher for reading, a second teacher for mathematics, a third for social studies, and so on.

At the beginning of this century most elementary schools went through grade eight, and most high schools included grades nine through twelve. As junior high schools developed in some school systems, they usually included grades seven through nine. Recently, there has been more interest in middle schools in some communities for grades five or six through eight, with grade nine again assigned to the high school. All of these patterns are still found in various school systems.

In a typical middle-school or junior-high-school day students would have from seven to nine class periods of thirty to forty-five minutes each. Each student would have one period for math, science, social studies, and language arts (English and reading). The language arts period might be a double period, and sometimes social studies and language arts are combined in a double period. One or more foreign languages are probably offered one period per day for those students who choose to take them. Physical education is probably required, but P.E. classes may not meet every day depending on the school's facilities. Art and music are probably required, but not necessarily for all students every year. Home economics and industrial arts will probably be available in some form. Students may or may not have study halls. Student schedules are usually individualized rather than by classes.

The junior high school usually has a variety of extracurricular (or cocurricular) activities, including interscholastic and intramural athletics for boys and girls. In most communities the junior high schools tend to mirror the academic and non-academic programs of the senior high schools.

The major difference in the academic programs of the senior high school and junior high school would be that the high school has considerably more curricular offerings. The high school usually has a college preparation track, one or more vocational tracks, and a general track. Students and their parents select the appropriate track, and once selected, this determines the courses that each student will take. These tracks result in academic segregation within the school. A vocational student and a college prep student would not be in classes together unless both happen to be in the band, chorus, or some other non-academic class.

High schools may have work-study programs in which a few students enroll for a half day of academic courses at school, and then work the other half day out in the community for pay.

Classes and schedules do not determine all that is significant in the students' school day or school year. The academic, extracurricular, and social interaction within the school are of great significance. The student role in the classroom at all levels is a passive one. Teacher talk takes up a greater portion of class time than student talk. Within most classrooms only a few students respond in discussions so that some students go through a school day without uttering a word in their classrooms.

For most students the most significant part of school is the peer group. Peers are probably much more important than teachers or subjects in the growing-up process. Most traditional schools tend to ignore this. Long after the Peloponesian Wars are forgotten, we remember a student who sat across the aisle in World History. The fascinating studies by Cusick (1973) and Keyes (1976) show how little students are affected by the academic curriculum and how much they are affected by peer status, peer pressure, and the total peer milieu of the school. This is probably true at all levels of schooling.

PROSPECT

The traditional educational system will continue to be the primary vehicle for schooling in this country for the foreseeable future. Certainly the majority of children and youth will be schooled in the traditional system for the remainder of this century.

Expert opinion, as exemplified by several major national studies of the schools since 1970, would agree that the traditional educational system is in need of immediate, dramatic reform. Public opinion, as reported by the Annual Gallup Polls of the Public's Attitude Toward the Public Schools, indicates waning confidence in and increasing concern for the schools, but there is no indication that the public in general or parents in particular are pressing for reform of the traditional system. The people directly involved in the schools—school board members, administrators, and teachers—are much more concerned with the operational problems of the schools than with short-range or long-range reform.

The traditional educational system has not changed dramatically in the last twenty-five years. It will probably not change dramatically in the next twenty-five. Words such as *change* and *reform* may be inappropriate in the analysis of a system which is several hundred years old, which has no central national control, and which performs a service to clients based on tradition rather than on client need (the postal service), client satisfaction (the automobile market), or professional research (medicine).

The traditional educational system will surely evolve into something in many ways quite different from the system we have now just as today's system is in many ways different from the educational system of 1880 or 1780 or 1680. Since this evolution is a gradual process, the signals of the coming evolution are probably present long in advance. Any reader of this book can and should look for these signals. To encourage readers to do so, four possible signals of the coming evolution in the traditional system of education follow:

1. A political signal

The current concern over declining test scores is forcing a much needed national dialogue on the effectiveness of the schools. To date the reactions of professional educators have been defensive. Educators should welcome those rare opportunities when schooling becomes a national issue and seize such opportunities to involve the public in a serious analysis of the educational system. The real problems of education are complex. There are no easy solutions, and there are no solutions without the involvement of the general public—citizens, parents, taxpayers, legislators, federal judges, etc. The current back-to-basics movement and the accompanying competency-testing movement are simplistic, superficial solutions to complex, deep educational problems.

2. A philosophical signal

The concept of alternative education presents a viable alternative to our hundreds-of-years-old philosophy of developing the one best system for all. The concept of a variety of optional schools, including the traditional school, suggests a way to strengthen American education without forcing families to send their children to innovative schools.

Action learning, one branch of alternative education that is endorsed by almost all recent national reports, provides a way to make schools much more than the traditional classroom learning experience.

3. A methodological signal

There are many signs today that some parents and some teachers would prefer to see emphasis in traditional schools shift from competition to helping relationships. If the schools are to educate all children and youth, the traditional competitive atmosphere must be modified for those who can't or won't engage in academic competition. This can and will be accomplished without the total elimination of competition.

4. A curricular signal

The curriculum will have to undergo a reorganization. New areas of study can't be added on to the traditional curriculum any longer. There is growing pressure within the society for including in the curriculum a number of areas that are directly related to the future survival of society—career education, conservation education, consumer education, death education, drug education, energy education, environmental education, health education, media education, nutrition education, parenting education, sex education, to name a few.

In this century the evolution of the traditional educational system was guided by a strategy based on industrial efficiency: large factories, uniform processes, quality control, uniform products. We are beginning to realize that industrial efficiency is the wrong model for developing compassion, wisdom, and all the other traits that are human. The system will soon abandon the industrial efficiency model. What will replace it is very much in doubt.

REFERENCES

Bailey, S. K., Macy, F. U. and Vickers, D. F. *Alternative paths to the high school diploma.* Reston, Va.: National Association of Secondary School Principals, 1973.

Bayh, B. *Challenge for the third century: education in a safe environment—final report on the nature and prevention of school violence and vandalism.* Washington: U.S. Government Printing Office, 1977.

Broad, L. *Alternative schools: why, what, where & how much.* Arlington, Va.: National School Public Relations Association, 1977.

Bruner, J. S. *The process of education.* Cambridge, Ma.: Harvard University Press, 1960.

Cawelti, G. *Vitalizing the high school.* Washington: Association for Supervision and Curriculum Development, 1974.

Coleman, J. S. *Youth transition to adulthood: report of the panel on youth of the President's science advisory committee.* Chicago: University of Chicago Press, 1974.

Cremin, L. *American education: the colonial experience 1607–1783.* New York: Harper & Row, 1970.

Cubberly, E. P. *Changing concepts of education.* Boston: Houghton Mifflin, 1909.

Cusick, P. A. *Inside high school: the student's world.* New York: Holt, Rinehart & Winston, 1973.

Elam, S. (ed.) *The Gallup polls of attitudes toward education 1969–1973.* Bloomington, In.: Phi Delta Kappa, 1973.

Fantini, M. D. *Alternative education.* Garden City, N.Y.: Doubleday, 1976.

Fantini, M. D. *Public schools of choice: a plan for the reform of American education.* New York: Simon & Schuster, 1973.

Gibbons, M. *The new secondary education.* Bloomington, In.: Phi Delta Kappa, 1976.

Glatthorn, A. A. *Alternatives in education: schools and programs.* New York: Dodd, Mead, 1975.

Goodlad, J. I., Klein, M. F. and Associates. *Looking behind the classroom door.* Worthington, Oh.: Charles A. Jones, 1974.

Hechinger, F. and Hechinger, G. *Growing up in America.* New York: McGraw-Hill, 1975.

Keyes, R. *Is there life after high school?* New York: Warner Books, 1976.

Medved M. and Wallechinsky, D. *What really happened to the class of '65?* New York: Ballantine, 1976.

Nachtigal, P. Attempts to change education in the sixties. *Changing Schools,* 1972, 1 (2), 8–11.

National Commission on the Reform of Secondary Education. *The reform of secondary education.* New York: McGraw-Hill, 1973.

National Commission on Resources for Youth. *New roles for youth in the school and the community.* New York: Citation Press, 1974.

National Panel on High School and Adolescent Education. *The education of adolescents.* Washington: U.S. Government Printing Office, 1976.

Overly, N. V. (ed.) *The unstudied curriculum: its impact on children.* Washington: Association for Supervision and Curriculum Development, 1970.

Passow, A. H. *Secondary education reform: retrospect and prospect.* New York: Teachers College, 1976.

Postman, N. Alternative education in the seventies. *The Last Supplement to the Whole Earth Catalog,* 1971, 3, 41–46.

Shane, H. G. *Curriculum change toward the 21st century.* Washington: National Education Association, 1977.

Smith, V., Barr, R. and Burke, D. *Alternatives in education.* Bloomington, In.: Phi Delta Kappa, 1976.

Smith, V. and Gallup, G. H. *What the people think about their schools: Gallup's findings.* Bloomington, In.: Phi Delta Kappa, 1977.

Stenson, B. *Research report: alternative schools.* Washington: National School Boards Association, 1976.

Task Force on Secondary Schools in a Changing Society. *This we believe.* Reston, Va.: National Association of Secondary School Principals, 1975.

Task Force '74. *The adolescent, other citizens, and their high schools.* New York: McGraw-Hill, 1975.

Tyack, D. B. *The one best system: a history of American urban education.* Cambridge, Ma.: Harvard University Press, 1974.

Woodring, P. *A fourth of a nation.* New York: McGraw-Hill, 1957.

CHAPTER 3

Individually

Guided

Education

JOHN M. BAHNER

DEFINITION

Individually Guided Education is a comprehensive, systematic manner of managing the learning environment in a school or related setting. It is applicable to all types of curriculum from "the basics" to a "humanistic approach". Teacher behavior is emphasized, but important ingredients also involve students and support persons such as school board members, administrators, and parents.

Individually Guided Education is primarily a series of processes to make better decisions about individualizing learning programs for students and instilling attitudes and skills necessary for continuous improvement in teachers and students. It is not another name for having students study independently, although learning in a group of one will occur at times in the system. It is not having students do only what they want to do, although the system does have students become increasingly responsible for decisions involving their own education. Rather, Individually Guided Education is a means of controlling many elements of the learning environment to match the learning styles of the students.

The basis of IGE is a set of 35 outcomes[1] which characterize the school when the system is fully implemented.

INTRODUCTION

Individually Guided Education was designed as a school improvement program emphasizing staff development. It is based on several concepts of what is idealized as good education, and it is based on theories relating to both change and learning.

Objectives Of Education

On almost everyone's list of educational goals is an item related to improving the quality of life of humans both individually and collectively. Learning to use basic tools skills such as reading, writing, and computing is obviously a major factor in good education. At least of equal importance are to think critically, to solve problems, and to become an effective decision maker. Furthermore, since life depends far more on cooperating with other humans than it does on competing with them, developing skills of interacting with one's fellow humans is a necessary ingredient to improving one's quality of life.

Education should help students develop an attitude of being life-long learners, should provide them with learning processes, and should help them to become cognizant of their full potential and the manner in which they use their talents. Somehow, many people in this country think of education as something which takes place during the first eighteen to twenty-two years of one's life, and that the next four to five decades are spent using that knowledge to earn a living. Formal schooling currently contributes to this restrictive view of education by emphasizing factual retention of knowledge and specific vocational skills.

Good education begins by helping a student develop a healthy self-image. This is not only a desirable objective in itself, but for most people it is prerequisite to learning in a social environment. Many of the practices which help develop a healthy self-image (e.g., providing enough successful experiences to keep the student motivated, helping the student receive positive feedback regarding his learning) also develop positive attitudes about learning and contribute to helping the student become a lifelong learner.

In the eyes of many, it is sufficient merely to know about something in an intellectual way. Of greater value is education which is internalized until it is useful. For most people, this means learning by doing and practicing it until it is part of one's lifestyle. Hearing, seeing, smelling, tasting, and touching may all be used in this process, but each learner uses them in different ways and to different extents. It is important that education help a learner understand the manner in which he learns in order to be more self-directed and to accept more responsibility for learning throughout life.

Learning is very difficult to force upon someone. Students drop out of school every day, some by absenting themselves from the premises and others by "daydreaming" during class time. Students must be helped to see that education is their responsibility, and this will not happen unless students are involved from the beginning of their formal schooling in decisions which affect their educational life.

Few people would deny the vital importance of acquiring basic tool skills in reading, writing, and computing. Yet, there is much debate regarding the next level of a good education. Factual retention of knowledge and other items commonly measured by most current standardized achievement tests are superficial at best. Far more important than these specific items are those processes by which the student learns. The means of becoming educated are the true ends of education.

Reasons For The System

Each of the many attempts to improve education in the past fifty years has tended to focus on a relatively narrow aspect of schooling. Many innovations fall by the wayside because there are too many variables to show significant difference for one element even if the element is a set of materials using a prescribed methodology. For example, Individually Prescribed Instruction may be the best way to teach some of the students some mathematics some of the time. But to expect a single approach to be the best method for all students for all mathematics at all times is to expect the impossible. Another example might be elementary science programs which have emerged during the past twenty years. Some of the research was based upon teachers who were insufficiently trained to conduct a new program properly but were included in the experimental group nevertheless. Seldom did the researchers go in and actually observe the extent to which teachers were using the new science programs in the manner in which they were designed prior to checking the effects of such a program. The amount of time devoted to science also varied considerably and contributed to conflicting results.

Other innovations fail to have lasting effect because related constricting factors were not taken into account. For example, differentiated staffing may have failed to become widespread because in school systems with expanding enrollments leadership personnel were taken from classroom assignments and promoted into traditional administrative positions as principal or supervisor. If the same idea were to be rejuvenated in the current scene of declining enrollments and relative staff stability, the effects might be quite different.

Another reason education has been relatively slow to change is that most innovations were conceived by academicians who were more concerned with new knowledge *per se* then they were with implementation of those innovations. A theorist may pursue his interests to the extent of seeing his model applied in a limited (often artificial) environment. But once the theorist has demonstrated its applicability (at least to his own satisfaction) he leaves widespread implementation to others—which usually means leaving it to no one.

Planned change, action research, and similar efforts have appeared in the professional literature frequently during the past 25 years, and almost invariably school improvement resulted in these limited areas. Unfortunately, ideas evolving from these movements seldom were incorporated into innovations advocated by theorists or other researchers. As a result, strategies to implement new ideas have seldom been a central concern of those involved with innovation and then only in localized situations.

Change from a narrow orthodoxy to a new but equally narrow orthodoxy usually lacks vitality, and the latter soon is replaced by still another new orthodoxy—and only if directly related does the new capitalize on the good aspects of the old. What has been lacking is a system which relates a number of proven ideas into an integrated whole and combines theory and innovative models with well designed implementation procedures. Individually Guided Education is designed to encourage peer supervision. This feature provides teachers with help they need and desire, and it is a motivating influence for school improvement in general. Individually Guided Education is also designed to foster the objectives of education discussed in the previous section. Teachers model decision making processes for students and help students become involved in decisions affecting their own education.

HISTORY

A wide array of concepts based upon research and practice in education over many years have contributed to the development of Individually Guided Education. Because this system is based upon sets of principles and not specifics, current operations prevail in a variety of forms and widely varying administrative structures.

Beginnings

One of the greatest inhibitors to individualizing instruction was the emergence of the graded school structure in the mid-1800s. Prior to that, education tended to be personalized if only because of such factors as small student populations, irregular school terms and pupil attendance, lack of commercial teaching materials, and little communication among educators.

Almost immediately after graded schools appeared and graded curriculums were identified with textbooks to help standardize content of a given grade, many attempts to thwart the graded system sprang up around the country. Some of these gained fame by being reported in the professional literature. The Pueblo Plan and the Batavia Plan of the late 1800s, the Platoon Plan of 1900, the Winnetka Plan and the Dalton Plan of the 1920s period, and the Dual Progress Plan and the Continuous Progress Plan at mid-century are mentioned in most books dealing with the history of American education. All these plans contained organizational aspects to make schools more flexible. Most of them also contained curriculum components designed to make school programs more appropriate for students.[2]

The traditional program of the elementary school and the classical program of the secondary school came under attack about the same time. Not only were new subjects such as social studies, vocational education, and foreign languages (supplementing Latin) added to the curriculum, but traditional areas such as science and mathematics had optional courses. At first these tended to be developed for the noncollege bound students, such as general science and general math. As sizes of high schools increased and proliferation became easier, a variety of courses in business and vocational education, English, social studies, music, and art emerged—soon to be followed by courses of advanced placement developed for academically talented high school students to enable them to undertake college work while still in the high school setting.

When selection from a variety of courses was added to administrative procedures which enabled a student to pursue course work at a pace which is appropriate for that particular student, then the nongraded high school evolved.[3]

Although rudiments of the organizational pattern occurred earlier, it was not until the late 1950s that examples could be found of teachers working closely together in a cooperative endeavor usually labeled team teaching. Regardless of other arguments for and against teaming, it soon became obvious that a greater variety of learning options could be offered by a group of teachers working together as contrasted to an elementary school teacher working in a self-contained classroom or a secondary school teacher handling all aspects of a course with a given group of students for a semester or year. Teachers working together found they could not only plan better but could offer a wider variety of learning options, provide a wider range of teaching methodologies, accommodate different learning styles better, diagnose more accurately, and in other ways take into account individual differences to a greater degree than working independently.

Most important of all, team teaching provided the means by which continuous improvement processes could be built into the planning, teaching, and evaluation aspects of the professional role using input from two or more teachers rather than having just selfassessment opportunities of the traditional organizational pattern.[4]

Also during the 1950s, scholars of school administration—drawing primarily upon research in business management—proclaimed the desirability of an administrative style which elicits participation of staff members in decision making processes. School administrators were urged to find ways to make institutional goals more compatible with personal aspirations of teachers.[5]

Theories of teaching and learning dating back to Socrates, but coming forth with more intensity in the past 50 years, are also in the foundation upon which Individually Guided Education is built. Those dealing with organizational structure and classroom management have explicit expression in the 35 outcomes of IGE. Those dealing with teaching techniques are implicit in examples of IGE portrayed in materials of the /I/D/E/A/ Change Program for Individually Guided Education.[6]

One of the major contributions of Individually Guided Education is the manner in which school personnel are trained in the new system. The roots of this training program reach back to a summer program to train teachers in the Graduate School of Education at Harvard University using the Lexington, Massachusetts public school system in the early 1960s. It was here that clinical training components which are now part of IGE were developed to continue the professional education of experienced teachers.[7]

For more than a decade, two organizations have been developing, implementing, and doing research on Individually Guided Education. The Institute for Development of Educational Activities, Inc. (/I/D/E/A/), the educational affiliate of the Charles F. Kettering Foundation has as its major purpose the reduction of the time gap between what is known about good education and what actually goes on in classrooms. As director of the Institute's Innovative Programs division beginning in the late 1960s, John M. Bahner was the chief designer of an IGE program to fulfill the Institute's purpose.

Simultaneously, the Wisconsin Research and Development Center for Cognitive Learning was working on a project then called the Multi-Unit School—Elementary with Herbert J. Klausmeier as principal investigator. The image of the "ideal school" perceived by the staffs of these two organizations was extremely similar. The Wisconsin R & D Center was working with schools in Wisconsin to make the image a reality. /I/D/E/ A/ was working toward the same goals with schools in five states. Changes in teacher behavior were guaranteed by /I/D/E/A/ for those school systems with which it had entered into a contract. At that time, federal funding did not provide for diffusion of programs developed by research and development centers. Thus, it was natural for the two organizations to enter into an agreement to develop materials based upon the theories and experience of the respective organizations. The name Individually Guided Education was coined as a descriptive title for the new system.

Within a year, it became apparent that although the main goals of the two organizations remained mutually consistent, differences in emphases and implementation procedures were becoming major. The Wisconsin R & D Center placed a heavy emphasis on curriculum materials for students, and indeed had already developed prototypic reading and math textbooks for early elementary school students. The R & D Center program also placed a heavy emphasis on organizational structure, and Center personnel apparently felt that the materials resulting from the agreement with /I/D/E/A/ would deal solely with the ideas generated in the Center and would reflect them accurately.

Development of curriculum materials was not deemed appropriate by /I/D/E/A/ staff members because they felt it was their task to help teachers individualize school programs by using whatever curriculum materials were available to a school. The materials which /I/D/E/A/ developed were to help teachers learn about and use processes to modify their classroom environment. Even here, however, the materials were decidedly subordinate to a clinical training program. These materials were made available to only those who had undertaken this extensive training.

Furthermore, /I/D/E/A/ was strongly oriented to processes rather than specifics and placed a major emphasis on change processes. At the time of the agreement with the R & D Center, /I/D/E/A/ was in the midst of a major study of change in its Research Division. Under the direction of John I. Goodlad, the research staff observed and analyzed over a seven-year period the actions of 18 school faculties in the Los Angeles area.

As a result of these differences, the Wisconsin R & D Center and /I/D/E/A/ parted company, and the two organizations continued working on IGE via separate but compatible routes. Because of this writer's heavy involvement with the /I/D/E/A/ system, this chapter is based entirely on the /I/D/E/A/ Change Program for Individually Guided Education. For a description of the Wisconsin R & D Center IGE Program, see the prolific writings eminating from that Center.[8]

Current Status

During the eight year period between 1969 and 1977, more than 1700 schools became involved with the /I/D/E/A/ Change Program for Individually Guided Education. These schools are associated in leagues of IGE schools coordinated by staff members, called facilitators, in approximately 250 intermediate agencies. Central offices of school systems, university schools of education, educational service centers, and state departments of education comprise the vast majority of intermediate agencies in this IGE network. Staff members in American sponsored overseas schools in more than 30 countries have also been trained in IGE. Growth is continuing both by the expansion of existing leagues and by identifying and training facilitators from new intermediate agencies.

Systematic data gathering is one of the cornerstones of IGE. In large measure, analyses of data obtained from students, parents, teachers and administrators are exceedingly positive regarding IGE.

One type of data provides feedback to the developers thereby enabling them to modify materials, training strategies, implementing procedures, and other parts of the system. Other sets of data provide descriptions of effects. A thorough assessment of the current status of IGE involves both types of data.[9]

Effects of IGE

IGE *per se* has no goals of raising achievement scores in specific subject areas or of making students happier in schools. On the other hand, most people involved with IGE desire higher reading scores for students; they want the students, parents, teachers, and administrators to be more satisfied with the school environment—to be happier individuals; they would like to see improvement in such tangential areas as attendance and school vandalism.

Student achievement

Schools using IGE are likely to show improvement in standardized achievement test scores according to samples of principals collected in a four-year period.[10]

The percentages for slight or significant increases, even though noteworthy, are deceivingly low because of the large number of schools that did no testing at all.

Data from a two year study involving 2800 personal interviews conducted by Belden Associates,[11] a research firm located in Dallas, showed both teachers and parents stated that students were doing better using the IGE system. Approximately 88 percent of parents were positive in their feelings about their children's progress in school. Just under 8 percent were somewhat dissatisfied and 3 percent were very dissatisfied.

A significantly larger number of teachers feel that students are learning and performing better since IGE was initiated. This is especially true in schools implementing most of the IGE program outcomes (high implementation) compared to schools that have not yet achieved most outcomes (low implementation).

TABLE 1
Reading and Verbal Achievement Scores

Response of Principals	1973-74 %	1974-75 %	1975-76 %	1976-77 %
"Scores are significantly higher since IGE implementation"	4	7	6	6
"Scores are slightly higher since IGE implementation"	13	21	27	35
"Scores have shown no significant change"	38	34	32	33
"Scores are slightly lower since IGE implementation"	1	3	5	1
"Scores are significantly lower since IGE implementation"	0	.3	0	.3
"We have not administered Standardized Achievement Tests"	34	28	24	20
No Response	10	7	6	5

TABLE 2
Mathematics Achievement Scores

Response of Principals	1973-74 %	1974-75 %	1975-76 %	1976-77 %
"Scores are significantly higher since IGE implementation"	3	5	4	7
"Scores are slightly higher since IGE implementation	12	18	24	29
"Scores have shown no significant change"	35	34	35	35
"Scores are slightly lower since IGE implementation"	2	4	4	3
"Scores are significantly lower since IGE implementation"	0	1	1	1
"We did not administer Standardized Achievement Tests"	34	29	26	20
No Response	14	9	6	5

TABLE 3
How Well Has Your Child Done in School This Year Compared to Last?

	Years Child in IGE		
	One Year	More than One Year	Total Parents
Learned more	38%	52%	43%
About the same	23%	33%	26%
Learned less	4%	4%	4%
No answer/not in this school last year	35%	11%	27%

Two trends are emerging: better academic achievement is attained through IGE processes, and more significant improvement occurs as the degree of implementation of the system increases.

IGE also improves attitudes toward school according to the Belden study.

Students react even more positively to their schools and their teachers than do their parents.

TABLE 4
Since the Adoption of the IGE Program, Do You Think Student Behavior
Has Improved, Stayed the Same, or Become Worse?

	Degree of IGE	
	High	Low
Improved	35%	26%
Stayed the same	48%	52%
Become worse	11%	11%
No answer	6%	11%

TABLE 5
Compared to Last Year, How Do You Feel About School This Year?

	More This Year	About The Same	More Last Year	Does Not Apply
Enjoyed school	43%	31%	8%	18%
Learned Subjects	63%	16%	3%	18%
Interesting	57%	20%	5%	18%
Like teachers	34%	40%	8%	18%
Like other kids	33%	42%	7%	18%

The above two tables are taken from the Belden study. Both these
phenomena were also observed in a study conducted by Fred W. Wood.[12]
In addition to the basic fact that attitudes of parents and students were
positive toward IGE and its effects, both the Belden and Wood studies
indicate that the attitudes become more positive the longer a student is in
an IGE school.

Data from annual surveys of principals[13] indicate that IGE is associated
with:

Improved student discipline
Reduced school vandalism
Lower teacher absenteeism
Lower student absenteeism
Improved school climate
Costs comparable to non-IGE schools in the same school system

Degree of implementation[14]

Schools participating in the /I/D/E/A/ Change Program for IGE monitor
their own progress. This monitoring is done by having teachers respond
to a "baseline" questionnaire prior to IGE implementation. Several months
after initial implementation efforts in their school and annually thereafter
teachers also respond to an "outcomes achievement" questionnaire. These
two instruments distinguish between situations where IGE processes are
in operation and where they are not in operation. Comparison of scores

between baseline questionnaires and annual outcomes achievement questionnaires indicates growth in IGE implementation during the intervening period of time.

Where schools are following the IGE system, evidence of change is definite. IGE schools that are a year or two into the program differ markedly from their status prior to IGE in terms of organization, use of staff resources, availability of various learning options for students, and leeway afforded students and teachers in selecting and pursuing learning objectives. These changes are evidence of progress in providing individualized learning, and some of the changes have been confirmed by the above mentioned studies as contributing to higher student achievement.

For most schools, rapid growth occurs during the first year they are in the program. The IGE implementation score attained by a school after approximately a year in the program is a reasonably good predictor of the amount of growth which will take place thereafter. To illustrate, a school which has an implementation score of 50 (out of a possible 100) is much more likely to continue growth than a school which has a score of 35. In fact, a school with a score of 35 is likely to regress during the succeeding two or three years.

Using data from a sample of schools involved in the program, the average implementation score during the 1976–77 school year was 58 and, based on previous years' growth, will increase about 6 to 8 points each year. The fact that schools which have been involved only two or three years score approximately as high as schools that have been in six or seven years probably reflects improved implementation and training procedures employed during recent years.

No school in the assessment sample has an implementation score above 80. This means that schools implementing IGE at the highest degree to date still have room for a 25 percent growth. The fact that schools with higher implementation scores show significant differences on student achievement and other factors mentioned above lends itself to a prediction that when schools finally implement all IGE processes the effects of IGE could be close to phenomenal.

THEORY

Individually Guided Education involves two different, but perfectly analogous, stages of learning and teaching—learning by teachers as they are taught by teacher trainers, and learning by students as they are taught by teachers.

Each theory of learning has implications for teaching. Thus, in the next section, each theoretical statement of learning is followed by discussion which contains its logical relationship to the teaching act.

IGE also is based on theory regarding the role of the teacher. A discussion of this is contained in the section on teaching.

Learning

Because IGE is applicable in a wide variety of settings, it can accommodate a wide variety of learning theories. Since some learning theories seem more appropriate with certain types of individuals than other theories, and since some learning theories are more helpful with certain content areas than others, it is the task of the instructor in an IGE system to select wisely using information at hand—to "wear the shoe when it fits". Nevertheless, there are a few theoretical concepts of learning applicable to all learners and therefore built directly into IGE.

> *Learning is increased when learners are clear about what is to be learned.*

If the learner knows where he is going, he is more likely to get there. Therefore, the IGE system advocates clearly specified learning objectives. The term "behavioral objective" does not occur in IGE literature because of the very specific connotation most people give to the adjective "behavioral". Rather, emphasis is on specifying the objectives sufficiently to insure that both the teacher and the learner have the same perception of what is to be accomplished. The language could be as detailed as performing 15 mathematical computations in a three minute period with 90 percent accuracy. Or it could be as general as reading sufficiently in an area to determine whether or not the learner wants to undertake a project in that area.

Whenever clarity is equated to measuring with quantifiable precision, the result is usually a focus on minutia—which may have no direct relationship to the student's broad objectives or schoolwide goals.

> *Learning is increased when learners are involved in helping to define objectives and activities to achieve those objectives.*

Obviously the ability of a learner to define learning objectives and learning activities are dependent in large measure on his mental age and experience. Therefore, the IGE system strives to have each learner increasingly involved in defining objectives and activities. Not only does this help to insure that the objective is clear and that the student knows what he is going to do, but it also helps develop commitment to his learning tasks.

A longer range purpose to having the learner involved at this stage is to assist him in learning how to learn. By clarifying what the student needs to learn and ways to go about it, the student is developing skills needed in later life when a teacher will not be present to offer direction.

> *Learning is increased when elements of the learning environment are matched to the learner's learning style and not to his age.*

A number of factors might be critical to a specific learning situation:

Previous achievement
Interest in the subject area
Time available
Sequence to be used
Peer relationships
Self-concept of the learner
Learning style of the learner

Merely knowing what a learner is able to learn next is not sufficient information for an instructor to plan properly for that learner. It is equally important to know how the learner got where he is. Under what conditions does the learner learn best? Is the task relatively difficult and therefore he should be using a learning style which is familiar to him? Or is the task at hand a relatively easy one for him and he therefore should develop facility in using a different learning style? Does the learner know how to work from facts to generalizations as well as deduce probable events from his knowledge of a generalization? These are the types of questions that must be answered by the instructor and increasingly by the learner before appropriate plans can be made for subsequent learning activities.[15]

Furthermore, it is no longer sufficient for a teacher to be assigned a group of students for administrative reasons and to have what is taught to that group to be decided by textbooks or curriculum guides. Nor is a single methodological approach sufficient in the IGE system. Such group-oriented education is outmoded.

Rather, instructional grouping must be the result—not the starting point—of planning. Thus, a learning group is composed of those who have been placed there deliberately as the consequence of considering all the factors noted above. The group remains intact only so long as it is deemed appropriate for those particular learners to remain together for the task at hand.

> *Learning is increased when the learner is in a supportive environment with at least one instructor particularly concerned with enhancing the learner's self-concept and with sharing accountability for the learner's learning program.*

Whether with a teacher learning new methodology or a pupil learning new subject matter, the instructor is there to support the learner until all concerned believe that the task has been accomplished. This in no way should detract from the learner accepting responsibility for learning himself. In some schools (and this includes schools of education at universities) the welcomed learner is one who is passive, who goes where he is told to go, who does what he is told to do, and who learns what is prescribed for him. Not so in an IGE school. Here each learner increasingly accepts responsibility for his own education. The instructor is there to play a very supportive role in regard to four basic areas. The first of these areas is the learner's self-concept. Whether helping the shy, meek learner build up self confidence, or whether helping the braggadocio to see that his true self need not be falsely enhanced, the instructor assists the learner to see himself as a worthy individual who can be successful learning on his own or in the company of others.

The second area involves the learner's interpersonal relationships. The instructor provides support by helping the learner interact in groups of his peers as well as with teachers and other adults.

The third area pertains to the learning activity. Here the instructor may provide instructional assistance or help the student evaluate progress and report it to his parents, to other teachers, and in his own record keeping system.

The fourth area is to help the student plan new learning experiences. This may take the form of an alternative learning activity if those tried at first were incomplete or unsuccessful. It may take the form of a reinforcing activity for something only marginally learned. It may take the form of a new and more demanding learning activity offering the student a challenge to reach new heights.

> *Learning is increased when feedback regarding*
> *learning is almost immediate, is constructive, and*
> *involves the learner in the assessment analysis.*

Humans have different degrees of tolerance regarding the amount of time they are willing to abide prior to getting information about their successes. In the IGE system, the learner is to be involved in continuous self-assessment. When the student is knowledgeable about the objectives he is pursuing, and if evaluative criteria have been built into his learning plan, feedback is immediate as he undertakes each learning activity.

Periodically the learner involves another person—the instructor whenever possible, but often this is another student. This could take the form of a test, analysis of a work product, or observation of the learner as he applies his skills to a situation which calls for their use. The learner first presents an analysis of his learning, and it is then the obligation of the second person to comment on the analysis with supporting evidence and to offer constructive alternatives.

> *Learning is increased when application accompanies*
> *or immediately follows initial knowledge and*
> *understanding; learning is further enhanced when the*
> *application is critiqued and a new cycle of planning,*
> *doing, and assessing further applications is commenced*
> *as soon as practicable.*

Learning by doing is an important element of the teacher training aspect of IGE as well as the learning of students in the classroom. An extremely important ingredient of this is that learning is done under the auspices of an expert who can tactfully offer constructive advice and bring about improvement as long as the learner is willing to stay with the task.

Even more important is the lifestyle which is engendered by this process. A willingness to try out new things, constantly analyzing how it is being done as well as how well it is being done, develops an effective learning process which retains its potential throughout one's life.

Teaching

In the /I/D/E/A/ Change Program for Individually Guided Education, the concept of teaching extends beyond the classroom. It includes the planning and evaluation that takes place before, during, and after the teaching act. It includes the relationships of all the teachers in the building. It includes the support and assistance a teacher receives from outside the school. The theory postulated in this section permeates all these dimensions.

Because IGE requires patterns of professional operation which differ from the way most teachers were taught in their teacher training years, underlying theory of IGE necessarily deals with the change process.

> *The individual school is the strategic unit of*
> *educational change.*

With the emphasis in IGE on the individual student, it would be easy to jump to the conclusion that changes involving the teaching staff should be focused on individual teachers. A study of change conducted by the /I/D/E/A/ research division indicated that individual teachers who want to try new patterns of instruction rarely succeed unless the school supports those efforts.[16] Try as the teacher might to adopt some interesting new ideas, attempts at change are easily frustrated when unsympathetic colleagues regard those changes as a threat to their own professional standing, or when an unsympathetic principal regards the teacher as "radical" or "unreliable" and translates this personal reaction into a denial of promotion or tenure.

Changing the professional staff of an entire school system is obviously cumbersome and unwieldy. However, the school has the elements necessary to carry out instructional and learning functions: pupils, materials, teachers, and instructional authority. Thus, each school is the optimal unit for bringing about educational improvement.[17]

> *Each school needs a process by which it can deal*
> *effectively with its own problems if it is to maintain*
> *continuous improvement.*

For almost two decades beginning with the late 1950s, school reformers advocated research-development-diffusion as the means by which schools could be improved. Emanating from industry with a scholarly base in scientific management, research-development-diffusion was completely logical. The trouble was, it didn't work in schools. Sometimes it worked partially but was short-lived when imperfect implementation showed no significant difference and was then discarded.

The fault did not lie in the products coming out of research and development projects. One of the problems was that the researchers did not communicate adequately with practitioners. When practitioners were not in a receptive mood, perhaps because maintaining the status quo was being rewarded, or when practitioners simply did not understand the language of the researcher, they could hardly see the relevance of the innovation. The diffusion aspect then broke down.

IGE advocates building a receptivity into a school staff prior to its receiving new ideas from the outside. This process includes having faculty members analyze their own goals, determine the extent to which they are now achieving those ideals, and then considering an array of new ideas (including the IGE system) and the potential each idea has to help the staff achieve its goals. Significant improvement begins when the process is used as the teachers consider adopting new school-wide policies and procedures. Further improvement requires that the process be used as teachers plan, teach, and evaluate the performances of themselves and their students as the new adoptions get underway.

Thus, heavy involvement on the part of teachers in solving their own problems is a fundamental ingredient of the IGE system. Obviously, the nature and quality of the various interpersonal relations among the staff members loom large as the determining factors in the success or failure to achieve a change. When the quality of these relationships is good, there will be a high sense of belongingness to the group and strong group cohesion which creates an atmosphere of permissiveness leading to creative expression and experimentation with new ideas without fear of repercussions either from the administration or from the group.

> *Basic changes in the effects of school (e.g., reading achievement, attitudes toward school) are lasting only when such changes include support of the administrative hierarchy and school board, when organizational structures are revised in response to the needs of the changes, when new modes of operation are assumed by the teachers involved, and when students modify their behavior appropriately.*[18]

Another reason for the failure of the research-development-diffusion change model was that a specific innovation dealt only with a relatively narrow aspect of school operations. Full implementation of the idea was hampered by other factors impinging upon it. A computer that could not handle certain scheduling demands, a clause in the negotiated master agreement with the teacher's organization, strict adherence to a graded curriculum concept, lack of understanding of school board members and parents, and many other factors not directly provided for by a new idea often hindered implementation of that idea.

IGE provides comprehensive, systematic analyses of the major aspects of schooling, participation in decision-making at appropriate levels from the school board to the students, and structures which facilitate incorporation of these analyses and participation into a way of life in the school. The system does not encompass all areas of schooling, but its comprehensiveness extends well beyond previous innovations. The system also accounts for each of the four support elements called for by the theory.

For example, the IGE system has as one of its initial conditions that the school district approve a school staff's decision to implement the /I/D/E/A/ Change Program for Individually Guided Education. It would be unfair to have a staff embark enthusiastically on a new program only to have the school board or superintendent object several months later to the fact that the school was employing multiage grouping practices. Agreements regarding the basic principles of the system are reached prior to implementation of the program.

An example of a support element at another level is the organization of teachers into closely knit groups of three to ten persons who work closely together in the planning, teaching, and evaluative phases of the instructional program. At another level of operation, teachers individually assume new modes of operation as they become more goal-oriented, see their role as providing assistance to their colleagues as well as to students, and design learning programs based upon individual assessments rather than on perceived group needs.

At still another level, the system calls for students to assume new roles in the learning process. They become involved in identifying appropriate objectives, in helping design learning programs, and in assuming responsibility for assessing what they learn and the manner in which they learn it.

These support elements involve aspects of a person's value system which are both peripheral and central. The peripheral aspects have less emotional involvement and are closer to the action level of the person. As such, changes involved in this region are relatively easy to achieve. The central regions involve deeply held values and beliefs; they are more personal, intimate, and private; they are less susceptible to environmental influences. Therefore, they are less accessible to action, but once change does occur in the central region, a difference in behavior will occur which is more enduring and sustaining than behavioral differences due to change in the peripheral region.[19]

Change agents for IGE thus advocate a two to five year period of intensive staff involvement before making claims that the system is fully installed in a school.

> *Most individual schools are not strong enough to*
> *overcome the inertia against change built into the*
> *typical school district and therefore require a*
> *supportive peer reference group.*[20]

Policies and procedures established at a certain point in time, usually for good reasons, evolve through the years into "the book" over which no individual teacher or school has control. What were once sensible guidelines can become cumbersome bureaucratic rules which few people have the authority or inclination to break even after those rules have outlived their usefulness.

Schools are organized into districts to promote some degree of uniformity in the allocation of resources, hiring and promotion policies, and the treatment of students. Principals perceive their tasks to be that of maintaining these uniformities, not challenging them. They may innovate here or there, but they tend to abide by an unwritten understanding that they are not expected or encouraged to change anything basic. A local school principal or group of teachers who deviate markedly from this established expectation risk isolation and censure.

No single school can, for any length of time, fight alone against the forces that resist change in a school district. The school must reach out to other change-minded schools that can offer it emotional and professional backing. It must find schools which can offer moral support because they themselves are changing and which can offer professional expertise at solving instructional problems. Sometimes this backing can be found from among schools within its own district; at other times, this backing is more likely found among schools geographically near but organizationally aligned in a different political subdivision.

In the /I/D/E/A/ Change Program, this supportive peer reference group is obtained through the formation of a league of IGE schools. A staff member, called a facilitator, from an agency affiliated with /I/D/E/A/ (a central office of a school, system, a university, a regional educational center, a state department of education) coordinates league peer interaction which many teachers say provides some of the most satisfying professional experiences in their careers.

Teachers learn new roles best when principles of
learning expressed in the previous section are followed.

In an IGE school, the teacher is a learner as much as are the students. Periodically, teachers are engaged in systematic inquiry into an area meaningful and relevant to their professional tasks. They consider a variety of alternatives offered by their own thinking processes, by their colleagues on the staff, and by persons outside the school. They apply the knowledge in new situations and analyze the degree to which they attain their objectives and the means by which they pursue it. Analysis of the new application triggers the cycle once again.

APPLICATIONS

The thirty five outcomes which define the IGE system are identical for elementary schools, for middle or junior high schools, and for high schools. Differences in application and emphasis occur from school to school, and the degree to which a specific outcome is implemented also varies from school to school.

The three vignettes presented in the next two sections are illustrative of IGE from the student's point of view. They present principles of the IGE system in three possible situations. Additional portrayals of the same principles are innumerable.

Curriculum, Academic

The IGE system makes no distinction between the "academic" curriculum and the "non-academic" curriculum. The system provides for the definition of curriculum goals as well as for identifying activities to achieve those goals. This is true of computational skills in elementary school arithmetic as well as in high school calculus. But it is also true of communication skills whether taught in a language course or in music, art, dancing, or dramatics.

The following description is an application of IGE in an elementary school. The academic areas are emphasized.

Eileen is an eight year old in Englehart School. She and her schoolmates arrive at the building intermittently between 8:00 and 8:20 a.m. Without assistance from a bell or a command from a teacher, they go to their working area and commence one of the several activities they have on their schedules to accomplish during the week. The items on the schedules vary from student to student and include activities that may be pursued independently as well as those that are achieved in small groups or with a teacher.

During the next 30 to 40 minutes while the students are thus engaged, the teachers are performing advisor functions. One may be talking to a child who has been absent, or helping another revise his schedule of weekly activities based on accomplishments or problems he encountered the previous afternoon. Another teacher may be working with a small group of advisees on a values clarification activity to provide feedback on a new learning program just designed by one of the group members.

Shortly after 9:00 without any audible signal, Eileen and five others from her learning community are working with a teacher on a reading comprehension skill involving root words. The ages of the children involved are seven, eight and nine. Two of them are getting their first formal instruction in roots of compound words. The other four are there because they need reinforcement of a skill for which they had specific instruction at least once previously in their school careers. The group is created specifically for this lesson and, if everything goes well, will not reassemble again.

While the teacher is working with this group, others are doing different language art activities. Some are reading for pleasure, others are working on written reports, several are working in a small group planning a skit, and a few are doing paper work involving the application of a skill they had received instruction on yesterday.

The teacher will handle two to four additional instructional groups during the hour and half designated as the language arts block of time. As one group is disbanded and another one is forming, the teacher circulates among the students working at their seats to provide any inspiration or help needed. The students are actually free to do anything they want provided they do not disturb others.

At 10:45 following a fifteen minute break on the playground, Eileen is involved with a group of seven other students working with a teacher on a new concept (for them) involving simple fractions and common geometric figures. The teacher anticipates working with this same group of students on this new concept for about 15 minutes each day throughout the week. Following her work with them each day, the students have related follow-up activities which they pursue individually or in small groups, according to their preference.

For approximately a third of the 45 minutes set aside for math each day, the teacher circulates among the students identifying problems they are having with seat work and pairing students who she feels would work well together. Sometimes these pairs consist of two students needing work on the same activity, and at other times the pairing is of an older student with a younger one for the purpose of providing tutoring.

Throughout the morning, students circulate from one room to another within the four rooms assigned to the learning community.

At 11:30, Eileen and 55 other students (half the learning community) work with a music specialist and an aide. This happens twice a week. The other 51 students in the learning community work with an art specialist and an aide at this time. The situations are reversed on two other days in the week.

Usually during these four days, the four learning community teachers have a team meeting between 11:30 and 12:15. However, twice a month the learning community teachers provide the instruction for music and art while the two specialists work with small groups who need remedial help or have special interest in the field. For example, last week Eileen and five other students—all monotones—had a special session with the music teacher.

Following lunch, and for most of the afternoon, the entire learning community is involved in a variety of activities having a common theme. Sometimes the theme has a science emphasis and sometimes it has a social studies emphasis. In either case, there is an attempt to integrate as many subject area fields as possible. Language arts and math are incorporated into the unit of study along with music and art activities.

The four classrooms of the learning community are replete with learning stations, interest centers, desks and chairs arranged for small group discussions, and work areas where the students may construct models, montages, or other projects.

Throughout the afternoon, groups of students leave the learning community and go to the gym for physical education. The schedule is arranged weekly and includes both remedial activities for those with physical development problems as well as typical physical education activities.

Back in the learning community, teachers circulate among the students providing instruction when necessary, and stimulating or assisting self-assessment as needed. They also coordinate or sometimes lead small group discussions and talk with advisees regarding program planning. Eileen is free to work with any of the learning community teachers, depending on the nature of tasks or problems she wishes to undertake.

Curriculum, Non-academic

It is the manner in which something is taught, not what is taught, which distinguishes an IGE school from a traditional school.Some teachers using the IGE system may handle guitar playing, cooking, scuba diving, repairing small engines, and the like as mini-courses or clubs within the school day. Other teachers using the IGE system will use the same format and add to a similar repertoire of courses or clubs such content as famous battles of the Civil War, computing in bases other than ten, Shakespearean plays, quantitative analysis, and other topics offered as parts of typical courses in a traditional school. Still other teachers using the IGE system will incorporate the same types of learning under traditional categories of English, social studies, math, science, etc.

Common to all IGE schools, and within them to all organizational formats, is the fact that students have long range goals, specific objectives for a given period of time, a variety of appropriate activities to help them reach those objectives, continuous assessment of the degree to which they are obtaining their objectives as well as the method by which they are obtaining them, and an increasing involvement of the students in all these decisions.

The following descriptions are applications of IGE to a middle school and to a high school. In these, an emphasis is given to those areas commonly labeled "non-academic".

Thurman is a thirteen year old in Thurston Middle School. He is in one of five learning communities each involving six teachers and approximately 160 boys and girls aged 13, 14, and 15. Like Englehart, Thurston Middle School begins the day with a thirty minute advisory period. This is followed by a two-hour block of time within which a social studies theme integrates several subject areas as the students pursue individual learning programs in small groups, sometimes by themselves, and less often in large groups. Interspersed throughout the three hours are four-week mini courses in English (e.g., paragraph writing, reading for meaning, speaking to small groups) and social studies (e.g., map reading and map making, group dynamics, geography of the state). Thurman and approximately half the students and teachers of his learning community are thus engaged.

In a nearby cluster of three rooms, the other half of the learning community is involved with a science theme. This theme also incorporates a multiplicity of projects encompassing various subject areas. The current theme places a heavy emphasis on critical thinking and problem solving skills.

Interspersed with the science theme during these three hours are four-week mini courses in science (e.g., weather prediction, heavenly bodies, simple machines, organic gardening) and math (e.g., multiplication and division of whole fractions, working with mixed fractions, word problems made easy, comparing prices in a supermarket, introduction to algebra).

Teachers in both groups are responsible for supervising learning stations and interest centers as well as assisting students as needed. They also have at least one mini course assigned as their responsibility. Students may go into special areas of the school for shop, home economics, art, and music equipment. These areas are staffed by teachers who maintain an open lab situation for students to work on special projects. These specialists also conduct specific instruction in basic skills, usually in small groups as the need arises.

Noon time is 70 minutes of special interest groups involving all teachers and students. Lunch is served on a continuous service basis and Thurman is responsible for scheduling his eating time when he is not in one of the special interest groups. These special interest groups are designed to stimulate student exploration in a wide variety of subject areas, some of which will be the focus of learning programs built into the morning and afternoon two-hour blocks of time. Guitar playing, gourmet cooking, chess, woodworking, lawn mower repair, choral singing, and still life painting are examples of some of the groups available to Thurman during this 70-minute period.

Following the noon hour the two groups of students reverse their assignments.

Compared to his experience two years ago in an IGE elementary school, Thurman is more involved in building his own learning program, selecting objectives to pursue, and arranging his daily schedule to achieve all his purposes. He is also more involved in school-wide decisions such as identifying special interest courses that are offered during the noon period, a project of the student council to handle racial tensions and cultural differences, and modifying the manner in which advisees are matched to their advisors.

* * *

Serge is a 17 year old at Stevenson High School located in a low social-economic urban area. The high school has more than 2500 students in it and has several types of learning communities.

In six learning communities, students are assigned on the basis of graduation date. Two of them contain only sophomores, two contain only juniors, and two contain only seniors. Most students spend about two thirds of their day within the learning community and teachers operate somewhat similarly to those in the Thurston Middle School plan. These students spend the remainder of the day in special resource areas, a term used to refer to those facilities which must be shared by students from many learning communities. Science laboratories, vocational education areas, music rooms, art facilities, and the driver education area are all examples of special resource areas.

All but these six learning communities are multiaged. That is, in the learning communities throughout the rest of the school, each teacher serves as the advisor to students encompassing all three age groups of this senior high school. In the majority of these learning communities, the teachers are all members of the same department. The schedule for students is similar to the traditional high school except the courses are nine weeks in length rather than lasting for a semester or a full school year. Teachers plan and critique each other within the learning communities, but they do not share a common set of students in the classrooms because the students come to them for classwork from most of the other learning communities.

Serge is in a learning community created for potential drop-outs. Serge and many of his classmates came to Stevenson from schools which were unresponsive to students with learning disabilities and low educational aspirations.

Teachers are assigned to Serge's learning community because of their talent for relating well to students. In addition, several of them can provide instruction in the basic tool skills (reading, writing, and arithmetic); others are teachers of subjects having a high interest level to this type of student.

Heavy emphasis is given to activities with potential for being highly relevant to the students—out of school learning in work related projects, community service projects, etc.—with remedial work in reading, basic computational skills, and mechanics of expression woven into the activities as needed. For example, Serge is learning to control variables while troubleshooting ignition problems in auto mechanics. His reading text is an auto service manual. The auto mechanics teacher can handle the math involved, but another teacher in the learning community comes into the auto lab to help Serge improve his reading skills "on the job".

It has taken several months in this learning community for Serge to realize his teachers are really not going to impose anything on him, but are willing to help him learn in areas meaningful to him. Serge responded by becoming quite task oriented. He gradually increased the specificity of his long range goals and short range learning objectives.

After six months, his interests have begun to extend beyond the auto shop and his day is becoming more diversified. His teachers suggest a variety of alternatives, and he finds he is improving his reading ability as he uses reading materials in areas of interest other than auto mechanics. Serge began the school year spending the entire day in the auto shop and gymnasium. (Class periods and courses do not exist in Serge's learning community.) He now spends half his day reading for pleasure (thirty to forty-five minutes), working with three other boys and girls on a social studies project involving the way the school system is set up to handle vocational education and adult education (two hours a day, three days a week), in a short course on mechanical advantages of gears (forty minutes two days a week and two hours three days a week), and in a special interest group for guitar playing (one hour, one day each week).

Student Evaluation

Student evaluation is another cooperative endeavor between the student and the teacher. Each is encouraged to devise a variety of options to assess the degree to which the student is achieving his learning objectives. The teacher and the student also evaluate the manner in which the objectives are being achieved. Or, in broader terms the student and teacher cooperatively assess the degree to which the student is learning how to learn.

Assessment is a continuous process with emphasis placed on student products and demonstrations of his ability to apply what he has learned rather than on paper and pencil tests of factual retention of knowledge.

Another principle of IGE is that student information is obtained and recorded systematically and that such information is used in planning future learning activities. Thus, information about the student's learning styles, peer relationships, interest, and other factors directly affecting learning are included in a student information system rather than, or sometimes in addition to, traditional letter grades allegedly describing achievement.

Record keeping in the IGE system is a constant process of improving the system of information gathered. As the schools become more sophisticated in the types of learning activities offered and in the degree to which students are involved, the record keeping system must be revised to include new information.

A student's record is always available to him and his parents. In fact, student files are usually used by the student and advisor as a resource in planning conferences with parents. If the student or parents come across something in the file that is upsetting or in error, their first step is to mention it to the advisor.

In many cases, the student's advisor might simply remove the offending item and nothing more would be said about it. However, if the person who inserted the item in the first place disagreed, the student and his parents could counter it with a rebuttal which then becomes part of the record. They, of course, have the right to petition the principal to have it removed or take the matter to a higher authority.

Records are kept to help students and teachers build a flexible learning program. Therefore, it is a policy to keep student records positive—to include only material which furthers this purpose. An attempt is made to keep the language simple, accurate, appropriate, and free of jargon so those who read it well have no doubt about what is being said.

In addition, it is the advisor's responsibility to keep each student's file current and to purge it of dated material. This enables the student, his advisor, and his parents to concentrate on current progress without getting bogged down in needless, out-dated detail.

Students are expected to take increasing responsibility for reporting to their parents. The pattern is to describe their past achievements, the learning objectives they are currently working on, and the reasons why these objectives were selected. They outline anticipated school experiences and explain why the plans are important to achieving their long range educational goals.

Counseling

In the IGE system, most counseling is done by the advisor within the Learning Community. Each teacher has a pro rata group of students whom he serves as an advisor—a warm, supportive person who helps the students to develop a good self-image, to plan and evaluate progress toward long range educational goals, and to report relevant information to parents and other teachers.

Much of the counseling is done in group sessions called advisement groups. These regularly scheduled sessions range from getting acquainted activities to values clarification activities. Learning programs are critiqued individually or in small groups and perhaps brainstorming is used to generate the goals and design of new learning programs. At other times, the advisor may be called upon to arbitrate differences between an advisee and a peer, between an advisee and a teacher, or between an advisee and his parents.

It is assumed that the vast majority of counseling needs are met by the advisement system in IGE. Only if a referral to a community social agency is needed, or if intense personal or social problems exist which require specialized training, is a counselor brought on the scene. However, a counselor would work behind the scenes to provide in-service training to teachers as needed.

Matching of advisees to advisors can be done in a variety of ways. However, common to all IGE schools is the condition that either the advisor or the advisee may terminate the relationship at any time. A new assignment is then made following procedures adopted by each school.

Advisement groups are multiaged. Assuming that the advisor-advisee relationship remains positive, the assignment continues for a two to four year period—depending upon the age range in the learning community. Career counseling is done by the person most appropriate for the student —a teacher, the advisor, or a guidance counselor. Advice about colleges may also come to the student from any of these sources. The only admonishment is that teachers and counselors do not exceed their own capabilities. They must recognize when referral to a person with more specialized training is necessary.

Discipline

For all but the most rare exceptions, discipline is handled within the learning community. When the advisor has full authority to modify the learning program of a student, and when the student is increasingly involved in decisions regarding his own learning, discipline problems seldom emerge. The IGE school is responsive to the student and at the same time expects the student to accept responsibility for these decisions and for his overall behavior.

Without question, a responsive school environment does help. In a pilot program in a New York City high school, an advisement system was inaugurated for the freshman class. In a two week period the average daily attendance increased from 57 percent to 86 percent. Since this was a class of more than one thousand students and since staffing was based upon average daily attendance, of the previous year, this phenomenon caused overpopulation problems—but it does demonstrate what happens when the students believe that someone cares about them as individuals.

In Houston, a Contemporary Learning Center was established for high school drop-outs and potential drop-outs. The program is highly individualized. Discipline problems are minimal in spite of the fact that more than 50 percent of the population have previously dropped out of school or have been assigned to the Contemporary Learning Center by court order. Of the remainder, a vast majority of these students were referred to the Center because they said they were going to drop out of their neighborhood high school.

Another factor which reduces discipline problems in an IGE school is the learning process itself. When learning objectives are pitched at a level to ensure success most of the time, when a student knows clearly what he is to achieve, and when he obtains feedback of his success in attaining the objectives, motivation and morale remain high and the major causes of school discipline problems have disappeared. Boredom and frustration are minimized; success is maximized.

A teacher's perception of what is a discipline problem may also change in an IGE school. Inactivity or time spent in a social center is acceptable provided other agreements of the student are met. Academic interaction and one student helping another are encouraged, not repressed. Self directed, student movement within the classroom and throughout the school is the norm, not the exception. Thus, what is seen as a discipline problem in a traditional school may be appropriate and even encouraged in an IGE school if it leads to purposeful activity toward agreed upon learning objectives and does not infringe upon the rights and property of others.

The emphasis on students accepting increasing responsibility in the IGE system apparently is paying dividends. This approach is dramatically in opposition to current trends in large urban schools which react to problems by imposing greater restrictions on students. High fences around schools, admittance by ID cards, armed guards patrolling the hallways, and similar tactics may possibly be justified as attempts to keep non-students from the premises. But when these tactics are accompanied by essentially an adult-run school program (e.g., teacher centered classrooms, locked restrooms, restricted student movement throughout the school, limited or non-existing options in learning program selections), the development of intrinsic discipline is extremely unlikely.

ROLES

There is a wide variation in the extent to which roles of persons involved in the IGE system differ from those exhibited before entering into IGE. Some administrators and teachers had assumed similar roles prior to using the IGE system. Most had not. The vast majority of students and parents have unfamiliar roles to play in IGE. The professional staff must provide orientation to these new roles and display patience as they nurture the growth of students and parents in unfamiliar patterns of interaction.

Administrators

Two primary tasks of administrators in the IGE system are to set expectations and to model desired behavior.

Teachers are more venturesome when they perceive their superordinates to be encouraging them to try new ideas. It is appropriate for an IGE principal to tell his staff: "I believe in the principles of IGE. The vast majority of this staff believes in the principles of IGE. Therefore I expect you either to implement the principles of IGE or to convince us you have some better ones towards which we all should be striving." Such a statement gives needed vocal support to teachers undertaking a new way of life, yet it also encourages them to seek even better ways of making the educational program more appropriate to the students.

IGE administrators also model three important types of behavior: (1) learning is a life long process, (2) critiquing one's own actions, (3) supporting others.

Few, if any, IGE principals can claim they implemented the IGE system when they were classroom teachers. Therefore, they model an adult learner role by participating with teachers in the clinical training program in the role of classroom teacher. This type of involvement also demonstrates to teachers that the principal knows the kinds of problems they are facing and the types of changes confronting them.

Administrators in the IGE system also ask a lot of "why" questions. This is the way they learn about what a teacher is doing and the reason it is being done. They paraphrase the responses to the "why" questions or in other ways demonstrate that they listen to and learn from their teachers. A desired by-product of asking these "why" questions is that it stimulates the teachers to analyze their own actions.

IGE administrators obtain feedback from staff members and students regarding their administrative actions. Principals see that process observers are present periodically at meetings which the principal chairs, for example, at meetings of the program improvement council. After a period of time elapses following one of their decisions, IGE administrators ask parents, students and teachers for an analysis of that decision and elicit alternatives which may lead to modification of the decision.

Principals participate on observation teams, provide substitutes, modify schedules, and in other ways demonstrate that they support the teachers' actions when a learning community team undertakes observation cycles involving critiques of their classroom performance. The IGE principal plays a supportive role in other ways, as well. He maintains a positive school atmosphere by being very positive himself. He publicly supports desired actions on the part of teachers and limits negative comments to an absolute minimum and then makes sure they are offered in privacy. He helps teachers think of an increasing number of alternative actions. He almost always offers a minimum of two alternatives himself so that the teachers must make choices and increasingly accept responsibility for decision making. He secures outside help when it is requested or is needed to give his staff members additional support. His chief resource in identifying consultants is his group of league principals who recommend key people on their staffs able to give consultant help not only to members on their own staff but to other schools in the league.

Teachers

The IGE teacher plays a multiplicity of roles. The IGE administrator sets the example, but IGE teachers are also expected to model for their students the same three traits of lifelong learning, subjecting actions to continuous assessment, and being supportive. An important role of the teacher is to provide a varied, rich learning environment full of alternatives which the teacher then helps the student make decisions about as the student's learning program is defined and executed. In performing this role, the teacher sometimes acts as counselor to assist the student to understand himself and make decisions about his school life. And other times the teacher assumes a didatic posture and lectures or demonstrates. At other times the teacher is a creative inventor offering options to provide for the wide range of learning styles and learning objectives of the students.

Another aspect of the teacher's job is to provide peer supervision in the broadest sense of that term. That is, there is a cooperative endeavor to improve the professional acts of one's colleagues. This may take the form of brainstorming new ways of teaching, suggesting alternative methods of working with a given student, or generating a complex schedule. At another time it may take the form of observing, analyzing, and providing feedback regarding a colleague's teaching in a constructive, tactful manner. At another time, it takes the form of participating in small group discussions and other staff development activities to solve problems identified within the learning community.

Although a parent organization and a school newsletter can help communicate with parents, the IGE system imposes a greater responsibility on learning community teachers to orient parents to the system and incorporate them into the planning and analysis of their child's learning program.

Other facets of the teacher's role in IGE are illustrated or implied throughout this entire chapter. To summarize, an outline of the six basic roles of teachers in the IGE system follows.

The teacher as an advisor
  Developing a healthy self concept and human interaction skills in each advisee
  Planning and assessing the learning program for each advisee
  Helping each advisee assess himself and report his progress to others
The teacher as a diagnostician
  Assessing the student
  • Where is he now?
  • How did he get where he is?
  • Where should he go from here?
  Assessing the learning environment
  • Does it provide for the range of interest and talents of all the students involved?

- Does it make provision for students progressing and ending at different times?
- Does it enable the students to achieve the objectives specified?
- What alternatives emerge to be incorporated now or the next time the unit of study is pursued?

Assessing group processes (appropriate for both groups of students and the teaching team, this is only a partial list of important items)

- Did all group members participate appropriately?
- Were contributions appropriate to the task at hand (e.g. brainstorming, constructive comments)
- What was the nature and effect of body language used by group members
- Were plans made to analyze decisions after an appropriate period of implementation?
- Was the process of decision making analyzed?

The teacher as a planner

Phase I

- prepare individually for long range goal setting and design
- interact with colleagues on long range goal setting and design

Phase II

- act as a resource teacher in area of competency to prepare a design for consideration by the entire group
- interact with colleagues regarding specific objectives related to long range goals and regarding elements of the classroom environment

Phase III

- prepare for individual teaching assignment thoroughly
- interact with students and colleagues to "fine tune" the learning environment making adjustments as necessary

The teacher as an environmental engineer

- provide instruction
- keep climate of classroom physically attractive and emotionally positive
- manage logistics of timing and movement based on individualized approach
- respond to conditions adversely affecting learning as students pursue learning programs

The teacher as a data gatherer

- records data in all areas mentioned in the above four roles
- makes records available to the respective students and parents

The teacher as a learner

- identifies and implements a personalized in-service program regarding IGE principles and other elements of professional responsibility
- participates in the learning community's inservice program
- tries new ideas and objectively assesses them
- elicits feedback from students, colleagues, and parents regarding all aspects of professional life

Students

One of the fundamental principles in the system of Individually Guided Education is that students become increasingly responsible for decisions regarding their own education. A growth factor is implicit. That is, students are not expected to be proficient in decision making at all times or in all subject areas. Rather, the student is gradually immersed into the decision making process with factors affecting those decisions increasing in number and in complexity as he progresses through his school career. As the student demonstrates his responsibility to handle these factors and to handle the consequences of poor decisions, he is encouraged to accept additional responsibility for making decisions which affect his educational progress. Teachers in IGE initially find themselves spending more time planning than in previous years. However, when students begin accepting more responsibility for decision making, teacher planning is severely reduced, and much of it is done when interacting with students rather than in the evenings.

Implicit throughout IGE materials is the expectation that students develop a healthy self-image capable of interacting constructively with staff members and other students.

The student and educational goals

In IGE terminology, a goal is a long range target which is never completely attainable. Thus, reading is an educational goal since everyone can improve on his ability to read no matter what his age or attainment at the moment. The role of the student is to relate his plans for learning to educational goals which he accepts. As he assesses his progress, he also relates his successes to his educational goals.

The student and learning activities

In the IGE system there is an attempt to bring to the conscious level of each student the various factors which comprise his learning environment. He is then encouraged to accept responsibility for defining those over which he may assume control. Thus, he makes decisions about such items as the length of time needed, the persons with whom he is going to work, the materials which are most appropriate, and the sequence to be followed. The older he is, the more he is encouraged to use community resources in the form of service projects, work experience, or observing and learning from every day operations of various community institutions.

Teachers can stimulate and motivate; some even demand. In IGE these might be means, but the end is to have the student accept responsibility for being self-motivated and self-directed. He pursues his learning program because it is meaningful to him and he wants to achieve the objectives for which his learning program was designed.

The student and assessment

In IGE, the role of the student is to become increasingly responsible for self-assessment. With the help of his advisor, he is to develop a systematic method of gathering information which affects his learning. He is shown how to use a variety of data sources such as records, samples of his own work, analyses of the way he has learned, and other factors which relate to what he has learned and the manner in which he has learned it. IGE assessment is continuous in order to provide immediate feedback and to influence next steps.

In IGE, the student accepts increasing responsibility for reporting his progress to his parents. Most IGE schools use parent conferences, and in these the student plays the lead role as soon as he is able to assume this responsibility. Although such reporting is a legitimate end in itself, there is an underlying assumption that students who can communicate with their parents regarding their school progress will also communicate to a greater extent with their parents on other matters and thereby help reduce the so-called generation gap.

The student and school wide policies

One of the outcomes of the IGE system is that students become involved in decision making regarding school-wide activities and policies. This is usually done through representative government on a school wide basis fed by learning community meetings as well as advisor-advisee group sessions.

* * * * *

Eleven of the thirty five outcomes which describe the fully implemented IGE system involve the role of the student. Outcome achievement data obtained from schools annually from 1973 through 1977 indicate that, as a group, implementation of student outcomes is delayed until after system components involving organizational structure, administrative support, and modifications in teacher action are dealt with. Since most of these data were collected in elementary schools, it could mean that these teachers do not see the appropriateness of these outcomes for children age 5 to 12. Or, the relatively low implementation could indicate that teachers may believe student outcomes to be important, but that other components of the system should receive their attention first. A third possible explanation is that many teachers do not have techniques needed to implement these student outcomes.

Parents

Most educators and PTA presidents would claim that the interest of parents decreases as their children progress through school. Perhaps it would be more accurate to say that the parents' interest remains the same, but the desire of the students to have their parents involved in their school lessens as they become older. Regardless of what has occurred in the past, in IGE the role of the parent is commom throughout elementary school, middle school, and high school stages.

Orientation to the program

The first task of the parent is to become acquainted with the way the IGE system is used within the school. Then, in much more detail, they become knowledgeable about specific applications of the system as it occurs in the learning community to which their child is assigned. Using films, film-strips, presentations, and discussion groups, the parents learn what is being attempted, how it is going to be brought about, and why the staff feels the system is an improvement over traditional schooling.

In many instances, parents are involved in the same IGE information program as is the staff when it is considering alternative ways of improving the school. These parents then become part of the decision making process to determine whether or not the school will adopt IGE in the first place.

Participation in setting goals and learning objectives

Parents, students, and advisors act as a triumvirate in program planning. Each of the three parties has a legitimate contribution to make in setting educational goals and identifying learning objectives for a student. Yet, each must learn to respect the views of the other two parties and know when to yield to superior knowledge or insight possessed by another. In traditional schools, parents are seldom involved in this process and all three parties may have difficulty participating in an efficient, effective manner.

Participation in the learning program

This third role of a parent in IGE can take on a variety of forms. Parents participate in study groups wherein they learn how to provide an intellec-tually stimulating home environment or, more specifically, how they can encourage more reading at home.

Some parents become more active in the learning program by assuming a teaching function. This might take the form of presenting a travelogue to an elementary school class, teaching gourmet cooking in a middle school, or providing a work-learn experience in a laboratory or automobile shop for a senior high school student.

Another opportunity for parents to participate in learning programs is as an aide or paraprofessional during regular school hours. Whether on a paid or volunteer basis, there are many tasks in an IGE school which an adult can perform satisfactorily without benefit of professional teacher training.

If nothing else, parents should discuss school with their child to demonstrate they have an interest in the student and the work he is doing.

SYSTEM IN ACTION

IGE helps change teachers from traditional patterns of operation to new patterns involving individualized instruction and continuous improvement. Its strategy of bringing about these changes is as important as the school processes and procedures the system implements.

Schools become involved in the /I/D/E/A/ Change Program for Individually Guided Education through the efforts of an intermediate agency—usually central offices of school systems, universities, regional service centers, or state departments of education. One or more facilitators on the staff of those intermediate agencies work directly with IGE league schools. /I/D/E/A/ provides training programs for these facilitators, and the training program models the process by which teachers are to be trained in IGE. There are two reasons for this: one is the belief that facilitators need to work with IGE processes in the classrooms with students in order to experience the same phenomena as teachers will; and second, the facilitators can learn the training procedures for teachers more easily if they actually undertake it themselves prior to working with teachers.

Facilitators participate in a two week workshop identical to the one that is described in the next section entitled "Getting Teachers Involved". Travel and living expenses of the facilitators are the responsibility of their respective agencies, and this itself is an expression of commitment on the part of that agency. This clinical training program is conducted by /I/D/E/A/ staff members or facilitators who were outstanding participants in previous workshops and who have subsequently worked with /I/D/E/A/ staff members until they are certified as facilitator trainers.

Three or four weeks following their clinical training, the facilitators complete their initial training during a three-day session in which they develop an understanding of their role as a facilitator.

Five outcomes constitute the agenda

> *1. The facilitator helps others to develop a commitment to the /I/D/E/A/ Change Program for Individually Guided Education.*

The facilitator learns alternative ways of helping school staffs examine their own educational beliefs and examine IGE to determine the extent to which the system can help them achieve their goals.

> *2. The facilitator trains staff to implement the*
> */I/D/E/A/ Change Program for Individually*
> *Guided Education.*

Here the facilitators examine their own training programs to insure they understand the reasons for the various activities pursued. Because it is not always feasible to conduct intensive two-week clinical training workshops for school staffs, facilitators explore options they might use to help staffs acquire the same understandings and demonstrate applications of IGE processes.

> *3. The facilitator establishes and maintains a league*
> *of IGE schools.*

A whole list of potential league activities is explored ranging from publishing a newsletter, to having monthly meetings with principals, to conducting in-service programs for teachers in response to requests for assistance.

> *4. The facilitator assists staffs to monitor the IGE*
> *outcomes.*

Since data gathering and analyses of those data as a basis for good decision making are essential parts of IGE, this monitoring function is an important aspect of the facilitator role. He learns the nature of data /I/D/E/A/ staff members desire for research purposes and how to encourage league schools to devise and gather data for themselves. More importantly he learns ways in which data, from /I/D/E/A/ and from individual school studies, can be analyzed and used by school staffs.

> *5. The facilitator participates in activities for*
> *continuous improvement.*

The facilitator is expected to model desired behavior and therefore he develops and pursues his own in-service program including annual meetings with /I/D/E/A/ staff members and other facilitators, self-assessment questionnaires with results shared with /I/D/E/A/, and observation cycles in which other facilitators and league personnel observe and critique him in action.

Teacher Orientation and Initial Training

The first contact teachers have with IGE is likely to be a "We Agree" Workshop. There are two target areas for these sessions. The first has to do with human interaction and developing better interpersonal relationships. The second has to do with goal setting and deciding what should be done about discrepancies between existing practice and desired ends. The sessions are also designed to have these two areas dealt with on two levels: teachers working with other staff members, and teachers working with students.

Team building is a term often applied to the "We Agree" area of interpersonal relationships. Participants become involved in activities to get acquainted with each other, to develop a sense of trust with each other, and to acquire group skills such as consensus building, brainstorming, and process observing. Both at the level of teacher to teacher interaction and at the level of teacher to student interaction, a real sense of team emerges.

As the participants learn how to brainstorm new ideas and make decisions collectively—moving first from non-educational issues into educational ones—they are approaching the goal setting aspect of the "We Agree" workshop. The group is asked to prepare statements of educational belief regarding six areas:

- Student-teacher relationships
- How students learn
- Parent involvement
- School and community
- School organization
- Curriculum

"We Agree" statements are developed in small groups. Usually each small group considers one topic at a time making lists of statements about that topic. All statements must meet the approval of all groups members. There must be total agreement, or at least the group members must trust one another enough to allow a statement to remain on the list. Any person can have a statement removed from the list. Statements generated are not meant to be operational rules of how the school functions; rather, they are highly general statements of a philosophical nature to which everyone can agree.

Many facilitators use a discrepancy model as the next step. That is, after the staff members have prepared "We Agree" statements, they are given a questionnaire to describe the current state of affairs in their own school. The questionnaire is based on the same six areas as the statements, which in turn are fundamental to IGE concepts.

Next, the teachers are exposed to the /I/D/E/A/ Change Program for IGE and any other system which the facilitator or members of the staff feel might help them close the gap between their idealized school and their descriptions of the status quo. At that point, the facilitator's role is to get the staff members to commit themselves to using one of the systems to improve the school—or to devise their own system. If IGE is selected, the next decision is to determine which 20 percent of the staff will undergo initial training in a clinical workshop involving a corresponding group from several other schools.

Throughout the above description reference is made to teachers. In many cases, representative parents and students participate along with staff members in the "We Agree" Workshop.

The clinical workshop

This event is designed to help the participants:

(a) become knowledgeable about the thirty-five outcomes of IGE
(b) demonstrate their understanding of the outcomes by applying them in actual school situations with students
(c) become capable of helping others to implement the outcomes

Because participants work in small groups involving people from other schools, the first several days of the clinical workshop include team building activities similar to those they experienced in the "We Agree" sessions.

Participants organize into learning communities and begin implementing the IGE outcomes dealing with school organization, program planning, student involvement, and peer observation. Each participant begins a personal in-service program to learn how to implement the IGE outcomes using the IGE *Implementation Guide*. This segment of the workshop takes two or three days.

The next eight days of the clinical workshop are spent in an actual school situation with students. Approximately two hours of each day are spent planning, two hours teaching, two hours observing and analyzing the teaching of others, and two hours engaging in individual and group inservice work.

During the last several days of the clinical workshop, participants are assessed on the degree to which they have attained the three objectives of the workshop.

In addition, participants reassemble themselves into groups involving only those from a given school. Here they spend several hours making plans to provide initial training to the remainder of the staff. Such training could take the form of a two week clinical workshop almost identical to that being pursued by this 20% group. An alternative is to reschedule the same activities which the 20% has just gone through, but provide these activities over a period of four to six weeks during the regular school term using their own students.

Regardless of the form initial training takes for school staff members, they all leave this stage of their training with a pattern for continuous staff improvement. This pattern consists of identifying IGE outcomes toward which they wish to make further progress, arranging to receive any outside input needed from college faculty members or other consultants, incorporating the outcomes into their daily working pattern, and assessing the progress they make.

Teachers in Action

As soon as possible after staff members have completed their initial training, they begin implementing IGE in their school. Since most of the 35 IGE outcomes involve decision making processes, the teachers are immediately confronted with a number of decisions to make.

Typically, one of the first considerations is to reorganize the school into learning communities consisting of a group of teachers and students who plan and work together for most or all of the school day. In elementary schools, the number of teachers working together is usually from two to five; in middle schools it is usually four to eight; in high schools it is usually six to ten. In a majority of schools, the students in a learning community are multi-aged encompassing two age groups—sometimes three or four age groups, depending on preferences of the teachers. However, a signficant number of schools delay working on the multi-age principle for one to three years.

A major tenant of learning communities is that each student has from among the teachers in the learning community an advisor responsible for helping him develop a healthy self-image and good interpersonal relationships, for planning his educational program, and for helping the student assess and report his progress.

IGE schools have a program improvement council which is a central steering committee establishing basic policies for the school. In practically all cases, it is chaired by the principal and is responsible for all areas involving two or more learning communities.

Another organizational decision to be made by the teachers is the extent to which they will participate in the league of IGE schools established and coordinated by their facilitator. They also select their representative to the hub committee which acts as the board of directors for the league.

Another organizational decision is the extent teachers are going to work with each other. For example, a few elementary school learning communities may have four teachers involved with a multi-age group of students who work closely together throughout the school day in all subject areas except music, art, and physical education. A more typical initial plan however, is for the teachers to limit their intensive involvement together to one subject area, such as reading, and move into other subject areas only when they feel that they are comfortably managing the reading program. It may take one or two years for them to try to incorporate all IGE processes throughout the entire school day.

In secondary schools, the range of teaming is even wider. Some high schools have multi-age learning communities primarily for advisory purposes and retain their departmental structure for planning and teaching together. Other high schools have learning communities composed of English, social studies, math, and science teachers, but limit the range of students to a single age group, e.g., the sophomore class. A very few high schools have carved out a segment of the school population, (e.g., potential drop-outs) to form a multi-aged learning community involving the four basic subject areas and have the students spend at least one half the school day in the learning community before they move out into special resource areas such as shop, out of school learning activities, distributive education, and similar areas.

After organizational decisions have been made, the teachers plunge into an area close to the heart of IGE—decisions regarding the instructional program. Central to this area is the planning process.

The planning process

The IGE system has a planning sequence which is a progression of three phases—each one involving both preparation and action. The preparation step involves the work of individual teachers, and the action step calls for the combined interaction of all teaching team members.

The entire sequence takes place within the context of the teachers' continually increasing knowledge of students, content, and resources.

Two functions—goal setting and design—take place in all three planning phases. They are used throughout the planning process, changing only in degree of specificity as the anticipated learning program progresses toward implementation.

The following describes a planning sequence in an elementary school. Planning in middle schools and high schools would be analogous and thus can be inferred from this description.

Phase I:—the Phase I stage is basically quite broad in nature:

- The overall goal setting for the students is determined
- Possible designs for it are examined
- The resource teacher for the learning program is selected

This first phase usually begins about four to six weeks before the teachers expect to launch the planned unit of study.

In determining the goal setting for a new unit of study, the first task of the teaching team is to explore possible directions to be taken—keeping in mind what the students have accomplished and what they might be able to accomplish in both the immediate and distant future. Each teacher is expected to contribute something because they have worked with their advisees and have intimate knowledge of the students' learning styles as well as the students' individual goals and objectives. The teachers also are thoroughly familiar with each student's educational progress through day to day contacts and assessment data.

Drawing on this broad understanding of student needs, each staff member considers the skills and concepts he believes should be emphasized and readies his own ideas for the upcoming interaction with the other members of the team. If the team member feels more up to date assessment information would be valuable, he sees that it is secured and uses it in working up recommendations for the new unit of study.

At the outset of planning, goal setting focuses on long range goals. Then as planning becomes more specific—during Phase II—the focus narrows to broad objectives appropriate for almost all students. And, finally, as student assessment data accumulates and students participate actively in the new program—during Phase III—the accent is on goal setting in the form of identifying and modifying learning objectives for individual students.

In Phase I, goal setting is long range in nature. It is the beginning stage of planning. Each learning community staff member brings his thoughts and ideas to a scheduled group discussion where team members compare ideas and make decisions for implementing them. As a group, their initial mission is to establish goals, brainstorm broad objectives, and indicate possible designs.

The resource teacher completes his proposal in sufficient time for duplication and distribution to the entire team at least two days before the first scheduled meeting in Phase II.

Phase II:—Phase II begins as soon as a resource teacher has been designated to design a given unit of study and present a comprehensive proposal. Phase II is in operation from the time the resource teacher receives guidance from the team and continues until implementation of the new unit of study begins.

As soon as the team members have the resource teacher's proposal in hand, they review it individually and make notes indicating additions and deletions they think may be necessary to modify it for use as a learning program. Then, at the first scheduled Phase II meeting, they collectively begin modifying the proposed learning program to team specifications. This process may go on for several meetings until the entire team is satisfied that the learning program is ready for implementation.

Throughout Phase II, advisors work with advisees until all concerned are convinced that—based on available data—the best possible match of students with activities and grouping and scheduling arrangements has been made. When all this has been done to the team's satisfaction, they are ready for Phase III—implementation.

Phase III:-During this phase, all planning and preparation is translated into action.

Daily situational conferences—involving students with teachers and advisors, or involving the team members with each other—are held to identify problems and make on the spot arrangements for solving them. Elements of the program's design are adjusted to keep them in line with the students' goals, and grouping and scheduling arrangements are modified to reflect student progress.

This final phase of planning lasts as long as the current learning program continues to meet the need that it was designed to fulfill.

Whenever any learning program is in progress, learning communities have three options:

1. They can continue in the same direction—extending the existing learning program and making appropriate modifications as described in Phase III planning.
2. They can go back to Phase II and make a major change in goal emphasis— revising the broad objectives and adjusting the design to reflect new information.
3. They can start again at Phase I and begin to work on a completely new learning program.

Planning and implementation go on continuously and concurrently in learning communities. Both are part of the regular operating strategy for all areas of the curriculum. While they are planning and implementing one program, they are also planning for succeeding ones.

PROSPECT

In 1969, the /I/D/E/A/ staff termed the emerging /I/D/E/A/ Change Program for Individually Guided Education a "starter model". That is, they perceived it as a system that would get schools started on processes of improvement which would lead to new and better systems. After almost 10 years, no comprehensive system has appeared on the scene to replace it.[21]

The principles of individualization are becoming more permanently imbedded in the annals of current educational practice. Federal legislation in the form of the Education for All Handicapped Children Act (P.L. 94–142) already mandates that principles of individualization be provided for handicapped students in the least restrictive environment. California and New Jersey have adopted legislation providing incentives to school staffs to develop programs incorporating these principles into operational plans. In the future, when the full impact of federal legislation is felt, state legislatures are likely to mandate these principles for all students. Parents of children without handicaps are going to demand the same type of educational opportunities for their children as handicapped students receive.

The research-development-diffusion model of past decades failed for one or more of the following reasons:

1. School staff members were not receptive to the idea promoted
2. Academicians and theoreticians who developed models could not communicate these appropriately to practitioners
3. Implementation procedures based upon change strategies did not accompany the models being diffused

If the /I/D/E/A/ Change Program for Individually Guided Education system is followed as recommended, research indicates all three of these obstacles are overcome. Staff members examine their own educational beliefs and insure that IGE is compatible before they undertake the system. Support materials in the form of easy to read booklets, filmstrips, and motion pictures convey the ideas in practitioner's terms. Carefully designed and tested implementation strategies insure that teachers learn the new system under conditions which make it directly applicable to their current teaching assignment.

There are several pitfalls in the system as it currently operates. One is the lack of specific help for principals. The building principal is considered a key figure in educational change within that building. In the IGE system he is given the same training as are teachers so that he can identify with their problems. Facilitators are to work with principals in monthly meetings and suggested agenda items are offered in IGE materials. In practice, many IGE principals have not accepted responsibility for being a key change agent in their buildings. Perhaps this is because the facilitator has maintained a too-prominant role. Perhaps many principals lack the ability to perform the key role. At any rate, there is a deficiency in the leadership provided by many IGE principals and the system has no specific help to overcome that deficiency.

A second pitfall of the system occurs when trainers do not emphasize processes sufficiently in clinical training programs and the participants come away with a cookbook of things to do rather than having internalized the processes sufficiently to apply them in new situations with resulting new decisions based upon current input. It is essential that directors of clinical workshops involve the participants in sufficient verbal interaction to insure they understand why they did what they did and have internalized the principles sufficiently to use them in new circumstances without the help of a consultant.

A third pitfall is the age of the materials. If a copyright is more than five years old, or if hairstyles and length of skirts portray a past era, some users of such materials may give less credence to the ideas contained therein. Few teachers change solely because of what they read or see. Yet if the materials stimulate discussions and offer alternative forms of action, they serve a vital function in a change process. But if the age of the materials distracts users from getting to the principles involved, the materials may become a liability.

Longitudinal evaluative data collected on the /I/D/E/A/ Change Program for Individually Guided Education over a period of years indicate that change is occurring in approximately 1700 schools in the United States and in American schools overseas. Data regarding the attitudes of parents, students, teachers, and administrators are highly positive. Data regarding student achievement ranges from neutral to significantly positive. Less than one percent of schools report significant declines in student achievement.

These results indicate that the /I/D/E/A/ Change Program for Individually Guided Education merits sincere consideration by any school staff interested in individualizing instruction and incorporating continuous improvement procedures into the lives of the staff and students.

NOTES

1. A list of the 35 outcomes is available from /I/D/E/A/, 5335 Far Hills Avenue, Dayton, Ohio 45429.

2. For a discussion of the history of non-gradedness and the emergence of the modern non-graded elementary school, see John I. Goodlad and Robert H. Anderson, *The Non-Graded Elementary School*, rev. ed., New York: Harcourt, Brace & World, Inc., 1963.

3. The first non-graded high school of this era is fully described in B. Frank Brown, *The Non-Graded High School*, Englewood Cliffs, New Jersey: Prentice-Hall, 1963.

4. For early descriptions of team teaching, see Medill Bair and Richard G. Woodward, *Team Teaching in Action*, Boston: Houghton Mifflin Company, 1964 (elementary school oriented); David W. Beggs, III, ed., *Team Teaching: Bold New Venture*, Indianapolis: Unified College Press, Inc., 1964, (high school oriented); and Judson T. Shaplin and Henry F. Olds, Jr., eds., *Team Teaching*, New York: Harper and Row, 1964 (theoretically oriented).

5. See especially Daniel E. Griffiths, "Administration As Decision Making" and Jacob W. Getzels, "Administration As A Social Process" in Andrew W. Halpin, ed., *Administrative Theory In Education*, Chicago: The Midwest Administration Center, University of Chicago, 1958, pp. 119–165.

6. Annotated lists of materials used by elementary schools, middle and junior high schools, and high schools implementing the /I/D/E/A/ Change Program are contained in the *Implementation Guide* for each of the three levels. These documents are published by Institute for Development of Educational Activities, Inc., Day-

ton, Ohio.

7. Detailed descriptions of the clinical training workshops are found in various materials of the /I/D/E/A/ Change Program. For example, see the filmstrip "Implement, Improve, Innovate (Part II)" in the series for ages 10–15. Two supervision books based on the same Harvard-Lexington Summer Program are Robert Goldhammer, *Clinical Supervision,* New York: Holt, Rinehart and Winston, Inc., 1969; and Morris L. Cogan, *Clinical Supervision,* Boston: Houghton Mifflin Co., 1973.

8. For example, see Herbert J. Klausmeier, "IGE: An Alternative Form of Schooling" in Harriet Talmage, ed., *Systems of Individualized Education,* Berkeley, California: McCutchan Publishing Corporation, 1975.

9. A comprehensive presentation of data gathered by /I/D/E/A/ is contained in Jon S. Paden, et al, *Reflections For The Future,* Dayton, Ohio: Institute for the Development of Educational Activities, Inc., 1978.

10. Jon S. Paden, *How Is IGE Doing In The Elementary Schools? A Four-Year Survey of IGE Principals,* Dayton, Ohio: Institute For the Development of Educational Activities, Inc., 1977.

11. Jon S. Paden, *A National Evaluation of the /I/D/E/A/ Change Program For IGE,* Dayton, Ohio: Institute for Development of Educational Activities, Inc., 1975.

12. Edgar A. Kelley, Fred H. Wood, and Ronald Joekel, *Teacher Perceptions of School Climate and the Implementation of IGE,* Lincoln, Nebraska: University of Nebraska, 1973.

13. Jon S. Paden, *How Is IGE Doing In The Elementary Schools? A Four-Year Survey of IGE Principals,* Dayton, Ohio: Institute For the Development of Educational Activities, Inc., 1977.

14. All research data in this section are taken from Jon S. Paden et al, *Reflections For The Future,* Dayton, Ohio: Institute For the Development of Educational Activities, Inc., 1978.

15. For a more thorough discussion of learning styles in the IGE system, see John M. Bahner, *Learning Styles,* Dayton, Ohio: Institute for the Development of Educational Activities, Inc., 1971.

16. See Carmen M. Culver, David A. Shiman and Ann Lieberman, "Working Together: The Peer Group Strategy" and Roger Rassussen and Adrienne Bank, "Mobilizing Group Resources for School Problem Solving", both in Carmen M. Culver and Gary J. Hoban, eds. *The Power To Change: Issues For The Innovative Educator,* New York: McGraw-Hill Book Company, 1973, pp. 73–122. Also see Richard C. Williams, Charles C. Wall, W. Michael Martin, and Arthur Berchin, "Role-Personality Conflict and Roles of Adaptation," *Effecting Organizational Renewal In Schools: A Social Systems Perspective,* New York: McGraw-Hill, 1974, pp. 43–75.

17. This is the first of eight postulates pertaining to school improvement set forth by John I. Goodlad as he reflects on the entire Study of Change. See John I. Goodlad, *The Dynamics of Educational Change: Toward Responsive Schools,* New York: McGraw-Hill, 1975.

18. For a similar theoretical position see W. W. Charters, Jr., and John E. Jones, "On the Risk of Appraising Non-Events In Program Evaluation," *Educational Researcher,* Vol. 2, November, 1973, pp.5–7.

19. Hubert S. Coffey and William P. Dolden, Jr., "Psychology of Change With-

in an Institution," *Inservice Education,* Fifty-sixth Yearbook of the National Society for the Study of Education, Part I (Chicago: The University of Chicago Press, 1957), pp. 67–102.

20. For a thorough discussion of this process and illustrations of its development as a theoretical position, see Mary M. Bentzen and Associates, *Changing Schools: The Magic Feather Principle,* New York: McGraw-Hill, 1974.

21. Perhaps this statement will be inaccurate as the Individual Education concept is further developed and adds a teacher training component. The reader is encouraged to speculate on this possibility by analyzing Raymond J. Corsini's chapter "Individual Education" in this book.

CHAPTER 4

Open Education

VINCENT ROGERS

DEFINITION

No definition of Open Education can be as precise as the reader might wish. It is at best a varied, shifting term, changing in its practical meaning from teacher to teacher. Nevertheless, it is possible to define the concept in a useful way by utilizing eight dimensions of classroom life developed by Katz (1967). In essence, Open education exists when:

1. *Space* is used in less rigid, freer and more flexible ways.
2. *The activities of children* are many and varied, including activities that are both active and manipulative as well as bookish and passive.
3. *The origin of children's activities* is more spontaneous, more child-centered, less adult-centered.
4. *The range of topics* studied is wider and more openended than in more traditional classrooms.
5. *Time* or daily scheduling is more flexibly rather than rigidly arranged.
6. *Interactions between teacher and child* are begun as often by the child as by the teacher.
7. *The teaching target* is more often the individual rather than the group.
8. *Interaction among children* is freer and less and less restrictive.

Open Education is, then, genuinely child-centered. It's practitioners seek to know the child as an intellectual, social, and physical being, as completely as possible. With this knowledge one identifies the child's developmental and other needs and creates a learning environment most likely to be responsive to those needs.

INTRODUCTION

Objectives of Education

Man has argued about the purposes of education for centuries. No doubt the most primitive caveman occasionally disagreed with his fellow tribesmen about methods of rearing the young. Certainly the history of western educational thought reflects this continuing controversy as one reads the challenges made by Socrates, Montaigne, Rousseau, Froebel, Whitehead, Dewey and others.

Clearly, this debate has continued into our time. One has only to read the voluminous educational literature of the 60s and 70s to recognize that we have not resolved this issue once and for all, and perhaps we never will.

One expects, of course, debate about the *means* of achieving educational goals. Technological change alone dictates a continuing reexamination of *how* we teach the young.

On the other hand, one would think that a society that is, with all its faults, committed to the democratic ideal would have greater consensus about the purposes of education.

We are a society, after all, that has evolved partially from the Judeo-Christian faith of the ancient Middle East. Among other ideas, that heritage places great value on the idea of the importance of the *individual* soul in the eyes of God—a concept as revolutionary as was Marxism in the 19th Century.

From Ancient Greece and Rome we have inherited a form of secular humanism that places great value on human observation and reason, and the idea of natural law in all human relations embodying the principles of justice.

The great documents and traditions of American life that evolved out of this heritage further develop many of these earlier concepts. We are, for example, a society that purports to place great value on individual freedom, equality before the law, the dignity and importance of the individual person, and the opportunity for each individual to develop as fully as his talents, abilities and interests will permit. In addition, we place great value on the abstract (yet still meaningful) concepts of liberty, justice, freedom and democracy.

In many ways it appears as if the modern American citizen suffers from a form of schizophrenia when he discusses the role of the schools. There is, of course, general agreement that certain basic skills should be taught to all children (although there is considerable debate about how that illusive goal should be achieved). Beyond that point of agreement, however, one finds considerable lip-service paid to the importance of rearing children to function effectively in a democratic society while educational practice often appears to be in direct conflict with such goals.

It is as if many Americans were quite content to live in a fantasy vis-a-vis the education of their children. The ideals and values outlined above are of course important, and we must tell each other this from time to time. On the other hand, those ideals need not clutter up the daily practice of education, nor in fact, our daily lives, and we prefer to believe that goals and purposes will somehow take care of themselves despite the things that happen every day in schools and out that may contradict those goals.

We say we believe that all men are created equal and entitled to life, liberty, and happiness, but we have no intention of applying that concept to education. We talk about the importance of things of the mind while emphasizing the rewards of more material things. We declare the importance of justice in public and private life, but practice injustice in our schools in a variety of ways.

The current conservative movement in American education clearly stands for more than a concern for literacy and numeracy. A desire for obedience, conformity, rigidity, and control seems to lie at the heart of the movement. These goals run a collision course with the most important values suggested by our traditions. Yet they are sought by educators and laymen alike who seem either to see no ideological conflict in such practices or assume that there is no relationship between what happens in schools now and the sort of human being one becomes following twelve years of schooling.

Reasons for This System

Proponents of Open Education believe above all that there should be consistency between the purposes of education and daily life in the school. (It would be better still if life in the society as a whole also supported the goals taught in the school. Unfortunately, we have little control over life outside the school, however, and therefore must concentrate on the institution we can influence, that is, the school). They believe this because they are convinced that children learn in holistic rather than atomistic ways and that the realities of daily life in the school will speak louder than classroom exhortations.

Apart from this belief, open educators believe that their system is genuinely faithful to the goals of a democratic society as outlined above. Open educators place great value on student freedom and choice in the classroom (although with some of the same, necessary restrictions to that freedom that other traditional values suggest, that is, concern for the freedom of others). Open educators place enormous, perhaps primary value on the importance of *individual* growth and development as well as the individual's right to be treated with dignity and respect. The concepts of justice and equality in terms of daily classroom living as well as democratic decision making are both educational goals as well as educational strategies for assuring this best possible life for children and adults in school.

In addition, open educators believe that the nature of both the present world we live in and the world of the future call for approaches markedly different from those followed in traditional schools.

For example, it appears as if we are living in an increasingly crowded and impersonal world. Advances in technology have added to the mechanization of American life, and many people feel the need for greater, more intense human interaction. While many traditional schools have themselves become ever larger, more departmentalized, and more dependent on technology, the open school places great value on smallness and close, relatively intense human contact.

Today's (and tomorrow's) children for obvious economic and other reasons are cut off from assuming genuine responsibility for performing needed, useful work in the society in which they live. Meaningless tasks abound, but in reality there is little that young people are *depended upon* for now in the way that they were 50- or 100 years ago. They are, in fact, *not needed* by society until they reach the age of 18 or so, and in the meanwhile are treated as dependent children throughout their years of traditional schooling. Open schools seek to provide the opportunity for service, responsibility and work in the school community and beyond, recognizing the importance of these responsibilities to the child's healthy growth.

Today's (and tomorrow's) children are too often segregated by age from older or younger children and from adults other than their teachers and parents. Open schools are organized so that children of many ages live, work, and share together. In addition, a variety of adults from many walks of life and age levels find themselves appearing regularly in open classrooms as teachers consciously attempt to bridge this very unreal and unnatural gap.

Ever increasing economic, social and technological changes are occuring in the world in which we live, and we have every reason to believe that the pace of such change will increase in the decades ahead. Rather than emphasize rigidity and conformity, it would seem as if flexibility and creativity are the characteristics called for in people who will live most of their adult lives in the 21st Century. Open schools value these qualities and provide children with many opportunities to develop them.

Perhaps a more general contrast between traditional and open practices may help to clarify further the reasons that many of today's teachers and parents have chosen open education as the system most suited to them or to their children.

The traditional teacher sees his task as transmitting knowledge and skills, the objectives for which are determined ahead of time with the curriculum essentially prescribed.

Tests can measure whether or not this has been accomplished. Grading can be based on the tests sorting out levels of achievement. The emphasis is on cognitive development; the life of the body, the senses and feelings, are secondary to what happens in the head. Correct answers still dominate. There is concern about being efficient and not wasting time. Content and skills tend to be compartmentalized for efficiency's sake. The excitment of learning tends to depend upon teacher stimulation and external motivation; it is the teacher who's primarily inventive and creative in the situation with the children following. A large part of the teacher's role consists of working hard to be inventive and to embellish the prescribed curriculum so it is interesting. Much of the emphasis is on preparing for the next step in learning and for the future in general. There isn't much trust that learning takes place unless the teacher does something that is highly controlled and orderly so that as much as possible he or she is on top of exactly what the children are learning. There are few loose ends. What a child *knows* is ultimately more important than what a child *is;* to the traditional teacher the quality of *knowing* is more important than the quality of *being.*

In open education the teacher is less content-centered and more person-centered. His task is to set up opportunities for learning experiences, both in and out of the classroom, where he can watch children and see what they respond to. While he has a good idea of the possibilities within the experiences he has set up, the actual questions brought to the materials or the activities by the children become the basis for the curriculum and much of the teacher's time is spent helping children pursue those questions, helping them to structure their learning. Consequently, curriculum is generated out of where the children are and what they bring to the situation and is not predetermined. It is difficult to test for this and even more difficult to grade it. No distinction is made between affective and cognitive development. Correct answers aren't so important as good questions; pursuing questions often results in dead ends which are not mistakes, and certainly not failures, but part of learning. This tends to minimize competition and promote collaboration.

Because it is this process that is important, rather than predetermined achievement or product at a prescribed time, there is more leeway with children to lose themselves in what they do without feeling they are wasting time. Leeway is also given for social time, for childhood is a valued time of life for its own sake. The excitement of the learning is less dependent on the teacher's input and motivational techniques and arises more from the actual engagement of the child with the learning experience which he or she has had a central part in initiating. There are more loose ends that the teacher cannot have control over, but there is a feeling that the teacher does not always have to be on top of everything for legitimate learning to take place. The teacher trusts that learning often takes place without him. Because the teacher cares about the children there are limits to their behavior. (A totally permissive adult or a totally authoritarian one really does not care much about the well being of children and the children know it.) For the open teacher the child *is* ultimately more important than what he or she *knows*.

Perhaps the basic question that we should concern ourselves with is: given the best traditional education and the best open education, do children arrive at different places after twelve years? In many respects, no. Both should have achieved their fullest in terms of skills in reading, writing, math, general knowledge, and cognitive development.

For many parents that is enough to make them choose the traditional which is more orderly and has fewer loose ends; that is, it is safer, more familiar. But as James (1968) points out there is a difference in the way lives are being spent. Do those differences matter at the time so that one group of children will have a different kind of childhood from the other? Over a long period of time, do those differences affect the way children go about learning, the kinds of questions they raise, the feelings they have of control over their own destinies, their willingness to ponder, the way they wonder about experience and the connection they make, their view of the resources within themselves and outside to draw upon?

Whatever the difference is between traditional and open education, they are qualitative not quantitative, perhaps observable but rarely measurable. Ultimately they come down to value judgments not only about two different processes of education, but also two different ways of spending one's youth.

HISTORY

Beginnings

The history of western educational thought is enormously exciting. By the standards of open education advocates, however, the history of western educational practice is dismal. As we shall see, thoughtful observers of children have protested against repressive and rigid schooling for centuries. Such schools, with rare exceptions, have dominated European and American education for as long as historians have taken the time to record and comment on such phenomena.

While it would be unfair and inaccurate to claim Socrates, Plato, Aristotle, Montaigne, Rousseau, and a host of others as advocates of open education, surely their thinking challenged the educational status quo of their time; more importantly, their challenges grew out of a deeper understanding of the interests, needs, and peculiarities of children.

Michel de Montaigne, for example, writing in the 16th century, condemned "cramming the memory with facts" and advocated instead an education that was to provide the basis for making sensible choices and decisions. He wrote (1899) that learning was "not so much for gain and commodity to (one's self) nor for external show and ornament, but to adorn and enrich (one's) inward mind, desiring rather to shape and institute an able and efficient man than a bare learned man . . . I would rather prefer wisdom—judgment, civil customs, and modest behavior—than bare and mere ritual learning."

He advocated an "activity" curriculum and believed that books alone could not provide an adequate education. He believed that real contacts with people and places were much more valuable than reading about them.

"Everything is good as it comes from the hands of the Author of nature; everything degenerates in the hands of man." So wrote Jean Jacques Rousseau (1911) in the opening lines of *Emile* in the 18th Century. For Rousseau, education was a hands-off matter. The child was naturally good, and this goodness should be free to grow and flourish in all spontaneity. Free play, free expression and the child's own natural inclinations would clearly dominate a Rousseau based school—although Rousseau himself never bothered to put his ideas to the test.

Pestalozzi's contributions to this ever expanding stream of thought included his use of "object teaching". Writing in the early 19th Century he believed that children should study the natural and physical world around them by making use of materials in the children's environment. Collections of materials of all sorts were made available to children, and outdoor observation became a major activity in his schools. In addition, oral language based upon the earlier sensory experiences of the children became a significant part of the Pestalozzi curriculum.

Froebel, the father of the kindergarten, believed that education was basically a process of creative self-development. A child develops when he is actively creating—and only then. "The purpose of teaching," he wrote (1892) "is to bring evermore out of man rather than to put more and more into man."

Maria Montessori built upon these ideas as she developed her "case dei bambini" in Italy. She recognized the importance of concrete materials in the child's learning, and the uniqueness, and individuality of all children. As did Rousseau, she had an optimistic view of the nature of man, but unlike him, saw the need for considerably more direction in the learning of the young child. "The teacher's task is not to talk," she once said, "but rather to prepare and arrange a series of motives for cultural activity in a special environment made for children."

It would be impossible to conclude this section without mentioning the contributions of the Swiss Psychologist, Jean Piaget. He is at once both a part of this short history as well as being an enormously influential figure in modern education. His early studies of thinking in his own children coupled with his later work and the work of his colleagues has led to the development of an impressive array of support for open education practice.

Piaget's work has revealed the importance of concrete experience in the learning of young children. Things need to be touched, felt, and manipulated; one does not know something until one acts upon it and transforms it; experience needs to be represented by the child in a variety of ways; children need the opportunity to experiment, to make mistakes; and, most important of all, children go through stages of cognitive growth, progressing gradually from a kind of thinking which is largely dependent upon one's perceptions to abstract thought.

In England, which is after all the major bastion of open education at this point in time, modern educators were of course influenced by all of the men and women who made their pioneering discoveries at an earlier time.

Unlike the United States, however, our English colleagues seemed to have moved rather steadily towards a freer, more child-centered education beginning, perhaps, around 1920. While they have attempted to escape from the shackles of formal education as symbolized by the infamous 11+ examination, America seems to have moved towards a far more rigid system.

These movements in English education may be correctly called evolutionary in nature rather than revolutionary. Gradualism has been the hallmark, while sudden shifts in one direction or another seem to characterize American education during the last twenty or thirty years.

Having traced earlier European origins in general as well as English beginnings in particular, it seems appropriate to turn our attention to the history of the open education movement in the United States.

There is no doubt that thinkers like Rousseau, Pestalozzi and Froebel influenced American educators who worked and wrote during the 19th Century - either directly or indirectly. It is safe to assume that this body of knowledge was part of the intellectual background of the formally educated citizens of those times. Horace Mann, Henry Barnard, Francis Parker and, of course, John Dewey as well as a number of others developed their ideas out of their own direct and vicarious experience.

Dewey's influence on the open education movement both here and abroad was (and still is) enormous. He gave the reform movement the intellectual leadership it lacked, and his presence is continually felt as dialogue about the purposes and nature of education continue.

The most succinct statement of Dewey's views is probably contained in his *My Pedagogic Creed* (1910). His fundamental beliefs can be summarized as follows: The school is basically a social institution as full of the vitality and stuff of life as is life at home or on the street. Education, then, is living, not preparing for life. The teacher should not impose his views but rather, *know* the child, select appropriate experiences on the basis of such knowledge and help the child to respond to such experiences.

A democratic classroom atmosphere is vital to Dewey's thinking, since he felt that anything less would be inconsistent with the tenets of democracy itself. Education, then, for Dewey, is the continuous reconstruction of experience. The processes and goals of education are, in fact, inseparable.

While Dewey is, of course, the giant of progressive educational thought, one can trace the roots of open education in this country to other, earlier American educators as well.

Francis Parker, for example, the dynamic superintendent of schools in Quincy, Massachusetts, advocated the use of field trips for children, teacher-made training materials, study of the local community, and the use of a variety of manipulative devices in the Quincy schools in 1875.

William Wirt, superintendent of schools in Gary, Indiana, was a student of Dewey's. He developed what was then a radical new educational plan for the city of Gary, which became famous throughout the world as the "Gary Plan". At its height, the Gary Plan was adopted by 1000 schools in more than 200 different communities. Its fame was further increased in 1916 when the *New Republic*—the same magazine that was later to publish Joseph Featherstone's influential series on English open schools—published a series of articles on the Gary Plan.

Perhaps the most outstanding example of successful open education practice in a school setting was the superb Dewey School at the University of Chicago between 1896 and 1904. This, from all accounts, was a school that successfully applied Deweyan educational principles. It gave the American reform movement something it badly needed—an outstanding example of progressive *practice*.

Apart from the schools themselves and the contributions of outstanding individual thinkers and leaders, one other early influence should be mentioned here. The Progressive Education Association was organized in 1919 to foster the cause of progressive education in America and abroad. It quickly became the focus of much of the intellectual dialogue that surrounded the movement at that time.

Despite some of the successes recorded above, one must recognize that progressive schools never represented more than a tiny portion of American practice at any point in our educational history. There was then as there is now, far more rhetoric than practice. Despite the continuing dialogue, schools in general changed very little indeed in terms of their basic purposes and methods.

The 1940s and 1950s saw a steady decline in the influence of progressive thought in American education, and it was not until the early 1960s that it surfaced again.

It is interesting to note, incidentally, that the phenomenon we call "open education" has, under one name or another, surfaced periodically in various times and places during the past 500 years. Despite its lack of universal adoption anywhere, it refuses to die, and its tenets seem constantly to be rediscovered by educators and others whose main concern is children.

During the 1960s a major social revolution occurred in American life. These were times when the unthinkable was thought, the unspeakable spoken. The pill, women's liberation, gay liberation, the sexual revolution, the general acceptance of drugs and marijuana among the young and not so young, rapid changes in family structure, serious pangs of conscience about Blacks, Puerto Ricans, Indians, and others, deep concern about the quality of life in our cities, and, looming over it all, the divisiveness of Vietnam were all challenges to the social and political status quo. Economically, times were good, jobs were plentiful, mobility was possible, and one could afford the luxury of challenging the system.

This period was a time, then, for opening up our minds to new possibilities; for embracing the concept of "progress"; for believing that change could indeed come about, that things did not always have to be the way they were. It was a time for action and involvement, a time for experimentation, a time for imagination, resourcefulness and creativity.

The schools, of course, reflected these changes and the open education movement was born (perhaps re-born would be a better word).

Jonathan Kozol (1961) and Herbert Kohl (1961) called for drastic changes in the education of America's urban young; John Holt's classic, *How Children Fail* (1964) devastatingly criticized traditional practice; William Glasser (1969) called for "Schools without Failure"; George Dennison (1969) wrote sensitively and convincingly of his "first street school" in New York City, and Lillian Weber began her "open Corridor" program in New York as well; Charles Silberman published his influential, *Crisis in the Classroom,* (1970) and I, along with a number of others, discovered and then advocated the methods practiced so successfully in English open schools for American children. (1970).

Both the lay and professional press reflected this interest, and one found it difficult to pick up a magazine or newspaper and not find articles either praising open schools or condemning traditional schools—often they did both.

"Open classrooms" sprung up in various parts of the country—many poorly conceived and badly managed, and a few that were enormously successful. Even at its height, however, it is doubtful that more than 1 percent of America's teachers and administrators made anything more than token movement in this direction. Once again, there was far more talk than practice.

Current Status

For those who have questioned the notion that education tends to reflect societal concerns and movements rather than change them, for those who have hoped, wistfully, that the schools might "dare build a new social order" or, at least, challenge the old—the past 15 years have been discouraging.

James Macdonald's (1975) perceptive essay dealing with open education's backgrounds and origins suggests that had open education not existed in the mid-1960s, we would have had to create or invent it.

"Open education is part and parcel of the social spirit and impulse for liberation that is reflected in such diverse phenomena as the counterculture's attempt to escape the dehumanizing and alienating role structure of our society; the New Left's attempt to stimulate participatory democracy . . .; minority group . . . demands for justice; a revulsion toward war and authoritarian power . . ."

One cannot in the late 1970s escape the feeling that large-scale, overt, and observable concern for and action about the causes of the 60s have gone largely underground. There is a different spirit pervading the lives of young and old alike—a cautious, frightened, suspicious, discouraged spirit that suggests a political, economic, social, and educational retreat from the ideas that moved both society and the schools in the 60's.

The *New York Times, Newsweek,* and other periodicals now write of the trend toward a "return to the basics"; music, dance, and drama are once again viewed as frills to be cut and pruned from ever-tightening educational budgets; and so it goes. In short, the times we live in seem to have encouraged both layman and professional alike, in Erik Erikson's words, "to search for smaller and often reactionary entities which will keep (one's) world together."

And so we move again in education, as we have so often in the past, from one extreme to the other, ignoring the collective insights of our profession and refusing to give extended and serious thought to the philosophy, theory, and assumptions that support our efforts.

This is not the place for a comprehensive treatment of what we know and what we don't know about children's learning, but surely even the most naive reader must recognize that children learn to read in a great variety of ways; that concrete experience is of vital importance to young learners; that rote memorization of grammar rules has little relationship to one's writing ability; that children learn better when they have some choice about what and how they learn; that success breeds success, repeated failure breeds further failure; that holistic learning is superior to fragmented, piecemeal experience; and, most important of all, that children differ in all sorts of ways from one another and cannot be taught effectively en masse, or held to arbitrary, adult-defined, grade-level standards.

There is, then, a body of knowledge that can and should serve as guidelines for those planning educational programs and experiences for children. That body of knowledge is largely apolitical, and ought to serve as a bastion against those who would change the schools out of political, social, or economic vested interest, fear, or prejudice. The ignoring of that body of knowledge by those who should know better—the buckling under to uninformed pressure—is perhaps the great tragedy of American education today.

Perhaps one should say "potentially great tragedy" rather than treat current trends as if they have already become dominant in educational practice. In fact, practice does not change that quickly, as many know who visited the schools and classrooms of the late 60s and early 70s. Open education (despite the *Times'* and *Newsweek*'s concerns) never became the major influence that recent mass media reporting suggests. Only a tiny percentage of America's classrooms are or have been truly open. Yet, the spirit of openness—the spirit of flexibility, of experimentation and innovation, of looking out rather than in, of seeking new and better ways, was an important influence on the lives of teachers and, ultimately, on the lives of children. It is the potential (and perhaps already real) death of that spirit which concerns most advocates of open education in America today.

Nevertheless, one cannot ignore the good things one sees and continues to see. Teachers have a way of riding out ideological and other storms, waiting for the wind to die down and in the meanwhile continuing to do what they think is best for children. America's teachers did not jump en masse aboard the open education bandwagon during the past 15 years, and they are not likely to move on a large scale to a 19th Century approach to learning and teaching in the 1970s.

There are for example a large number (still a tiny percentage of the total) of outstanding open classrooms that exist in America today. Surely, compared to the situation, say, in 1964 or 1965, we have many more successful working models of good practice—and these models exist in virtually every size and type of community, in all parts of the country. The continued existence of such models is indeed a healthy sign, since they are of great importance to the vitality and growth of openness.

Open education advocates in other parts of the United States seem to share the view that, despite conservative (perhaps reactionary is a better word) pressures from a number of sources, those teachers and administrators who came to open education with something more than a superficial interest have tended to reinforce and support their beliefs and practices through the years. There is a cadre of informed and successful practitioners in the schools who, unlike Tom Paine's "summer soldiers and sunshine patriots," will not give up their deeply held beliefs simply because the *Times* and *Newsweek* tell them they should.

THEORY

Learning

Perhaps one of the great weaknesses of American education is our eagerness to adopt the new and discard the old. Unlike our English colleagues, who seem to move at a more studied pace, Americans in and out of education are convinced that better solutions to most problems are not only possible, but that they lie just around the corner, waiting to be discovered and utilized.

Thus almost any new idea—team teaching, the non-graded school, flexible scheduling, differentiated staffing, career education—is seen as a possible solution to the problems that ail us. We jump rapidly on the new bandwagon, often with little genuine understanding of it. Change generally comes from the top down. The people who have the greatest impact on the success or failure of educational practice—classroom teachers—are neither comfortable with the new idea nor convinced of its worth. A year or two or three and the new approach is often abandoned. Perhaps it was carried out ineffectively; perhaps there was too little in-service education to prepare teachers to use the practice; perhaps teachers never wanted it in the first place. In any case, it doesn't matter a great deal, since another new program inevitably waits in the wings, soon to be heralded as the new savior.

These pendulum-like changes in American education tend on the whole to be superficial in nature. They are generally more cosmetic than substantive, and in many ways the basic purposes and methods of schooling go on much as they did before.

Nevertheless, this tendency to look superficially and uncritically at new methods and programs damages virtually all new approaches, those that are superficial and those with more substance. Thus when a concept such as open education is written about at length in educational documents, discussed at conferences, and reported in the media, many are quick to adopt its most obvious features—adding some old furniture, putting a rug on the floor, and bringing in gerbils. Thus one appears to be "with it" without making any significant change in ones basic educational goals or methods. *If* teachers and administrators were to look beneath the surface of a concept such as open education, they might find that they do not believe in or support its basic assumptions about the nature of knowledge itself or how children learn. If they are in agreement with such basic ideas, their chances of making the new practice work are infinitely better.

It was in this spirit that my friend and colleague Roland Barth (1972) embarked upon an intensive study of the assumptions underlying the practice of open education. Barth studied the literature of open education and identified twenty-nine assumptions or assertions that appear to underlie the practice. Barth's monumental work, perhaps the most significant analytical writing done on open education, is unquestionably the major source for theoretical comparison of this concept with others. In this section we will state Barth's assumptions as he wrote them. A brief clarifying paragraph by the writer will follow each assertion.

1. Children are innately curious and will explore without adult intervention

Children are not passive, disinterested creatures waiting for the world to be defined and explained to them. They are in effect aggressive and natural learners if they are allowed and encouraged to learn. Continuous and exclusive teacher direction, then, is *not* the sine qua non of effective teaching. On the contrary, children need time to experiment with materials to discover their proportions and relationships on their own. In Piagetian terms, they need and welcome the opportunity to act upon and transform knowledge. Centuries of perceptive observations of children at play support this view. Children apparently have an innate, instinctive drive to explore the environment that surrounds them; this seems a part of their very nature. This drive is a powerful aspect of children's behavior and can be utilized effectively in schools.

2. Exploratory behavior is self-perpetuating

If we assume that the child's innate curiosity is encouraged, that the environment for learning is designed and organized to encourage exploratory behavior, and that the teacher plays an integrative rather than dominating role, one can expect that such behavior will be extended and indeed multiplied with time. Such behavior is intrinsically rewarding to the child, and is therefore continuously reinforced. For the child, learning may be perceived of as a series of encounters with the environment, nuclear rather than linear in nature. That is, exploration leads to further exploration in the same or in different directions. There is little closure, and the answer to one question leads to new questions. The role of teacher and schools is to provide the kind of environment that will indeed extend and challenge the child's interaction with the physical and social world.

3. The child will display natural exploratory behavior if he is not threatened

Open educators have given a great deal of thought to the elements of a social environment that would encourage children's exploratory behavior. Experience and practice have led to the conclusion that a supportive, non-threatening environment is essential; otherwise, other, more pressing needs of the child will take precedence. For example, if a child is anxious about pleasing an overly critical, judgmental teacher, or fearful of punishment (or of *not* receiving a reward of some kind) or concerned about doing something better (or worse) than others, or, most importantly afraid of failure, exploratory behavior will be curtailed, if not eliminated. As open educators see it, the concept of failure has no place in a classroom that purports to encourage and support exploratory behavior.

4. Confidence in self is closely related to capacity for learning and for making important choices affecting one's learning

Helping children develop positive self-concepts is an essential element of the social environment of the open classroom. All children must have the opportunity to succeed in school, whether they are mature or immature, quick or slow, socially and emotionally maladjusted or well adjusted. The learning environment must be structured to provide opportunities for success regardless of the child's stage of development. Thus rigid standards, lists of competencies or skills to be mastered by a given age and other methods used to "guarantee" learning have no place in the open classroom. By their very nature they guarantee, rather, that *some* children will not achieve the standard; that some will have their confidence destroyed. Once a child begins to think that he cannot learn, it is unlikely that he will learn.

5. If a child is fully involved in and having fun with an activity, learning is taking place

Open educators believe that involvement in learning and obvious pleasure in that involvement inevitably leads to learning—almost by definition. It is difficult to prove this or demonstrate it experimentally. It seems more a matter of subjective evaluation on the basis of shared observation of children in classrooms. To further clarify, if a child is involved, i.e., caring about what he is doing, undisturbed by distractions and eager to continue the activity for a lengthy period, maximum learning is taking place. On the other hand, if a child is indifferent to the activity and must constantly be urged to continue the task; if he is anxious to change or drop the activity, then minimal learning is taking place. Clearly there is an unwritten assumption made concerning assertions #1 through #10 about the role of the teacher in exercising control over children's learning. While a great deal of choice is obviously valued by open educators, they also recognize that choices are often made among the options provided by teachers. If this is so, it suggests a more important role for teachers than may appear on the surface as one reads these assertions.

6. Concept formation proceeds very slowly

Advocates of open education appear to place far more value on the fullest possible development of a relatively small number of concepts as opposed to the superficial "mastery" of many. They recognize that genuine understanding is difficult for children and adults alike. To know something, to paraphrase Piaget, is to construct and reconstruct it, to explain it, to organize and reorganize it, to act upon it, to see and understand it in its many dimensions. A chair is more than something to sit on; it is wood, glue, paint, nails, shape, form, design, length, height, width, weight, color, smell, feel, and more. To know a chair is to know it in all its dimensions; to know the number 4 is also to know it in as many dimensions as possible. The same is true of concepts such as "mountain", "river" or "plain", as well as more abstract concepts such as "justice" or "equality". It is generally accepted in open classrooms, then, that children need time to do things thoroughly and well. A flexible schedule which allows for long periods of concentrated work is preferred over a day divided into 30 minute periods. Children are more likely to be encouraged to stay with an activity even though it means lack of "coverage" of other material.

7. Children learn and develop intellectually at their own rate and in their own style

Once again, open educators borrow heavily from the work of Piaget as they develop and act upon this assertion. They are particularly affected by his conclusion that children go through developmental stages as their thinking develops from the concrete to the abstract. An acceptance of a Piagetian conception of intellectual growth leads clearly to a recognition of the uniqueness, the individuality of each child. It becomes, then increasingly important to know each child, his strengths, weaknesses, interests, needs, and stage of *intellectual development* if one is to teach him effectively. Teachers thus become students of children, and the insights gleaned from such study form the basis for much of the teaching that goes on in open classrooms. In addition, a recognition of these ideas further supports patterns of school organization such as mixed-age grouping that encourage and enhance individuality.

> *8. Children pass through similar stages of*
> *intellectual development—each in his own way, and*
> *at his own rate and in his own time*

Piaget is fond of mentioning what he calls "the American question" whenever he speaks in the U.S. In essence, the "American question", asked over and over again by our teachers, parents and administrators is "how can we push the children through your stages more quickly?" Piaget's answer is simple—"you can't". Children need time to grow and develop. Open educators place great value on this insight and are hesitant to hurry children through a curriculum, to "cover" material rapidly. They prefer instead to offer rich, "horizontal" learning opportunities that are appropriate for the stage a child is in, confident that movement to the next stage will inevitably come when the child is clearly ready to move on.

> *9. Intellectual growth and development takes place*
> *through a sequence of concrete experiences followed by*
> *abstractions*

Piaget has often expressed deep concern over the tendency of many teachers to be satisfied with verbal association rather than genuine conceptual thinking on the part of their pupils. To talk about is not necessarily to know, and open educators therefore place great emphasis on experience *preceding* abstraction. They believe (and their beliefs are supported by Piaget's research) that most elementary school children have great difficulty thinking abstractly. Thus schooling shall place a major emphasis on providing concrete experience *as the basis for later abstraction.* Experience by itself, without the opportunity to examine it, weigh it, evaluate it, relate it *and* talk about it is surely not enough.

> *10. Errors are necessarily a part of learning; they*
> *are to be expected and even desired, for they contain*
> *information essential for further learning*

In most traditional schools, errors or mistakes are to be avoided. Right answers are valued, and those that come up with right answers quickly and with a minimum of error are the most often rewarded. Yet if a child (or an adult) is working on a genuine problem, i.e., a question for which there is no obvious solution, the making of errors is almost inevitable. It is part of the trial and error process that must go on in any authentic problem-solving situation. Open educators place great value on this process. They believe that teachers should develop a willingness in children to go out on a limb, to be intellectually daring even at the risk of initial failure.

> *11. Those qualities of a person's learning which can be carefully measured are not necessarily the most important*

Perhaps in this case an illustration drawn from practice will serve best to clarify this assertion.

A fourth-grade teacher had invited a blind high school student to visit her class and show her children some Braille books, writing and note-taking materials, etc. As the children became more comfortable with this engaging, open, and personable youngster, they began to ask questions about blindness itself. What is like to be blind? What does one "see" in one's mind? The discussion continued for nearly an hour. Clearly, this experience grew and developed out of a plan with relatively modest goals on the part of the teacher. "Objectives" that the teacher never planned for were undoubtedly achieved by some children. Some children were touched by the experience in ways that cannot be measured now, for only in time will the experience become a part of their way of looking at the world and in fact affect their behavior. Each student interpreted the experience differently, for each student brought with him his own experience and perceptions. Was the experience worthless? Open educators would consider such activities among the most valuable in a child's education. Surely one should encourage them, even though their results are difficult if not impossible to measure.

> *12. Objective measures of performance may have a negative effect on learning*

Objective measures such as standardized achievement tests, the Scholastic Aptitude Tests, school or district wide tests such as the N.Y. City Regents' examinations, and other similar measures tend to pit child against child in a highly competitive, academic race. Since open educators believe that an important goal of education is to help each child to grow and develop optimally as an individual and without regard to the achievements of others, they look with great disfavor on such tests. They believe that schools do not exist to rank and sort individuals, but rather to help each child grow to be the best he can become.

Teaching

1. Active exploration in a rich environment, offering a wide array of manipulative materials, facilitates children's learning

This assertion is of course, supported empirically by the observations of Piaget. On the other hand, many teachers were well aware of the importance of concrete experience for learning long before they were aware of Piaget's work. That is, informal practice preceded research. Open teachers believe that concrete experience brings meaning to abstraction, and that this is true for all children, older and younger. The child cannot learn in a vacuum. He must have something to think about, write about, sketch or draw. Unlike the materials used in Montessori schools, those used in open classrooms should be relatively open-ended, allowing for imaginative use. Children's perceptions of the world and the things in it are not the same as adult views, and they will often use materials in quite unpredictable ways. It is not enough, then for the teacher to manipulate or demonstrate; the child must do these things for himself.

2. Play is not distinguished from work as the predominant mode of learning in early childhood

Many teachers and parents make an unfortunate distinction between a child's play and his work. Play is something done at recess, in the gym or after school. Play-like activities during other times in school (playing with dolls, dressing up, puppet play, "messing about" with clay, etc.) are frowned upon by many adults in and out of education. Work, on the other hand is seen largely as two-dimensional, paper and pencil activity, usually done quietly at one's desk. Such distinctions are unfortunate. Open teachers believe that play is the most natural way for young children to learn—indeed, that play *is* child's work. Through play children imagine, fantasize, try out new roles, develop concepts and learn to discriminate. Opportunities for such play abound in open classrooms. Open teachers are careful observers of children at play since their activities tell the adult a great deal about the intellectual, social, emotional and physical development of the child.

3. Children have both the competence and the right to make significant decisions concerning their own learning

This is in part a philosophical-moral issue, that is, *do* children have the right to make any decisions related to their own learning and/or schooling? Surely one cannot resolve this problem (or other questions related to children's rights) in an empirical way. If one accepts the notion that children should be treated with respect and dignity, it follows that they should have some responsibility for making important decisions related to their lives at school, especially since young children, after all, spend a major portion of their waking hours in school.

> *4. Children will be likely to learn if they are given considerable choice in the selection of materials they wish to work with and in the choice of questions they wish to pursue with respect to these materials*

Again we are struck with the importance of open-endedness or flexibility in the use of materials with children in open classrooms. This is not merely a matter of being nice to children, of making their lives more pleasant or palatable. It is in fact a learning strategy based upon decades of observation of children at work and at play, in and out of school. *If* children can choose among many alternatives, they will likely choose those activities that are of most interest and importance to them. If they are allowed to further decide how they may work with such materials (as opposed to constant strict and rigid definition of use) they will not only choose those activities that are of interest to them; they will, in fact, in the long run, learn more effectively by following this process. Thus again it is worth noting that much of what goes on in many colorful, material-laden, active open classrooms is not occurring simply to make things pleasant for children; those activities are based upon a firm belief that they will lead to deeper, longer lasting learning.

> *5. Given the opportunity, children will choose to engage in activities which are of high interest to them*

This assertion was explored to some extent in the paragraph dealing with assertion #8. It is important to note here that open educators accept as a given that activities of high interest to children are per se better than other activities. It is therefore important that children be allowed such choice whenever possible.

> *6. When two or more children are interested in exploring the same problem or the same materials, they will often choose to collaborate in some way*

Children learn not only from teachers, books and materials, but also from each other. Children themselves are in fact, a valuable resource in any classroom if one chooses to organize so that these resources can be used. Many English primary schools utilize the form of classroom organization known as family or mixed-age grouping. Children aged roughly 5 through 7, or 7 through 9, or 9 through 11 are mixed in the same classroom to encourage maximum interaction. The importance of this assertion in the eyes of open educators in general also explains their objections to much of the teaching that is carried on under the heading, "individualized instruction". Such programs often sacrifice collaborative learning in their attempt to teach the individual child "at his own pace," often utilizing specially prepared packets of sequentially organized materials which the child is expected to work on alone. In open classrooms, it is thought to be a good thing when children help and cooperate with each other. Conversely, competitive learning is downgraded. Open educators appear to place a value on collaboration not only because they think it encourages learning, but also because they are willing to make the value judgment that collaboration is in fact a good thing.

> *7. When a child learns something which is*
> *important to him he will wish to share it with others*

If, as we stated above, cooperation and collaboration are valued in open education during the course of an activity, it also follows that sharing—a broader form of cooperation involving more children than may have participated in the original activity—is also of value. Sharing of this kind involves the use and development of spoken language, representational skills, and mutual, critical give and take.

> *8. Verbal abstractions should follow direct experience*
> *with objects and ideas, not precede them or substitute*
> *for them*

Much of what was written in the discussion of assertion # 9 above obviously applies to this assertion as well. One might add that most open educators see this sequence of events (i.e., concrete experience followed by verbal abstraction) as important to adolescents and adults as well as children. Although high school aged children and adults, in Piagetian terms, ought to be far more able to think abstractly—to be less tied to their perceptions—deeper meaning and understanding comes to them as well when experience is involved in a new learning situation. To put it another way, learning for older children and adults does *not* consist of exclusively abstract thinking based upon the concrete experiences of childhood.

9. The preferred source of verification for a child's
solution to a problem comes through the materials he
is working with

Right answers come not from authority but from the way things work or don't work. Structure and order come about by a process of hypothesis experimentation, evolution, additional experimentation if necessary, until one has verified or discarded one's initial hypothesis. Open educators believe the child is capable of making such assessments. Every question of course cannot be handled in this way. A child cannot verify all his questions with direct experience. It is important, however that the child have the opportunity to identify these questions that can be dealt with in this way because of the value placed by open educators on process as well as product.

10. Evidence of learning is best assessed intuitively,
by direct observation

Let us assume that by learning we mean more than academic learning; rather, we are assessing the totality of learning in a comprehensive sense, including physical, social, and emotional as well as intellectual growth. Given this conception of learning, open educators believe that what might be called the quality of life in classrooms is the best measure of learning in the inclusive way we conceive it. Is there excitement, enthusiasm and interest on the part of children? Are they involved, happy, and challenged? Do they cooperate and share? How do they react to new materials, novel situations? What do they do with their time when they have a choice? Do they read, write, measure and compute? Open educators seem quite willing to assess the overall quality of learning by studying what might be called the classroom's ambience. They feel this is more revealing than the results of tests or other objective measures.

11. The best way of evaluating the effect of the school
experience on the child is to observe him over a long
period of time

There is an ever glowing body of literature both here and abroad which concerns itself with the performance of individuals over a long period of time. The major conclusion of such research is that there is little relationship between test score performance and success in one's field. Outstanding physicians, artists, scientists, teachers, and many others showed little *formal* evidence of their eventual success in early life. There was much cumulative evidence, however, in the subjective observations of these individuals to indicate the likelihood of such performance. This data was gathered over long periods of time and, when pieced together, gave a coherent portrait of performance. Open educators believe that short term evolution yields few useful results. It is only in time with the cumulative gathering of data that an accurate profile of one's pupils begins to emerge.

12. The best measure of a child's work is a child's work

Open educators believe that through observation of the child at play, in dance and movement exercises, reading, sharing, probing, sorting and organizing he reveals what he is doing, how he is thinking, how he is growing. Through examination of the child's writing, drawing, painting, sculpting, measuring and weighing, teachers can see growth or lack of growth in their pupils. This common-sense observation is of great importance to open educators, for they believe that many traditional teachers fail to see the forest for the trees; i.e., they seem satisfied with their teaching because of satisfactory test performance even though the sort of observation described above might reveal glaring deficiencies if applied. It is equally true, of course, that such teachers might fail to notice the progress their pupils may be making despite low test scores if they did not use these procedures.

13. The quality of being is more important than the quality of knowing; knowledge is a means of education, not its end. The final test of an education is what a man is, not what he knows

The traditional education enterprise in the U.S. which, of course, is the dominant approach, places great emphasis on knowing. We are clearly a credential-based society, and most of our "credentials" are earned by taking a series of tests of one kind or another. The purpose of education thus would appear to be the gathering of knowledge so that one may pass certain tests—and gain entry to or promotion in one's chosen field. Open educators are not willing to accept this limited view. Does a scientist display in his everyday work the qualities we associate with the scientific profession i.e., objectivity, thoroughness, curiosity, and a continuing search for knowledge? Did the many trained lawyers convicted on various charges associated with the Watergate scandal display in their work a concern for justice, fair play, and the law? Clearly they possessed knowledge—but just as clearly, knowledge was not enough.

14. Knowledge is a function of one's personal integration of experience and therefore does not fall neatly into separate categories or disciplines

It is doubtful that children see the world compartmentally. Indeed, it is doubtful that adults do. Scholars, for convenience, categorize knowledge into various disciplines, but the problems and questions which concern all of us both academically and in a more general sense inevitably cut across such arbitrary lines. Surely unemployment in the U.S. is more than a question of economics; an urban redevelopment project is far more than an engineering problem; and the admission of blacks and other minority groups to professional schools is more than an educational problem. Open educators believe that wholeness is vital to the study of most problems children encounter in school. Children should see the world whole rather than in parts, and the relationships *among* categories of knowledge are more important than the individual disciplines themselves.

> *15. The structure of knowledge is personal and idiosyncratic, and a function of the synthesis of each individual's experience with the world*

Each child brings to school his own personal experience with the world. As teachers teach, the child interprets what is taught in terms of his personal experience, filtering what is taught through his own intellectual lenses. Thus group teaching, while convenient, offers no guarantee of uniform learning; nor do test scores. Children discover their own structures, their own concepts—and the teachers job would seem to be, in Piagetian terms, creating situations where structures can be discovered rather than transmitting them whole.

> *16. There is no minimum body of knowledge which is essential for everyone to know*

Open educators tend to view the world as an almost infinite source of data, problems, movements, organizations, creatures and places—all interacting with one another. There is more to be learned than any individual can hope to master in a lifetime. What is most important is that children study questions and problems thoroughly and well that are of interest to them and of social, scientific, artistic, moral or ethical value to the larger society. Thus open educators refuse to arrange content in some sort of academic hierarchy. On the other hand, they do apply the test of overall societal significance to what is studied, and thus becomes at least a broad limitation to what is contained in the curriculum.

> *17. It is possible, even likely, that an individual may learn and possess knowledge of a phenomenon and yet be unable to display it publicly. Knowledge resides with the knower, not in its public expression*

The display of knowledge in a public sense seems vital if the individual living in modern America wishes to make "progress" or "get ahead". There is nothing inherently wrong with this view; it is however a limiting view. Knowledge does not depend upon public expression for its existence. Helen Keller's understanding of human society was hers, as she experienced it, whether or not she was able to display it to the outside world. An American Indian child may be reluctant to display his knowledge publicly for a variety of cultural reasons. This in no way diminishes his understanding of the problem he may have been asked to solve. Knowledge is above all, a personal thing. One cannot assume it exists or does not exist purely on the basis of its public expression. Open educators are willing to recognize this phenomenon and thus become even more sensitive to the subtleties of their relationships with and observations of children.

APPLICATIONS

Curriculum, Academic

Let us begin by describing some activities that took up a good deal of the school time of a group of several 8- and 9-year-old children over a three- to four-week period a few years ago.

A dead owl was found in the woods by two of the children. They, with two of their friends, brought the owl to school. After some discussion with the teacher, it was agreed that the four would boil the owl, get rid of flesh and feathers, and examine the skeletal structure of the bird. This was done. The bones were carefully organized, then mounted with wire on black construction paper.

This experience led to a further study of the life-ways and habits of owls. Since a simple reference book had mentioned that owls eat a great many mice, owl pellets were gathered, opened and examined. Tiny bones were found; verified as mice bones; categorized into shoulder bones, leg bones, etc.; and also carefully mounted. A short but very specific book was written and illustrated by the four children concerning the habits of owls, and two of the children made a lovely "batik" of an owl sitting in a tree.

During the course of this study, the children shared some of their findings with other boys and girls in the school. The younger children were particularly moved by the older children's guesses about how the owl had met its death (its head was badly bruised by a blow that could have been made with a stone or stick) and considerable discussion followed (in which the teacher played a significant role) concerning the cruelty of those who killed wantonly, and the fact that killing owls was against the law.

This very real incident illustrates in concrete terms the essence of curriculum-building in open classrooms. The questions raised by the children during the owl experience as well as the activities they engaged in were partly social studies, partly science, partly reading, partly writing, partly skill development, partly art and partly ethics. There was a wholeness or unity in their learning. In Piagetian terms, they learned or "knew" by acting upon, modifying and transforming reality rather than by "copying" it. The experience surely involved cognitive growth, yet it also touched the children's feelings and emotions. In addition, these activities entailed much sharing and interacting among children and teacher, emphasizing human contact with each other. The children had a considerable degree of choice over their activities, and they worked for intrinsic rather than extrinsic rewards. Most important, the learning represented the genuine and personal concerns of the children themselves.

Open educators, then, conceive of the curriculum as a series of starting or jumping-off places. An idea, a question, an observation—child's or teacher's—acts as a stone thrown into the middle of a quiet pond. The ripples begin, one idea leads to another, and a study is under way. In contrast, traditional educators seem far more concerned from a curricular point of view with identifying and then covering in some particular order or sequence a series of ideas, concepts, generalizations, or skills that (theoretically) form the backbone of the curriculum in any area. There appears to be very little content that is regarded as "basic" and "essential" in the eyes of the open teacher. While he tries to understand the nature of the broad academic fields in which he works, he tends to see them largely as possibilities rather than as prescriptions. He tries to challenge and stimulate within a broad framework of cultural and societal significance, but he does not pre-plan to the extent that beginnings, middles and ends are clearly laid out in six-week study "units." The curriculum then emerges through the mutual interests and explorations of children and their teachers working together; occasionally in large groups, sometimes in small groups, and often as individuals.

Another characteristic of the open curriculum which was alluded to above has to do with the eagerness of teachers to cut across subject-matter lines in their handling of any study that may evolve in their classrooms. Art, music, history, poetry—all are brought to bear on a given problem or topic, and it is often difficult to tell whether children are studying history or geography, art or science. This freedom tends to give a wholeness to learning that must be lacking in more compartmentalized curricula, and it helps support and build the image of the school as a place where lifelike questions may be investigated as opposed to questions that may appear to be narrowly academic.

Let us now look more specifically at the ways in which various specific aspects of the curriculum are organized and taught.

Reading

Open teachers pride themselves on being both willing and able to draw from a large number of methods and techniques as they attempt to meet the individual reading needs of children. Since children differ in terms of learning rates and styles, interests and needs, and in a number of other ways, it seems appropriate to be willing to fit the method to the child rather than the child to the method.

Nevertheless, the dominant method, and surely the method that is used at the initial stages of reading instruction is the language-experience approach.

Simply stated, the language-experience approach is based upon the belief that children respond to what is meaningful to them. Since a child's oral vocabulary far exceeds his written or reading vocabulary, and since his own personal experience has the greatest meaning to him, these elements become the basis for teaching the child to read.

Children are introduced to reading through the use of a variety of experience stories. The child dictates his ideas to the teacher, the teacher writes them down, and this material, together with his illustrations, become the focus for the child's beginning reading.

Later, stories are extended in length as the child matures, and ultimately even very young children may read and write three and four and five page stories of their own creation. Personal word dictionaries soon become a part of the child's reading material, as are "word banks", or collections of words a pupil can recognize by sight.

When a child has built a sight vocabulary of perhaps one hundred or so words, the teacher may introduce him to a conventional basal reader.

Older children, once they have become more than beginning readers, are expected to spend much of their time writing about their in and out of school experiences, writing descriptions, gathering and organizing social studies or science data and then writing books or reports utilizing such data. Throughout the elementary school years—and indeed, even in high school—experience, meaning and relevance are the key words in the language experience approach.

Mathematics

In more traditional schools, "mathematics" may be best translated as "arithmetic". Open educators, however, are more interested in the broader implications of mathematics. They are concerned about topics such as computation and structure, pictorial representation, and shape and size. They are also concerned that children learn to think logically and to approach new problems with confidence and enthusiasm.

As in reading, concrete experience forms the basis for mathematics instruction, particularly in the early years. The environment both in and around the school serves as a source of mathematical problems and data and is used extensively.

Young children (ages 5–7) spend much of their time sorting and classifying sets of objects according to properties such as color, shape and size. Stones, shells, buttons, sticks, beans, macaroni and other commonly available items are weighed and measured.

Pictorial representation in the form of graphs is very common. It is not at all unusual to see child-made graphs of the number of trucks, automobiles and other vehicles that may have passed by the school during a given time period. Graphs are made of weight gain and loss for animals and people, the growth rate of plants, and many other topics.

Commercially made equipment is also utilized extensively—particularly with older children. An abacus is standard equipment, as are geoboards, trundle-wheels, Cuisenaire rods, pattern blocks, stop watches, scales, measuring cups and many other items.

Clearly, there is a different emphasis in the teaching of mathematics in open classrooms. That emphasis does not, however, eliminate much of what is taught in more traditional classrooms. Children still learn to add, subtract, divide and multiply. At the same time, however, open educators are attempting to broaden their pupils understanding of mathematics, while providing them with experiences that should help them to learn to think mathematically as well as gain pleasure and enjoyment from their work.

Writing

While the basic point of view of a writing program in an open classroom has been suggested in the section on reading, a few additional comments should be made concerning this area of the curriculum.

Writing is of course of great importance to both children and adults. It is also one of the most neglected and poorly taught skills in both elementary and secondary schools. It is important not only because of its utilitarian value but also because of its close relationship to growth in language development and reading ability.

In open schools, children write in order to communicate rather than to simply perform a set of exercises. Teachers believe children learn to write by writing, and they provide endless opportunities for children to develop and utilize this skill. Letters, announcements, party invitations, lost and found notices, class newspapers, labels, descriptions of real objects and events, reactions to poetry and music—all are used to stimulate thoughtful written communication.

Curriculum, Non-Academic

Social and environmental studies

Environmental studies are the natural outgrowth of the ideas of Pestalozzi, Froebel and others who placed great value on learning based in the real world.

Thus children in open schools study churches, shops, post offices, cemetaries, nursing homes, dumps, woods, fields and marshes as they push out in to the environment that surrounds them and away from the confines of the four walls of a classroom.

These activities are of course consistent with movements in other areas of the curriculum where first hand experience has taken precedence over purely abstract study. Open educators believe that concrete experience should precede abstraction in studies of the social and physical world as well as in mathematics.

In addition, studies of the local environment enable teachers to cater to the individual needs and interests of their children. These activities bring children into close contact with the community and its people, with their hopes and aspirations, problems and fears. Dealing with this set of reality provides endless opportunities for *genuine* inquiry. Children hypothesize, gather data, categorize, organize and generalize. In short, open educators believe that this approach is much closer to the reality of social science than are the largely second and third hand experiences studied by most children in more conventional schools.

Music, movement, drama and art

In open classrooms, the arts are vital. They are central to the curriculum and have become the integrating force that often unites it. Teachers believe, above all, that they and the school itself teach as much by example as by instruction. Thus open schools and classrooms are colorful, attractive places. Paintings and wall hangings are attractively mounted and displayed. A piece of sculpture or a pottery display sits on a table, while flowers, a nature table with shells, stones, sticks, bark, or other items are interestingly arranged. There will be trays of sand, a water table, clay, paints, charcoal, weaving apparatus, lino and other print materials, "junk" of all kinds, a dramatic play or dress-up center, etc.

All of this is designed not only to encourage children to participate, to *do*, to become involved—but also to absorb the arts as a natural part of their every day lives. Open teachers believe that ugliness breeds more ugliness—while beauty, sensitivity, and taste in one's surroundings breed more of the same.

Children are expected to become comfortable with a wide range of materials. Poets, potters, dancers, and other artists are regular visitors to such classrooms as teachers try once again to relate all areas of the curriculum to the real lives of the community and the people living and working in it.

Music, dance and movement receive a great deal of attention in open schools as children learn that expressiveness and agility with their bodies is as important as—indeed, is clearly related to—expressiveness and agility in their minds.

Science

All of what has been said about other areas of the curriculum applies equally well to science. Firsthand experience is emphasized; children work on problems of significance to them; children study science problems in relation to other aspects of the curriculum i.e., holistically; and good, effective work in science naturally leads to the need for and desire to communicate with others.

Thus the classroom may contain scales, ropes, pulleys, magnets, magnifying glasses, bones, gerbils, hamsters, insects, and other creatures, as well as an almost infinite number of other things. Teachers work in personalized, individualized ways, and children draw, sketch, and describe their work. Once again it is process rather than product that dominates.

Student Evaluation

One of the fundamental assertions underlying the practice of open education is, "the best measure of a child's work is a child's work." That is, if one wishes to gauge the progress and growth of a given child, the best way to do this is to be completely familiar with what the child does in school (and sometimes, out of school); what sort of "work" (in the broadest sense of the term) the child produces, and how that "work" changes as time goes on.

Open educators place far less value on standardized and other "objective" tests than do their traditional counterparts. They feel such tests often generate anxiety, foster competition, and enforce conformity. In addition, they question the validity of such tests, feeling that they do not really measure very well what they purport to measure.

Thus, open educators rely more on what is now commonly called the documentation of a child's growth. Samples of a child's work are kept and commented on as the year progresses. Teachers' anecdotal comments are filed on all aspects of a child's life in school; check lists of skill development are kept, conferences and interviews are held with the children (and ultimately with parents), the children keep journals of their activities, and teachers keep journals of their perceptions of children's work. All of this activity is geared to allowing the documents to reveal insights about the intellectual, social, emotional and physical growth of a child. Rather than measure a child's adequacy against an arbitrary standard or norm, the child is measured against himself. Open teachers are interested in a child's growth as measured against his own potential for growth.

A practical example of documentation as carried out by an elementary school teacher was recorded by Pederson (1977) as follows:

Not long ago I discovered I could evaluate the teaching and learning in my classroom by using a form of documentation that would assess the learning taking place. One of my former college instructors suggested I begin by just observing the activity in my classroom for short periods of time each day. I made anecdotal records of my observations in a notebook.

I used my notes to make some specific observations about children's activity and their learning. The results were not astounding but the entries helped me to confirm many of the notions I had and also raised some questions.

After making many broad observations ... I decided to investigate ... math because that subject was least appealing to the children. I began observing and recording both my activities and the children's ... my observations indicated an inconsistency between my philosophy and my practice. In spite of my strong belief that manipulative math experiences help children to understand math concepts, I was doing little in the way of teaching with these materials or encouraging their use in independent study ... Some new directions were begun. Since my first attempt as a teacher-researcher, I have continued to experiment with alternative manipulative experiences in math, using a variety of settings and age levels. Through careful observation and recording, I have come to more specific conclusions about the purpose and use of manipulative experiences. Using the same process during the past five years I have also been involved in research on lab approaches to social studies and science, vocabulary development, language experience, parent-child-teacher conferences, values clarification, multi-age grouping, parent meetings ....

Counseling

Walberg and Thomas (1971) have outlined a number of specific aspects of the open teacher's role in the classroom. It would be valuable to examine these teacher characteristics as we consider the role of the *teacher* vis-a-vis the dimensions of humanness, respect, openness and warmth. Such an analysis should clarify the counseling function in open schools.

1. The teacher respects each child's personal style of operating—thinking and acting.
2. The teacher rarely commands or reprimands.
3. The teacher values the children's activities and products as legitimate ex-

pressions of their interests, not simply as reflections of their development.

4. The teacher respects the children's ideas.

5. The teacher respects the children's individuality by rejecting ability grouping, group norms, homogenization.

6. The teacher takes children's feelings seriously.

7. The teacher recognizes and does not hide her own emotional responses.

8. Children generally do not try to suppress emotions.

9. The teacher strives to recognize emotions differentially and to act as a stabilizer upon whom children can depend when the going is difficult.

10. Conflict is recognized and worked out within the context of the group, not simply forbidden or handled by the teacher alone through punishment or exclusion.

11. There is no abdication of adult authority and responsibility.

12. The class operates within clear guidelines, made explicit.

13. The teacher promotes openness and trust among children and in her relationship with each child.

14. In general, relationships are characterized by warmth and affection.

15. The teacher recognizes and admits her limitations when she feels unable to give a child the help he needs.

16. In evaluating children's work, the teacher responds honestly, based upon a real examination of the product and a sensitive judgment about the particular child and circumstances.

17. The climate is unthreatening; fear of failure is absent.

This description makes it clear that the relationship between teacher and child in an open classroom is a broader and deeper relationship than in conventional classrooms. In fact, teachers are expected to assume responsibility for all aspects of a child's growth—academic and non-academic. This implies a close, personal relationship between teacher and child, since it is not possible to deal with the broad spectrum of student problems and concerns if one knows the child only superficially.

This dimension of *teacher* role clearly overlaps the guidance-counseling role often assumed by specialists in conventional schools. The *teacher*, not an out-of-the-classroom specialist, assumes the responsibilities as a normal part of his role. He is slow to label children as "problems" and slower still to refer them to specialists who have little first hand knowledge of the behavior of a specific child.

The techniques employed by teachers in these areas are eclectic in nature, ranging from highly personal, individual conferences to various group counseling techniques.

Discipline

One of the most common misconceptions haunting the open school is the notion that there is little or no "discipline" in such schools—that children do as they please in a completely permissive atmosphere, with little regard for the needs and rights of other children or adults.

In practice, nothing could be further from the truth. If we re-examine the quadrant outlining the relationship between teacher and child in four different types of schools (p. 138) we see that in open schools there is a *sharing* of responsibility by student and teacher. That is, the teacher has in no way abrogated his responsibility as classroom leader or adult authority figure.

Open classrooms do not consist of Mark Hopkins sitting at one end of a log and a single student sitting at the other. On the contrary, most open classrooms consist of children who are there, in ratios of 25, 30, or more, to one adult, because the law says they must be. Given this situation, it is impossible to carry on without rules and regulations of some kind.

On the other hand, open teachers have a Deweyan conception of the meaning of the word, "discipline". To them it means an ever-increasing development of a sense of personal responsibility for one's own actions—a steady movement towards self-discipline.

Thus as few rules as possible are devised by children and adults in open classrooms. In some situations, rules are broken down into something as simple as, "we must not injure or damage other people or other people's work or property".

Obviously, this allows for considerable freedom as well as personal responsibility. In both open classrooms and in open schools, children have more freedom of movement. Bells are not generally rung to signify the start or end of classes or the beginning and concluding of the school day. Students do not need "passes" to go to the lavatory, library or gym, and teachers do not "police" the corridors and washrooms.

In addition, students are expected to share a sense of ownership vis-a-vis the building they spend so much of their time in. It is *theirs* as well as the teachers'; *they* help to make it a warm and attractive place to be in through displays of their (and other's) art. They help design classroom space and often contribute prized personal possessions (books, posters, artifacts, collections, etc.) in order to make the classroom a more interesting, livelier place for everyone.

Clearly, it is difficult to make these arrangements work to everyone's satisfaction. It would, of course, be easier to run things in more authoritarian ways.

This is particularly true when children come to an open classroom from a situation in which strict and rigid discipline has been the rule. A child learns to behave in given ways in the culture of the school i.e., he learns what is expected of him as "student". It is not easy to break down these expectations, and it may take a long time indeed before such a student learns to accept the behavior called for in his new situation.

Nevertheless, the goal of self-discipline is constantly in the minds of open teachers, and movement towards that goal, however slight in some cases, is a vital part of the growth and development of children in their classrooms.

ROLES

Principals

The principal's role in an open school is difficult to define. He shares, of course, some of the functions outlined below for teachers. In addition, however, the building principal in order to be effective, must assume responsibility for the following roles:

The principal as intellectual leader

Assuming that one places great importance on the quality of the intellectual cultured life of the school, it becomes obvious that the man or woman chosen to be an open school's leader should be someone who has shown some evidence of intellectual concern and involvement in his professional and personal life. Is he a collector? A tinkerer? A poet? A painter? What does he care about? Does he have some passionate interests and concerns? To use Lillian Weber's phrase, "Is he alive and in love with life?"

The quality of the intellectual and cultural life of a school depends quite heavily on the quality of its leader. We cannot expect a school to become a challenging, stimulating place where ideas are valued if these matters are of no real concern to the school's principal.

The principal as educational philosopher

John Goodlad (1974) recently described his experiences with a number of principals who responded eagerly to his researcher's request to list the kinds of problems they were encountering in their schools. Rather than attempt to develop ideas for the improvement of their schools, however, they consistently asked what others were doing around the country. Presumably, if others were attempting to meet certain problems by making greater use of drugs with hyperactive children, or awarding tokens and prizes for greater achievement, or dividing their children into family groups, or going back to more emphasis on penmanship and grammar drills, these solutions became viable alternatives simply because they were being tried by someone, somewhere.

One might well ask whether some principals believe in anything; whether they have an educational philosophy that guides them, a set of values that helps them judge the overwhelming number of innovations that pervade education everywhere. Do we adopt team teaching, nongrading, greater use of educational TV, mini-courses, and on and on? If so, for what purpose?

In far too many cases, there is no overall purpose or aim in developing school programs other than responding to immediate needs and pressures. To be the leader of an open school, one must know where one is leading. One must have some vision or ideal of what schools should be like for children—and be prepared to say, if necessary, "This we cannot and should not do."

The principal as student of children

Principals of open schools need a deep understanding of what might be broadly called child development. Simply stated, we know a number of things about the way children grow and learn. We do not know everything, but we do know, for example, that concrete experience is of great importance in the education of primary school children. Therefore, even if one cannot reject increased paper and pencil drills and workbook exercises for six-year-olds, for example, on purely philosophical grounds, one should be prepared to reject such proposals vigorously on the basis of current professional knowledge.

The principal as developer of a sense of community

Perhaps nowhere was this role illustrated better than in John Dewey's famous University of Chicago Laboratory School. Teaching and learning *can* be very lonely occupations. Dewey developed a school in which social interaction among teachers, administrators, parents and children took place on a genuine and regular basis. *Ideas* rather than trivialities were discussed at teachers meetings; data were gathered relative to children's learning which became the focus for professional seminars and other meetings; teachers had enough free time to enable them to visit and learn from other teachers; parent study groups were formed that concerned themselves with issues closely related to teaching and learning rather than fund-raising and entertainment.

It is of great importance that a school's educational leader know what is happening in the classroom and, more importantly, in the minds of teachers and parents. An open school is a place in which everyone shares responsibility for its growth and development. The principal, however, is responsible for creating the kind of climate or atmosphere in which genuine exchange of ideas is possible.

The principal as instructional leader

If the principal of an open school is to become a respected and sought after leader of teachers, he needs to have a degree of competence in the classroom that is not generally possessed by most administrators. It is difficult, indeed, to gain credibility as a school's leader if one is inept at, and relatively ignorant of, good classroom teaching procedure. Lacking such skills, the principal is likely to fall back on that which he feels he can do well; that is, paper work, scheduling and rescheduling, and so forth. This is not to say, incidentally, that an open school does not need to be "managed" or that certain housekeeping chores do not need to be performed. It is, rather, a matter of degree or of putting things in perspective. If a principal feels unable to cope with difficult problems involving the changing of teacher behavior or the honest and sincere complaints of parents, he will probably crawl more and more into his protective housekeeping shell.

The principal is non-threatening, supportive authority

Minimizing the principal's traditional power and evaluative role is also of great importance to the open principal in terms of his relationships with classroom teachers. English open schools have made considerable use of nonevaluative advisors whose job it is to help classroom teachers improve their skills if and when the teachers request such help. The head is a strong authority figure in the school; nevertheless, many heads are able to work in relatively non-threatening ways with their teachers despite the fact that they are very much in charge. It is as important for open principals to work with teachers in a humane, thoughtful, sensitive, and dignified manner as it is for teachers to work with children in these ways. In both cases, it is clear where the authority rests; it is possible, however, to work with other human beings in ways that do not abuse that power.

Other administrators

In addition, it is important to point out that open principals need the support, security, faith and confidence of their superiors in precisely the same way that teachers need the principal's support. Once selected for the job, the principal needs to work under the assumption that he is competent, is a professional, and can do the job. He cannot be treated as a convenient scapegoat by those above him; he cannot have the rug pulled out from under him at the least sign of parental unrest. If we expect him to assume real responsibility for the growth and development of an open school, we must grant him the freedom and the support that will make it possible for him to do so. This does not mean, of course, that everyone appointed to the principalship of an open school and who is granted such support will rise to the occasion and become an effective leader. It does, however, create the conditions that allow for educational leadership. Any other position relegates the principal to the role of clerk-manager-housekeeper.

Teachers

The people who matter most in open schools—apart from the children themselves—are, of course, classroom teachers. This is not necessarily true of all systems, as can be seen by examining the classification scheme developed by Bussis and Chittenden (1976).

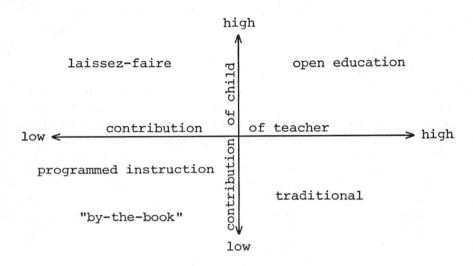

FIGURE 1

Double Classification Scheme Based on Extent to which (1) the Individual Teacher and (2) the Individual Child are Active Contributors to Decisions Regarding the Content and Process of Learning.

In this model, there are four basic modes or types of schooling. In the quadrant on the upper left, teacher input vis-a-vis decisions relating to the content and process of learning is minimal, while the child's input is maximal. This leads essentially to a hands-off role for teachers; a role emphasizing watching and waiting rather than active participation in the teaching-learning situation.

In the quadrant on the lower left, neither teacher nor child have a great deal of input. Decisions are made by higher ups, and total programs are adopted for all children. The teacher's role becomes more mechanistic, and he concentrates on following directions.

The quadrant on the lower right represents a maximal role for the teacher, and a minimal role for the child. The teacher makes virtually all decisions concerning content and process, and the child does as he is told.

The quadrant on the upper right represents open education. The teacher's contributions and the child's are at parity in this model. The teacher has fundamental responsibility for making ultimate decisions—but he does this only after seeking the fullest possible understanding of the needs, interests, wishes, and capacities of children.

Thus Bussis and Chittenden suggest a role for teachers in open classrooms that includes functions such as facilitator, research assistant, diagnostician, fellow learner and friend.

Walberg and Thomas (1971) have elaborated on this concept by developing a set of themes and characteristics that further delineate the role of the teacher. While space does not permit complete reproduction of their materials, seven relevant themes will be included together with sample characteristics that illustrate each theme.

Provisioning for learning

1. Manipulative materials are supplied in great diversity and range with little replication; *i.e.*, not class sets.
2. The environment presents a balance of commercially prepared materials and materials brought in or developed by teacher and students.
3. Materials are readily accessible to children.
4. The teacher constantly modifies the content and arrangement of the classroom based upon continuing diagnosis and reflective evaluation of the children.
5. The teacher permits and encourages constructive unplanned use of materials.

Diagnosis of learning events

1. To obtain diagnostic information, the teacher takes an *involved* interest in what the child is doing.
2. Diagnosis is based upon attention to the child's thought processes more than his solutions.
3. Errors are seen as desirable, as a necessary part of the learning.
4. Fantasy is valued; it is another way of knowing about the child and a means the child may use for learning.
5. Children do not always depend on teacher judgment; they also diagnose their progress through the materials they are working with.

Instruction—guidance and extension of learning

1. The teacher becomes involved with the child diagnostically before suggesting any change, extension, or redirection of activity.
2. The teacher plans instruction individually and pragmatically, based upon reflective evaluation of each child's particular needs and interests.
3. The teacher becomes "actively involved in the work of each child . . . . as one who seeks to help him realize his goals and potential."
4. The teacher tends to give individual children small concentrated amounts of her time rather than giving her general attention to the children as a class all day.
5. Instead of giving assignments, the teacher amplifies and extends the possibilities of activities children have chosen, through individualized conversation, introduction of related materials.

Reflective evaluation of diagnostic information

1. Evidence of learning is assessed through direct observation of what the child does and says and produces.

2. The teacher avoids traditional testing procedures and tests.

3. The teacher's record-keeping consists of individual histories chronicling the child's development.

4. The teacher keeps a collection of each child's work and makes use of it as the appropriate measure for his evaluation.

5. The teacher uses evaluation to provide information she will use in seeking better ways of encouraging and providing for children's development.

Humaneness—respect and openness and warmth

1. The teacher respects each child's personal style of operating—thinking and acting.

2. The teacher rarely commands or reprimands.

3. The teacher values the children's activities and products as legitimate expressions of their interests, not simply as reflections of their development.

4. The teacher respects the children's ideas.

5. The teacher respects the children's individuality by rejecting ability grouping, group norms, homogenization.

Seeking opportunity to promote growth

1. The teacher seeks further information about the community and its physical and cultural resources.

2. The teacher seeks information about new materials.

3. The teacher experiments herself with materials.

4. The teacher enjoys on-going communication with other teachers about children and learning.

5. The teacher attempts to know more about her children, by getting to know their parents or relatives and their neighborhood.

Self-perception of the teacher

1. The teacher views herself as an active experimenter in the process of creating and adapting ideas and materials.

2. The teacher sees herself as a continual learner who explores new ideas and possibilities both inside and outside the classroom.

3. The teacher values Open Education as an opportunity for her own personal and professional growth and change.

4. The teacher feels comfortable with children taking the initiative in learning, making choices, and being independent of her.

5. The teacher is able to recognize her own needs (*e.g.,* for importance, recognition) and restrain herself from intervening in children's activities based on these needs rather than the children's.

6. The teacher accepts the legitimacy in the classroom of her own feelings.

Students

The following comments were recorded by Rogers (1970) during a teacher-pupil planning session with a group of nine-year-olds in an English open school:

Daniel: I think we should learn to do long division next.

Gerald: What's that?

Daniel: Well, I don't really know but they're always asking me at home if I have learned it yet. My brother can do it, so I expect I could if I tried.

Audrey: How long would it take us to learn it, Miss X?

Miss X: I should think most of you would manage it in about two weeks, if you worked at it for a little while every day.

John: Supposing we worked at it all day? Would we learn it in about two days then?

Miss X: I think you might get rather tired of it if you did it all day. Wouldn't it be better to do a bit each day?

Gerald: Oh no, if we really made up our minds we could do it all the time and learn it quickly.

Christine: What use is it—what do you do with it when you know it.

Gerald: I don't know, but I expect Miss X knows.

John: Well, things you learn aren't always useful just when you learn them. Sometimes you have to wait and find out when they're useful.

Robert: Perhaps it's useful for when you do exams for 11+.[1]

Christine: Is it, Miss X?

Gerald: I think we should find out all the things we should know for 11+, and make sure we know them, even if they are not very interesting. Then we shall see how much time we have got for interesting things.

The discussion illustrates the role children are capable of vis-a-vis making significant decisions about their own learning. More elaborate illustrations of children's involvement may be found in the section, "System In Action".

In open classrooms, children are expected to take an active part in their own learning. Learning is something children do, as opposed to something that is done *to* children. Therefore they are expected to share in decisions related to the organization of the physical environment for learning. In addition, they take some responsibility for the content of their learning, and considerably more responsibility for how and when that learning should take place.

Therefore, rigid schedules or time-tables are inappropriate in open classrooms. Work may be carried out intensively, for long periods of time, or be spaced or divided into smaller units. Often students agree on week-long "contracts" developed together with their teachers. Such contracts may specify what is to be achieved, but leave the timing and methods largely up to the students. Older children, of course, may develop contracts covering much longer periods of time.

The child, then, is expected to play the role of active *learner*. He makes significant choices about his own learning, he participates, he becomes deeply involved.

He is also expected to share and collaborate with others. Thus, many open classrooms group their children in "family groups" of say, seven, eight and nine-year-olds, or nine, ten and eleven-year-olds. Such cross-age groupings encourage children to learn from each other.

Children are expected to learn to play the role of researcher-enquirer as opposed to being "receptacles of learning." Questions are posed, data gathered and evaluated, and conclusions are drawn. All of this is done in a non-competitive atmosphere in which individual growth is valued as opposed to being "better" than others. The atmosphere is purposely cooperative rather than competitive, and children are given many opportunities to help each other.

Older students in particular are expected to play an active, participative role in student government. In genuinely open schools, students help make meaningful decisions about the rules and regulations that govern their lives during the school day.

Parents

Openness implies new roles for parents as well as for other adults in the community. To be open means that parents are welcomed as partners in the teaching-learning process. Parents are rich sources of information about children—information that can prove invaluable to child-centered teachers. Parents share in the dialogue about goals and methods and play the role of learner and teacher during such discussions. Parents share many of their skills and experiences with children as well, adding dimensions to classroom life that would be impossible without them.

Similarly, other adults—painters, poets, potters, mechanics, carpenters, waitresses, the young and the old—are invited to share their lives and occupations with children as the school opens itself to the realities of the community that surrounds it.

Many open educators recognize the need for parents to become more sophisticated, more knowledgeable about the learning, growth and development of children. If parents behave on the basis of limited, fragmented, or inaccurate knowledge, it is unlikely that they will either understand the teaching-learning processes carried out in an open school or be supportive of such programs. Thus, for the child's sake and for the school's, formal and informal parent-child education programs are often a part of open school activities.

Such programs are generally carried out through the mutual initiative and involvement of parents and professional staff. They usually cater to parents of children from infancy through seven or eight years. Seminars, workshops, discussion groups, film showings, and other activities are offered at the school, at times convenient to working parents.

With or without parent education programs, open teachers insist upon close personal contacts with parents through the use of regularly scheduled conferences. These meetings serve as the major means of reporting children's progress to parents, and often serve as a substitute for conventional report cards. At such meetings, teachers share their anecdotal records of all aspects of the child's life in school, including social, emotional and physical as well as academic performance. In addition, teachers share and discuss selected samples of children's art, writing, project work, and other materials which illustrate the child's growth during a given period of time.

In these ways, open education changes the traditional roles of both parents and adults in general vis-a-vis their relationships to schools and children.

SYSTEM IN ACTION

So far we have necessarily described open education in terms of disparate collection of pieces. This has of course been necessary since we have been trying to analyze this system, look for its origins, and gauge its possibilities.

At this point, however, it seems appropriate to try to fit those pieces together. This can be done most effectively by going through a detailed description written by an informal observer (Grugeon, 1971) of the morning activities of a group of thirty-five five, six and seven year old children in an English Infants' school. The teacher is mature and experienced, the environment challenging and stimulating, the school building relatively old, the school budget very, very tight.

"One of the children had brought a newt to school. When I arrived, the teacher had just found an aquarium to house it, and a group of children were crowded round the milk table. 'Why does he have that big stone in there?' someone asked. 'He's like us at the swimming pool,' suggested another child. 'He likes to get out and jump in again.' The boy gave an action demonstration, and the teacher carried the aquarium to a table in the classroom, which already housed some tadpoles. The newt became a focus of attention for all the children throughout the morning.

Outside, five children settled down at the table to have their milk in a leisurely and civilized way. (The school encourages this, as a number of the children have inadequate breakfasts.) Inside the classroom, four children had already started work with a selection of books about newts, tadpoles and reptiles. When two girls asked a question about the newt, their teacher advised them to ask these children. Carolyn and Mary returned to the newt's tank with a book, so as to compare their newt with the pictures.

Four of the younger children, dressed in rubber aprons, went to play at a metal sink of water just outside the door. They chatted as they filled and emptied containers. Two older boys were busy making a model of the Mayflower, working with a collection of books on sailing ships and on Elizabethan history.

Three boys were working at a task which took all morning and, as it happened in the central space of the room, became a centre of interest for the whole class. Using two long wooden measures (one in inches, one in centimetres), they were measuring and recording the height of every child in the class. They worked systematically, requesting each subject to remove his shoes, and to lie on the floor with feet turned up at right angles; they then drew chalk lines along a ruler placed at the top of the head, and another placed against the feet. Meticulously measuring and recording their findings required concentration and cooperation, particularly since, at any one time, individuals or groups would be watching, speculating, and contributing ideas, while their friends were measured.

The wendy house was typical of those in every classroom (containing dolls, two dolls' prams, a small table with a cloth, pots and pans, and dressing-up clothes neatly hung on hangers), and it was already occupied by a group of girls. One of them left, shutting the door and saying, 'I'm just going to see the newt.'

The headteacher came in with some chopped worms. She and some of the children had been to find these after an earlier discussion, when she looked in and they had been wondering what to feed the newt on. A group gathered to see whether the newt would eat, and then dispersed, leaving two very small boys who speculated about the newt being hungry when it wasn't lunchtime, and discussed what they hoped they would have for lunch that day.

A girl brought in the plastic plates which had been used for biscuits and crisps at the milk table, and washed them up at the classroom sink. A seven-year-old (Clinton) was working on his own in the quiet corner, writing laboriously. He was making a book about deserts. He had drawn a recognizable camel, and was writing on the page opposite. 'The desert is very hot. All the people were rags even the chief and the byoutefull ladies is well and the loutenet. They all were rags.' He was so absorbed in writing this that he was quite unaware of my taking it down. Occasionally, during the morning, he got up and had a look to see how the measuring project was going, and then returned to become absorbed in, writing. Near him, in the quiet corner, a girl was looking at an illustrated alphabet. In the brick corner, stretched out on a rug, two boys were building a garage for some Dinky cars.

It was 9:45, and everyone was occupied. There was an atmosphere of busy concentration. The girls in the wendy house were dressing up. The drama they were involved in seemed fragmented, but they were obviously satisfied by it.

'I'm only going out for two hours,' said one. 'We're going to the pictures,' said another. Later, I heard one announce, as they came out dressed in assorted finery, shutting the door carefully on their domain, 'You're going to see your gran.'

9:50:The cry of 'There's a little fing moving', drew eight children to the newt's tank. It was a bit of worm, the teacher joined the group, quietly drawing their attention and to the number of 'fingers' on the newt's feet, and the way he moved in the water. She suggested that they look at what Carolyn and Hilary, who were still at work with the newt and reptile books, were doing. They all moved to the books, and began to look at them with interest.

The girls in the dressing-up clothes seemed to be structuring their drama: 'You've got to wait here,' I heard one say. The two boys working on the Mayflower were still very busy while, out in the corridor, the group of youngsters who had been at the water sink had moved to the sand tray.

I left to watch another class working on the apparatus in the hall, returning at 10:25. Clinton was still writing about the desert, but some of the girls from the wendy house were sitting at a table, drawing. Four girls had taken over the brick corner and had constructed an elaborate and symbolic bus out of the largest bricks and blocks. A large block with smaller ones on top was the driver's cabin, a parallel row of large bricks represented the seats. The girls were sitting quietly inside this construction, while one drove. During the time I had been away (about thirty minutes), some of the children had been painting; careful coloured prints, of hands and abstract patterns, were lying out to dry on the paint table.

At playtime, the children left the room unhurriedly. Clinton, who had now been joined by Martyn, remained in the quiet corner. They were talking about lakes. Martyn had drawn a picture of the newt and, at the top of the clean page opposite, written 'The', obviously intending to write about it.

11.00–11.15:The children went to join another class, to watch a television programme about reptiles. I was in their room when they came back. Four children went straight to the quiet corner, took out books and sat at the table. Two girls wedged themselves into the armchair and began to take turns to read aloud to each other from a book. The boys involved in the measuring project resumed work as if there had been no interruption. Three girls and a boy unhooked overalls from the corner by the sink, and went to the clay trolley, where, they told their teacher, they were going to make crocodiles. Martyn and Clinton went back to their writing. Two boys took out their interest books, and began some writing about reptiles. Four of the younger boys began building in the brick corner, while they were waiting to be measured. They built an ill-defined enclosure, talking a great deal before they all got inside.

11.20:The teacher sat in the book corner, hearing children read aloud to her. A group of girls settled down at the table outside the wendy house. 'I'll do the picture, you do the writing,' said one. By now there were five in the brick construction, a little noisy and unruly, but involved in a complex game. 'That's our radio,' I heard one say.

The two boys who were measuring now had a large audience; they were discovering, as they moved on to the younger group, that height is not absolutely related to age. A lively discussion took place, going from the relation between age and height to the relation of their height to that of their parents: 'My mum and dad are both tall.' 'Wesley's mummy's not very tall.' 'I take after my dad.' They drew their teacher into this discussion for a while.

The boys in the brick corner, uninvolved in all this, were purposefully removing their shoes and storing them in one of the hollow blocks which they had turned on its side to make a locker.

The teacher moved to the clay group, who were referring to a book, since they wanted to establish the difference between crocodiles and alligators and needed her help. The girls who were drawing were all drawing castles. This related to a television programme seen earlier in the term, and a number of children were still thinking about it, as I discovered later. A small boy was beating out a careful rhythm on the xylophone, repeating it gently and thoughtfully over and over again. Two girls were helping each other into overalls to start painting.

11.35:The measuring project reached the youngest children, and enlisted the teacher's help to line them up in order of size. There was much argument among the children, and the measurers were still surprised to find that five-, six- and seven-year-olds can be the same height.

I moved to a table where four boys were now writing in their interest books, and attempted to record what they were writing and saying, and generally how they worked. I stayed with them until the morning ended shortly before noon.

They already had their books out. One said, 'I am going to do two pages of writing.' All four proceeded to count the number of pages left in their books; this was becoming rather competitive, until one of them said cross-ly: 'Shut up, you're putting me off', and they settled to work amicably. While I was there, I recorded what three of them were writing about. (First, it was about subjects that they were already preoccupied with; secondly, they had all already done drawings to illustrate the writing; and, thirdly, none of them approached the teacher at any time.) They seemed very relaxed and businesslike. In about ten to fifteen minutes, Wesley wrote; 'This is the wor between england and france attacked the english in the castale', Graham wrote, 'The Apollo 13 splashed down in the Pacific Ocean on', and Stephen wrote, 'The England Knights are going to fit the french.'

The fourth boy abandoned writing for very detailed drawings related to the programme they had just seen. He talked to himself as he drew, 'This is an iguana.' He asked me the name of a reptile I had never heard of. I suggested that he had got the name wrong but he insisted on 'gully monster'. Graham asked the others to spell 'splashed down' and they told him it was up on the wall. He took a notice down from among a collection of pictures of Apollo 13, and brought it back to the table. Wesley said, 'Mena, how do you spell "attached"?' They looked back through Mena's book and found it in a recent piece of writing. Wesley wasn't satisfied. 'That's "attacking"; he said scornfully, but managed to adjust it to what he wanted. Graham got up again, after the others had ignored his question, 'Where did Apollo splash down?', and came back triumphantly with another card. 'Pacific Ocean', he told them, getting out his personal dictionary and turning to 'P'. He asked me to write it in for him, and then realized he could copy it himself. Wesley, suddenly bored, persuaded Stephen to put his book away and go with him to the clay table. There was no room there, and they quite happily came back to writing. Stephen showed me his drawing of the English and French at war, (minute little men in chain mail, very carefully drawn in pencil, with the English and French helmets very distinctly different). By now Mena had drawn a chameleon, a snake, a lizard, and a tortoise very accurately, and all from memory. He showed them to the teacher, and they both looked up 'iguana' in an encyclopedia of reptiles. He was delighted to find the 'gully monster' and brought the book to show me,—a gila.

The drama in the brick corner had become more peaceful and purposeful, but it was time to pack up for lunch. Mena worked on until the last minute, leaving the room last, muttering in a satisfied tone 'gila monster'.

How typical a day is this? How much can one generalize from it? Probably very little in specific terms. Surely there is nothing sacred about newts, measuring one's height, or writing about deserts.

It would be fair to say, however, that the attitude displayed by the teacher (*and* head teacher or principal), the relationships that existed among adults and children, the emphasis on individual work, the concern for children's interest, the emphasis on the concrete and the real—all of these are typical of the good open classroom.

PROSPECT

It is clear that the open education movement has failed to live up to the hopes of its most ardent advocates. Neither has it supported the skepticism of its sternest critics. The movement in the United States has surfaced again as it has in the past. Its ideas have had an impact upon many teachers and administrators, but the schools have not changed on anything approaching a large scale. While this current surfacing may have already had its greatest effect—perhaps in 1971 or 1972—its ideas continue to influence the schools in a variety of ways. There will be countermovements in education—new ideas, new forces, new directions. But the ideas that have been associated with a more humane, responsive, and child-centered education—from Rousseau through Froebel, Montessori, Dewey, Piaget, and Isaacs—are inexorably a part of American educational thought in the 1970s.

How these ideas will influence schools and at what magnitude is far more difficult to determine. Nevertheless, one might predict the following trends:

1. It seems quite likely that we will opt more and more for the notion of "alternatives" in the public sector of American education. Monolithic change seems neither possible nor desirable. There is a values question involved in the movement toward openness, and choice for parents, teachers, and children may become increasingly important in the future.

2. It is quite possible that the concept of the "community school" may become increasingly important as time goes on. Those who have called for a much closer relationship between schooling and the total life of the community see great possibilities in the community school concept as it has been developed in Jarva, Sweden, for example. Here an elementary school is conceptually woven into housing, recreation, and social patterns. The school exists side by side with medical, dental, and social facilities, commercial shops, clubs for the elderly, and library and recreational facilities.

3. Closely related to the community schools idea is a movement toward greater community service, whether such service originates out of a "community school" or an ordinary school. That is, we may see a time when, as a part of the daily life of the school, children engage in activities such as aid to the elderly and/or urban poor, the construction of community playgrounds and other facilities, publicizing of problems such as lead poisoning or alcoholism, serving in hospital apprenticeships, providing legal aid for teenage defendants, and developing counseling centers for runaways. Certainly these services are needed, and certainly children can be involved in providing them. It seems a natural extension of the ideas of open education to include more and more of this kind of service activity in the programs of elementary and secondary schools.

4. Open education may have its greatest impact in the future on the education of mature adults. As the percentage of older citizens increases, as life expectancy grows, and as the need for greater richness and fullness

in people's private and professional lives becomes increasingly recognized, the demand for life-long learning opportunities should increase significantly. Much of this demand will be met through experimental, student-based programs rather than through formal, narrowly academic approaches.

5. As research continues on the complex questions related to childrens learning, we may expect considerably more support for methods generally associated with open education. Current research on the diverse functions of the left and right hemispheres of the brain, for example, indicates that the visual-spatial abilities of most children are seriously neglected because of the current, almost exclusive emphasis on symbolic-analytic learning.

6. It is quite likely that a significant, positive economic shift in the American economy accompanied by a period of stability and confidence in government might lead to a more flexible, less rigid attitude towards schooling than currently exists in this country and in others. If, as has been argued earlier, trends in education reflect the social and economic trends of the community at large, we might well expect a period of innovation to follow current, conservative movements in education.

Clearly, these few, isolated ideas do not represent in any sense a program or manifesto for change. They are simply an attempt to stop, take stock, and look, however tentatively, into the immediate past and not-too-distant future. Perhaps these ideas will contribute toward a more reasoned approach to change in American education and help to counteract our self-defeating tendency to move with fad and fashion from one extreme to another, learning little from the past and sometimes, in the long run, harming those whom we want most to help—America's young.

REFERENCES

Barth, R. *Open Education and the American School.* New York: Agathon Press, Inc., 1972.

Bussis, A. and Chittenden, E. *Analysis of An Approach to Open Education.* Princeton, New Jersey: Educational Testing Service, 1976.

Dennison, G. *The Lives of Children.* New York: Random House, Inc., 1969.

Dewey, J. *My Pedagogic Creed.* Chicago: A. Flanagan Co., 1910.

Froebel, F. *The Education of Man.* New York: Schocken Books, 1966.

Glasser, W. *Schools Without Failure.* New York: Harper and Row Publishers, 1969.

Goodlad, J. Speech delivered at American Association of Elementary, Kindergarten, Nursing Educators. Washington, D.C., 1974.

Grugeon, D. *An Infant School.* New York: Citation Press, 1971.

Holt, J. How Children Fail. New York: Pitman Publishing Corporation, 1964.

James, C. *Young Lives at Stake.* New York: Schoken Books, 1968.

Katz, L. Research on Open Education—Problems and Issues. In D. Hearn, J. Burdin, and L. Katz (Eds) *Current Research and Current Perspectives in Open Education.* Washington, D.C.: Association of Elementary-Kindergarten-Nursery Education, 1967.

Kohl, H. *36 Children.* New York: New American Library, 1967.

Kozol, J. *Death at an Early Age.* Boston: Houghton-Mifflin Company, 1967.

MacDonald, J. Perspectives on Open Education: A Speculative Essay. In B. Spodek and H. Walters (Eds) *Studies in Open Education.* New York: Agathon Press, 1975.

Montaigne, M. *On the Education of Children.* New York: D. Appleton and Co., 1899.

Pederson, C. *Evaluation and Record Keeping.* Grand Forks, North Dakota: Center For Teaching and Learning, University of North Dakota, 1977.

Rogers, V. *Teaching in the British Primary School.* New York: The MacMillan Co., 1970.

Rousseau, J. *Emile.* New York: E. P. Dutton and Co., 1911.

Silberman, C. *Crisis in the Classroom.* New York: Random House, 1970.

Walberg, H. and Thomas, S. *Characteristics of Open Education: Toward An Operational Definition.* Newton, Mass.: Educational Development Center, 1971.

CHAPTER 5

Montessori
System of Education

URBAN H. FLEEGE

DEFINITION OF EDUCATION

The term education embraces all the influences and experiences that prompt and enable a person, young or old, to develop his* physical, intellectual, emotional and social potentialities. Education is an active process; it implies immanent activity. Unless the learner is interacting, no lasting learning takes place. To the extent that the learner is intimately involved in the learning activity, resultant changes in behavior are correspondingly small or large.

Education in essence is functional in intent. Education aims to help the child develop his potential. There are developmental goals to be achieved: ideas to be grasped, appreciations to be developed, skills to be acquired, attitudes and habits to be formed ... all useful resultants enabling the individual to function more fully as a person. Effective education at levels involving the higher mental processes requires the learner to internalize the learning experience; without internalization, sensitivity to application in varying situations will be lacking.

Education, as viewed by Montessori, is a system in which everything

---

*The masculine pronoun is used throughout this selection as a generic term referring to both sexes.

In this chapter we assume that education refers to persons as distinguished from the lower forms of life in which the term "training" is sometimes used.

relevant to the life of a child, at his particular stage of development, is provided in an appropriate, stimulating environment in which learning through discovery is facilitated. The teacher, as a key influence in this environment, serves as a catalyst. Every child, in Montessori's view, possesses an inner, dynamic spirit which, if given the appropriate environment, shows itself in a desire to learn.

INTRODUCTION

Objectives of Education

The overriding objective of education is to help every individual become a fully human person. The ultimate purpose of education is twofold: (a) to help each individual become aware of himself, accept himself, like himself and believe in his own worth as a person, and (b) to help him develop his various potentialities so that he becomes as fully as possible the person he is capable of being. The inner residual of all educational efforts should be a positive self-image, the key to a person's personality. The habitual way a person thinks, feels and believes about himself is a primary determinant of his approach to learning as well as of his behavioral response in any given situation. Educational experiences, which do not result in positive feelings about self, negate efforts toward self-actualization. Consequently, the dominant purpose of any educational program, at least up to and probably through the teen years, is to prepare the individual for life, but in the process also to foster the development of a positive self-image.

Education should help prepare people to achieve happiness. Many of the major religions, in answering the question *What is man's purpose on earth?*, cite the rationale for man's existence in terms of his pursuit of happiness. One of the principal religions of the world, the Roman Catholic, states man's purpose simply: "God made me to know Him, to love Him, to serve Him and to be *happy* through Him in this world and with Him forever in the life hereafter."

Every human being experiences the desire to be happy. Happiness is an inner residual dependent upon the quality of what one is, what one strives for and what one does. Education leads the young person to appreciate the fact that the actualization of one's potentialities is the essence of human happiness. Thus, education ties in to man's life and purpose by facilitating the development of his potentiality.

Man is social by nature. The architect of human nature so designed man that he can reach the fullness of his being only in a social milieu. Education, therefore, aims to assist the child in discovering and developing guidelines for living in a changing social world. This means developing interpersonal competence, an essential element in becoming an adequately functioning social being.

To function adequately as a responsive and responsible social being, the child must develop: (a) sensitivity to the feelings and rights of others, and (b) skills and attitudes requisite for adjustment, adaptation, cooperation and initiative in social situations. This requires education to focus, not only on the child's physical and intellectual development, but on his emotional, moral and social development as well.

In a changing society, education focuses on developing problem-solving and decision-making skills. A person unskilled in analyzing complex situations, innovative schemes, or puzzling problems, is unprepared for living in an increasingly complex society.

The development of intelligence is a residual of activities engaged in when confronted by problems demanding the interrelating of insights and the drawing of conclusions. In the process of thinking and solving problems, the child is actually structuring his own intelligence. Existing constructs, or *schema* as Piaget referred to them, are in a state of change, revision, expansion, as successive relevant experiences are grappled with by the curious, exploring, solution-bound mind. This most distinguishing, unique cognitive feature of human beings is, therefore, central in the educative process.

Education aims to encourage creativity in *every* child. Every child is born with the potentiality of being creative. Every child has the power of fantasizing, imagining, formulating new combinations and permutations. Some possess these potentialities to a lesser degree while others possess them to a greater degree; every child, given the appropriate stimulation and opportunity early in life, can utilize and develop his creative powers.

Education aims to provide a curriculum of experiences appropriate to every child's needs so that the development of his whole person will be facilitated. Society has the duty of providing educational opportunities designed to meet, in an adequate manner, the needs of today's children so that the persons peopling tomorrow's world will enjoy a larger measure of human dignity.

Education fosters the acquisition of core academic skills, which become the tools for a lifetime of creative learning. In a highly verbal society, as is ours, and where everything is quantified, communication and mathematical skills must be developed in every person capable of assuming responsibility for his own life. An integral part of education in the core areas is the concomitant development of positive attitudes toward one's ability to perform effectively in these areas. A prerequisite to the development of the core of academic skills is the development of perceptual discrimination. *Nihil in intellectu quod non prius fuerit in sensu.* (Nothing is in the intellect which was not first in the senses) Where young children have not enjoyed an enriched, stimulating home environment, a program of supplementary enriching experiences should be provided by the schools.

More sophisticated knowledge and use of communication skills, a love of reading, an appreciation of health, science, literature, history, art and music, as well as a deeper grasp of mathematics are objectives as the child advances in structuring himself through his learning.

Since man needs to earn a living, education assists in helping him develop habits of initiative, a "marketable skill," and a sense of responsibility. A mature adult is prepared not only to attain and maintain satisfactory human relationships, but likewise is able to sustain himself and contribute to the sustenance of others.

Education aims to help each child experience success within a framework of internalized ethical values. Given modest satisfaction of man's lower needs on the human hierarchy of drives, as outlined by Abraham Maslow, (1970) every person craves success. The drive for success can become "success at any price," unless an appreciation of and experience in the application of ethical values is a prominent objective in the educational program. A person with a perceptive mind and sharp skills, but lacking the guidance and control of ethical, moral values, is dangerous to self and others because he is unpredictable. Because there is general agreement in many areas of life as to what is right and what is wrong, what is good and what is bad, education should foster the examination and appreciation of ethical and moral values in the school program.

Reasons for the Montessori System

Apparent inability of existing educational programs to meet the varying needs of young children lowers morale in the public at large and prompts parents and teachers to explore Montessori schools because they provide a learning environment geared to individual needs.

Montessori's observations led her to conclude that every child possesses an inner psychic pattern guiding his development, a "spiritual embryo" which seeks expression (Montessori, 1970, p. 42). Basic in the Montessori system is the conviction that every child is born with a desire to learn. Emphasis is on recognizing this inner motivation by providing an encouraging learning environment. Montessorians approach education with the conviction that every child has the responsibility of constructing himself.

Existing traditional educational programs do not provide the administrative structure, the curriculum, the learning environment, the materials and activities, the methods of teaching and manner of relating to the child which Montessorians see as necessary if the child is to be helped in his task of developing himself. Montessori views education as a process of aiding the child to construct himself, for he possesses within the potentialities of the person he someday will become. Teaching, as traditionally understood, functions as an external force. The psychic reactions of the child, which are initiated in response to inner promptings when confronted by appropriate stimulation from the environment, are frequently interfered with by the traditional teacher.

Because Montessorians feel that most child and educational psychologists have overlooked the inner workings of the child's psyche, a system of education which recognizes a unique guiding pattern within the child is necessary. If the child is to develop his human potentialities, he needs to be assisted in an educational system designed in keeping with his uniquely human characteristics. Laws of learning, and their implications, suited to creatures possessing a nature different from that of man are inadequate for assisting man in realizing his full potential.

For a person to assume responsibility for developing himself, a sense of responsibility must first be developed in the child. This is possible only in an environment characterized by freedom and discipline, simultaneously present. The child must be free to choose from the learning environment that with which he will work. The call of interest comes from within the child in response to a developmental need. He must be free to interact with what he has chosen as long as he savors satisfaction. He must not be hurried, forced, or expected to engage in that which has no meaning for him.

In addition to making discoveries through his work about the nature of things, how they respond and why, the child reaps residual feelings of joy, satisfaction, increased interest and the conviction "I can do it!" Thus self-esteem is nurtured as the child, through daily successes, comes to be more clearly aware of himself and what he can do. He comes gradually to feel and think positively about himself, thus constructing within his self-image.

The child can develop himself fully only in a social setting. Consequently the necessity of the second prerequisite in an effective learning environment: *discipline,* or in Montessori language, *ground rules.*

To safeguard the rights of others, to maintain order where all are free, to clarify what is expected by way of routine operations, ground rules are stated simply, clearly understood and consistently implemented. For example, in a classroom where there are hundreds of materials in easy access to all, there has to be a place for everything and everything must be returned to its place.

Underlying the rationale of the Montessori system is an ethical philosophy of life which conceives of the child as possessing a spiritual destiny destined ultimately for a life beyond the present life. Montessori takes issue with the dualistic Descartian view of man as divided into the intellectual and the physical. The hypostatic union of body and mind necessitates physical activity for the full development of man's psychic powers. As Montessori says, "One of the greatest mistakes of our day is to think of movement by itself, as something apart from the higher functions . . . Mental development *must* be connected with movement and be dependent on it. It is vital that educational theory and practice should become informed by the idea" (Montessori, 1964, p. 140). "Movement is a part of man's very personality, and nothing can take its place" (Montessori, 1970, p. 103). Learning tasks calling for the child's active participation are fundamental in a Montessori learning environment.

How the child comes to feel about himself, as he is assisted in the process of developing himself, is more important than what he is learning to accomplish. In Montessori schools children are encouraged to express their feelings, in a manner appropriate to the situation. In the self-learning environment children are loved, trusted, encouraged. Gradually children show more initiative, confidence, persistence in their behavior as they find themselves confronted by fascinating materials and activities with which they become involved—until their habitual behavioral response becomes an asset in any learning or problem situation. In short, the Montessori self-learning environment fosters the gradual acquisition of the habits requisite for a lifetime of learning. Values, like other elements in the environment, tend to be caught rather than taught. A four-year-old approached his Montessori teacher one day, "Virginia, you must love us very much." "Why?" "Because you have so many things here for us—and I *love* to work with them!"

Since every child possesses the potential for being creative, the "freedom within limits" environment in Montessori fosters, rather than stifles, this fragile aptitude. Montessori serves the unmet needs of the community by providing a form of child-care service (as more and more Montessori is being incorporated into day care) which provides an educationally stimulating environment beyond nursery care.

While insufficient longitudinal studies have been undertaken, partly because Montessori has come into its own in America only within the past decade, observational evidence abounds attesting to the effectiveness of Montessori in equipping children with effective tools for further learning. Follow up research studies utilizing tests by Gross and Banta (1969), Sciarra and Dorsey (1974) and by Fleege, Black and Rackauskas (1967) found Montessori children to be performing at superior levels, especially in verbal and math areas, when compared with students in control groups.

HISTORY

Beginnings

At the turn of the century, Maria Montessori, a young physician with an interest in anthropology and psychology, was confronted by the problem of what to do with retarded children in a state orthophrenic school who were considered "unable to learn." This problem set her to applying her scientific bent to observe the so-called "idiot" as well as the normal child. To her amazement she found all of these "idiots" could learn in an environment suitable to the child's needs, when obstacles and threats were removed.

Her lifelong work as an educator began in 1907 when she established her first "children's house," *Casa dei Bambini,* in a Rome housing project in the San Lorenzo slum. Then, as today, in Montessori schools throughout the world, children's interests and enthusiasm blossomed as they tasted success in working at their own pace with materials from their environment so constructed as to isolate and clarify the skill to be mastered or the insight to be grasped.

Maria Montessori, born in 1870 in Ancona, Italy, as a young girl in Rome became interested in mathematics and biology. In 1896 she became the first woman to graduate from the University of Rome Medical School. Shortly thereafter she joined the staff of the University's Psychiatric Clinic where her duties brought her into contact with mentally defective children. Convinced that these children could benefit from some type of special education, she travelled to London and Paris to observe the pioneer work of Jean Itard and Edouard Sequin. Utilizing insights thus gained, she developed and experimented with materials for the children in the State Orthophrenic School of which she had been appointed director in 1898 by the Italian Minister of Education. Of this experience she wrote:

"I succeeded in teaching a number of the idiots from the asylums both to read and to write so well that I was able to present them at a public school for an examination together with normal children. And they passed the examination successfully ..." (*Montessori* 1964, p. 38). This set her to wondering why normal children were not achieving more. She continued, "I became convinced that similar methods applied to normal children would develop or set free their personality in a marvelous and surprising way." (p. 39). Her interest in education ripened as she returned to the University of Rome to deepen her psychological, anthropological and philosophical insights. Meantime she was doing research on nervous diseases of children, serving on the staff of the Women's Training College in Rome, practicing in hospital clinics, and carrying on a private practice.

As a professor of Anthropology, an appointment she received in 1904 when she was 34, she was asked to set up and direct a day-care center for 60 children, ages three to seven, in a slum housing project. This was accomplished in 1907. She described her children as "tearful, frightened ... so shy that it was impossible to get them to speak; their faces were expressionless ... They were indeed poor, abandoned children who had grown up with nothing to stimulate their minds." (*Montessori*, 1970, p. 129). She had no system or method in mind. She wanted merely to compare the reactions of these children with those of the mental defectives as she presented them with the various materials she had designed. She provided a simple, natural environment where everything suitable to the child's development was made available. At first most of the materials were sensorial in nature. Obstacles and distractions were removed. Montessori became fascinated as she discovered differences in the children's reactions. Her observations led to a number of discoveries which so amazed her that for some time she was left incredulous. The children became absorbed in working with the apparatus provided; their degree of concentration was far beyond that of the mentally deficient children. Instead of putting the materials away when the task was completed, they repeated the work over and over again, moving to another task only when some internal hunger had been satisfied. Instead of appearing tired at the completion of a task, the children were relaxed, rested, peaceful, happy.

Similarly other reactions surprised her. Once, someone forgot to close the cupboards housing the materials. Upon arrival, the children selected their materials and initiated work on their own. This led to open shelves with materials arranged in an orderly manner at children's height. One day a mother brought her six-month-old baby to the center. The children fascinated with the silence of the baby imitated the silence, enjoying their feeling of accomplishment as they held their impulses to be noisy in check. This led to the "silence game" now found in Montessori preschools. (Lillard, 1973, p. 6) Similar discoveries led to the introduction of writing as a preliminary step to reading and to hundreds of other auto-education exercises.

Before the end of 1907 a second Montessori school was founded. In the following year she established schools in Milan and Rome. By 1909 many schools in Switzerland were incorporating the Montessori system in their orphan and "children's houses." As schools were founded from other socio-economic levels of society, further experimentation was undertaken with consequent discoveries. For example, the immediate interest evidenced by the slum children was not the response of the more affluent child; but after a few days or several weeks, the materials caught their interest likewise. The reactions thereafter were similar to those noted in the first "Children's House" in the slum district: First there was the cycle of repetition accompanied by concentration and relaxing satisfaction. This led to increasing inner control, competence, self-confidence and an evident preference for purposeful activity. When a child arrived at this stage of his development, Montessori said the child was "normalized."

As schools multiplied, word of the success of "Montessori children" spread. Persons from all over, including America, came to see for themselves what was so unique about these non-traditional schools. Dr. Montessori became a popular figure, being invited to intellectual as well as social gatherings in Europe and America. She became a world traveler, giving lectures, establishing schools and teacher training programs, writing articles for journals. In 1909 she wrote the first extensive account of her work, *The Montessori Method*. Twenty years later she surveyed how her ideas had spread: "There is not one of the great continents in which (Montessori) schools have not been distributed—in Asia from Syria to the Indies, in China and in Japan; in Africa from Egypt and Morocco in the north to Cape Town in the extreme south; the two Americas: in the United States and Canada, and in Latin America." (Montessori, 1967, p. vi)

Montessori paid her first visit to the United States in 1912. Received at the White House, she gave her first lecture in Carnegie Hall, stayed at the home of Thomas Edison and helped found an American Montessori Association with Mrs. Alexander Graham Bell as president and the daughter of President Woodrow Wilson, Margaret, as secretary. (Standing, 1962, p. 63) So pleased was Dr. Montessori with her American reception that she returned in 1915 to give a training course in California and she set up a demonstration class at the San Francisco World's Fair. Educational journals as well as the popular press popularized Montessori. Teachers attended training programs weeks in length. Failing to grasp in depth what Montessori was all about, many obtained the Montessori materials, but used them as a teacher would use visual aids rather than as intended. As a result, the hundreds of Montessori classes that sprang up were short-lived.

A major factor in Montessori's early demise in America was the publication, in 1914, of William Kilpatrick's book, *The Montessori System Examined*, in which he concluded that Montessori had little to offer educators. At the time, the trend was toward emphasizing the socialization of the child; school was not to be a preparation for life but to be life. The school was to be a miniature society. Kilpatrick found Montessori's materials emphasizing individual learning—"they should be stressing social cooperation." He saw in Montessori's training of the senses an adherence to "outmoded faculty psychology, based on an outworn and cast-off psychological theory . . . worthless." (p. 52). Kilpatrick agreed, however, with Montessori's concept of self-education. He viewed with favor her practical life exercises. In comparing Montessori and Dewey, he wrote: "The two have many things in common. Both have organized experimental schools; both have emphasized the freedom, self-activity, and self-education of the child; both have made large use of 'practical life' activities. In a word, the two are cooperative tendencies in opposing entrenched traditionalism." (Kilpatrick, 1914, p. 40). Being labelled "worthless" by the reigning educational pontiff was too severe a blow for the fledgling movement. Mention of Montessori in the American press dwindled along with Montessori schools.

Kilpatrick's verdict stood unchallenged in America for forty years while Montessori continued to spread in other parts of the world. Seven years after Dr. Montessori had been nominated for the Nobel Peace Prize and five years after her death in 1952, Nancy Rambusch, a fiery young mother, who had discovered Montessori while traveling in Europe and where she later secured her Montessori training, established a Montessori class in New York. This auspicious "second beginning" was to become later the Whitby School in Greenwich, Connecticut, the first of over three thousand Montessori Schools currently functioning in America.

Current Status

Montessori from the beginning had been a source of controversy in education. Avid advocates of Montessori ideas contend that Dr. Montessori recognized forces present in early childhood which most educators ignore or misinterpret. Critics, then as well as now, find her insights too simplistic and idealistic. Despite criticism, Montessori schools continue to expand throughout the world. Parental dissatisfaction with existing educational programs, the interest and satisfaction children evidence in a Montessori learning environment, success in learning and personal development, achievement and fulfillment in later life—seem to be some of the main factors responsible for Montessori's continuous expansion.

Montessori schools are found in practically every country of the world, even in developing countries of the so-called third world (*Association Montessori Internationale*, 1972). A major factor accounting for the missionary-like zeal characteristic of many Montessori advocates is the charismatic personality of the founder of the Montessori system. In 1923 she founded the *International Montessori Association*, which, until her death in 1952, helped her exercise control over "the purity of her method" in the Montessori teacher training centers which were established in many of the larger cities throughout the world. Upon her death, her son, Mario Montessori, became head of the Association (AMI) and continues to this day to be, a board member of every AMI-recognized teacher training program with the right of refusing approval of any Montessori training program which does not conform to standards set by the international organization. As general director of the AMI, Mario Montessori appoints national AMI representatives, approves of training programs and determines who is qualified to serve as Montessori examiners of candidates for an AMI diploma.

This rigidity of control for the sake of maintaining "purity of Montessori doctrine" has been challenged in many countries, especially in the United States. Consequently, there are several interpretations of Montessori theory with resultant differences in Montessori schools in America as well as elsewhere.

When Montessori experienced a rebirth in the United States in the late fifties, there was a growing dissatisfaction with life-adjustment education. The launching of Sputnik by the Russians alerted parents to question more seriously the validity of public education. Arthur Bestor had just published a book (1953) in which he labelled the public schools "educational wastelands" (*Educational Wastelands: The Retreat from Learning in our Public Schools*) while Mortimer Smith (1949) was emphasizing that "the school must educate the whole child; it must be so organized that it meets the developmental demands of every side of the child's nature, intellectual, emotional, spiritual, physical. The curriculum must be based on the child's needs, interests and abilities." (p. 105). Other authors were explaining research findings pointing to the need for early education of the child. To many parents Montessori appeared to be the answer. To fill the requests for Montessori teachers, Nancy Rambusch applied in 1960 to the AMI world headquarters in Amsterdam, Holland for permission to train Montessori teachers in America. Her request was approved along with the stipulation that Elizabeth Stephenson, an approved AMI trainer, would head the training program. Another stipulation was that ten percent of the income would be sent to the headquarters of *Association Montessori Internationale* (AMI). Rambusch was appointed the AMI American representative (Rambusch, 1977).

Seeds of rebellion sprouted early. Rambusch and board members of the *American Montessori Society* (AMS) which she had founded, viewed Montessori as a social movement; teacher training should reflect, not only American culture, but recent research in child psychology as well. AMS viewed training, not as "mystical initiation," but as professional development. Means should be found for introducing Montessori into the mainstream of American education rather than founding schools distinct from but parallel to existing schools.

While articles were appearing extolling Montessori insights, Rambusch was speaking all around the country. Petty politicking and squabbles over teacher training, democratic representation and inadequacy of funds brought differences of viewpoints to a head which culminated in AMS splitting from AMI in 1963. Two major factors were responsible for the break: trans-ocean control over the content of teacher training and the American rejection of the concept of "closed-shop" Montessori.

The two major Montessori organizations in the U.S. are the *American Montessori Society* with headquarters in New York and the *American Association Montessori Internationale* in Washington, D.C. Both organizations set standards for teacher training programs and schools which each supervises, both publish literature, sponsor in-service workshops, regional seminars and national conferences. AMS-trained teachers and schools tend to be somewhat more open to incorporating whatever is relevant to the life of the child into the curriculum, provided it is justified by its contribution to the pupil's all-round development. AMI training tends to be more circumscribed and somewhat rigid. There are also "Montessori-like" schools which do not meet the standards set by either of the two major American Montessori organizations. They may call themselves Montessori but frequently a visit will reveal the differences: some or many of the Montessori materials may be present but there is disorder, the teacher is teaching rather than facilitating; the majority of the children are not absorbingly involved, a joyful atmosphere of work is absent. In a good Montessori school, one detects a busy hum of activity with the children happy and interestingly involved, the majority initiating their own activity. The teacher is usually not immediately in evidence. The atmosphere is attractive and bespeaks care. There is freedom of movement, yet there is order and respect for the rights of others. Gimmicky exercises of the "busy work" type, sloppy materials and external discipline are conspicuous by their absence.

In most countries there are several varieties of Montessori. In almost every country exist schools that use the name of Montessori, but fail to function with its principles thus constituting a roadblock to the clear understanding of what Montessori education really represents. Teacher education programs which grasp Montessori's insights as to the nature of the child and how he learns produce teachers that are anything but rigid.

The majority of Montessori schools are geared to the young child of three to six years old. It is the firm belief of Montessorians that it is during these years that the individual's future, both as student and adult are determined. In the United States, there are roughly ten Montessori preschools for every Montessori school geared to the older child. In other countries this ratio varies somewhat, favoring more programs for the older child. The Montessori approach is designed for all levels of education up to age eighteen when the university welcomes the young adult. (Montessori, 1976, p. 129). In Montessori secondary schools (more prevalent in Europe than America) the main Montessori characteristics of freedom, individualization, learning through discovery and a deep personal respect for the student are in evidence, but the dominant feature of uniquely designed materials so characteristic of Montessori learning environments for the younger child is less in evidence.

The nearly forty AMS or AMI teacher-training programs in America are unable to train sufficient teachers to meet the expanding demand as more communities seek to establish Montessori schools. In recent years requests for incorporating Montessori in Head Start, day-care and "toddler" programs have added to the demand for well-trained Montessori teachers. In greater Chicagoland, for example, where the first of the ninety-plus Montessori schools in the area was established in 1963, there are three AMS training programs, the largest of which, the *Midwest Montessori Teacher Training Center,* prepares an average of seventy certified Montessori teachers a year. While some American Montessori teacher training programs are at the undergraduate level, the majority of applicants for Montessori teacher preparation are college graduates. The training lasts a minimum of twelve months. Prospective teachers must possess personality qualities requisite for working effectively with young children.

The majority of Montessori schools in America are non-profit, controlled by a private or parent board, financed by a tuition charge which currently varies from less than $300 per year to over $1200. The average tuition cost in Chicagoland is currently $750 for the 3-to-6-year-olds attending five half-days a week for the academic year. For the nine Montessori elementary schools in the Chicagoland area the average tuition for the academic year is about $1200.

About fifty per cent of American Montessori schools are in University or suburban communities, twenty per cent in general metropolitan areas of our large cities and twenty per cent in the "inner city." The latter are usually financed by a combination of charitable donations, fund-raising and in some cases by government aid. About ten per cent of the schools are found in small towns. College-university communities have been in the forefront in establishing Montessori schools.

Life within Montessori policy-making circles is anything but static as AMI functions to protect Mario Montessori's right to determine what conforms to Dr. Montessori's original method while AMS confronts challenges to render Montessori insights and principles more relevant to the American child. Innovations, some promising, others not, are found on the cutting edge of experimentation in trying to make Montessori maximally relevant to the child in his task of self-development. Montessori continues to enjoy the stimulating prods of critics who find the Montessori approach too structured for fostering creativity, too academic to develop the arts, too individualized for developing the social side of a child's nature. Convinced that every child has a right to reach his full stature as a person, teachers who have caught the spirit of Montessori keep an open mind for discovering even more effective ways for assisting the child in actualizing his full potential.

THEORY

Learning

Montessori theory of learning is rooted in a conviction that the mind of the child is dynamic, not static . . . that intelligence is not pre-determined by heredity but results from activity prompted by confrontation with reality. Learning is the result of activity, a matter of developing awareness and sensitivity to the nature of the task confronted. Sensing key elements in the problem as a result of previous experience triggers insight and approaches to be tried. Learning does not result in connections but rather in the formation, extension or change of schema within the person. These schema constitute the guiding patterns for behavioral implementation. Within the child there is the human psyche, a spiritual entity, which provides a guide for development.

1. Learning is functional; that is, transferrable to other situations

Learning in essence is a process of changing behavior. Learning which is not functional in some manner is useless and does not belong in an educational curriculum. Everything in a Montessori learning environment is designed for its relevance to life. That which confronts the child in a Montessori classroom provides experience in coping with life situations while at the same time aiding the child in constructing himself. "Behavior is always in reference to something and has meaning." (Montessori, 1976, p. 37). To the extent that elements and relations in one's world are understood, to that extent will what is learned, function.

2. Learning is a dynamic process in which the whole personality of the child must be actively engaged

The psychosomatic unity of man must be recognized to understand effective learning. Man is body and mind functioning as a unity. Learning is an integral process in the formation of the total personality. How we think and what we think affects what we feel and how we feel, what we value, what we do and how we do it. "A child's constructive movements have a psychic origin and are of an intellectual nature. Knowledge always precedes movement . . . A child's imitation is never purely mechanical" (Montessori, 1970, p. 103). How he perceives (sees and feels) the situation enters into determining his reaction. The end-products of learning are everything that affects feeling, thinking, valuing, choosing, doing.

3. Man is a social being by nature and consequently requires a social environment in which to learn and develop

Human beings need each other to realize collectively the possibilities of human potentiality. Man is different from animal, which reaches the limits of its development shortly after birth. The child is dependent on his social surroundings, not only for his survival, but for his psychic and spiritual development. Animal comes equipped with instinct to guide behavioral response. Man possesses potentially higher powers of intellect and will, which when developed enable him to analyze, judge and choose. "The continuity in human history is a cultural continuity, whereas the continuity in the animal world is in principle biological . . . Man's behavior is only partially determined by the laws of nature. Insofar as he has alternatives (which he is capable of creating) he must make choices " (Montessori, 1976, pp. 36–37). Man lives in a dynamic psychosphere, animals in a static biosphere. Because of difference in kind, not only in degree, laws of learning applicable to animals, such as in conditioning as outlined in stimulus-response theory, are inadequate and when explaining man's higher mental processes are erroneous when applied to man.

4. Learning is an active process

Montessori sees man as an initiator of actions, an active being, not a passive, S–R mechanism. A child constructs himself through work in response to inner urges to utilize his expanding abilities. Man's behavior is not so much dependent upon what happens to him but rather upon how he *interprets* the stimuli and the consequent meanings and feelings thereby generated within. "A psychic event only acquires meaning when it is related to a higher totality, in the final analysis, to the personality as a whole" (Montessori, 1976, p. 40). How the child perceives himself in the confronting situation determines his behavioral response. A person's self-image is a key factor in determining the meaning of an experience and one's consequent response.

5. Motivation for learning is primarily from within

Every human potentiality presses for actualization. The eye wants to see, the fingers enjoy manipulating objects, the mind wants to know. Even the infant in a crib is wreathed in smiles as he pulls at an object extended to him, enjoying his newly developed ability to grasp. Thus it is with every potential possessed by man. It is a law of human nature that man enjoys interacting with his environment when the situation at hand provides opportunity to exercise one or several of his abilities. The more involved the interaction, the greater the effort and the deeper the satisfaction. Montessori believed that man's nature was designed thus; consequently she stressed the necessity of a free, appropriately enriched environment which would "call to the child," eliciting his interaction. His inner developmental needs are manifested to the observer through his spontaneous activities.

The pattern of the child's unique response through which he develops ability is guided by an inner psychic determinant indigenous in the child. Montessori's concept of a "spiritual embryo" within the child lies at the heart of her theory of learning and development. This inner guiding force is a dynamic element with which the environment must cooperate. The subtle guiding urge from within can be stifled by an emaciated or restrictive environment. The significant adults in the child's life are key elements in his environment.

6. External reward and punishment have little or no place in learning

Since motivation for learning and development is primarily intrinsic, the inner rewards and satisfactions resulting therefrom are more enjoyable and intense than external rewards, which at best are extrinsic to the task. External rewards, whether gold stars behind one's name on the blackboard, a physical reward, or even "That's nice, Johnny!" are not necessary in an appropriately enriched learning environment where the developmental needs of the child are matched with the kinds of materials and activities needed at this particular juncture in the child's development. A good measure of the adequacy of the total learning environment is the extent to which children enjoy the opportunity to learn through discovery without the prodding of external rewards. This statement is not to be interpreted as frowning on encouraging or appreciative remarks by significant adults. Such verbal "rewards" however should not become habitual lest the child's need for inner personal approval be blocked by the shallower satisfactions of such external motivation.

There are times when a child needs to be made keenly aware that his behavior is not acceptable. Physical punishment is not the answer because it calls forth negative, hurt or hostile feelings in the child. The effect is the opposite of that intended by the one administering the punishment. Punishment should be related to the situation at hand and never be physical. A child desires to be free to achieve that which brings inner satisfaction. Depriving a child of his freedom at the moment he has overstepped a given commonly understood "ground rule" is effective because it is immediately meaningful to him; he easily relates his disapproved behavior with the dissatisfying feelings of loss of freedom. Isolating the child from the learning environment is one means of "withholding the child's freedom" momentarily.

7. Cognitive concepts posit a spiritual side to man's nature

Abstract ideas and insights can be described, but the specific nature of an abstract idea escapes absolute definition. The specific nature of man's "spiritual principle of life" lies outside man's grasp. Because we have difficulty in describing the "definitive essence of man's soul" is no reason to deny the spiritual element in man's nature. Montessori recognizes this spiritual element as central to understanding man's uniqueness among all creatures in the universe. Through careful observation of man's actions we discover the nature of man. Since man is capable of conceiving abstract concepts (possessing none of the delimitations of physical material properties), the nature of the conceiver must likewise be non-material, at least that element of the conceiver responsible for the non-material function.

The term *spiritual soul* calls forth a scratched nerve response on the part of many modern psychologists. We do not know the true nature of electricity, though we describe it as a flow of negative electrons; but that does not stop us from exploring its function. Montessori, in acknowledging the spiritual nature of man's soul, the source of his power of acting from within, found what she termed the "secret of childhood." Acknowledging this uniquely human force, a spiritual inner guide, she arrived at the conclusion that the child could construct his own development. To do this, however, the child needs to be given the proper assistance through the provision of appropriate opportunities to interact with an environment through which he will discover meanings.

Montessori agreed with Aristotle's statement that there is nothing in the intellect which does not first come through the senses. Hence she devised materials through which children, via the use of their senses, sharpened their perception of the nature of things. As the child develops, these impressions become clarified, interrelated and meaning blossoms. What specific psychic form these developing insights take no one knows for sure. Psychologists coin various terms and theories. Montessori is close to Piaget's theory of "developing schema" that become more complex and adequate as successive experience necessitates adjustment and accommodation.

8. Retention and forgetting is a matter of clarity or confusion in psychic schema

The clarity and meaningfulness of an experience determine whether what has been experienced will be remembered or forgotten. Montessori is most careful in structuring learning experiences so that each step in the process is clearly presented, as well as the relationship of each step to the whole. First the whole framework, of which a given task is a part, is presented. Gradually, refinements are introduced. Psychic activity which is not a part of a dynamic whole is like a branch laid in the crotch of a tree; it soon withers. When experience is a functional part of a meaningful whole or schema, the part is like a branch of the tree thriving on the life-giving sap. Experiences, meaningfully understood, become a living part of flexible schema which thrive on expanding experience and use.

Forgetting occurs primarily because of a lack of clarity of meaning in the learning experience. The resulting schema is inadequate, fuzzy, only partially formed, lacks tie-ins with related ideas, or schema, and hence ceases to function dynamically. Sometimes forgetting is caused by certain elements in the schema which are similar to elements in other schema and hence confusion results. When the differences between similar ideas or experiences are not clearly distinct, or when similar but different experiences occur in close succession, a form of proactive or retroactive inhibition takes place, interfering with the dynamic psychic process which results in an indistinct schema. Consequently reproduction from memory is difficult if not impossible.

Teaching

The principles in Montessori teaching theory center around the child, the environment and the teacher; the latter serving as a go-between or catalyst leading the child to interact with a prepared learning environment. How the child learns and develops, his needs, what attracts his attention and what does not, the rate at which he assimilates new elements in his environment, what frightens or pleases, how he feels about himself, every aspect is the center of focus. The child is the teacher's textbook, her consultant, her teacher. With the child as her guide, the teacher selects from the cultural milieu in which the child lives, those materials, situations, activities familiar to the child and designs exercises, which when engaged in, answer inner developmental needs of the child. The teacher or "directress" thus does not teach in the traditional sense. Sensing the child's needs, she introduces him to an exercise, allowing him to interact at his own individual rate and thus make a new discovery. In keeping with the concept that education is an aid to the child's development, Montessori views teaching primarily, though not exclusively, as a matter of *facilitating* individualized learning.

> *1. The Montessori method of instruction is primarily*
> *that of assisting the individual in learning through*
> *discovery*

Since each child is different, possessing unique potentialities, developing at his own rate, each coming from a uniquely perceived background, teaching must be predominantly individualized. The teacher does not teach directly; she serves as a facilitator or catalyst. She prepares the confrontations which will entice the child's activity, leading him on, through programmed materials and exercises, to make one discovery after another. She rarely presents a new learning exercise to a group, since the members of a group do not arrive at a respective readiness at the same time. This is not to say, however, that there are no group activities. Group involvement has its place but not as a rule in learning skills and acquiring insights.

Since education is viewed as an aid to the process of self-development, a prepared learning environment constitutes the heart of a Montessori school. The teacher is primarily responsible for preparing the learning environment, for determining the layout of the resource areas so as to facilitate use, for selecting relevant materials, for clarifying ground rules necessary to preserve an atmosphere of freedom, for making the classroom attractive and beautiful, for introducing the materials and their use to individual children as needed, for maintaining a friendly atmosphere of joyful activity. The teacher's role is more indirect than direct.

Whatever is relevant to the life of a child is made available in the learning environment. What is found in the classroom on any given day in no way represents all the materials available for the children's use a month later. The environment must be simple, orderly, adequate, attractive; but not cluttered with materials not currently being used by the children. An overabundance of materials confuses the child and tends to interfere with his task of categorizing his world. Those materials in the environment which children are no longer using are removed; others, the next step up the ladder of complexity of the materials and exercises in given areas, are added. Thus the learning environment is anything but static. This requires the teacher to be a shrewd observer. She always knows where each child is in his process of gradually mastering the tasks in each area of the environment.

2. Meaningfulness to the child determines the nature and content of the learning curriculum

The learning environment is organized so that order and continuity simplify the student's grasp of all that is available to him. The pre-school environment contains six or seven easily distinguished curriculum areas: 1) practical living, which helps the child become independent through acquiring such skills as buttoning, tying, pouring; 2) sensory discrimination, which challenges the child to distinguish similarities and differences using his various senses; 3) communication and language, wherein the child finds materials and exercises preparatory for and involving writing, speaking, reading; 4) mathematics, wherein ingeniously designed materials introduce number concept and the various arithmetic functions; 5) science, which contains natural, biological, social learning materials, including globes and three-dimensional maps; 6) music and art corners where easel, clay, musical instruments invite individual or group participation, and movement-muscle-balance areas, wherein group activities tend to predominate. Weather permitting, the learning environment extends to the outdoors. Hammering nails in a log, gardening, nature walks, caring for plants and animals, anything relevant to the child's life is incorporated into the learning environment and, if possible, structured into a meaningful activity. Gimmicky items such as a wind-up toy or busy work which leads nowhere has no place in a Montessori classroom.

3. The residual feelings aroused by a learning task
are more important than the knowledge gained or
skill acquired

The Montessori teacher maintains a keen awareness of the affective reactions of children in the learning environment. How a child comes to feel about himself as a learner and about the task at hand, whether it be geography, language, mathematics or music, is important as an end-product because his residual feelings tend to shape his self-image. If the child gains confidence in himself in a given area, his future success in this field is practically assured; if his experience has been unfortunate, he perceives himself as inadequate in this kind of activity and avoids anything resembling this area of activity in the future. For this reason the teacher studies the child's spontaneous activity for detecting the subtle responses that reveal his needs. She then asks the child if he would like to be shown a given exercise. Proceeding to demonstrate in a quiet, simple manner, she again notes the child's response. As soon as he grasps the idea of the exercise she withdraws, permitting him to make the discovery on his own. Doing so, he smiles, becomes excited and repeats the exercise over and over until the inner need has been satisfied. In the process he has become absorbed, oblivious to surroundings, concentrating on the task at hand. Such repetition is evidence that self-discipline is in the process of being established (Montessori, 1964, p. 275).

Should, however, the child not be attracted by the material, or initiate the activity but not complete it, the teacher does not pressure the child nor does she correct him. She merely suggests that he put the exercise away and maybe some other day he may want to work with it. The affective reactions in a learning situation are of primary importance in the child's efforts at undertaking his own development.

4. The learning environment must provide for every

child a match for his developmental needs

Learning does not take place in a vacuum. While the child possesses potentialities pressing for actualization along with an inner guiding psychic pattern, human development takes place only when the child is assisted in his self-construction. A social setting, geared to the child's developmental needs, is required to awaken and provide opportunity for the child's self-activity. J. McVicker Hunt called this element in learning the "problem of the match."

Every child is unique. No two, other than possibly identical twins, develop at the same rate or possess identical needs. Consequently each child needs to have the opportunity to learn through interacting with that which answers his specific needs at a given specific time. Group instruction, while administratively more feasible and economical, ignores this basic fact in human development. The results are evident: educational failure for a large percentage of children.

The moment of need can be discovered by the teacher only through consistent observation of children engaged in spontaneous learning activity. Noting the need, the teacher matches the child to an exercise designed to answer this need. She asks him whether he would like to be shown how to work with a given learning material; e.g., a geography puzzle map, the binomial cube, the moveable alphabet, a box of language matching cards. Knowing what each child has been working with to date and knowing the progressive steps of difficulty represented by each piece of self-teaching material in each curriculum area, the teacher is able, with minimum time and effort, to match up a learning activity with the child's specific need and readiness level. In Montessori language, "the material calls to the child," it arouses his interest. The result: increasing concentration, inner satisfaction, a sense of achievement, growth of self-confidence, a favorable attitude toward school and further learning.

5. The pupil is led to assume responsibility for his own education

A basic principle in Montessori is, that since the child possesses a non-material guiding pattern within for his unique development, he must construct himself. Initiative and responsibility for this development must be fostered and encouraged. The Montessori teacher never does anything for the child which he can do for himself. Whenever the child is engaged in a meaningful task the teacher is careful not to intervene. She stays in the background, mindful that a word, gesture, even a look may disrupt the absorbing psychic activity (Montessori, 1964, p. 264).

This insight into the inner nature of the child likewise underlies Montessori's emphasis on respect for the child. Montessori teachers are asked to reverence the uniqueness of every child. To develop into the unique person he is someday to become, the child must assume more and more responsibility for his present and future development. To the extent education is initiated and pressured from without, to that extent a child misses the opportunity to develop himself into the unique, genuine person his various potentialities fit him to be.

6. Grouping of children is flexible, according to level of development

Chronological age or standardized test scores are not used in grouping children in Montessori; instead a combination of factors, largely arrived at through observation of a child's reactions in a prepared learning environment, determine group placement. Usually there is a three to four year age spread in any classroom group even among children in a Montessori pre-school. Membership in a group is not static. A child may advance rather rapidly and be placed in a more mature group if he seems to be more at home with the children and materials in the older group. In some schools, certain children are free to go to another group for certain work. Sometimes where siblings are close in age, or where one of two close friends is a follower, the children are placed in different groups.

Where physical facilities provide an unusually large environment, teachers use a team approach in dividing responsibility for given areas. At the pre-school level a teacher with twenty children will have an assistant; with thirty, two aides who work with her as a team.

Because children continue to work with a given exercise as long as their activity satisfies an inner need, they master each step with considerable thoroughness. Confidence in their ability to work with materials completed prompts them to help others who may be a bit puzzled when initially interacting with a new exercise. Peer teaching is a common experience in a Montessori class.

7. Motivation is aroused through assisting children in setting realistic goals

A person has as many potential motives as there are practical goals for actualizing his various potentialities. A child feels "edgy," uncomfortable, bored when he fails to perceive an appealing goal-activity as an outlet for his unidentified inner urges to actualize one or several of his potentials. Herein a perceptive teacher plays an important role: she identifies the specific needs implied in the child's behavior and introduces the child to a relevant activity with a specific, realizable goal. The appropriateness of the task awakens inner interest as the child sets for himself the suggested goal. Utilizing previously acquired facility, the child accepts the challenge with which he is confronted, achieves the goal and savors the inner satisfaction consequent upon every human, meaningful achievement.

Thorough knowledge of the learner, refined perceptive ability and ready-at-hand self-discovery learning materials are the three elements requisite if the child's inner potential motives are to be called forth by the Montessori teacher. While praise is available, it is utilized only infrequently as a means of tapping inner motives.

For the teacher to be effective in helping the child set realistic goals, she must accept and respect each child as he is, and show love, trust and empathy in her relations with the children. Her whole attitude is one of encouragement. Her expectations for each child are realistic and portray confidence in his ability to respond successfully. Confidence begets confidence as acceptance begets acceptance.

8. An effective educational program requires the close cooperation of school and home

Since parents are the child's most influential teachers, schools have no choice but to work with the home. Parents have the inside track with young children because of the natural ties of love and attachment. Where the atmosphere in the home is at variance with, or contrary to, that of the school, even effective teachers will have difficulty in eliciting the child's cooperation.

The Montessori staff gives considerable time and effort to working with parents, clarifying Montessori objectives explaining the nature and purpose of the variety of materials in the learning environment, sponsoring regular parents' meetings at which discussions are held explaining children's needs and why they behave the way they do. Many Montessori schools have an "open-visitation" policy; some schools require parents to observe the children while school is in session. Parent conferences and parent study-groups are standard procedure.

Some schools utilize a specially-designed two-way child report form in which observations are made on various aspects of the child's total development; instead of merely signing the form, parents check their observation of changes noted in the child's behavior in the home. Since the child lives in both worlds, mutual sharing is necessary.

Dr. Maria Montessori emphasized the importance of the mother. She felt it her obligation to educate parents toward a better understanding of their children. In her inner-city school in a Rome slum she required the parents to confer weekly with her teachers.

APPLICATIONS

Curriculum, Academic

In a Montessori school there is no fine distinction between the academic and non-academic curricula. Curriculum content is not presented in truncated subject areas, but rather centers on learning exercises, activities, or problems rooted in life situations. Many of the non-academic or co-curricular areas intertwine daily with the learning of academic skills. Learning areas are fluid, natural, functional. Since Montessori views learning as self-construction, carefully structured series of learning materials (each leading the child to discover and develop step-by-step more complex insights and skills) are made available in each major area of learning having relevance to life.

Helping the child establish confidence in his own ability to learn, whetting a child's interests, fostering a sense of order, encouraging habits of initiative and concentration through intriguing tasks, enticing a child to sharpen his discriminative capacities . . . these are some of the outcomes deliberately sought through the Montessori curriculum for the young child. Practical life sometimes identified as independence-developing activities, and uniquely designed sensory discrimination tasks help the child acquire essential elements for developing basic academic skills, the "tools" for later learning.

The quality of a child's earliest overall experience in school, as well as in each of the areas of the curriculum, is most important in determining later response. In introducing the child to numbers and later to arithmetic functions and geometric figures, Montessori presents the child with a variety of three-dimensional materials which he handles; for example, there are ten rods, each one unit longer than the other. The child places the first on top of the second as the rods are lined up, shortest to longest; he discovers that the "1" rod when added to the "2" rod is the same length as the "3" rod; he makes other arithmetic discoveries in manipulating the other rods. Another manipulative exercise enables him to discover not only how many each number from one to nine represents, but likewise the meaning of "0." This exercise consists of a box with ten partitions, each labeled from "0" to "9." The child is given forty-five sticks. If he does not place the correct number in each partition, he will not have nine for the last partition; thus, the material has a built-in control of error, enabling the child to learn by himself and know when he has done the exercise correctly. Coming out with just the right number as he counts "seven, eight, NINE!" . . . he glows with pride and proceeds to do the exercise over and over again. With the assistance of hundreds of similar auto-education learning materials, the teacher introduces the child to understandings and skills in each area of the curriculum. In this way children in a Montessori school acquire insights, master the basic skills and, at the same time, acquire positive attitudes toward the subjects learned—a natural result of enjoyable work.

In the communication arts, after children have learned to associate the appropriate sounds with the color-coded sandpaper vowels and consonants, children are introduced to writing, a preliminary step to the more complex task of reading. Through detailed step-by-step exercises involving matching cards, sounding out letters and words, building words with a moveable alphabet, watching and listening to the teacher as well as other children read words and stories, the child makes the discovery of the meaning of certain hieroglyphics. He can scarcely contain his joy as he blossoms into reading.

Interlacing all the activities and interpersonal relations is a conscious intent on the part of the teacher to choose and use language appropriate to the child's level of comprehension. After most of the children have experienced their peak of activity with individual work for the day, children are invited to join a circle with the teacher for a variety of activities involving oral communication, story-telling, listening, singing, rhythmic movement, walking on the line (a challenging muscle coordination exercise), or the "silence" game. Spelling is learned gradually and naturally, but never at the expense of feeling seriously embarrassed.

Affirming that every child possesses some potential for being creative, Montessori fosters creative expression through painting, music, movement, drawing, carving, innovative design. An atmosphere of freedom encourages an easy, open, free expression of feelings.

While the Montessori teacher's handbooks for each area (which she prepared during her year-long training beyond college) constitute a general curriculum guide, her observation of the spontaneous activity of the children provides her with more specific directions. Their curiosity about other lands and people, their questions about birds, rocks, plants in their environment direct her to introduce children to a time-line enabling them to see the time relation between events in history. Responding to their cues, she adds geography puzzle maps, globes, land-forms, and so forth, to the social science resource alcove. In the science area there are simple devices illustrating the inclined plane and air pressure; in the biology area, besides specimens, there are plaster reproductions of parts of the body, furnishing tie-ins with health; collections of rocks, minerals, pictures of plants and birds along with a terrarium and aquarium invite exploration of natural science.

A reading corner with little chairs and tables along with pillows on the rug along the wall invite children to curl up with a book of their choice, selected from open shelves which partly wall off the area, giving an aura of semi-privacy. Books from home and library keep the shelves interesting to the young readers.

Children are not required to break off their concentration at a given time in the day's schedule in order to shift to another activity. In a Montessori school there is no set schedule directing the children to spend a specific amount of time each day on specific subjects; instead, each child selects his own work. He may spend the entire morning in math, on language, or art; or, he may put in a half-hour's work on a given exercise or project. When his inner need is satisfied, he chooses another piece of work from the open shelves, where materials and exercises are placed in sequence, according to order of difficulty.

The majority of children work in several curriculum areas each day along with participation in at least one group activity. If a child comes to school preoccupied with what happened at home earlier, the teacher, after a short period, asks him if he would like to be shown how to work with a specific exercise one step up from where he was involved yesterday.

Materials and tasks designed in keeping with the developmental needs of the child lead him to interact with all learning areas meaningful to his world.

Everything relevant to the life of a child is welcomed as part of the Montessori educational program. Where experiences cannot be conveniently brought to the school, the school goes to the community.

Curriculum, Non-Academic

Field trips to museums, factories, art institutes, the zoo, the farm expand the child's introduction to and preparation for life. These excursions are prepared for in advance and discussed afterwards. Children are taken to visit a lake steamer, for a boat trip on the river, for a ride on the subway, a visit to the fire department. Plays appropriate to children are attended, opportunities to listen to music selections are provided. Educational films and slide presentations are made available at suitable times.

Community resources in the form of parents and others with expertise and appropriate experience are part of the school program. A manager of a food store may introduce the children to the economics of running a business, a banker may explain about money, a mother may involve the children in mixing cake batter or preparing a loaf of bread, a carpenter may demonstrate the proper use of tools, an electrician may reveal the secrets of a light switch or explain what makes a motor run, someone's big sister may demonstrate how to hem a skirt or sew on a button.

Where weather is feasible, easy access to an outside working area is available for sensory-motor coordination activities such as walking a plank, climbing, hammering and sawing. In the spring, a garden plot invites children's initiative with tools and seeds. Animal care is a spring-time addition to the curriculum where health regulations do not permit animals in the classroom.

Physical education includes simple games and the usual playground equipment. Many Montessori schools have the Porter gymster apparatus, which is collapsible and therefore easily moved from place to place and stored. This equipment, for both inside and out, is used for both diagnostic and remedial small and large muscle work with children. The nature of a child's coordination difficulties can be discovered with the equipment and appropriate exercises prescribed.

Daily living skills are broken down into step-by-step tasks so that the pre-school-age child can master with relative ease such skills as buttoning, lacing, tying, buckling, snapping, washing, pouring, dressing. Cutting, brushing one's teeth, and other more complicated self-care skills follow as uniquely designed exercises confront the child with such tasks.

Appreciation of the beautiful is achieved indirectly by surrounding the child with an environment that speaks of good taste. A sense of beauty is caught rather than taught. The learning environment is neatly arranged; replicas of great works of art hang on the walls; the teacher's dress and manner bespeaks self-respect. The choice of decorations is attractive. Music records of children's classics are available for leisurely listening.

While the majority of Montessori schools are non-denominational, they nevertheless implement an appreciation of religious values, respect for the dignity of every person, recognition of a moral code which holds truthfulness and honesty in high regard and provides for the discussion of truths held by various religious groups. Some Montessori schools are denominational and thus provide experience through which children discover a deeper meaning of their particular faith. Such Montessori schools, although a minority—less than ten percent in America—usually provide opportunity for occasional participation in liturgical services. All Montessori schools rely heavily on the good example of staff members with whom children have a warm, open and trusting relationship, for inspiring their pupils with high ethical and moral standards.

Drama, dance and music presentations provide additional avenues for personal expression, while at the same time enabling the participants to experience the advantages of poise.

Student Evaluation

Ability identification lies at the heart of the Montessori approach in education; yet, reliance on standardized tests and test scores is de-emphasized as a means of identifying needs of the learner. In a flexible curriculum, expectations and confrontations must reflect changing levels of the child's development. Herein lies one of the Montessori teacher's major responsibilities: to help the child set goals for himself in the various areas of the curriculum she must be able to assess not only the nature and extent of the child's potential talent, but likewise his preferred way of learning and where he is on the learning continuum in each curricular area. This calls for shrewd observational skill, developed through training and experience, coupled with a thorough understanding of how young children develop, how personality is formed and how early learning takes place. Heavy reliance on formal tests is impractical in an effective learning environment where the inner status of the child is continuously changing. Montessorians believe there is no substitute for shrewd, continuous observation of the child engaged in a variety of tasks for discovering the "teachable moment."

The observer-catalyst role of the teacher underlies the fluidity of groupings in a Montessori school. Children are moved easily from group to group when the rate of an individual's progress warrants a change; thus the rigidity of student placement, sometimes consequent upon categorization in accord with test results, is avoided. A chronological age-spread of three to five years is not unusual in a Montessori class.

Where a child appears talented in one area but not in another, or where either unusual difficulties or striking progress is in evidence, a variety of tests may be utilized to gain deeper insight into the child's response. With a very young child, one of the self-concept scales may be used along with an intelligence test, such as the Peabody Picture Vocabulary Test. In most instances, an individually administered test is chosen. As children advance in curricular areas, teacher-made as well as standardized achievement tests are given. Little weight is placed on scores, however, for Montessori views competitive comparisons as more harmful than helpful, even when shared with parents. Where Metropolitan Achievement Test scores of Montessori-educated children have been compared with those of children in control groups, the former have been found to score higher, especially in math and verbal areas (Sciarra and Dorsey, 1974).

Some schools, at parents' insistence, issue scholastic grades on report cards, but the majority of Montessori schools depend on either regular parents' conferences in which the child's progress is discussed individually, or, they have devised a report form that reflects the child's progress in all areas of his development, academic as well as non-academic; some Montessori schools in the Midwest use a form that requests parents to report back to the school their assessment of the child in such areas of his development as adjustment to school, his developing interests, evidence of initiative and change in attitude (Fleege, 1974).

Frequently these report forms do not carry letter or number grades but rather a series of code checkmarks that indicate quality of response and progress. Where a child is not achieving as well as expected, parents are informed as to the probable cause, indicating what steps should be taken; e.g.,where a child seems to be suffering from inferiority feelings, probably because an older brother or one of the parents is hounding the child for his mistakes, parents might be advised to focus instead on areas wherein the child is doing well.

Montessori schools emphasize the cooperative role of parents in assisting the child in his arduous task of developing himself. To minimize problems in the parent-child relationship, school personnel insist on parents observing the school in action. (See later section on *parents* in this chapter.) Many schools are equipped with one-way glass so children can be observed without their knowledge. In this way parents learn firsthand what the school is attempting to do, what is expected of their child . . . and where a problem exists, secure a better grasp of factors contributing to the child's problem.

Montessori teachers report that a common misunderstanding of parents centers on failure to appreciate the validity of individual differences among children, especially among their own. Observation of a class of twenty to thirty children, working individually and in small groups, each at a different pace, evidencing different styles of learning helps parents develop a more positive approach toward their children. Observation sessions are frequently used to counsel parents while both teacher and parents are observing the child's reactions.

Counseling

The theory underlying counseling in Montessori schools is dominantly eclectic. No theorist's model is adopted hook, line and sinker. Most Montessorians feel comfortable with the ideas of Alfred Adler, Carl Rogers and Albert Ellis. Karen Horney's stressing the dignity of the person and his striving for perfection and happiness, along with her acknowledging the reality of the inner life of the child, correlates well with similar views held by Montessori. Erik Erikson's stages of development and his optimistic, creative view of the person as the captain in charge of personal development fits well with a central insight of Montessori, namely, that the child possesses within a guiding pattern for his self-construction. This is not surprising, since Erikson received his own early education in Montessori schools. Tenets held by these and other humanistic or phenomenological psychologists are interwoven almost imperceptibly with Dr. Montessori's views on child development and human behavior. Counseling is viewed as a means of leading the child to understand his behavior and functioning in a way that self-help will occur.

Most counseling with Montessori children is carried out on an individual basis. It is part of the catalytic process in the day-to-day functioning of the teacher-child relationship in the learning environment. The child is guided into activities which will enable him to savor the thrill of success and thus build up competence, self-acceptance and confidence.

Where lack of self-understanding lies at the root of a problem, non-directive counseling is usually preferred. Basic to any effective one-to-one relationship is the establishment of a friendly, trusting atmosphere of personal acceptance. The child must feel that the teacher or counselor wants to help him help himself. The child is led to comment on what he thinks about a given problem situation, how he feels about everything impinging on his behavior through which he revealed his difficulty. The adult is shocked at nothing the child says. Display of feeling is encouraged. If the child finds difficulty in expressing himself, the adult waits patiently, careful to show no sign of impatience or disgust. Above all he is a good listener. The teacher-counselor may suggest to the child how he sometimes feels in a similar situation, thus giving the child courage to voice his own hostile, hurt or confused feelings. At times the adult may volunteer how it seems to him the child may view the situation.

Once the child discovers why he behaves the way he does, the adult asks the child what he thinks or feels he should do. Where the child is puzzled, a choice of one or several specific options is suggested, leading the child to make the decision. While the counselor is patient, friendly and helpful, the help offered toward the solution of the problem confronting the child is limited; the solution, to be effective, must be wholeheartedly embraced by the child. In this aspect of assisting the child, Montessorians are in agreement with William Glasser's (1969) "common sense reality" approach: the child is led to set a goal, formulate a plan, determine what is to be done, where, how and when it is to be done. Depending on the strength of the child's self-image, the adult now becomes firm in refusing to accept nonsense excuses should the child lack seriousness in his campaign for change.

An adult hoping to qualify for working in a Montessori school must have a thorough knowledge of the psychology of child behavior and a grasp of how early learning takes place. The psychology of child development and implications for the adult-child relationship interlace every facet of the Montessori teacher's preparation. Other prerequisites include emotional and social maturity, a love of children, patience and objectivity. While the nature of Montessori education requires every teacher to work individually with children, some possess the desired characteristics in greater measure and consequently are given more responsibility in the counseling area. Since most Montessori schools are small, they do not have a full-time psychologist on the staff; they do, however, have school or clinical psychologists on call, or, to whom they refer special children in need of professional counseling.

Group counseling is utilized with children only when behavioral insights are of general relevance to all. Common expectations, general ground rules for facilitating the smooth functioning of the learning resource areas, insights into feelings shared by all are some of the input of group counseling sessions. Group counseling of parents, however, is regarded as a necessity in every Montessori school. Parents are recognized as having an influence equal to or even greater than that of the school; hence, insights centering on the nature of the child, his uniqueness and implications flowing therefrom, the importance of a positive approach in relating to the child, the question of "how much freedom, how much discipline," characteristics of a favorable home atmosphere are some of the topics discussed in group sessions with parents. Specific, practical examples keep the advice offered from remaining ineffectively in the realm of theory.

Discipline

Montessori views discipline as a point of arrival, rather than a point of departure in the education of children. The term is not used to denote the unpleasant implications of punishment as it does in the minds of many who speak of disciplining children. A disciplined child in Montessori terms is one whose behavior is directed from within in accord with given rules and expectations. In accomplishing a task or achieving a goal he utilizes his abilities, keeping his impulses under control, in keeping with the ground rules governing the situation.

Discipline and freedom go hand in hand in a Montessori school. It is impossible to have one without the other. Freedom without the implementation of principles governing freedom results in chaos. Discipline without freedom may achieve outward conformity, but inner discipline is never acquired. Self-discipline is learned, but learning is an immanent activity. An inner change in behavior cannot be accomplished by pressure from without (Fleege, 1974, xx-3).

Children need to experience freedom and inner control at all stages of their development. At each stage Montessori provides experience in several types of behavior through which children develop inner discipline and grow in assuming responsibility inherent in the wise use of freedom. The types of behavior they need to experience at each stage of their development are: a) responsible behavior insisted upon out of necessity; e.g.,avoiding specific behavior because of inherent danger; b) opportunities to exercise choice within controlled situations;e.g.,choosing learning materials with which to work; c) opportunities for complete freedom of choice; e.g.,what he chooses to paint; d) opportunities to assume responsibility for his behavior when in a group that establishes and regulates its own response. To the question "How much freedom and how much discipline should be given a child?" Montessori responds: as much freedom as the child can handle at his level of development and as much external guidance or discipline as is required to provide the appropriate experience and environment conducive to discovering the satisfaction of successfully taking charge of himself. Freedom and discipline are both means and ends in the vital process of becoming mature.

For Montessori, discipline, in the sense of limits, guidelines and expectations, resides in three areas: (a) in the prepared learning environment, (b) in the design and use of the learning materials, (c) in the relations of the teacher to the child. For children to be free to interact in the environment, simple, clear, consistently implemented ground rules governing the child's behavior in the learning environment are necessary. Children are led to understand clearly what is expected of them: materials must be put back in the place from which they were taken, never bother another unless you are invited to share in his work; you may talk and express your feelings provided you do not interfere with the rights of others; you may choose your own work and work area.

Self-learning materials are designed with specific goals in mind. To achieve a specific objective, the teacher introduces the child to the work material, suggesting initial steps to be taken which will lead to discovery. Thus discipline is indirectly present. The teacher maintains an open, accepting, encouraging relationship with the child, exercising care not to help beyond the point where the child catches on to what is expected of him. She is equally cautious not to intervene and thus frustrate the child when he is slowed by a difficulty. Inner discipline is a prerequisite in a Montessori teacher.

Ground rules limiting the freedom of children are discussed democratically, leading the children to ask questions, to express their opinion why these are necessary if they are to be free to work on what they choose and finally to voice their acceptance. Where inappropriate ground rules are proposed by some of the children, discussion leads to their rejection. The focal point of discipline is within the child himself, stemming from absorbed attention in an appropriate learning task. Self-discipline is a natural result where interest, competence and concentration are called forth by learning tasks and materials designed to answer inherent developmental needs. Opportunities for extending inner control to varying life situations enables the child to assume expanding responsibility for his behavior.

An effective Montessori teacher seldom finds discipline a problem. Exceptions occur when children transfer from situations where problems have existed in home and/or previous school. Care is taken to clarify to the transfer pupil what the rules are and why. At the first failure to respond with the expected behavior he is told that he will lose his freedom if he does not observe the given rule. Deprivation of freedom may take a variety of forms, depending on the individual and the situation. He may be assigned specific work apart from the others, be kept in the office with nothing to do and no one to talk to, or be asked to accompany the teacher as she goes about the room. After a short period the isolated child is asked if he thinks he can comply with the rules. In practically all instances his reply and cooperation are positive. Physical punishment is never used. Suspension is rare and a last resort. Where suspension for a few days is initiated, it is for the purpose of eliciting more cooperation from the parents.

School vandalism, truancy, racial problems are conspicuous by their absence in Montessori schools because enrollment reflects the ethnic constituency of the environment served and likewise because most schools are private and have a limited enrollment. Some Montessori schools have a dress code; most merely suggest "dress in keeping with good taste."

ROLES

Administration

Since most Montessori schools are small, not-for-profit and established by interested parents, administrative procedures are simple, yet functional. Municipal and state requirements help provide the guidelines for outlining responsibilities that have to be met. A formally organized board establishes policy determining who will be specifically responsible for what has to be done. The school board is the legally responsible body accountable for meeting licensing requirements, which include safety, sanitation, food and health laws, adequate space, qualified staff, a defensible curriculum.

Most Montessori school boards consist of five to seven members, democratically chosen by and from parents. When a school is first established the board frequently includes a much larger representation of parents. Differences of opinion and experience usually reduce the number on the school board to seven within a few years. The minority of Montessori schools incorporated for profit usually have a minimum number of board members, namely three. Most of the larger schools include a Montessori teacher and only occasionally an administrator on the board. Quite frequently the majority of board members are representative of the helping professions. Membership is rather equally divided among men and women.

The administrator usually has several responsibilities in addition to being the chief executive officer in the school responsible for implementing board policy. In a small school the administrator may be responsible for a half-day class or at least assist in one in addition to being responsible for recruitment, interviewing parents, admitting children, collecting tuition, paying the bills, keeping the books and reporting on all operations to the board. In some small schools where there are only three or four classes, the head teacher also doubles as administrator. She usually assumes responsibility for arranging for parent meetings, providing instruction to parents for the better understanding of their children and undertakes whatever public relations program the school may have. Where the school has half a dozen classes or more, the administrator functions in the role of school principal.

As the school increases in size, committee heads or faculty members are assigned responsibilities for various areas such as parent-education seminars, in-service meetings for staff, editing a school newspaper as part of a public relations program, liason person with a fund-raising committee of parents, follow-up evaluation studies, coordinator of resource centers, materials-making librarian, attendance coordinator, bookkeeper, treasurer.

Regardless of how the administrative responsibilities are delegated, the principal administrator has the responsibility of coordinating those to whom she has delegated responsibilities and of being the responsible person who reports directly to the school board. In some schools the board assigns the financial responsibilities to a board member who has to okay all purchases above a given single item figure (e.g.,fifty dollars) pay bills and give a monthly or quarterly report to the chairman of the board. In small non-profit schools interviewing and hiring of teachers is the responsibility of the board; in other schools this job falls to the administrator.

The majority of Montessori non-profit schools rent, rather than own, their buildings. Where the building is purchased by the school, parents generally purchase an interest-free bond when a child is enrolled. The bond is repaid when the child leaves the school and another parent supplies the bond. The bond is over and above the tuition cost.

As a matter of policy, children are admitted to Montessori schools irrespective of race, color or creed. Since the Montessori program is designed primarily for the early education of children, the age and readiness level of the child enter into determining whether the child is sufficiently mature to benefit from the school experience. Usually children are admitted at the age of two years nine months to three years old. Occasionally a child of two or two and a half proves to be ready for interacting on his own in the Montessori environment. Part of the admission procedure is a visit by mother and child to the school on a "try-it-out" basis. The child is permitted to observe the children going about their work. If the child is ready he shows an interest; he may ask if he can stay and "play" with the materials or he may wander over to an open shelf and select something that has caught his attention. At this point, or, if interest is evident but the child is shy, the teacher asks if he would like to be shown how to work with a given item. In most instances the child stays and becomes absorbed and, to the surprise of most mothers, forgets about her for the time being. If the child is not ready he shows little or no interest, frequently clinging to the mother. At times, however, the child is ready but the mother fosters the clinging behavior. In such cases the mother is asked to observe from behind a one-way glass or to leave for a while. Children are admitted whenever they are ready, irrespective of the time of the year. This is possible since the learning environment is designed to meet individual needs. Since children are admitted regularly through the year, an additional class or two is formed frequently around mid-year.

A minority of Montessori pre-schools have toddler classes which meet one to three days a week, primarily for the purpose of educating mothers of children eighteen to thirty months old. Mothers come with their toddler, frequently with another child, an infant, in their arms. The sessions are usually two hours long with the mothers observing while the little ones are interacting with the materials and each other in the specially prepared environment. The purpose of these classes is twofold: to lead the parent to a better understanding of her child and his needs; and to assist the child in developing self-help skills in response to his needs.

Because Montessori-educated children tend to perform in a superior manner academically, a popular misconception has arisen that only brighter children are admitted. This writer knows of no Montessori school that has such an admission policy. All children are admitted, even special (handicapped) children, provided their disability does not interfere with their benefitting from the program offered. Most Montessori schools have several special children enrolled. These may have partially impaired hearing, sight, muscular coordination, or be identified as hyperactive or with Down's Syndrome. The presence of a special child is considered an advantage in most Montessori schools since young children respond with unusual considerateness, thus facilitating the development of thoughtfulness of others. The seriously handicapped, such as the autistic or emotionally disturbed child, are usually not admitted.

The average class size is between twenty-five and thirty children, depending upon room size, state regulations, availability of qualified personnel and a waiting list of children seeking admission. A class under a dozen provides less mutual stimulation than a class twice that size. In an individualized learning environment, the number of children present is less a determining factor than is space and materials available, assuming there is an adequate staff. A class of seventy-five children functions beautifully in a learning environment laid out, for example, in a former gymnasium where several Montessori teachers and assistants can work as a team. Moveable open shelves, containing learning materials laid out in sequential order from simple to more complex, form resource centers, giving the environment a children's house atmosphere while at the same time controlling traffic patterns. The absence of visual obstruction enables teachers to observe the entire environment and be readily available where a child gives evidence of needing help.

Montessori consultants are available for assisting the administration in evaluating the effectiveness of the staff as well as the total operation of the school, including the quality of the learning materials and the functioning of the learning environment. Consultants are available both regionally and nationally. Schools affiliated with the *American Montessori Society,* for example, are entitled to periodic consultative visits as part of their annual affiliation fee paid to the national organization, which has as one of its functions, the maintaining of professional standards. A similar consultative service is offered by the headquarters of the *Association Montessori Internationale.* Montessori teacher training centers offer in-service training locally along with several evaluative visits a year to schools cooperating with the training center. Some, provide regional teacher seminars throughout the year together with a consultation and evaluation service.

Montessori teacher training centers which are approved by the *American Montessori Society* must meet quality standards set by a national teacher training committee which is made up of representatives of approved training centers. Field evaluation teams, representative of the broad field of education, check on performance as a means of maintaining high standards. Before a Montessori teacher is recommended for certification she must not only meet all the academic requirements, but must be able to demonstrate through performance in the classroom that she can function successfully as a catalyst in a Montessori environment. The Montessori Teaching Certificate is issued only by the national organization. Practices differ somewhat from country to country, but in general, the authority to issue the Montessori teaching credential is closely guarded. Teachers in elementary schools and above likewise hold required state certification.

All schools maintain confidential records on staff as well as on children. Teachers' records are also maintained in the offices of the national organization conferring certification.

Faculty

The majority of teachers in Montessori schools are women, although in recent years an increasing number of young men are entering the field. The major incentive for becoming a Montessori teacher is not money. Love of people, especially children, and the desire to spend one's life in work where one will be able to leave the world a somewhat better place for all, is the dominant motive of most Montessori teachers. This non-materialistic motivation and concomitant dedication is without doubt a contributing factor to the success of Montessori schools.

In some areas the salary of a Montessori teacher is equivalent to that of teachers in other schools in the area with comparable background and experience. In large cities, however, the majority of teachers in non-profit Montessori schools earn a salary comparable to that of parochial school teachers, considerably less than that paid in tax-supported systems.

Incentive lies primarily within the teacher. She strives to improve her effectiveness because she is convinced that it is during the very early years that the child is constructing not only his present but his future. Motivation is further stimulated by opportunities for self-growth provided through in-service seminars, institutes and advanced courses in Montessori training.

Love of independence and freedom is a trait found more frequently in Montessori teachers than in the average person. This desire to be free from the restraints and conformities inherent in a large organization prompts many to look forward to the day when they can have their own school. The vision of establishing a Montessori school in one of the thousands of communities still waiting for Montessori is an appealing motive to improve oneself professionally. While scales of monetary increases in salary exist, they are not a major incentive for the average Montessori teacher.

Every aspect of a teacher's role befalls a Montessori teacher: she is not only responsible for all the children in her class, but likewise serves as counselor to parents, diagnostician in analyzing the child's behavior, curriculum planner and improvisor, maintainer of the environment, maker of learning materials, record-keeper and repairman when materials get broken. Because she is responsible for so much, she finds her work stimulating, challenging, and although tiring, nevertheless most rewarding. Her work is never done. If not experimenting with changes in the learning environment, she is sharing ideas with fellow staff members in a planning session or providing evaluative feedback to the administrator.

Most Montessori schools welcome observational visits from teachers and others. Prospective new teachers are usually invited to spend some time observing in a school before deciding on Montessori as a career. School policy usually provides for staff to visit innovative school programs as well as other Montessori schools as a means of professional stimulation.

Most states require an adult for every ten children under five years old in a classroom. In Montessori pre-schools this means three adults in a class of thirty children. Occasionally this would include two certified Montessori teachers and either a Montessori intern or an assistant. Usually one

Montessori certified teacher with two trained assistants or interns would staff a class of thirty pre-school age children. All the adults in the classroom need special training if the environment is to function effectively.

Students

Montessori views the student as responsible for his own development. Everything is planned to facilitate this task. The atmosphere of the school, the opportunities, materials, exercises provided, the accepting relationship between teacher and pupil, the realistic expectancies, all nudge the child toward accepting his role of educator of self. To assist him in assuming this role the teacher tends to remain in the background. She does not instruct in the traditional sense; instead she prepares the path, encourages, refrains from interfering, does not expect a report as to accomplishment; yet, she stands ready to assist with a directive question should help be needed.

From the first moment, the learner in a Montessori school is presented with opportunity to experience freedom. He is free to choose from a variety of attractive-looking materials; he may work fast or slowly as he savors the satisfactions he is reaping from his activity. He is accepted as he is, is trusted to handle the material by himself. Subtly, but nonetheless convincingly, the feeling that his teacher believes in him and has confidence in him grows and takes root as it were in his own feelings about himself. Thus he comes to accept his role of being personally responsible for his own education.

Participation in every kind of activity relevant to the life of the child is the essence of the Montessori approach to life. Initially, with the younger child, the majority of learning activities are individualized. There are opportunities, however, for group participation; e.g., the various line and rhythm activities, but the pre-school age child loves to do things by himself. Older children are more comfortable with a larger measure of group work, but still enjoy assuming the full responsibility for a learning task. Role-playing, exercising initiative, assuming leadership, cooperating with others provide the needed balance in activities if the pupil is to bring about his all-round development. Mastery of what might be termed the academic phase of the curriculum goes forward as fast as the student prefers; hence, problems of placement or acceleration do not exist in a Montessori school.

Student organizations, advocacy groups, community service committees are as varied in a Montessori school for older students as are the problems in the community and the issues in the world at large.

Parents

The home is looked upon as the child's most important educational influence because it is during the early years of a child's life that his self-image is formed. The atmosphere of the home environment, especially the parent-child relationship, determines how the child comes to feel and think about himself: accepted, liked, able, or disapproved, rejected, incapable. During the early years the child is interested in discovering the nature of everything: what is heavy, hard, smooth, breakable, sweet, hot, bitter, short, round, sharp. He wants to find out what fits, stacks, bends, springs. He tries to find out why this does not fit, why that works, why this happens when he does that.

From the very beginning the child is in the process of constructing his own intelligence. Parents need to understand what the child needs, and why, if they are going to provide the help and environment conducive to the child's all-round development. Consequently, Montessori schools sponsor home study groups among parents for the purpose of making parents aware of the importance of the early years and to acquaint them with what they might do to be more effective in assisting the child. Adults need to recognize that a child is usually more interested in the *process* of what he is doing than he is in what he is *accomplishing;* hence he is not in a hurry to finish the work in which he is engaged. Unless parents understand this difference between child and adult, they will find it difficult to be sufficiently patient with the child's activity.

In preparing parents for relating more understandingly and effectively to their children, either through study groups, parent meetings in school, family or individual parent counseling, directed reading from Montessori books along with current writings by humanistic child psychologists are relied on for providing background for further discussion. Montessori's *The Secret of Childhood,* 1970; Fisher's *Montessori for Parents,* 1965; Lillard's *Montessori: A Modern Approach,* 1973, are some of the books used to acquaint parents with the Montessori approach. Fisher's book is excellent for the skeptical parent who is full of questions about Montessori. The author lets the reader discover the answers to his questions as he examines, through her eyes, how the children function within a Montessori environment.

Most Montessori schools are the outgrowth of parent interest in providing an educational program for their child that will challenge him while at the same time recognize his uniqueness. This interest prompts parents to assume responsibility for learning about Montessori. This same interest motivates their attending school board meetings, heading committees and even engaging in fund-raising. The majority of Montessori school boards are made up of parents and as such have the legal responsibility for the school. Where a small board sets policy, an advisory committee of parents provides input to the school staff and volunteers help in securing community cooperation in areas beneficial to the school.

Parental involvement is welcome in the form of planning, in secretarial work, issuing a newsletter, accompanying children in emergency situations as well as on field trips, participating in cultural events and, if qualified, assisting in the learning environment. Parents with a particular expertise are utilized in the classroom, in such areas as art, music, drama, dance, foreign language.

While most schools have a policy of welcoming parents to visit and observe at mutually convenient times, some schedule regular bi-monthly visits. Most schools likewise have a "fathers' night" and a "mothers' night" where children attend school in the evening from seven to nine or ten. This is necessary where parents work during the daytime. Usually only half the class attends on a given evening since the parent is free to have his child show him personally the various tasks he can perform. Both staff and parents find these evenings most informative and helpful. Minor misunderstandings are readily cleared up on the occasion of parents' visits. Grievances of a serious nature are a rarity, but where they do occur and the administrator cannot resolve the difficulty, the matter is taken to the board, which may seek the advice of an outside consultant or arbitrator if deemed advisable.

Regardless of how interested parents may be in their child's education, Montessori staff find considerable advantage in offering parents, in addition to the above, regularly scheduled lecture-discussion sessions throughout the year. These discussions are planned to highlight various aspects of child development, kinds of parent-child relations and their corresponding effect on the child, the need for freedom, limit-setting and order in the child's life, characteristics of an appropriately stimulating home environment, the rationale for the learning materials in the child's Montessori classroom, the teacher's role and her expectancies and means of fostering carry-over to life outside of school.

The desire of parents for more knowledge of the Montessori approach to the child has led, in some communities, to Montessori training programs for parents offered in the evening or during the summer by a local teacher training center, university, or by the more experienced members of a regional or national Montessori teachers' association.

National as well as regional Montessori societies provide opportunity for parent membership which entitles parents to a regular newsletter plus other publications. A section of the annual national Montessori seminar schedules leaders to develop topics of interest to parents. Schools likewise collaborate in sponsoring local and regional institutes geared to parental interests.

SYSTEM IN ACTION

Ancillary Services

Montessorians conceive of education as a help to life. Adults have a responsibility to help young persons to bring to full functioning everything that they are capable of doing, being and becoming. As a doctor only assists nature to bring about health, so likewise a teacher assists the individual to discover knowledge, develop talent, apply skills. The young person needs assistance in the process of actualizing his potentialities so he may live life more fully. Consequently, wherever human services of an educational nature are appropriate, a Montessori program in some form may be found.

Montessori philosophy is implemented in various areas of human endeavor: in programs designed to assist retarded, emotionally disturbed, blind, crippled, autistic, gifted, Down's Syndrome children. There are day care programs for working mothers, home-bound instruction for mother and child where the child is seriously handicapped, classrooms on wheels, learning apparatus libraries, infant classes for mother and child, instructional programs for young and prospective parents, family counseling . . . in addition to Montessori pre-schools, elementary and secondary schools and undergraduate and graduate teacher training institutions. The large majority of Montessori-trained personnel, however, are engaged in programs designed for the average young child. This is more true in America than in other countries of the world. In Dublin, for example, a Montessori training program specializes in the preparation of teachers for the special child. In Munich, a children's center works with pre-schoolers suffering from serious social maladjustment; intensive social therapy is prescribed, using parents and siblings as co-therapists.

Although a wealth of helpful measures lies in the Montessori approach, not only for the normal but likewise for the handicapped child, there have been, unfortunately, too few Montessori schools established in the United States for the special child.

Many Montessori schools have a small lending library utilized by parents and study groups. Others help the local library stock books on Montessori and participate in discussion programs open to the public. Staff members with particular training, such as in counseling therapy, child behavior, reading difficulties, muscular coordination, music and art serve as consultants to groups and programs in the community, interpreting their expertise in the light of the Montessori approach to the child.

In inner-city areas where poverty and limited educational background of parents deprive the child of appropriately stimulating experience, some Montessori organizations have cooperated with government funding in establishing Montessori pre-school programs. In addition, some help equip a bus or van with Montessori auto-education materials which circulates among the homes weekly, permitting parents to borrow, free of charge, self-teaching devices appropriate to their children's level of development. The van operates like a library on wheels.

An apprenticeship program is available in many Montessori schools wherein young men and women may get first-hand experience in working with young children in a self-learning environment. The program enables the recent college graduate to discover whether or not he is fitted for this kind of work. Qualified undergraduates, as well as mothers who no longer have children at home, are likewise welcome to take this first step before undertaking formal training.

Some of the larger Montessori teacher preparation programs offer a variety of educational courses designed for parents, counselors, teachers with other than Montessori orientation. In addition most provide seminars and institutes throughout the year, each focusing on a specific aspect of human development from a Montessori point of view. Major emphasis, however, is on fostering a better understanding of the child as a means of providing appropriate assistance to the child in his task of developing himself.

For a qualified person desiring to become a Montessori teacher, professional preparation consists of three parts: 1) a good foundation in general education, which generally means a college degree; 2) a curriculum of professional areas with emphasis on Montessori insights and the means of their implementation; 3) an academic year of internship which culminates in the prospective Montessori teacher being required to pass both a written and a performance evaluation in the classroom. In *American Montessori Society* schools, pressure is building toward a policy of granting only a temporary teaching certificate upon completion of training. The ability to demonstrate effectiveness in the learning environment coupled with continued professional growth would qualify the new teacher after one to three years for a regular Montessori teaching credential. Failing to meet this criteria, the ineffective teacher would be dropped from recognition. Professional standards in Montessori training in other countries of the world vary; in some areas, a teacher with little more than a secondary education undertakes Montessori training and is certified for teaching children under six.

Physical facilities

The utilization of space is a central factor in facilitating the effectiveness of the freedom which characterizes a Montessori learning environment. The ideal classroom starts with a large open space; for example, a rectangular room forty by twenty-five or thirty feet. This permits about thirty-five square feet per child. The open shelves housing the materials are arranged so that children have easy access to their use and the teacher is able to observe what is going on at all times. For example, "L" shaped shelves in three corners of the room may contain in sequenced order the math, language and practical life materials. In the center of the room another "L" shelf with sensorial materials is so arranged as to prevent "runways," yet not obstruct an easy flow of activity. Areas along the sides may, along with tables within the room, contain resource materials in art, music, science, geography.

The arrangement must be fluid; children are constantly changing as they work through the environment. Early five-year-olds who worked mainly as individuals in the early part of the year may prefer the give-and-take of their peers in small groups by Christmas. Larger tables and working areas are necessary to accommodate their developing social awareness. Shelving must be sufficiently low so as not to obstruct the view of the insecure child who needs the supporting comfort of seeing the teacher present. Strategy calls for creating a living environment for the child which provides freedom, fosters a sense of order, satisfies a need for discovering the nature of reality, stimulates an appreciation of beauty and promotes the child's experience of community life.

Children need to move comfortably throughout the environment using all curriculum areas appropriate to satisfying their needs while at the same time being socially mobile. Periods of non-teaching observation are necessary for the adult to evaluate how the environment is functioning. An insufficiently illuminated corner of the room may be avoided by certain children; another area may attract running or unnecessary congregating. To maintain an accommodating environment, that is effective in meeting the learners' needs and abilities, necessitates continuous observation and change.

Perhaps the most unique feature of the Montessori system is the content of the learning environment: the sequenced auto-education materials. Without materials, in which each new step in the learning process is isolated and presented in a way that the child can make the discovery by himself, the open classroom approach would fail (as it has in schools other than Montessori). Starting with the simple manipulatives which Dr. Montessori contrived during the seven years she worked with mentally deficient children, she and those she trained, developed and experimented with thousands of materials designed to confront the child, step by step, with practically every aspect of the world having relevance to life. Today thousands of these uniquely designed materials in all the areas of the curriculum lead the child in the interesting process of discovering the world. In so doing he simultaneously is not only constructing his own intelligence but developing every facet of himself.

PROSPECT

A prevailing objective of many Montessorians is to introduce the Montessori system into the mainstream of public education, especially at the pre-school and elementary levels. As long as Montessori remains predominantly in private or independent schools, Montessori influence will be limited. In some Asiatic and European countries, Montessori is used to some extent in government-supported schools. In the United States, however, the inclusion of Montessori in public schools at the primary level is spotty and just beginning to be adopted in only a few states. What lies ahead?

Three factors favor an optimistic outlook for Montessori playing an increasingly influential role in American education: 1) the large number of children coming up through public inner-city schools with inadequate reading skills and a distaste for learning, 2) an increasing number of mothers sending their children to pre-school or day care programs as they seek fulfillment in activities outside the home, and 3) the necessity of providing effective intervention programs for the culturally disadvantaged as a means of helping these children develop positive attitudes and the "tools" for enjoying learning. Montessori is proving effective in providing solutions to problems posed in all three areas.

One of the obstacles to Montessori expansion into the mainstream of education is a tinge of clannishness on the part of many Montessori teachers. Convinced, on the basis of personally witnessed evidence that Montessori brings results superior to that of other systems, many feel they have the answer to what makes for effectiveness and therefore do not feel the need to participate in developments across the broad field of education. This has a double adverse effect: cutting off a mutually beneficial, stimulating interchange while blocking the development of possible avenues of influence on public education.

Currently a movement is under way for improving this situation. In addition, the United States Office of Education is meeting with Montessori representatives, asking them to examine in greater depth their own teacher preparation programs as a step toward unifying the two major Montessori organizations in the United States through agreement on a single certifying process in accord with a yet-to-be-established National Accrediting body. This would help pave the way for greater acceptance on the part of public educators and eliminate some of the "closed shop" aura that hangs over Montessori at the present time. If these developments do not materialize, Montessori expansion in America will be slowed considerably.

There are three areas in which Montessori could easily expand: (a) day care, (b) programs for the special child, and (c) pre-schools for the culturally disadvantaged. In the first area Montessori will continue to expand as more and more existing Montessori schools extend their programs to all day, thus providing day care service. Growing community pressure for more day care facilities along with dissatisfaction stemming from a lack of enriching content in existing day care programs will result in the establishing of an increasing number of Montessori facilities. Infant and toddler programs, where mothers come to observe while being instructed, will continue to grow along with day care.

An important area in which Montessori has demonstrated effectiveness is in programs for the special child. However, until Montessori makes its way into the arena of public education and has more ready access to government funding, Montessori programs for the special child will not flourish.

The third area in which Montessori has much to offer is in the cultural intervention programs for the disadvantaged. Again, because of inner-city families lacking funds, tuition-supported Montessori is unable to fill the evident need. If Montessori were incorporated into the stream of public education, Montessori would be able to supply much of what many feel is currently lacking.

The future of Montessori as an influence in education is hazy; it could be bright if *all* concerned took an objective look at the child and his needs and acted accordingly.

ANNOTATED BIBLIOGRAPHY

Lillard, Paula Polk. *Montessori: A Modern Approach.* New York: Schocken, 1974.

An excellent introduction to the Montessori movement in education. Presents a clear description of Montessori's perceptive observations of how children learn. Provides the reader with an understanding of how and why Montessori works in the classroom with American children.

Montessori, Maria. *The Montessori Method.* New York: Schocken Books, 1974.

This book is a principal source of Montessori's ideas. When first published in 1912 it carried the additional title: *Scientific Pedagogy As Applied to Child Education in "The Children's Houses."* In outlining the education of children 3 to 6, Dr. Montessori discusses the roles of freedom, observation, activity and discipline. The role of the teacher is described as a "stimulator of life" who guides the physical and psychic development of the child. This basic text has been reprinted in recent years by various publishers.

Montessori, Maria. *Spontaneous Activity in Education: The Advanced Montessori Method, Vol. 1.* New York: Schocken Books, 1964.

This volume describes the education of children ages 7 to 11. Montessori calls for an interdisciplinary approach in fostering the child's self-development. In describing the new direction education should take, she discusses such topics as the preparation of the teacher, freedom, attention, will, imagination, development of the child's intelligence and moral character along with a description of materials she designed for educating the older child.

Montessori, Maria. *The Montessori Elementary Material: The Advanced Montessori Method, Vol. II.* Cambridge, Mass.: Robert Bentley, Inc., 1964.
Basically, this volume is an illustrated manual of educational programming techniques for assisting the six-to-eleven-year-old pupil in developing skills in math, language and the arts. Ten per cent of the book is devoted to explaining the use of Montessori materials with the special child.

Montessori, Maria. *The Secret of Childhood.* Notre Dame, Ind.: Fides Publishers, 1970.
This book outlines Montessori's views of the psychology of the child. The adult's most important role, according to Montessori, is to recognize and nurture the inner, dynamic force present in every child. Because of this psychic force the child is capable of constructing the person he some day will become. In developing this theme Montessori focuses on the unique role of the child's psyche, his development and adult-child relations.

Montessori, Maria. *From Childhood to Adolescence.* New York: Schocken, 1973.
The first part of this volume discusses the characteristics and needs of children seven to twelve years old. In the latter part, which first appeared under the title *Erdkinder and the Function of the University,* Montessori proposes a plan for reforming secondary education wherein pupils would be exposed to science in a natural environment. Her approach is similar to that of Jerome Bruner's spiral curriculum.

Montessori, Maria. *To Educate the Human Potential.* Adyar, Madras, India: Kalakshetra Publications, 1956.
In this book Montessori outlines strategies for stimulating the child's imagination as a means of developing a reverential respect for life and nature. She describes her *Cosmic Plan* for enabling the older student to study developing civilizations, the nature and evolution of man in society and the effect of nature's elements in shaping the earth. This book ties into her *Education for a New World.*

Montessori, Maria. *Education and Peace.* Chicago: Henry R. Regnery Co., 1973.
Based on her conviction that the only avenue toward peace in the world is through the education of the child, Montessori outlines her educational insights and her plan for educating children. Her commitment to religious values is present as an undertone as she explains why children need social and moral models in a suitable environment if their inner nature is to be oriented in the direction of peace.

Montessori, Maria. *Pedagogical Anthropology,* New York: Frederick A. Stokes Co., 1913.
In the heavily documented references, Dr. Montessori, a lecturer in anthropology at the University of Rome in the first decade of this century, outlines her views on science, philosophy and the arts. She examines the research and writings of nearly 200 writers in the field during this period. In reflecting on the education of man, she emphasizes the necessity of objectivity and exactness in arriving at a method of education. Bearing in mind that the material is dated, the reader gains

a respect, however, for Montessori's scientific leanings.

Montessori, Mario M. Jr. (Ed.: Paula P. Lillard). *Education for Human Development,* New York: Schocken, 1976.

This book by Maria Montessori's grandson, a practicing analyst, assesses Dr. Montessori's contributions in the light of modern psychology and current education. He analyzes the place of work and values in education and emphasizes that educators who would be true to the spirit of Montessori must be continuously open to the findings of science. With Montessori's books translated into twenty-two languages, he views from the 70s the expanding Montessori movement.

Rambusch, Nancy M. *Learning How to Learn: an American Approach to Montessori.* Baltimore: Helicon Press, 1962.

A book by the author who launched Montessori's rebirth in America in the sixties. A cogent discussion of Montessori's theories and educational materials. In outlining Montessori's conviction that every child is born with a desire to learn, she argues for the Montessori approach. A bibliography of 481 Montessori books and articles in English from 1909 to 1961 is included.

Standing, E. M. *Maria Montessori: Her Life and Work.* New York: New American Library, 1962.

A warm and at times sentimental biography written by her friend and disciple of thirty years. Through quotations from letters and diaries, Dr. Montessori emerges as a perceptive, forceful yet self-forgetful physician-educator consumed with a desire to help all children achieve more of their potential. Montessori materials are described in the process of relating hundreds of classroom anecdotes. The "discovery of the child" is Montessori's greatest achievement, according to the author.

REFERENCES

Applebaum, P. *The Growth of the Montessori Movement in the United States, 1909–1970.* Ann Arbor, Mich.: University Microfilms, 1971.

Association Montessori Internationale. Reports of National Montessori societies. *Communications.* Amsterdam, Holland: 1972.

Baines, M. R. & Snotum, J. R. Time-sampling analysis of Montessori *versus* traditional classroom interaction. *Journal of Educational Research,* 1973, *66,* 313–316.

Banta, T. J. The Montessori Research Project. *The American Montessori Society Bulletin,* 1967, *7,* 1–16.

Berliner, M. S. Reason, creativity and freedom in Montessori. *Education Forum,* 1975, *40,* 7–21.

Bestor, A. *Educational wastelands: The retreat from learning in our public schools.* Urbana: University of Illinois Press, 1953.

Boyd, W. *From Locke to Montessori.* London: George Harrap & Co., 1917.

Boyd, W. (Ed.) *Towards a new education.* New York: A. A. Knopf, 1930.

Cole, L. *History of education: From Socrates to Montessori.* New York: Rinehart & Co., 1950.

Dimoff, E. Effect of initial structure upon children's divergent thinking. *Graduate Research Education,* 1975. *8,* 45–67.

Elkind, D. Piaget and Montessori. *Harvard Educational Review*, 1967–68, *37*, 535–546; *38*, 352.

Fisher, D. C. *The Montessori manual for teachers and parents.* Cambridge, Mass.: Robert Bentley, Inc., 1964.

Fisher, D. C. *Montessori for parents.* Cambridge, Mass.: Robert Bentley, Inc. 1965.

Fleege, U. H. (Ed.) *Building the foundations for creative learning.* New York: American Montessori Society, 1964.

Fleege, U. H. *Guidelines and techniques for healthy child development.* Chicago: Success Research, 1975.

Fleege, U. H., Black, M. & Rackauskas, J. *Montessori pre-school education.* Washington, D.C.: U.S. Department of Health, Education and Welfare, Office of Education Bureau of Research, 1967.

Fleege, V. B. *Standard Montessori operating procedures.* Chicago: Montessori Publications, 1974.

Gardner, R. A psychologist looks at Montessori. *Elementary School Journal,* 1966, *67*, 72–83.

Gitter, L. L. *The Montessori way.* Seattle, Wash.: Special Child Publications, 1970.

Glasser, W. *Schools without failure.* New York: Harper & Row, 1969.

Gross, Michael J. *Montessori's concept of personality.* Washington, D.C.: University Press of America, 1978.

Guidubaldi, J. *et al.* Evaluation of Montessori and day care programs for disadvantaged children. *Journal Education Research,* 1974, *68*, 95–99.

Hainstock, E. *Teaching Montessori in the home. The pre-school years.* New York: New American Library, 1968.

Kilpatrick, W. H. *The Montessori system examined.* Boston: Houghton Mifflin, 1914.

Kramer, R. *Maria Montessori: a biography.* New York: G. P. Putnam, 1976.

Lillard, P. P. *Montessori: a modern approach.* New York: Schocken Books, 1974.

Maslow, A. H. *Motivation and personality* (2nd Ed.) New York: Harper & Row, 1970.

Montessori, M. *The absorbent mind.* Wheaton, Ill.: Theosophical Press, 1964.

Montessori, M. *The child in the church.* (Ed.: E. M. Standing). St. Paul, Minn.: Catechical Guild, 1965.

Montessori, M. *The child in the family.* New York: Avon Books, 1970.

Montessori, M. *The discovery of the child.* Notre Dame, Ind.: Fides Publishers, 1967.

Montessori, M. *Education for a new world.* Wheaton, Ill.: Theosophical Press, 1964.

Montessori, M. *To educate the human potential.* Wheaton, Ill.: Theosophical Press, 1963.

Montessori, M. *The formation of man.* Wheaton, Ill.: Theosophical Press, 1969.

Montessori, M. *From childhood to adolescence.* New York: Schocken Books, 1973.

Montessori, M. *The Montessori method,* New York: Schocken Books, 1964.

Montessori, M. *Pedagogical anthropology.* New York: Frederick A. Stokes Co., 1913.

Montessori, M. *Spontaneous activity in education. The advanced Montessori Method, Vol. 1.* Cambridge, Mass.: Robert Bentley, Inc., 1964.

Montessori, M. *The Montessori elementary material. The advanced Montessori method, Vol. 2.* Cambridge, Mass.: Robert Bentley, Inc., 1964.

Montessori, M. *Reconstruction in education.* Wheaton, Ill.: Theosophical Press, 1964.

Montessori, M. *The secret of childhood.* Notre Dame, Ind.: Fides Publishers, 1970.

Montessori, M. *What you should know about your child.* Wheaton, Ill.: Theosophical

Press, 1963.

Montessori, M. M. Jr. (Ed.: Paula P. Lillard). *Education for human development.* New York: Schocken, 1976.

National Association for the Education of Young Children. *Montessori in perspective.* Washington, D.C.: 1966.

Orem, R. C. *Montessori and the special child.* New York: G. P. Putnam, 1970.

Rambusch, N. M. *Learning how to learn: An American approach to Montessori.* Baltimore: Helicon Press, 1962.

Rambusch, N. M. The "American Montessori" experience. New York: *The American Montessori Society Bulletin,* 1977, *15,* 1–28.

Rusk, R. R. Montessori. Chapter 12 in *The doctrines of the great educators.* London: Macmillan, 1954.

Sciarra, D. J. & Dorsey, A. Six-year follow-up study of Montessori education. *The American Montessori Society Bulletin,* 1974, *12,* No. 4.

Smith, M. *And madly teach.* Chicago, Henry Regnery Co., 1949.

Stodalsky, S. S. & Karlson, A. L. Differential outcomes of a Montessori curriculum. *Elementary School Journal,* 1972, *72,* 419–433.

Standing, E. M. *Maria Montessori: Her life and work.* New York: New American Library, 1962.

Standing, E. M. *The Montessori revolution in education.* New York: Schocken Books. 1966.

UNESCO. *World survey of education, Vol. 2: primary education.* Paris: 1958.

Weill, B. C. Validity of the Montessori method for special education: a case history. *Journal Special Education Mentally Retarded,* 1974, *10,* 130–140.

CHAPTER 6

Individual Education

RAYMOND J. CORSINI

Individual Education, a system suitable from pre-school through high school, is based on the humanistic democratic model of man found in Alfred Adler's Individual Psychology. It operates on the notion of the absolute equality of parents and children, faculty and administrators in a school learning situation. Adults provide facilities and services (including teaching and counseling) but the children have the absolute right to learn or not learn. Adults are specifically prohibited from "motivating" children to learn through rewards (such as "good" grades) or through punishment.

The curriculum of Individual Education schools has three elements: (a) academics, (b) "creative" courses and (c) socialization activities. Children can "manipulate" (a) and (b), but must participate in socialization activities.

The specific goals of Individual Education to which all activities and relationships are directed are Responsibility, Respect, Resourcefulness and Responsiveness (social interest). These goals are for children and adults alike.

Results based on six schools indicate in comparison to traditional education (a) children actually learn more of academics in less time and enjoy such academics more, (b) schools are happy places with little violence or vandalism, (c) children are overall better prepared for life, (d) home life is happier, (e) adults (faculty and parents) benefit, (f) this system is suitable for a wide range of intellectual, motivational, cultural and personality variables, and (g) the system is economical and simple to operate.

INTRODUCTION

Objectives of Education

There are two contending views about education. The first is that the sole purpose of compulsory education is to give children only the basic tools that they can use for further learning. The most restrictive view would be that schools should only teach the so-called three r's of reading, 'riting and 'rithmetic. A somewhat liberal view would include exposure to science, social science and the humanities. The second point of view is that compulsory education should give children skills and attitudes to succeed in life in a world of social forces. This point of view considers teaching "the whole child"—and the utmost view would be to prepare the child psychologically, socially, philosophically to meet the world.

There are strong positions taken by proponents of both views. Some considered the economic costs; some other people are concerned about schools serving as propaganda agencies. In any event, the whole issue of what schools should teach is not yet settled. Cynically, we can say that many schools say that they teach "the whole child" thereby satisfying the liberals, but only teach the "three r's" thereby satisfying the conservatives.

Those who argue, following the concepts of John Dewey's books *School and Society* (1899), *Democracy in Education* (1916) and *Experience and Education* (1938) that the true purpose of education is the preparation of the child for life, state in effect that training children only in the academic 3 r's is not what education is all about; it is not what the children need; it is not what society needs.

There are three possible views of the objectives of education:

1. *To please parents.* This would be equivalent to the concept of taking a dog to an animal trainer who would then ask the dog's owner what he or she would wish the dog to learn.

2. *To serve society.* Schools can be seen as an instrument for the benefit of the society, to prepare citizens to be patriotic and law-abiding; training workers to be skilled and capable; and parents to bring up children to be an asset to the community.

3. *To maximize childrens' abilities.* This third view would be concerned with doing what is best for children, looking ahead to their future roles in life and in society.

These views need not be incompatible. In a good social system, a school would meet simultaneously the needs of parents and society and children. However, it is our judgment that traditional schools do not meet any of these needs to any worthwhile degree, which is the reason for considering educational innovations, and, of course, Individual Education, which purports to be a superior system.

Reasons for This System

The primary argument for Individual Education is that the traditional system of education in the United States has uniformly been accounted a failure by those individuals who have examined and evaluated it. The various accounts of Glasser (1969), Hentoff (1967), Holt (1964), Illich (1970), Parker (1970) and Silberman (1970) as well as others uniformly add up to an indictment of our present educational system which is labeled, among other terms as emotionally harmful, undemocratic, unfair, inefficient, ineffective, overly expensive, unresponsive to human needs, inflexible and generally a colossal failure in practically all respects. A close examination of some alternative systems such as Behavior Modification shows that many of them are merely "clever" ways of attempting to "motivate" children—that is, to force children to do what they don't want to do, and that they are only variations on the same theme as traditional education.

Individual Education claims as Dewey did, that education is for the whole child in a democratic society, and its argument for being considered is that it actually achieves what traditional education attempts to achieve —and much more—but simply, cheaply, easily, due to its superior philosophy, theory and operations. It is especially critical of traditional educational practice which it sees as effectively discouraging children, making them "hate" education, and generating all kinds of psychological distance between children and adults, and also between parents and faculty members.

It criticizes restrictive schools which feature mindless conformity under the heading of "discipline" as authoritarian, principally teaching children to obey regardless of reasons and it criticizes progressive schools of the Summerhill (Neill, 1960) type as essentially anarchistic—teaching disorder, selfishness and disobedience. Individual Education criticizes the so-called traditional schools as being half way between authoritarianism and permissivism, as having no character as it were, bland and standing for nothing. On a hypothetical triangle with one corner being labeled Authoritarianism (West point type of school), another corner being labeled Permissivism (Summerhill type of school), Individual Education sees itself in theory being at the third corner labeled Democracy. Traditional Education is seen somewhere in the middle, equi-distant from each of the three corners (Figure 1.)

We have several reasons for advocating Individual Education.

1. Children who come out of our schools are more mature, more sensible, more capable of taking care of themselves than are children from other schools. This is agreed to by nearly all parents and all faculty members. Consequently, Individual Education helps children become more responsible. It becomes a kind of place

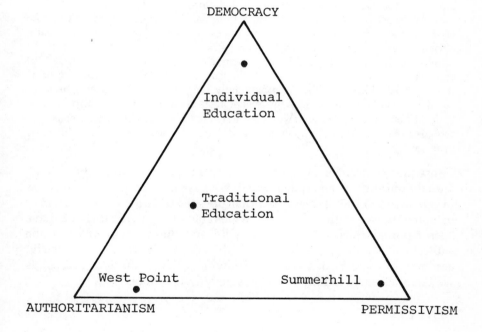

FIGURE 1

Map of relationships expressed by various schools with corners labeled
Democracy, Authoritarianism and *Permissivism.* Traditional schools are
somewhere in the middle, possibly at the lower left as indicated by dot.
These dot placements do not refer to any particular schools but rather
to the system as a system.

where children can grow up.

2. Our schools are happy places. Practically one hundred per cent of the thousand or so visitors to our schools who have filled out questionnaires state that the relationships they observed between children and children, and children and faculty, were pleasant and cooperative.

3. Our children learn a good many things during the regular school day in our "creative" program: life-coping skills that most schools do not teach, vocational and avocational subjects. Children are truly prepared for life much better than in traditional schools.

4. The homes of children who go to Individual Education schools are much more disciplined, orderly, happy and have a spirit of cooperation. Of all the school systems, only in Individual Education must all parents take a course in parenting to enroll their children. The nature of the relationships between the "school" and the "family" is considerably different from that in any other school. We respect the parents and we demand respect from the parents, and we also respect children. As a consequence our families are much happier since we all operate in concordance with the Adlerian theory of human relationships.

5. As an academic delivery system, Individual Education appears to be more efficient and more effective than traditional education in that children actually appear to learn more of the traditional 3 r's in this system than they did in the traditional system. An unpublished research by Don Warren (Corsini, 1977b) shows that a sample of students who had spent five years in an Individual Education school had accomplished approximately ten percent more learning as measured by standard scholastic achievement tests than expectation. Also, in Our Lady of Sorrows School over five years, in comparison with 26 other elementary schools in its district this school had moved up six academic rank orders from its prior rank.

Consequently, were one to be only concerned with the capability of Individual Education as an academic delivery system, it appears this method overall accomplishes its aim better than does the traditional system. It may be noted, however, that extremely wide ranges of individual efforts have been reported: thus, some children will learn three or more years of one subject and very little of other subjects in any year. However, statistically, academically the evidence is that Individual Education does at least as well as traditional education in considerably less time.

HISTORY

Beginnings

The writer does not know whether in the history of educational innovations the beginning of any system can be so definitely pinpointed as can be done with Individual Education. Possibly, some systems "just grew" over time, with changes being made from time to time; in contrast, Individual Education was deliberately designed.

The beginnings of Individual Education took place in Honolulu in August, 1968. The writer there accidentally met Sister Joan Madden, principal of Our Lady of Sorrows Elementary School, who had been his student some two years previously. During a discussion that took no more than ten minutes, the decision to develop a completely new educational system was broached and decided on. On being asked how her school was going, Sister Joan stated, "Terrible. Children are resisting learning and are restless, the teachers are listless and discouraged, and parents are angry and puzzled." The writer suggested that the problem most probably was due to an improper system. On being told (a) that it was the same system that we had ourselves been taught in and (b) the same system as in other schools, the counterargument was that (a) times had changed and (b) other schools were in the same sad predicament.

Sister Joan asked whether there were any better academic systems available, but the reply was that none of them seemed either philosophically or theoretically superior to the traditional system, with some alternative systems having serious deficits. On being challenged to develop a scientifically and philosophically correct system, the writer accepted the challenge then and there, and said that he could and would develop a new and better educational system based on scientific knowledge and the personality model of Alfred Adler! Sister Joan said: "Do so and I'll put this system in my school."

The developmental process took approximately three years, with considerable readings, conversations with educators, visits to all sorts of schools, conversations with parents and students, leading to a series of propositions, some 300, each of which was defended in one page essays. Examples of these propositions are:

IN AN IDEAL SCHOOL

Children should not be taught what they cannot learn.
Children should not be taught what they already know.
Classroom offenders should be sent out of the classroom.
Non-Academic subjects should be taught during the school day.
Specialist fragmentation should be avoided.
Every child should have a close personal relationship with one teacher.
A simple logical uniform disciplinary system should be developed.
There should be no rewards or punishment.
Children should get frequent information about academic progress.
Children should have reasonable freedom of movement.
Children should have freedom to go to a quiet place at all times.
Every child should be permitted to go academically as fast or as slow as he wishes.
Parental pressure on children should be minimized.
Children should have the right not to learn anything.
Children should have the right to learn anything.

Each proposition was discussed with associates and teacher-acquaintances. Generally, there was approval of most propositions. About the only proposition to which there was strong opposition was the opinion that teachers should be paid a base salary plus a bonus for their popularity as demonstrated by class sizes and number of children in their homerooms. None of the educators consulted liked this concept. Practically all other propositions seemed reasonable and rational. Finally after three years, the new system, then called *Rational Education*—as a kind of dig at traditional education—was finally ready for tryout.

The writer then met with the faculty of Our Lady of Sorrows and in three two-hour sessions explained the system in detail. At that time, the faculty consisted of exactly ten people. Nine of them loved it. One of the faculty, a middle-aged woman, stated that the system made no sense to her, "but go ahead," she said, "put it in, I'll cooperate." The principal, however, stated she wouldn't put the system in until there was complete concensus. The recalcitrant teacher finally resigned, and the system passed its first test—complete approval of the faculty. Approval of the pastor of the church and the superintendent of Catholic Education was quickly obtained. Approval by the school board was another matter. Highly conservative, mostly military Catholics, they weren't going to approve readily anything so radically different from what they were used to. Three two-hour sessions took place, and finally one hundred per cent approval was obtained, and in September 1972, Individual Education was finally installed at Our Lady of Sorrows just about four years after the initial decision to develop a new system.

The school board insisted that the new system would be evaluated at the end of the first year, and if the evaluation was favorable, it would be permitted a second year; and then there would be a second and a third evaluation. A local attorney agreed to head an evaluation committee. At the end of the first year the three committees gave their reports:

The psychometric committee reported that the children in this school made normal academic progress.

The consensual committee reported that parents preferred Individual Education over the traditional system.

The professional observation committee reported that their drop-in visits showed the school operated well —everything was orderly—and that a good deal of varied learning seemed to be going on.

It was the intention of all concerned with Individual Education to not report anything in print for five years, and consequently the very first publication was issued in the fall of 1977 (Manaster, 1977) five years after the first Individual Education school opened.

In the meantime, three other schools decided to take on this model. The first was Our Lady of Good Counsel (1974), also an elementary school at the K-8th grade level, then Hale o 'ulu (1976), a special school for delinquent and disadvantaged youths, age 12–18, and finally, Ke Aala Hou, a K-to-3rd grade primary school in 1977. In 1978 two public schools, Haaheo in Hilo, Hawaii, and Forest Park in Joliet, Illinois, took on this system.

Current Status

As of the time of this writing (Fall 1978) six schools mentioned above are functioning. A seventh and an eighth school are preparing to convert to Individual Education in the near future.

It may be worth discussing one school in some detail, to show what Individual Education can do. In the special issue of *Journal of Individual Psychology* already referred to, eleven prominent educators were asked to give their opinions about Individual Education. Two people commented on the type of students that might not be suited for this kind of school. Robert J. Havighurst, Professor Emeritus at the University of Chicago wrote, "I do have some questions which I suppose the other readers will share. One has to do with the applicability of this kind of school to a lower working-class population. It seems well suited to a lower-middle class family population ..." (Havighurst, 1977, p. 403). Don Dinkmeyer, a well-known Adlerian educator (Dinkmeyer, 1978), states in reference to the disciplinary system, "Discipline is handled in a systematic fashion. The three simple rules establish their own consequences. The disciplinary process sounds too simple if brought to the inner city of one of the cities of the United States." (Dinkmeyer, 1977, p. 3850).

In view of these somewhat dubious views relative to the suitability of Individual Education to hostile populations, it will be interesting for the reader to know something about Hale o 'ulu. It is a special school for disadvantaged and delinquent youth from 12 through 18, and runs from intermediate through high school. The principal, Richard Whittington (1977), wrote, "Several delivery methods were tried to provide for academic and social skills development, but at no time did our staff feel grounded in terms, of really knowing how to fulfill our goals ..., Our program simply moved from one student crisis to another. Fights, verbal abuse, and destruction of personal and school property were common occurrences." (Page 356)

Now, this must certainly sound like the kind of students that Havighurst and Dinkmeyer are concerned about.

Continuing with Whittington's account,

"During the first several months students and staff were learning what agreements and responsibility really meant ... At the same time we experienced an incredibly strong feeling of growth and accomplishment. The system was beginning to make sense to us ... The effects of the new learning and feeling of unity that staff experienced began to show in student behavior. During the last 5 months of our first year, class participation picked up to the point where for days, no students spend time in the game room. Violent episodes dropped to zero. Violation of rules dropped by more than 50 percent, and parents began reporting remarkable behavior changes in their kids at home." (Page 357)

Consequently, in terms of the fears expressed relative to Individual Education working with difficult children, the evidence we have at Hale o 'ulu school is that this system works very well.

Currently, a group of individuals, including the editors of this book, Dr. George Gazda, Dr. Guy Manaster, Dr. John Platt and Dr. Frank Walton are busy arranging training seminars, workshops, etc., to bring to the attention of educators the benefits of this system. On-site-training for interested educators is available at Our Lady of Sorrows School in Wahiawa, on the island of Oahu in Hawaii. A complete training package is being prepared by Dr. Edward Ignas through the University of Chicago. In short, vigorous efforts are being made to explain and to expand this system.

Research

From the very beginning, evidence of the value of Individual Education was required by members of the school boards and desired by its backers. Educational research to be meaningful should be well planned and should be comprehensive. Since there has been no funds available for research, whatever has been done in this regard has been done in terms of what was feasible. A minor point may be made here: the writer was adamant about not wanting financial help of a temporary nature either for faculty salaries or for research or for equipment, etc., in the realization that Individual Education might flourish if helped financially and then might wither if "soft" money would be withdrawn. Consequently, in discussing research, it should be kept in mind that the various studies to be reported here were all done with a minimum of cost.

After considerable reflection of the realities, the final assumption was that three aspects should be simultaneously evaluated: (a) how much academic learning has actually occurred as a result of children attending an Individual Education school? (b) what are the attitudes of three classes of people towards the school: parents, teachers and visitors? and (c) what are the opinions of knowledgeable school visitors about the on-going program?

Below is a summary of research findings: At the end of the first year: three research teams reported (a) on the basis of test–re-test results, over a 12 month period the children who had been tested in May 1971 and May 1972 had improved academically exactly 1.0 years; (b) in terms of telephone interviews with 50 percent of parents done in May, nine months after school had been on Individual Education, the parents indicated they preferred the new system six-to-one over the prior one, with the parents reporting that their children liked the new school more and that their children were simultaneously more cooperative and more independent; and, (c) a visiting team of teachers who made unannounced visits to the school reported that the level of activity in the school was good, children appeared to be learning and that teacher-student and student-student relationships were good.

Perhaps the most important research evidence, however, comes from reports of 1060 visitors as of the end of 1977 of Our Lady of Sorrows School. These visitors, some of whom observed this school in action from as short a time as a half day to as long as a week, filled out report forms summarized in two separate articles by Muirhead and Fong (1977) and by Kozuma (1977). Well over 95 percent of the reports were highly favorable with typical statements commenting on the good relationships, the order-liness, the atmosphere of learning evident as well as comments critically contrasting other traditional schools with this one.

So the research evidence available while thin is highly favorable. Here is the kind of additional evidence available. In meeting with the faculty of Hale o 'ulu, the consensus of the faculty estimated that prior to the installation of Individual Education that that school was functioning at a 15 percentile level of desirability. Six months later they felt the school was now functioning at the 75 percentile level.

In summarizing, it can be said that there are currently (1978) six schools, one in its seventh year, one in its fifth year, one in its third year, and one in its second year and two in their first year. The faculty, the children and the parents are all strongly in favor of these schools. Moran (1976) found that Our Lady of Sorrows School graduates did better than average academically and socially when they went on to high school.

From the point of view of the writer of this chapter, the best proof of the value of Individual Education does not come from results, such as those cited above, but rather from the theory of Individual Education! That is to say, were the reader of this chapter to make selection of one of the various systems in this book, the decision would probably best be made in terms of the logic of the system rather than on statistically-based research efforts of the objective type! Now, this is not an anti-research position, but rather the writer's belief that the apparent success or failure of any system might be due to a wide variety of causes that have nothing to do whatever with the value of the system itself. The theory and the philosophy of the system would seem to this writer as the method of choice for selection, rather than "results" which can be contaminated by all kinds of irrelevant matters. Our appeal would be to the reader's convic-tion that what counts is the logic of a system rather than such facts as the number of schools that use the system, or the endorsements, or how much academic learning has been crammed into children. If we want research, the only kind that would make sense would be evaluation of the products, i.e., the students some 20 years after exposure to two or more systems, measuring what is important, that is to say, success in life. Such a research would cost several million dollars over at least a twenty year period. Lacking such proof for any system, the discriminating reader in a position of making decisions should best use of her judgment—and her judgment should not depend as much on "facts" such as research results but rather on the intangibles of the theory, the philosophy and the procedures of the system!

THEORY

Every school system, paradoxically, is solidly based on two insubstantial elements: philosophy and theory. By *philosophy* is meant the values of the school—what the people who organize and run the school expect the school to do—its goals. By *theory* is meant how these values are to be achieved. Most people in education disregard both elements—thinking perhaps that both are obvious: a school is to prepare children for life by teaching them the three r's and that if one prepares a good environment and hires capable teachers and attempts to motivate children to do well by rewarding or punishing them, that this is all that there is to education.

In Individual Education we have four goals, the four R's of Education. Were the reader to accept these goals, he or she could then create an Individual Education school independently simply by arranging procedures to achieve these goals. For this reason, careful attention to our goals is called for—and then if accepted as *the* valid goals, even more careful attention is needed to see if the reader agrees with our methods of attaining these four R's.

The four R's are Responsibility—Respect—Resourcefulness—Responsiveness.

Responsibility

Our first goal is to make children self-sufficient, preparing them to go out into the world on their own; to make them able to take on their proper duties; to become as mature and as self-reliant as soon as possible. We see any system that infantilizes a child as wrong. Our system maximizes the child's self-determination.

Respect

Our second R is respect, meaning by this we want to develop in children feelings of self-and other-respect. We know that many school systems make children feel inferior, and tend to make them think of themselves as unsuccessful. We believed that a system based on rewards and punishment—praise and dishonor—was morally incorrect, and essentially disrespectful. If a child were born with lack of academic potential or if born in an environment that did not stress the importance of academics or if the child had other ambitions rather than academics in life, we saw any system that systematically insulted him as wrong. And so, our second goal is to develop respect for one's self and for others.

Resourcefulness

The third of our four R's is resourcefulness, a term which has two concepts. The first of these is that every person has certain innate talents, or certain specific abilities stronger than others. Thus, young Mozart had potential to be a great musician; young Bertrand Russell had the talent to be a great mathematician. So, whatever resources a person might have, a good school should permit expression, whether academic or non-academic. So, if Mike Angelo wants to paint, and has that talent, let him paint to his heart's content, even if this means as a result he might not learn how to solve square roots. Who can tell what is more important in life?

The other aspect of this concept of resourcefulness is that in terms of Adlerian theory, every human has three main tasks in life which measure his success as a human person: (a) the family, (b) society, and (c) vocation. That is we all must succeed in a relationship with *family*—meaning a sexual relationship with another adult, and with one's children, as with *job*—some means of contributing to the world, and also with *society*—that is to say other people.

Responsiveness

Basic to Adlerian theory is the concept of *Gemeinschaftsgefühl,* usually translated as Social Interest, meaning concern about others. Call it love, esprit de corps, altruism or whatever, responsiveness to us means responding to the needs of others. It is seen in school spirit, in love for family, in patriotism. We felt that no matter how well an individual develops in terms of responsibility, respect and resourcefulness, that person is not a complete human being unless he also cares for others.

The above represents the philosophy of Individual Education—the goals that we go after. Below may be the single most important statement about Individual Education.

> *Every single feature of Individual Education should*
> *contribute simultaneously to all four goals—no feature*
> *should in any way impede any of these four goals.*

Consequently, any educational system which explicitly aims for these four goals in all respects *is* Individual Education! Individual Education is *not* necessarily the procedures to be described in this chapter but rather the desire of those who run a school to have an institution that will maximize childrens' responsibility, respect, resourcefulness and responsiveness. Let that system be called whatever one wishes to call it, but if all four of these goals are aimed at, and if in logic they do appear to support these four goals, then it *is* Individual Education. Individual Education has flexibility. The procedures we have developed are only our vision of how to achieve these four goals. So, if the reader believes that these are indeed the proper goals of education then the question is how to best achieve these goals. Below will be found our vision of how to achieve these goals.

Learning

Individual Education's theory of learning comes from Alfred Adler's view of human nature. Ansbacher and Ansbacher (1956) in their *Individual Psychology of Alfred Adler* give the following proposition as the first of Adler's thinking:

> There is one basic dynamic force behind all human activity, a striving from a felt minus situation towards a plus situation, from a feeling of inferiority towards superiority, perfection, totality (p. 1)

The implication is that all human beings at all times want to grow, develop, improve, succeed, become more perfect. This adds up to *learning*. In short, all people at all times want to learn. We are all attempting to be better, to be stronger, smarter, wiser, cleverer—constantly in search of self-improvement. We want to gain attention, to gain power, to be successful. We are dissatisfied with ourselves and want to look better, to earn more, to make a better impression on others—this is a natural human condition. This is true for all—children and adults. We do not have to try to motivate children to learn: they want to learn anything that appears to be helpful to them. This becomes our real problem: to communicate that what we want to teach them will help them achieve their personal goals. Achieving goals is what education is all about.

Why do you study bridge columns in the newspaper? *To improve your game.* That means learning. Why do you take tennis lessons? *To play tennis better.* Why do you read the latest novel? *To learn what everyone is talking about so that you too can participate.*

Feelings of inferiority (not to be confused with the inferiority complex) are normal and natural and universal. They cause tension, and unease. To compensate, adults as well as children take pains to improve: to become better.

"Yah, yah, you little baby, you can't ride a bicycle", taunts a child of another. This statement hurts the other child, who now wants to learn how to ride. Or, a child sees some adult playing a game, and so he too wants to play that game.

The importance of these statements is that we don't have to motivate children to learn. They are already motivated. The most universal of all motives of people is to improve—to learn.

Now, as every parent and every teacher "knows", the above is just not true. Children struggle not to enter schools, children do not pay attention in class, children "fool around", children "play hookey" and children want to be elsewhere rather than in classes. How can we handle this discrepancy between the "universal" statement that everyone wants to learn and what we actually see?

The answer comes from a second proposition stated by Ansbacher and Ansbacher:

The striving [of superiority] receives its specific direction from an individually unique goal or self-ideal, which though influenced by biological and environmental factors is ultimately the creation of the individual. Because it is an ideal, the goal is a fiction. (page 1)

Now, this statement is extraordinary, and if understood will explain why traditional forms of education do not work. It says in effect that every human being *interprets* how to attain this goal of superiority in a unique way. A child feels inferior and wants to be superior, and so will want to do *something* to achieve superiority. If the felt inferiority has to do with reading, then the child gladly wants to learn how to read because he is now aware that reading makes him superior. But if another child does not have this felt need to learn how to read, then it has no motivation to learn how to read.

Suppose you are offered a free scholarship to learn (a) how to play the tuba, (b) how to read Turkish, (c) how to play polo, (d) how to solve quadratic equations, (e) how to reduce weight, (f) how to make better investments, (g) how to be a more effective parent, (h) how to fix automobiles and (i) how to arrange flowers—how would you react to each proposition? This writer, for example, would be interested in a—c—e—f—h, but not in b—d—g—or—i. Now, let us suppose that I was forced to go to classes (as say I were in the military and assigned to school) and say that my academic courses were to be Turkish, quadratic equations, parenting, and flower arrangement, I would be most unhappy. The reason is that while I do want to improve (in general) that I also have very specific concepts of what will improve me. Financial investing that interests me, not flower arranging!

This is exactly the situation with children. Billy will want to learn numbers, Sally wants to learn colors, Frances would like to be able to read,

Johnny wants to learn how to sew. They have their specific goals, what is important for them.

This issue discussed in the next section, is how to match what the child wants to learn with what the school wants to teach.

Putting these two ideas together we come up with the following: as a result of every individual feeling inferior and wanting to become superior, every person wants to move upwards. Among the various ways of self-improving is through learning—but each individual develops through his environment and through biology and through his own interpretations, some goals and some concepts of how to attain these goals—and if what a school offers and what the child wants *co-incides*, then the child is motivated to learn and will learn!

What this means then is that if a school offers a variety of subjects, children will apply themselves to learn what is taught for a variety of motives. Some children may be pleasers and they will simply learn what they are taught, to appease parents. This is the message that John Holt (1964) gives in his book *How Children Fail.* They are so interested in pleasing adults that they will learn anything—and they will then quickly forget what they have learned since they really don't have an intrinsic desire to learn what is taught. But if they learn what they want to learn, they then are truly motivated and will work hard.

Self evaluation

We come now to another important issue relative to a theory of teaching. The child knows best what he wants to learn, but also when to learn, how to learn, how long to study, under what conditions, and so on. To the extent that a school system limits the individual, to that extent the system harms his learning. Child B can study ten minutes at a time and child M can study three minutes at a time, while child R may be able to study for forty minutes. Child A wants to study alone in absolute silence, Child K prefers to study with the radio going on, and Child X likes to study in a room with a lot of people. Child P would like studying early in the morning and Child F prefers it late at night.

Now, how can we accommodate all these different preferences, how can we individualize instruction? How can we help individuals learn what they want to learn in the fastest manner?

We do this in Individual Education by putting the child in charge of his own education! We say to him something as follows: This is unit X—we think it is important for you to learn it. When you do learn it, if you want to be tested, let us know, and we will test you to see if you have accomplished it.

If the child says: "How can I learn it?" We would answer, "Well, one way is for you to go to classes. This week we will be teaching unit 19 in room 217 every Monday, Wednesday and Thursday from 1:15 to 2:00. Or, if you don't like to go to classes, you can learn it in the study hall. Ask the study hall supervisor for help and she will help you learn it on your own, or with other kids. Or, you can look at the Unit curriculum sheet and go to the library and study it on your own. Or, maybe you will find a teacher who will tutor you during her tutoring hour. Or, maybe you will find a friend who will teach you, or maybe one of your parents will teach you—or any combination of the above."

In other words, learning any unit is not only the responsibility of the child but also—*how* he learns it is his responsibility. (Incidentally, we find that most kids given all these choices, overwhelmingly perfer to learn academic units in classes—which is a substantiation of the value of learning in groups.)

Subject areas

The typical academic program for kindergarten through high school is trade-training—to be a teacher! However, some kids don't want to be teachers. Thy are not interested in learning how to convert fractions into decimals, assuming (probably correctly) that they will never have to do this; or they may be disinterested in locating the sea of Marmora thinking (probably correctly) that they will never have to find this body of water; or that they never will conjugate French verbs (probably correctly) in their real life. However, they may think that it is important to know how to read road maps, how to work out Income tax forms, how to fill out job applications, how to drive a car, how to apply for a job—and so these "useful" things, as they see it, are more important than "useless" things such as scanning poetry or parsing sentences.

In Individual Education we state that any child can learn whatever he wants—and that we will help him to learn what he wants. This is the reason for our *Creative Program*, which attempts to match teachers' and childrens' interests. Our secondary reason for having such a program is not only to teach children what they want to learn, but also to help them realize that learning is fun. We try to make scholars out of them. We think that schools with rigid schedules of curriculum, and so forth, are harmful to a love of learning.

Homework

Our view on homework is that it is almost always harmful, if homework is defined as assignments selected by the teacher for the whole class, as when a teacher says to children on a Friday afternoon, "On Monday bring in answers to pages 37 and 38 in your math textbook." Despite the common belief by almost every parent and many teachers that homework helps children, objective evidence is that it does not help at all—or at best very little.

Here are our ideas about homework.

1. It can generate dislike for schooling.

2. It can generate conflicts in the family. "You can't go out until you do your homework" mother says.

3. It leads to lying and cheating. Children will say they don't have homework when they do; and they will copy from one another the answers. When asked why they didn't bring in homework, they will give all kinds of tall tales.

4. Children may not study at school, figuring they will learn in the evening— and then they don't do it at home either. Or, they may use their parents as tutors.

5. Homework may distract from chores and other home-related activities.

6. Bright kids find homework a meaningless chore; dull kids just don't know how to do it.

7. Homework can not be done effectively in many homes: too many distractions, other children, television, etc.

8. Students may ask parents for help, but their help may not gibe with teachers' methods, and cause confusion.

9. Homework interferes often with a students' social life.

10. Most children do homework mechanically, not caring, just wanting to get it over with. They don't enjoy it; it just is a chore.

But the biggest reason against homework is this: children can not study effectively more than perhaps two hours a day: and to impose some extra hour or so of homework on top of six hours a day of schooling is just plain cruel. It makes them dislike learning.

The big problem in learning is motivation: the child has to want to learn. Extrinsic learning occurs when one learns just to pass a test, or to please a parent, or to get a good grade. Motivation comes from within. This means that children must be permitted to make a choice, to make selections, to make decisions. In Individual Education every child at all times, without exception has choice: he can go to the library or to the study hall, or to a creative class (see curriculum: non-academic), or may, depending on the school's schedule go to a play room or to the gymnasium or to a game room or outside to the playing field—and he is never forced to study anything he doesn't want to. He can enter or leave classes at all times.

Progress chart

In Individual Education we are not unmindful of the importance of academic subjects. We realize that success in academics is important for success in the next school as well as in life. Because academic subjects do not have inherent interest for many students, some sort of evidence of progress helps students move along. This is a function of the Progress Chart.

Every child in an Individual Education school has a progress chart,

which may look as Figure 2. Each number represents a "unit of instruction" and whenever a student has finished a project or has taken a test
which indicates he has learned that unit, this is indicated on the chart. A
copy is in the child's possession; one is in the office and one is in the
counselor's possession. The progress chart is an unofficial indicator of the
child's academic progress. In the typical elementary school every child is
expected to do a unit a week in each of the various subjects, thus typically
a student will pass a unit in Language Arts, Arithmetic, Science and Social
Science weekly.

Frequent feedback tends to encourage students, bright and dull, they
constantly see progress. So, the bright child might have four or more units
a week if he wishes to go rapidly and the dull child may have fewer, but
nevertheless he can see progress rather than ratings of "C", "D" and "F."

Level of functioning

The academic process is based on the theory that every child is likely to
function in each of the academic subjects at different levels. For this
reason, on entering the school, every child, whether a transfer student or
an old student is given scholastic achievement test, whereby each level of
actual knowledge may be ascertained. Stuart Dent on entering school early
in September takes this test, and within a week this ten year old boy, who
would ordinarily be pegged at the fifth grade level, learns that he is
reading at the seventh grade level, is doing math at the fourth grade level,
that his science level is third grade and his Social Science level is 9th grade.
On the basis of this information his counselor advises him to work at
various levels which she thinks are appropriate for him, so that he will be
at the "growing edge" of his ability rather than say being put at the fifth
grade level for everything. By doing so he would be bored to tears in
English which would be too easy for him and just tortured by math which
would be too difficult for him.

The reader should know that the counselor (whom he selects himself as
indicated in the section on counseling) only advises, but that the student
makes final academic decisions himself.

To summarize this section on the theory of learning in Individual Education, *the student is in charge of his own education.* The analogy is that of a
cafeteria, where one picks and chooses what one wants to eat, and then one
eats in whatever order one wishes, and leaves whatever one doesn't want.
As part of the Adlerian concept of the dignity of individuals and the
importance of freedom, the student can learn what he wants, when he
wants, where he wants, as much as he wants—and he need not learn
anything that he doesn't want. School is the child's business. Parents send
him to school, because they must—it is the law. Teachers teach him as best
they can, because it is their profession. Counselors advise him as best they

SCHOOL PROGRESS CHART

STUDENT *Jim Slack*   COUNSELOR *Pat Yuen*

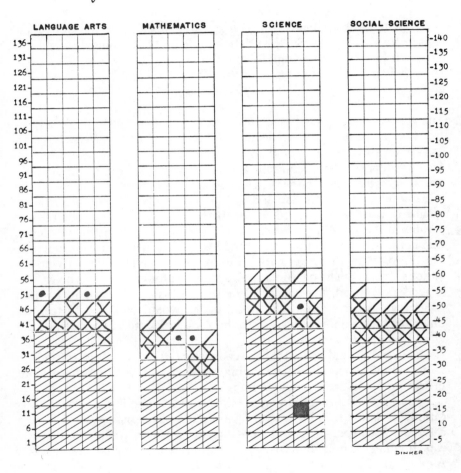

FIGURE 2
Individual Education Progress Chart

By a glance the teacher/counselor can tell immediately the child's academic situation. Please examine the chart on the opposite side of the page. You will notice five different "signals" given on the chart. *Blacked out portion of the Progress Chart.* (e.g. Items 1–39 for Language Arts, items 1 to 28 for Math.) This refers to how many units the child had succeeded in as of the end of the prior academic year. In Science, this child last year had accomplished 43 units. In Social Science 35 units.

Empty box. For example, item 55 in Language Arts. This means that we have no evidence whatever that the child has gone to any classes or taken any tests for that unit.

A dot in a box. As seen in Language Arts unit 51 and Math units 38 and 39. This means that the child took but did not pass these unit tests.

A slash line. As seen in Science items 54–55–56–57–59. This means that the child has taken and passed these units but has not yet had a conference with the teacher/counselor.

A cross in the boxes. These represent units that have been passed and have been counseled for. Thus, this year, this student has passed Math units 29–30–31–34–35–36–37—and has been counseled since passing them. In this example, the teacher/counselor may wonder and inquire why student has not passed Language Arts unit 47, why the student has not tried Math unit test 32, etc.

We have blacked in the Science unit 14 since we shall show later what a Curriculum unit sheet looks like.

can, because it is their work. But the final decision about learning is and must be—the child's. Actually it is so in any school—but only in Individual Education do we make this concept explicit.

The result—children like our schools and they actually learn more—academically, vocationally, socially.

Teaching

Below we shall discuss a variety of concepts relative to teaching in Individual Education. It is important to understand from the very beginning that we visualize teaching as a cooperative process. The teacher is not "above" the student in any sense of the word: it is a meeting between equals: those who want to learn and those who want to teach.

Methods of instruction

Every teacher has complete freedom to teach her assigned subject as she wishes. Teacher A may like to do a lot of lecturing while teacher B may prefer group discussions. Teacher C may like roleplaying and teacher D may prefer audiovisual aids. Teacher D will use a textbook while Teacher E may not use them. Teacher F may like to give daily classroom tests while teacher G may never use tests at all. Teacher H may tell a lot of jokes and be "interesting" while teacher I may be serious and solemn. Every teacher uses whatever method she prefers. And, every child has a selection of whatever teacher he prefers to go to.

Curriculum

The curriculum of an Individual Education school has three components: academic, creative, social. The academic aspect is usually established by a school board. This is their right and privilege. The creative aspect is dependent on the combined desires of children and faculty. The social aspect is the only mandatory part of Individual Education.

In terms of academics, children can learn the very same academic subjects as they do in any other school. In traditional schools children are forced to attend classes, and the impression is thereby gained that they will learn everything on the curriculum. This just is not so! We openly state that it is all right for students to refuse to learn anything on the academic curriculum if they don't want to.

Classroom environment

Every teacher has complete control of the classroom, since simply by pointing her finger, the misbehaving child must leave the room silently and immediately. (See section on Discipline). In this manner she establishes an environment she prefers. Some teachers want absolute order, while other teachers prefer spontaneity. Some students prefer the first kind of teacher, some the second kind. As a consequence, after a bit of time, students tend to gravitate to those classes run in a manner that satisfies them. Individual Education does not attempt to establish any form of classroom control. This is up to the teacher.

Ability grouping

As far as the teacher is concerned, she teaches her subject as indicated by the curriculum sheet. So, whether one child or a hundred children come into her room, her task is to teach that unit as best she can. She may deviate and give special attention to some children, but ordinarily she will not do so when the child is considerably out of line. To give a simple example, say she is teaching multiplication and a child says that he does not yet know how to add. The teacher may inform him that to learn multiplication presupposes that he understand first how to add, and that she will not teach adding at this time since this is not in her unit.

By sticking to her curriculum unit, children who already know the unit, will tend to not attend and the same will be true for children who are not prepared to learn the unit. The class will tend to have children who "belong" at this level of instruction, and so they tend to arrange themselves in ability groupings. Should a child operating in respect to math at the 2nd grade level attend a sixth grade math unit find he will not understand what is going on, and if he fails the unit tests, he will soon realize that he is attending at the wrong level. In discussions with his counselor, he will realize that he must do something to bring himself up to whatever level he would want to be at, and this will motivate him to use his ingenuity to achieve this aim. Thus, in collaboration with his counselor, he may set on a program of studying on his own, in the school and at home; he may attend tutoring classes, etc.

We don't have "ability tracks" in which the teacher's efforts are distributed to two or three "parallel" groups in the same room at the same time.

Individualized instruction

The word "individual" in the title of this chapter refers to two things: (a) that this system is based on the Individual Psychology of Alfred Adler and (b) that this system is individualized. We have discussed aspects of this before, but another aspect will be valuable. The child is in charge of his own education, and so he individualizes his program with the advice but not necessarily the consent of his counselor. So, a child might well be taking only science courses, disregarding mathematics or language arts or the social sciences. Or, he may have a balanced program. Or he may not take any academics at all. Or, he may take nothing but academics. We have seen every one of these "programs" that children will establish for themselves. We prefer to see children take charge of their education since the first goal of Individual Education is responsibility. Actually, we think that too many children, sheeplike, just go to classes routinely, establishing a pattern suggested by their counselors. It calls for courage for a child to break loose from a pre-established schedule and take charge of his own education. So, contrary to the opinions of some people who think that children in an Individual Education program will just do what they want, and run about wildly, the plain fact is that over 90% of children in our schools follow a close routine most of the time.

So, the child has the chance to individualize his own education, and sooner or later most children do set up a program that meets their needs.

Teachers' attitudes

We expect faculty members as teachers to play a somewhat different role from their role as counselors. The statement, "The teacher teaches the *subject* and the counselor counsels the *child*" can refer to the same person. Thus, Miss Miller as teacher, teaches children how to do long division; but Miss Miller as counselor, deals with Stuart Dent and his personal and academic problems. So, a teacher is a teacher and a counselor is a counselor. As a teacher Miss Miller has one major intention: to teach her unit as efficiently and as effectively as possible, to all present who want to learn. So, if Stuart, her counselee, is in her classroom and if he disturbs her or disturbs others, she simply points him out of the room. Later, in her role as counselor she may discuss her attitudes to him and listen to is attitudes to her, other students and the class.

As a teacher Miss Miller is neutral and tries not to be affected by the emotional ups and downs of her students. She concentrates on teaching, not on counseling, when she is teaching. This bothers some people, since they can't understand how a faculty member can play two such contrasting roles. Actually, it is not a difficult thing to do. Just as you operate differently when you eat at a picnic from when you eat at a formal banquet, so too you will function differently when you are standing in front of forty children who have come to your class to learn about photosynthesis (say this is the unit you are to teach) from how you will function when you are in the homeroom where there is nothing formal to teach; so too, you will function differently if Stuart acts up in the homeroom (which is OK) from how you will act if he acts up in the classroom (which is not OK). In one case you have one goal—*instructing a group*—and in the other case you have a different goal—*helping children socialize*—and since you have different goals, you operate differently.

Encouragement

In teaching, while we expect the teacher to be relatively neutral, and not get over-involved emotionally with any child, keeping in mind her primary responsibility is to the total group, she should always be ready to encourage children. "I know this is hard to catch on to, but I am sure if you try, you'll get it after a while" a teacher may say to one child, or to the entire class. "Yes, you got all the examples wrong," her comment may be to a child who failed either a classroom test or a unit test, "but if you keep at it, I am sure you will learn." Or, she may say, "Why don't you see me in my tutoring room, and we'll go over this ..." to a child who is having difficulty. As Adlerians we don't believe in praise, since we see praise as reward. Also, we don't believe in punishment. But we do believe in encouragement, which goes to those who are troubled, worried or who have failed.

Motivation

Learning is intentional not incidental. You only learn if you intend to learn. How many times have you sung the various stanzas of the Star Spangled Banner? Can you now sing it or say the words? If so, it is because you intended to learn. As a child I must have said a particular prayer ten thousand times. I am not sure I can say it now. And yet, I can recite, practically perfectly, in French, LaFontaine's poem about the ant and the grasshopper. The difference is that in one case I had no intention of learning it; while in the second case I did want to learn.

Through a variety of procedures and attitudes, such as making classrooms interesting, through educational games, or using audiovisual equipment; through proper attitudes towards children of acceptance and empathy, expressed as sympathy and understanding, attempting to encourage those who are not doing well; being ready to listen to children when they struggle with learning, being ready to meet their needs; but also taking a hard-headed attitude in terms of children's readiness, aptitudes and actual capacities, so that concern for any child will not harm the rest of the class, the teacher in Individual Education can maximize learning.

As a result of these attitudes, and this system, the evidence we have at hand is that children in two hours a day of academic instruction, and without homework, will actually learn more than children in a traditional school doing five hours daily. We not only have a happy and orderly school but an effective and efficient school.

APPLICATIONS

Curriculum (Academic)

Individual Education has nothing to say about *what* should be taught; only *how* it should be taught. Every school establishes its own curriculum, whether it is to be heavy with the three r's to the exclusion of other things or whether to concentrate on vocational subjects, or whether to be focused on the arts and sciences, etc.

This writer believes that a school should prepare a child for life through as complete a basic academic curriculum as possible, meaning basic academic skills such as communication skills (reading, writing, auditing and speaking), mathematical skills such as computation and mensuration, and cultural information skills such as knowledge of art, science, music, history, biology, politics, psychology, etc. The usual curriculum found in most academic schools from pre-schools through high schools seems reasonable enough. But to repeat—Individual Education is not concerned with *content* but rather with *process*—not what one learns but rather how one learns.

Units

We do not like the usual method of teaching academics. The general process, as far as we are concerned, is illogical. In the typical school a child is placed in a classroom on the basis of his age which in the case of a transfer student usually means the number of years he has attended classes. Then, all students in that class are exposed to the same instruction, given the same homework, and then later given the same tests and then graded in terms of a combination of test evaluation and teacher's impression of the child's efforts, deportment, etc.

In Individual Education we break the academic curriculum into bite-size pieces, usually week-long units, and each unit is later objectively evaluated. Thus we have the following situation.

Curriculum Unit and name
Math 15   Addition of two digits whose sum does not exceed 9   (e.g. $-4+3$)
Math 16   Addition of two digits whose sum exceeds 9   (e.g.—$5+8$)
Math 17   Addition of one digit plus a two-place digit   (e.g.—$13+9$)
Math 18   Addition of two two-place digits   (e.g.—$27+34$)

Consequently, a student is exposed to math unit 15, and later takes unit test M-15; and then goes on to math unit 16, and takes test M-16, and so on, so that the child progresses unit-by-unit, knowing at all times just where he is. (See Fig 2, page 218.)

A child can go whereever he wants in an Individual Education school. Let us say that a student takes Math test 15 and fails it. He can then go on to 16. And if he fails that he can still go on to 17, etc. However, he gets feedback on his lack of progress and so does his counselor, so that he always knows what and how he is doing.

Curriculum guides

Available to every child, every faculty member and every parent is a set of curriculum guides (see Figure 3). These guides are usually kept in loose-leaf books, and inform everyone just what is the content of the particular unit, so that if Ms. Supernant is to take over Mrs. Muirhead's class at the beginning of the week, all she has to know is that she is to teach Math unit 37 and so will be prepared.

Children can use these guides as a textbook! Or they can study on their own, using the material in these guides and in reference books listed in the guides as indicators of what to study.

In a real sense, in Individual Education, students make up their own curriculum, decide what to study, when to study and where to study. The school provides the child with the "materials"—that is to say the teacher, the books, the classrooms, the counselor, the units, the unit tests, etc., which the child can use. If the child rejects everything, this is his privilege. If he accepts everything, this too, is his privilege. But we provide the child with everything—counseling, teaching, materials for him to learn what he wants to learn.

To summarize our teaching process goes as follows:

FIGURE 3
Sample Curriculum Guide

Science 14—Insects (Part A)

Objective: To gain an understanding about insects: what they have in common, how they differ from other forms of life, in what ways they are valuable and in what ways they are dangerous to humans.

Specific goals may be:
1. To be able to name social insects, such as bees, etc.
2. To name insects that eat other insects.
3. To show the value that some insects have for humans.
4. To show some harmful insects.
5. To explain methods of insect control.

Process: Lectures, board illustrations, samples of live and mounted insects, possibly films. Children may be asked to collect insects: cockroaches, ants, etc. A fine way to study live insects is to make an ant farm.

Example Name three social insects?
How do insects help pollinate plants?

References: *Concepts in science,* Harcourt, Brace & Jovanovich, pp. 242-243 and 256-257.
Science–far and near, Heath, pp. 125-128.
Wild flowers, Ferguson, pp. 47-49.

1. We test the child to see exactly where he is on each subject taught.
2. The counselor informs him of the facts relative to grade levels.
3. The counselor then advises him where to go academically in terms of equivalent units.
4. Where the child actually goes is up to him.
5. He is tested, objectively, for every unit.
6. If he passes or fails is made known to the counselor, who so records this on the child's progress chart.
7. Information, week-by-week, is given to the child, who may adjust his academic program.
8. Periodically, once a month, the child and his counselor review the child's progress, and the counselor will advise him.
9. The child makes up his own mind what to do about his own education, and may continue, drop down, go faster, go slower, drop out, etc.

Curriculum, (Non-academic)

An Individual Education school's "curriculum" can be divided into three parts: (a) academics, (b) creative subjects, and (c) socialization activities. The faculty, overall, spends generally approximately an equal amount of time over the semester in these three areas, and children usually also spend an equal amount of time, about two hours daily in doing academic work, creative work, and socialization activities. In this section we shall discuss what we call "creative" activities. We have already taken up the academic curriculum and we shall discuss the socialization program under counseling.

The creative program

Above we put the word *curriculum* in quotes relative to the creative program, because unlike the academic program where everything is preplanned in terms of units with unit tests, and the like, the creative program is really quite different, as will soon be seen. The motto of this program, to parents, to teachers, and to students is: "We will allow you to teach or learn whatever you want—and we will help you." So, let us say a teacher would like to learn how to bake cookies. The school would permit her to teach/learn this as part of the creative program. Say that a group of boys would like to learn to play the Indian game of lacrosse. The school would attempt to help them to get the equipment and instruction. Say that a child would like to learn how to speak Romanian, the school would attempt to help him learn this language.

Mechanics of the program

Essentially, all concerned parents, children, teachers will get a notice which might go as follows:

CREATIVE PROGRAM

The F. E. Peacock Intermediate School of Itasca, Illinois is pleased to announce that we intend to establish a creative program. We wish to ask every one: parents, teachers, children to write to us, letting us know what you would like to teach, what you would like to learn and what you would like to teach/learn. Thus, a child might like to learn how to do handstands, a teacher might like to learn how to paint and a parent might like to teach table tennis.

So, please do the following: using 3×5 cards, available from the office, write down your name and the name of your counselor if you are a student, or your name and telephone number if you are a parent, and on the card write the word LEARN and put under that word what you would like to learn and then if you wish to teach something write the word TEACH on the other side of the card and under that write what you would like to teach. We suggest that all teachers include tutoring as part of their creative teaching.

We shall attempt to satisfy as many people as possible. So, if you are interested in teaching or learning sports, such as fencing and archery; in music, such as playing an instrument or appreciating opera; in art, such as cartooning or sculpting; in handicrafts, such as making paper maché masks or weaving; in academics, such as history of Europe or advanced mathematics; in science, such as astronomy or chemistry; in foreign languages, such as the ability to read Latin or speak Greek; whatever you would like to learn to teach or to learn or to teach/learn, please let us know.

Now, if such a notice were to be sent out, a committee would attempt to find teachers for those subjects of greatest interest, and keeping in mind availability of space, would establish a number of "courses" which might run for a specific period, such as six weeks, or which might be of the "open ended" type.

An alternate way to handle a creative program might be to ask teachers what they would like to teach, and then to put up sign-up sheets for children to write down their names, indicating that they will register. An announcement might look as follows:

Magic Tricks

My hobby is magic, especially tricks with cards. Some very easy card tricks are very hard to figure out. Some call for hand dexterity. I will be happy to teach all interested a dozen of my best tricks. This can be an interesting hobby for you, and you can always entertain others. Come to room 302 Monday, October 28 or Wednesday October 30 at 10:15 am and I will give a demonstration of some of my easy and some of my difficult tricks. I can only register 15 students, and this course will be on Mondays and Wednesdays for six weeks, from November 4 to December 11. You can sign up at my demonstrations. Material costs will be two dollars per student.

Henri Niedzielski, French instructor.

Tutoring

We expect every teacher to schedule herself for at least one period weekly as a tutor in her own major subject. Depending on student need, teachers will be able to contract or expand their tutoring time. Thus, perhaps Miss Lester will have two periods of tutoring in social studies while Miss Condrey will have eight periods weekly in mathematics. Through conferences faculty members will have opportunities to learn about variable needs of students in this respect.

Areas of instruction

While we do want to leave the "nomination" and the selection of creative courses to the student and faculty, we see it as perfectly proper for the "administration" (meaning by this the school board, PTA, principal, superintendent of schools, etc.) to attempt to insert items in the creative program, whether it be vocational subjects, such as typing; or whether it be Boy Scouting or history of the United States; or public speaking or whatever may be in the minds of those who have administrative authority. However, the general policy of letting children and faculty have freedom of choice always holds. While this may be a problem in some schools, such as parochial schools where religious training is considered mandatory, nevertheless, we believe that freedom is called for, and that any highly desired course can be made interesting so that students will take it willingly. In one Catholic school, eight teachers taught religion simultaneously. Nothing else was available to students at that period, except the library or the study hall. After several weeks, five of the teachers gave up, since attendance was very low in their classes, while the other three persisted since they had good attendance.

Gazda (1977) suggests that all schools teach life coping skills such as health maintenance and family relations. We would consider these subjects most valuable and would suggest that they be added to the creative curriculum, and efforts made to get children to participate in such skills.

Naturally, the creative program affects the academic program. Thus, a child who takes a course in cooking finds that reading a cook book is necessary and that a knowledge of mathematics is important in cooking. The young mechanic soon finds that a knowledge of physics and chemistry is important. The child who would be an athlete will learn the importance of hygiene and proper diet, and so on.

Student Evaluation

Individual Education is at the same time humanistic, having a concern for the individual's growth and development in all areas, and scientific, searching for truth, efficiency and effectiveness. We strongly believe in the importance of proper evaluation and in proper communication of evaluation. We do not believe in competition between students, nor in public awards to children who are outstanding. We want every child to develop his unique abilities. So, if Tony will eventually become a success-ful plumber, if Harold will become a good hair dresser, if Peter will become a salesman and if Thomas will eventually become a professor, each has the right to develop as best he can—and proper evaluation is called for. In Individual Education we define 5 kinds of tests.

Classroom tests

These are made-on-the-spot tests during classroom instruction. Say that a teacher is trying to explain how to do square roots. She may first decide to see whether her students can square a number, and so she may direct all students to square the number 11. They go to work and she goes up and down the aisles to see whether they all know how to do this. She may help some children who are having problems. If some just don't know what to do, she may inform them that unit 115 takes up to problem of squaring and that they should study that unit, etc.

Unit tests

These tests given generally on Friday afternoons represent a measure of whether students have learned particular units taught that week. Thus, this Friday Math units 37–54–68–77–98–113—and 117 might be given. Any child may take any unit. These tests are not proctored. They are only for information for each child and for the counselor, to show how the child is progressing.

Review tests

Some tests that end in a 0 are review tests, means, For example, unit test 40, will contain elements of unit tests 31 to 39. While unit tests are short (generally taking about 5 minutes) review tests are longer and will last up to a half hour.

Practical tests

A third kind of test may be called a practical test, and may be inserted in the Progress Chart anywhere, but most likely will be in " 0 " series above. Here are some examples of practical tests:

Language Arts 170:

"Go to the library and find reference material to write a 100 word essay on each of these subjects:

—The Haymarket riot

—The black hole of Calcutta
—Rudolf Dreikurs

Language Arts 190:

Fill in this employment application for a clerk.

Math 165:

In this envelope you will find Income Tax form 1040 and a sheet of information about John Doe's income and expenses. Figure out his income tax.

Standard scholastic achievement tests

These commercially prepared standardized tests are among the very best tests that psychometricians have developed. They can do several things: (a) give the counselor a general picture of the overall academic level of any child, such as 6.3 overall academically; (b) a more detailed picture of the child's pattern of abilities, such as

Reading	7.3
Grammar	6.4
Spelling	5.9
Arithmetic	2.4
History	6.8
Science	7.1

The above pattern informs the counselor that the child is seriously deficient in mathematics.

And (c) these tests can sometimes be diagnostic. Thus, through checking the teacher/counselor may come up with such information.

Difficulties for Stuart Dent
Can not multiply with a zero in the middle of the multiplicand (Unit—M 37)
Can not carry over nines (Unit—M 22)
Can not subtract when nines are in the subtrahend (Unit—M 24)

We can see then that the counselor can pin point which units the child will need to be able to move forward academically in arithmetic.

Reporting

Every child is normally expected to pass one unit weekly in each subject area. Information, *pass* or *fail,* is sent by the examiner to the counselor, who then transfers this information to her copy of the child's progress chart, and she later informs the child of results. In this way the child learns weekly about his progress. If he has taken many tests (theoretically he can take all the tests in the whole academic curriculum in one week!) he learns how many he has passed. Reports are made only to the child—not to the parent. The child informs the parent, not the "school".

Student variability

Students vary considerably in terms of academic abilities. This variation probably depends on a complex of interrelating factors such as genetic potentiality (intelligence), family attitudes, community attitudes, early life experiences, illnesses, emotional status, etc. In any case, it is not unknown for children of apparent normal intelligence to come out of schools practically illiterate, unable to compute, not knowledgeable about science or social science. Such children skillfully and successfully resist all attempts to make them learn.

In Individual Education because of heavy concentration on tests, the learning situation for any child becomes clear very soon to all concerned. Counselors are alerted rather quickly, something that just does not seem to happen in traditional education with its illogical evaluation and teaching system. Counselors can now call the faculty consultant who in turn now can call in specialists in reading, social workers, psychologists, physicians, etc., as needed. As far as academics go, we in Individual Education are able to monitor closely every child. We pick up the bright, the average and the below average, the low and the high achievers.

However, our school situation is such that practically every child is motivated to develop academically. No child is lost. No child is permitted to wander about intellectually. Every child is watched over carefully by his counselor. And every deviating child is counseled, and if a serious problem, the counselor consults with the school faculty consultant who in turn has a variety of professionals to whom she can turn to for special help.

Counseling

Perhaps the most unique as well as the most important feature of Individual Education is its counseling program. Every faculty member[1] serves three functions, each taking about the same amount of time weekly: (a) she is an academic teacher, (b) she is a creative teacher, and (c) she is a counselor. In addition, in every school, there is a faculty consultant, a full time or part-time adviser to counselors. The "counseling" function works as follows: the faculty consultant counsels with teachers; the faculty as teacher/counselors counsel with students. We shall discuss the functions of the teacher/counselor first, then the consultant, who is more-or-less equivalent to present-day school counselors.

Teacher-counselor

As a counselor, every faculty member serves five functions: (a) homeroom participant, (b) one-to-one academic counselor, (c) small group facilitator, (d) disciplinary problem advocate, and (e)liaison with parents. We shall examine these five functions in detail. But first an explanation of how a child gets a teacher/counselor, his school parent.

Selection process

In an Individual Education school every child has the right to petition any faculty member to be his counselor. The faculty member, in turn, has the right to accept or reject this invitation. Once the child is accepted, how-ever, only the child can make further counselor changes, not the faculty member! Should the child want to change counselors, he simply petitions any other faculty member, who has the right to accept or reject his propos-al; if she accepts him as a counselee and wants to be his school parent, she simply obtains any materials on the student from his prior counselor.

Children coming into the school for the first time who do not know any of the faculty may be assigned to a homeroom, but as soon as they wish to make changes, they can petition any other faculty member. The control of the number of students in the homeroom is up to the faculty member. Say you are on the faculty of a school and say that the teacher student ratio is one to 25. Say that you have 18 students in your homeroom, and therefore you are seven below the average expectation. If a child were to ask to come to your homeroom and be your counselee, you might be likely to say "Yes", but if you had 32 students, your answer would probably be "No."

So the child proposes, and the faculty member disposes.

The relationship between the child and his chosen counselor is the single most important part of Individual Education. He can keep this same counselor as long as he wants. So, in an elementary school he might have the same counselor from age 6 to 14. Indeed, this counselor becomes his school parent; and generally the counselor gets to know and to love this child who she will see growing from practically an infant to practically a man. Let us now examine in some detail the five functions mentioned above.

Homeroom

This first period of the day is a full 40 minutes in length, and now the faculty member is an equal among equals. She can *not* keep order; she can *not* send a child out of the room; she is made deliberately helpless. She can only intervene in the case of violation of Rule 1 (Danger and Damage). Otherwise, she has no especial status in the classroom except that she happens to be an adult. She can not reprimand, warn, threaten or other-wise use any force. She can't get rid of any child who has selected her. She is put on a plane of equality—and she must operate in terms of her wits, her social skills, her friendliness, her love and other personal qualities.

About the only thing she is asked to try to do is to establish a democratic class council. This should never be done by fiat: "I am going to start a council" or "I am asked by the principal to start a class council" but rather should be done indirectly, subtly, such as: "We have so much disorder here, do you think that maybe we should start a class council?" Or, "Why don't we have a democratic meeting to settle this issue of which park we will visit next week?"

In the homeroom, considerable "misbehavior" must be tolerated by the teacher/counselor including loud noises, disrespectful behavior, scuffling, curses, bickering, etc. The reason for this is not "to allow children to blow off steam" but rather to permit the group to establish its own standards, which inevitably will happen. Bullies, braggarts, noisy children, etc., will eventually run afoul of the majority of the group who will begin to stand for "law and order"—and the wise teacher/counselor will allow bad homeroom situations to get worse so that they can get better from within. For a teacher who has been used to rigid disciplining of children through threats, the homeroom can be at at first a traumatic experience.

The counselor may suggest games, such as blind man's buff, twenty questions, pin the tail on the donkey, spelling bees; or may try to organize the group to establish some sort of class project, such as planning for some entertainment for the Christmas season, etc.

In the homeroom all kinds of activities can be done, including days when the counselor will do absolutely nothing, just read a book while the counselees play among themselves, form little groups, etc. In short, the homeroom is a kind of laboratory of human relations, in which the counselor as a human person participated with equals who happen to be younger than herself.

No child is pressured to do anything. So a child may come to the homeroom sit in a corner and read the whole period. It is his prerogative never to participate in any activity.

The counselor has an unparalleled opportunity to see children in interaction in a permissive situation during the homeroom period. At the bell, the homeroom breaks up and every child now goes wherever he wishes, and the adult now becomes a teacher when the next bell sounds—and lo— relationships are completely different! She is now in full charge of the room, and any child who misbehaves is pointed out of the room. As a counselor, the adult person is permissive but as a teacher she is restrictive. As a counselor she is at the mercy of the kids, she is relatively helpless; but as a teacher she is in charge of her classroom and no one can remain who doesn't behave properly!

Academic counseling

At least once a month every counselor schedules a private interview with every child using the child's Progress Chart to give her information how he is doing academically. She takes the attitude of helpfulness, but not authority. She advises, but does not demand. The child has the full responsibility of his own education. She gives her opinions, her suggestions, but what the child does is up to him. Should she want to discuss personal matters, such as his behavior in the homeroom, she can do so. She may ask the child to change homerooms, but he only does so if he wants to. Only he can divorce her! He doesn't have to follow her advice about anything. We have found that over time, relationships become strong, and most children will listen and will follow their counselor's advice.

Small groups

Practically the only feature of Individual Education that was not originally planned for and which developed out of necessity, was the use of small groups. The way this happened is as follows: Eli, a ten year old boy, always was chased and beaten by other kids. His mother came to the school and complained bitterly, arguing that we were not protecting her child. Upon questioning, she admitted that the same pattern had occurred at the child's prior school, and the conclusion reached was that Eli was a "victim"—one who provoked others to attack him. To punish these "tormenters" would do little good—which is what the mother demanded. More important it was to find out what Eli did to provoke others and how his pattern could be solved.

Six of his major "enemies" were formed into a group to have a discussion about the problem. Each of the aggressor kids spoke up against Eli, and pointed out the things that Eli did to "bother" them. After an hour session, it was suggested that they meet again, this time with Eli present. There was an agreement to do so. At the next meeting, Eli was attacked by the others—this time verbally—and Eli defended himself. We decided to have a third meeting. The result of this *ad hoc* group was highly favorable. Eli stopped being a pest and became one of the "gang". Since there was a certain amount of tension and difficulties at the school with a number of other problem children, the faculty decided to try having small groups for discussion purposes.

They worked out very well, and such discussion groups have become an integral part of Individual Education. Essentially, they are started by x fiat. The principal asks all students and all faculty for all students in each home room to self-select themselves into groups ranging from as few as four to as many as eight, so that the faculty member can meet with each group for one period once weekly.

These groups are for personal discussions. The analog is group therapy. The faculty member plays a supportive, permissive, empathetic role, perhaps interpreting behavior, giving advice, and perhaps even discussing her own problems and difficulties. We can give little advice about handling these groups. We know that they are one of the most important parts of the program: and they generate strong loyalties. What we have done is to take potential gangs and socialize them through developing group solidarity in a group in which a responsible adult is a member.

Advocacy

Should a child be in serious trouble (see next section on discipline), the counselor acts as the child's lawyer. She now plays a kind of double role: she is, after all, a loyal member of the faculty, but she is also that child's school parent. A child in serious trouble now has a friend when he is in court. As his school parent, she may take some criticism from the principal etc., because her "school child" has not adjusted well.

Liaison

The counselor is the one person in the school who gets to know the child best. She is his counselor, sees him daily in the homeroom, interviews him monthly about his school academic progress as well as other aspects, sees him weekly in a group, discusses him with other teachers informally and in faculty meetings, deals with the school consultant about him when necessary, and so is highly knowledgeable about him, while he may be only a face to the various academic teachers who see him only in a class-room situation.

If a parent wants to get information about the child or if the counselor would want to meet the child's parents, both of them operate through the child. The counselor and the parents can not meet unless the child is present and willing to have this conference. Faculty members are not permitted to discuss children with parents, except at the direct request and in the presence of their own superiors, who in turn should protect the counselor-child relationship.

It sometimes happens that a child does not want his parents and the counselor to meet. In such cases, the consultant or the principal (not the counselor!) can meet with the parents to give them advice how to change the child's attitude. Parents can get some information—which is some-times their legal right—about their children, but such information should be given only after explanations why it is important to try to change the child's attitudes to the parents. This is often a very ticklish task. Say the parents are very anxious to know how their child is doing. The child gets a weekly Progress Chart which he does not show them. He tells them practically nothing. They don't know what he is doing all day. They may be afraid he is wasting his time in school. But if their relationship is such that he will not inform them, the problem is not solved by giving them information, but rather it is solved by changing his attitudes towards them, which is what the counselor can do, by employing Adlerian counseling such as suggested by Dreikurs (1964) or Corsini & Painter (1973) or Rogers (Rogers, 1942) or other counseling procedures.

But ordinarily, the three parties: parents, the child and the counselor meet in amity and have fruitful discussions.

Discipline

If there is one thing that impresses visitors to Individual Education schools it is the orderliness of the schools, the pleasant, friendly ambience, the spirit of discipline. How do we achieve this remarkable degree of discipline? The answer does not lie in the faculty being better educated, or more tolerant, etc. The answer lies in the system of Individual Education as a whole: its admission process, its freedom in the homeroom and control in the classroom, the children's ability to move around as they wish; the few rules rigidly enforced; the fact that the school is solid in terms of philosophy, theory and practice. However, according to John Milton's poem *Paradise Lost,* even in Heaven, the angels didn't act like angels, and they revolted, so too we can expect that some children will, especially at first coming to an Individual Education school, become disciplinary problems. To meet these contingencies, we have a three-partite system of discipline: (a) information, (b) rules, (c) consequences.

Information

During the admission process, the rules of the school (three in number) had been explained to the child, and the child was accepted only if he gave positive evidence that he (a) understood the three rules and (b) that he thought them to be valid and logical. Also, the parents were informed of the rules. At that time, depending on circumstances, children and parents might be informed of the consequences of rule-violations. Usually we don't stress these consequences, since we don't want to be too negative, or make the school sound like a prison. Within a few days children learn from other children what are the consequences of breaking rules will be.

Rules

In an Individual Education School we have three rules.

1. Do nothing that *could* be dangerous or damaging to yourself, others or property.
2. While in school always be under supervision.
3. Leave the classroom immediately and in silence if a teacher points to you and then to the door. (Go Signal)

While an Individual Education school might set up other rules in addition to the basic three, we would discourage this, finding that these three are sufficient. The success of the school depends on every single faculty member undeviatingly reporting any violation by any child of any of these rules. We learned from sad experience that if even one teacher refuses to enforce these rules, the whole school is negatively affected. This came about when an emergency-hired teacher refused to use the pointing method (Go signal) and shouted at children. The whole school was in an uproar. When this teacher was told she should use only the GO signal and no longer her voice, she resigned. Another teacher took over, and the school settled down within a few days.

Consequences

Let us imagine a disturbed child, undisciplined, negative, hostile, a real problem child who when asked if he wanted to enter this school said "yes". When the rules and consequences were explained to him he said he understood them and accepted them. He gave all the right answers, and was accepted, but immediately and persistently began to break rules. Let us follow what happens.

Violation 1. Walked off the campus. Sent to the office. Disciplinarian asked him if he did walk off the campus. Child trys to explain why. Disciplinarian not interested in knowing why. Only interested to know whether it is true that he was off campus. If child says "Yes" then note is put on card that as of this date he violated rule 2. Only *then* will disciplinarian listen to *why*. There is NEVER an excuse for violating any of the three rules. Should child deny the violation, disciplinarian will meet with teacher in presence of child and make her own determination of guilt. The only consequence of violation of a rule the first time is a disciplinary note on the child's record.

Violation 2. Child threw book (rule 1) at another student. Child admits doing this. Note made. Then—if the child wishes—he can explain his reasons. But an explanation is NEVER an excuse.

Violation 3. Teacher pointed him out of the room, but he said: "I didn't do anything" as he walked out. Teacher reported him. Again, the sole issue is fact. Did he indeed talk after being pointed out? Only after making the notation will the explanation be heard, *but an explanation is never an excuse.*

Consequence

After three violations a conference is set up with the child's counselor and the principal (or the principal's agent, such as the vice principal, the disciplinarian, etc.).The purpose of this conference is to try to discover, if possible, reasons for the child's violation of the rules three times. The disciplinarian may direct herself more to the child's counselor, with questions such as: "What do you think you can do to help Mike get along better in this school?" or to Mike: "Is there anything we can do about the school to make it better for you?" and usually, the problem is put on to the counselor: "Do you think that having some personal discussions with Mike and his parents might help? Would you like that, Mike?"

So, this meeting following a third violation is a friendly helpful meeting.

4. *Violation 4.* Same as for violation 1.

5. *Violation 5.* Same as violation 1.

6. *Violation 6.* Now, the parents are called in for a conference, preceded by the child and the parents listening to a long dull tape-recorded explanation of the whole disciplinary process, including discussion and explanation of the suspension and expulsion aspects (to be taken up soon.) After the child and the parents have listened to this tape, they meet with the principal and the counselor. At this time, there is a discussion of what will happen if there should be a ninth violation—*the suspension process.*

The suspension process is the following. Should a child violate rules a ninth time, he is sent to and must remain in the office, in silence, until one or both of his parents or guardians come for him. In ABSOLUTE SILENCE they are to take him home. He is to go to his room and remain incommunicado, without using a telephone, listening to a radio, watching TV. He is to have his meals in his room. No friends or siblings may talk to him until the next morning. The purpose of this suspension procedure is to permit the child to contemplate the reasons for his suspension and to decide whether he wants to return to this school.

The suspension procedure must be accepted as logical by the parents and also by the child. The parents agree to pick up the child if there is a ninth, tenth and an eleventh violation, take him home in absolute silence, lead him to his room, keep others away from him, and if he should violate the suspension procedure they are to report it to the school. The child is to agree to wait in the office in silence until his parents come for him, and to remain in his room at home without talking with anyone.

The purpose of the suspension procedure is explained in detail to help the child decide what he wants to do with his life, and not as punishment. If the child or the parents do not accept this procedure, the child is transferred to another school. After a suspension, the child returns to school the next day.

Violation 7. Same as for violation 1.

Violation 8. Same as for violation 1.

Violation 9. Suspension procedure put into effect. He is sent to the office and told to remain there in silence. Parent called to come get him. Should he talk with anyone, or refuse to remain in silence in the office, immediate expulsion and transfer occur.

When it comes to discipline, we just don't fool around. We have a permissive system when it comes to learning; we are inflexible when it comes to discipline. Our schools are exceptional places to learn and to live. We want to keep the atmosphere friendly and conducive to learning. Any child who can not or will not adjust to our simple rules just must suffer the agreed-upon consequences.

Violation 10. As for violation 9, suspension.

Violation 11. As for violation 9, suspension.

Violation 12. Special meeting called for. Parents not present, but child is present throughout. Child's counselor present as his advocate. Issue is whether to expel child. Child can speak up. Principal alone makes decision. Should there be a thirteenth violation, principal alone makes decision. Every case of expulsion is judged by the principal upon its own merits.

It is important to remember in any case of expulsion, that it is the child who calls for expulsion, not the faculty! Also, expulsion may be the best thing for any child. It will give him a taste of reality, may lead him to a different kind of school in which he may adjust better, etc.

An expelled child may re-apply for admission. Alone, not with parents, he can be interviewed by a committee established by the principal. If accepted, he is not have same counselor. Concensus of committee is called for. Former counselor not to be on this committee. If his application to return is rejected, he can still re-apply at a later date.

Individual Education has some apparent contradictions: full freedom of the mind (study or not study); limited freedom of behavior (go from room to room if you wish); but absolute limitation of violations of rules of behavior.

We find that children and faculty adapt to these rules readily. We balance our considerable freedom of what is to go into the mind with the limited freedom of action that we permit children in terms of movement and the uncompromisingly rigid system of rules and consequences. Our system of discipline, simple as it is, held to firmly, contributes considerably to the happy and relaxed ambience of the school, since every student knows exactly what he can do and what he can not do, and is never in any anxiety that maybe he is doing the wrong thing.

Our system of discipline works very well because it is based on logic and reason, and every child and every faculty member knows completely the rules and the consequences. Moreover, every child and every parent has had an opportunity to agree or disagree with the rules; and the child is accepted only if and when the family accepts the rules as logical and reasonable.

To end this section, we differ completely from those schools that operate as part-time prisons (you have to go to this school!) or as part-time insane asylums (you have to keep this child in your class). We see early life education as a voluntary association of equals, who operate together in an atmosphere of mutual regard and respect on the basis of agreements freely and openly arrived at, with logical consequences upon violation of the rules. Children who are desperately unhappy to the extent that there are delinquents or crazy just do not belong in schools. They should be treated for their psychopathy outside of the school, and admitted to schools only when they are ready to do what schools are for—to learn!

ROLES

Administration

By "Administration" we refer to the support aspect of the school, running from the principal through the clerks. Administration deals with three classes of individuals: (a) faculty, (b) parents and (c) school board/superintendent, etc., primarily; also, of course at times with the public, visitors, vendors, salesmen, etc., but herein we shall concern ourselves only with the three primary groups.

Faculty

Essentially, administration serves to support faculty—not the other way around. The principal should see herself in the same way that a hospital administrator sees himself: he is to serve the doctors, and the principal is to serve her teachers. She should have three primary tasks: selection of her personnel, training them and supervising them. This means she herself must know the philosophy and theory of Individual Education thoroughly, and should understand that part of the purpose of our schools is the enhancement and growth of the faculty, through their having full academic freedom. This does not mean that the principal will support the faculty at all times. This is especially true in her judical function having to do with complaints of faculty against the students. For example, one teacher in one of our schools reported a child for violation of rule 1 (Danger and Damage) by claiming the child was chewing gum in classes. The principal ruled against the teacher, telling her she could send the child out by means of the GO signal but that she could not cite the child for a rule violation since gum-chewing was neither dangerous nor damaging.

The principal is a supervisor, not a snoopervisor. However, she should keep records of class and homeroom attendance. Popularity of a teacher should be the main evidence of a teacher's effectiveness. So, if the average number of students in teachers' homerooms is 25, and Miss Finnigan has only 12, this tells us something—students don't like her. If Ms. Jones' arithmetic classes average 35 and Ms. Gedan's only 20, this too tells us something. Such unpopular teachers may need counseling or instruction. One way to help lowranking teachers is to suggest that they sit in classes of more popular teachers. However, the initiative and responsibility for training is up to the faculty member. The principal is a helper.

Parents

The principal serves a valuable role vis-a-vis parents. Frequently, parents dissatisfied with lack of information about their children or frustrated by the fact that their children will not permit parent- child-counselor conferences, will come to the principal for information. The principal may be obligated by law to give this information. If so, we recommend a showdown: first, inform the parent why they should not have this information; but if the parent(s) insist, then call in the child and the counselor for a discussion on the matter to see if the counselor and the child will agree to allow the parent the information and then give this information in the presence of both child and counselor. This can be done in such a manner to support all: the child who wants privacy; the counselor who wants to protect the child; the parent who honestly feels she needs this information and is entitled to it legally. The administrator is in the middle then between child, counselor and parent, and so in trying to satisfy all contending parties has a difficult situation.

For this reason, the principal, and not the consultant or anyone else should be in charge of parent training, although the consultant may be the most logical person to conduct such training. The more informed parents are about how Individual Education works and the more they trust their principal, the less likely it is that there will be difficulties. Consequently, the alert principal will make certain all parents get training so that every parent will understand the philosophy, theory and procedures of the school.

Children

The administrator of the school generally has few direct contacts with children except under disciplinary situations. As such, in general keeping with the philosophy of Individual Education, she is concerned primarily with saving the school, and making certain that any very difficult child is (a) removed from the school and (b) given appropriate referrals through the consultant for proper treatment. She has the final authority whether to re-accept any expelled child. The old concept that a child must stay in the school in his district is out in Individual Education. The welfare of the faculty and other children must be weighed against the interests of any single family or child.

Faculty

The faculty member in an Individual Education school plays a number of roles. In the homeroom she is an older equal among equals, and must survive there in terms of her wit and her social skills; as a counselor, she should be well versed in the realities of life in terms of academics and occupation; as a small group counselor she should be a practical psychologist; as a creative teacher, she should be an enthusiast about whatever she will be instructing; and as a classroom teacher she should have competence in her field and be able to intrigue and motivate children.

She is always under pressure, in a sense, in view of the fact that children have the option to avoid her. She no longer can count on some anonymous clerk assigning children to her. She must be alert and must convey to children she has something to offer them. Teaching is no longer a matter of simply conveying information, in the same sense that a record player does.

In short, in Individual Education, teaching is a lively occupation, with a lot of different things going on all the time. The teacher's day is spent in four activities, usually about equally divided in terms of time: (a) she is an academic teacher, and may face from one to perhaps one hundred children in her classes; (b) she is a creative teacher and may in the same week teach knitting and diving; (c) she is a counselor and will be dealing with a variety of problems of children in a one-to-one situation, in small groups and in the homeroom room, and will also possibly meet with the principal and parents for disciplinary conferences. Also, in her functioning as a member of the faculty she will be on various curriculum committees, will make up tests, and will spend time in faculty meetings. She may be on the school council and there represent the faculty point of view in a group consisting of parents and children as well as other teachers.

Possibly the best part of teaching in an Individual Education school is the fact that every single child in her room is there voluntarily, since every child can be somewhere else. But the best part of being a faculty member, for most teachers, is the free relationships with those children who are her counselees who she sees daily in her homeroom, weekly in her small groups and once a month in private academic interviews. Over the years, these children will become part of her "school family" and she is likely to keep in touch with them years after they have left the school. And, we should not neglect the very important part that the creative education program plays in the life of a teacher: she can spend about two hours a day teaching something that really interests her, some skill or hobby or subject that she finds of interest. Indeed, in contrast to the more-or-less deadening routine of most schools with the relatively little freedom given to teachers, personnel who work in an Individual Education school find their day most pleasant and exciting, but not exhausting.

Students

The basic purpose of an Individual Education school is to make children more responsible, more respectful, more resourceful and more responsive. The child will find that right from the beginning, he is treated with deference. "Do you want to come to this school?" the principal asks and only if the child says "Yes" is he accepted but only if he gives evidence that he understands the school's rules and if he agrees that the rules are sensible. He may be put into the hands of one of the faculty who becomes his teacher/counselor, but he can change counselors. He can associate freely with his friends, getting into the same homeroom with them. He can move about the school freely, going to whatever classes he wishes, and avoiding those that he does not want to attend. His counselor is his friend and meets with him periodically to review his scholastic progress. He can ask for practically any subject he would like to learn, and will be given consideration and assistance in learning. He can go as fast as he wishes academically. Or, he can take his time.

In this school he is never criticized, never compared, never made to feel superior or inferior by the faculty. On the other hand, he finds that if he is in violation of any of the school's three simple rules, that the consequences are unvarying and inevitable.

He can more or less do whatever he wants but he can not violate the rights of others. Should he want to stay in the library all day and look at the ceiling, no one will bother him. Should he want to be in the study hall and talk with his friends, this is fine and dandy with all concerned. Does he want to read, good! Does he want to listen to music, fine! So long as what he does is not destructive or annoying, no one will stop him from what he wants to do, but he must go to the homeroom, he must attend small group meetings, and he must see his counselor individually.

The child's day rotates about the counseling program in a sense. In the homeroom, he can express his opinions about the school and about the homeroom. He can be elected through the class counsel to membership in the School Council, where his opinion is listened to by others, and so he has a voice in the school as a whole. There, in the homeroom, he can complain about other students, or can help plan for picnics, visits to various sites of interest, or he can socialize—just as he wishes. In the small group, he can get to learn about others in depth, and get to know his counselor as a person. In one-to-one conferences, he will be given advice by his counselor.

If there are difficulties academically, his counselor will call in the school faculty consultant, who may meet with the counselor and the child. If necessary, with everyone's agreement, the consultant may take over the child for some specialized counseling, or may make arrangements for intelligence testing, physiological evaluations, hearing and vision tests, etc.

Perhaps most important to the typical child is the creative program. Say that the child has interests in muscle building. He asks for this—and lo, something is done about it. Or he may want to become an astronaut, and lo—a program is developed in this area. In contrast to his cousin whose school program is strictly academics, he can have any variety he wishes.

In an environment of this type, the child is likely to find that he likes the school, his teachers and his fellow students. Morever, he will find that his parents, who have taken a parenting course through the school, are much easier to deal with than the parents of children who go to other schools.

In short, the child is in an environment conducive for self-expression and learning. He is encouraged to go as fast as he wants in any direction he wishes. His counselor closely monitors his personal, social and academic progress and becomes in effect his "school parent" watching over him closely, and she intercedes or coordinates with him relationships with the principal and/or parents relative to behavior and growth. On the other hand, there is a simple but very rigid set of rules with very clean and clear-cut consequences unvaryingly applied. If any child desires to test these rules and consequences, he can do so by doing dangerous or damaging things; by going out of bounds; or by refusing to obey the only orders that faculty members are empowered to give—the GO signal.

Our findings are that many children who were rebellious in other schools, refused to do homework, were school phobic, etc., find that there is no need to rebel in an Individual Education school. The story of Amy is an example.

Amy

A ten-year old girl, Amy had already been expelled from two other schools, when the mother inquired what could be done with this "impossible" child. The recommendation was to send her to an Individual Education school. Mother went to the school with Amy.

First visit. After the principal explained the system to mother and child, both showed interest, but when the three rules were explained, Amy stated that rule 3—the GO signal—might be unfair. "Suppose I did nothing," she asked, "and the teacher points her finger at me, why should I leave?" "That's our rule" replied the principal. "It makes no sense," Amy replied. The principal explained the reason for this rule: that it was used to preserve order; that it was used rarely; that no one complained about it; that while mistakes might be made, that in practice this practically never happened; that a child sent out of the room in this manner could return right away if he wished, etc., but the explanation did not convince

Amy, so the principal informed mother and child that the interview was over, and Amy would not be accepted.

Second visit. The next day mother and child re-appeared and this time Amy stated she would obey the rule. "Do you think it is a good rule?" "No," Amy replied. "Then we will not accept you. This is not a prison. This is a school based on good sense. If you don't accept or understand our rules, then we just can not have you." Amy asked again for an explanation of the reasons for this particular rule. Finally, she stated that she accepted it. "Now," asked the principal, " are you absolutely sure you understand that whether or not you did anything that the teacher has the absolute right to send you out for any reason and even for no reason? The classroom is hers. You are only in the room if she will allow you. She could not even let you enter if she didn't want you in it." Amy finally stated she understood.

Adjustment. Amy was in this school two years, and during this time was never once sent to the office for any violation. The mother, who had been the recipient of practically daily phone calls and letters from other schools, and who had to go to the principal's office at least once a week before, now never heard a word from anyone at the school. Amy went happily to school, made normal progress, and when finally her parents moved away, she was in tears at leaving her beloved school.

Such incidents, in one form or another, are common. Children do want to conform; they do want to learn; and if the system is rational they will adjust beautifully. Such has been our experience with Individual Education.

Parents

The role of parents relative to children's education is quite different in Individual Education from that in traditional education. In the traditional system, the school acts as the parents' substitute, and indeed the statement, "The school and the home should work together" is frequently heard. Most schools are highly sensitive to parental pressures, and it is highly possible that some highly questionable educational practices, such as homework and report cards (to parents) and parent-teacher conferences are mostly pushed by parents rather than by teachers.

In Individual Education we take the following general attitude:

We wish first of all for parents to have full freedom to veto their child going to any school, including Individual Education schools. Since we are philosophically against compulsion, unless absolutely necessary for life or freedom, we want parents to have freedom to choose schools for their children. Wealthy parents do have this right, since they can select any of the various private schools in their locality, but poorer parents ought also to have this right, even if it were through a voucher system. We see the present system as undemocratic: all children deserve the best possible education and the current district type system does not provide this.

So, philosophically, and there is nothing we can do about this except in the negative sense of not taking in any child whose parents object to Individual Education, we permit parents to veto their children's entrance to this type of school.

Then, if a parent does want this school, regardless of reason, perhaps because it is convenient, we require the parent to be exposed to at least one hour of explanation of how Individual Education works. Our experience is that it is precisely those parents who will not find time to attend such sessions are the very ones who will make trouble: so our absolute rule is that no child is taken unless we have evidence that his parents understand the system. To ensure this, we recommend that every parent sign a kind of contract or agreement. Even then we will find parents complaining about "what is the reason my child does not have homework?" Although they signed an agreement that this school would not force homework on children.

Moreover, every parent is informed that any time without any explanation his child may be removed from the school immediately, simply upon the parent's request. An Individual Education school is always an alternative school—for parents—for faculty—for students. There never is any compulsion. The school is held together by love and understanding and mutuality, not by force. We are more than happy to let out any one who does not want to remain. Unfortunately, as far as children are concerned, it is often those who need this type of school most, who are taken out by their parents.

But this is not all, as far as parents are concerned. For them to keep their kids in the school, they must agree that the rules of the school are sensible and also the consequences—and more than that, they must agree to cooperate with the school in terms of the suspension procedure which as indicated on page 238 calls for parental involvement of a somewhat unusual kind.

Now, let us assume that the parent understands the system, accepts it, wants his child entered, agrees that the rules make sense and also the consequences, what is it that will be different as far as he or she is concerned?

In Individual Education, as far as parents are concerned:

1. Children do not bring home school work assigned to them.
2. There are never any calls from teachers either reporting that their child is not behaving well, or not learning, or asking parents to help their child in spelling, etc.
3. There are no report cards to the parents.

4. Parents are not called for conferences with teachers or counselors.

5. Children do not inform the parents of high grades that they have made on tests.

6. Children are never singled out for their superior abilities.

Here are some elements of Individual Education different from what is found in Traditional Education.

1. Children may bring home weekly Progress Charts which show what unit tests they have passed. Parents can obtain curriculum books which will tell them that if their child has passed Math 36, this means that he can now add numbers, carrying nines.

2. The parent can have joint conferences with the child's school parent (teacher/counselor) and the child, but all three parties must be there willingly. Thus, the child is the mediator for these conferences.

3. The parent can become a member of the School Council, a group of people elected from their constituent groups: classrooms (in the case of students), from the faculty and from the parent-teacher association.

4. Parents may teach a wide variety of creative courses and they may have faculty members and children as their students.

In other words, the roles of parents viz a viz the school as an institution, the faculty as individuals and their children, is considerably different from the roles found in a traditional school. We feel that it is the child's business what he learns and how he learns and when he learns and even whether he learns—and the faculty of the school is not there to cajole the child, to "motivate" him, pamper him, or otherwise baby him. School is a place for learning, and any child who wants to play can do so, so long as he doesn't bother others. If he does not conform to the school's very reasonable rules, and if he deliberately provokes the situation, he will simply be suspended and eventually expelled according to an agreed-upon schedule.

The faculty sees itself as professional, not parents' underlings who must do their bidding, responsible for and to the children, and not to the parents. The parents take care of the child in the home, and we faculty take care of the children in the school.

Now, if this attitude seems unusual, it is so only because we have seen too many cases of children harmed seriously by the over-ambition of their parents, who torture the children relative to their education. We know that not all parents are unreasonable, but since we can not know in advance which parents are likely to interfere with their children's learning, as a matter of policy we draw an iron curtain between the home and the school in some respects.

Parent training.

Perhaps the most radical step we take has to do with parent training. We accept no child unless his parents will agree to attend five sessions of parent training, except for very unusual cases. We recommend not accepting any child unless *both* parents attend five sessions of parent training *before* registration. The reason is simple: it is those parents who do not attend who tend to cause the most confusion.

Our parenting sessions essentially relate to how the Adlerian philosophy of human relations operates, not only in the school but in the home. For this reason, we employ as our textbook any of several Adlerian texts, such as Dreikurs' *Children: the challenge* (1964), Dinkmeyer and McKay's *Raising a responsible child* (1973), Beecher and Beecher's *Parents on the run* (1955), Grey's *Discipline without tyranny,* (1972) or Corsini and Painter's *The practical parent* (1975). However, should those responsible wish to have other texts, such as Ginnott's *Between parent and child* (1963) or Gordon's *Parent effectiveness training* (1970), this would be perfectly acceptable, even though we would prefer an Adlerian-oriented text since then the philosophy and theory of the home and the school would be identical.

INDIVIDUAL EDUCATION IN ACTION

To see how an Individual Education school works, let us follow one student, Stuart Dent for a week.

Monday. The week begins with Stu age 11 going to his homeroom. Miss Miller is his counselor. There are 22 other children in this homeroom, most of them about eleven years of age. The youngest is nine and the oldest is 13. During this homeroom period, Miss Miller asks children who want to know what they did on their unit tests of Friday to come to her desk. Stuart gets in line with his own copy of his progress chart(see figure 2 for Stuart's chart). Miss Miller informs him that he passed Language arts Unit 56, failed Math units 38 and 39 but passed Math 40, and that he passed science 57 and 59 and social science 60. He makes a slash line on the units he passed and a dot for math 38 and 39 indicating that he failed them. At this point his progress chart and Miss Miller's are the same.

The reason for taking three math tests last Friday is that as can be seen on his progress chart on page 250 he is considerably behind in math, and has been going to tutoring to catch up.

After this, Stu went over to some of his friends and they began to talk. Stu complained how tough math is. "I find it very hard, too" Alan stated, "but I want to be a pilot and my father tells me it is necessary to be good in math to be able to be a commercial flyer. . . . " While the conversation was going on, the bell rang and Stuart went to his first academic class of the day, Language Arts 50 which was on the use of commas and semi-colons. He felt this unit was very easy and so decided to cut that particular class next Wednesday in the second period but planned to attend it on Friday. Notice on Figure 4 (p. 250) that in the second period on Wednesday he went to the library instead of class. Following Language Arts he planned to go to Math 41. He had made a mistake in his scheduling, and instead found he was in Math 61. He got up, left this room and went to the proper room where Math unit 41 was in progress. (In an Individual Education school any child can leave any room at any time, but entering is dependent on the teacher's permission. The same is true for the library and the study hall.) Following the math period, Stu went to Science 54. At the end of the period was lunch time, and he had completed his academic class work for the day. Following lunch he went to Miss Inlay's room. She was one of the math teachers, and in this room in the sixth period she did math tutoring as part of her creative course teaching. He asked her for help on Math unit 38—which happened to be multiplication with a 9 in the multiplier, a unit that he had studied, been examined on, but had failed. (See Fig 2, and notice the dot in unit 38.) Following this tutoring period, he went to his first creative course of the week, a two-period course in cooking. Together with seven other students and the teacher, he prepared a meat loaf, which he brought home carefully wrapped. A short final period of ten minutes in his homeroom ended the day.

Tuesday. In the homeroom, a class council was scheduled, and the major topic was a visit by the homeroom class to a public building. Stuart wanted to visit a court, seeing justice in action, and he made a motion to that effect, but the majority wanted to visit a jail instead, and a committee was established to make arrangements if possible.

Then he attended Math unit 40, Social Science 60 and Science 54 before lunch time and in the 6th period went to his guitar lesson taught by Roberta Rigney, then to a Spanish class taught by Eileen Sarber, and then on to his typing class taught by one of the mothers, Mrs. Elizabeth Stickney. As usual, back to his homeroom for clean up of the room, and free for the day.

Wednesday. Following homeroom which was kind of slow, with the kids in small talk-groups, Stuart decided not to go to his Language Arts class. He felt that it would be a waste of time, that he knew about commas and semi-colons, and so went to the library, and after looking around selected *The Red Pony* by John Steinbeck. He found it a bit hard to read, and started to talk with Aldo Lavaggi, a boy who was in his homeroom. Suddenly he saw that the librarian was pointing him, the GO! signal. Immediately, Stuart got up, followed by Aldo and the two of them walked out. Once outside the library, Stuart said "Guess I'll go to my math class, after all," and took off for room 114. After that class, he went to Math 41, and realized that taking two math classes in sequence was just a bit too much,

FIGURE 4

Weekly schedule for Stuart Dent (9th week of year)

Period	Monday	Tuesday	Wednesday	Thursday	Friday
1	HOMEROOM	HR	HR	HR	HR
2	LA 50	M 40	Library	M 40	LA 50
3	M 41	SS 60	M 41	SS 61	M 41
4	S 54	S 54	S 54	S 54	S 54
5	L u n c h	L u n c h			
6	Tutoring Math	Guitar	Small group	Tutoring Math	Play Rehearsal
7	Cooking	Spanish	First Aid	Testing	Play Rehearsal
8	Cooking	Typing	Library	Tennis	Conference
9	Homeroom	HR	HR	HR	HR

but after all, he did want to catch up. Then he went to Science 54. After lunch, he went to what was the high point of his week usually, the small group. In this group were John Bond, Richard Adler, Rick Whittington, Mary Lock and Charlie Clark. This week, for a change, the discussion was not a gripe session. "Susan," Stuart asked of Miss Miller, "why do we spend so much time on these academic subjects? I enjoy the afternoons, but not the mornings!" This statement started a discussion with only Charlie strongly supporting the importance of academics. It was a good meeting even though nothing was definitely settled.

Stuart then attended a first aid course given by Mrs. Vickie Hill, a nurse, and the mother of one of the children in the school. Stuart volunteered to be bandaged, and soon he had "a broken arm" with a bandage around his neck. Following this he went to the library, browsed around a bit, and read some more of the *Red Pony*. He began to get into it, like it so much that he asked the librarian, Miss Lindquist, whether he could take it home. She checked it out to him. Following this—back to the homeroom to clean up.

Thursday. The big thing today was a game called "Ask me another." Miss Miller found an old book with that title which had series of 20 questions. The members of the homeroom when they heard of the book and Miss Miller's suggestion that a contest be started, agreed, and soon two teams were chosen by chance. Miss Miller would ask a question and if a person didn't know the answer he or she got a pencil to hold. When one had 3 pencils, one had to sit down, having made three mistakes. Four children missed this question: "Who is the supreme commander of the military forces of the United States?" One said the Secretary of Defense, another the Chief of the Joint Chiefs, another said the General of the Armies, another said the Chief Justice—but when this question came to Stuart—he knew the right answer, the President of the United States. But Stuart was not the last one to drop. It was Kleona Brown, the smartest girl in the class. She was always reading. Following the homeroom, he went to the same schedule of classes as on Tuesday (see Figure 4) and after lunch went again to tutoring. This time he saw Miss Toby Metcalfe, and went over the very same things as he had done on Monday for tutoring. Following this he went to the study hall where that hour was set for special testing—that is to say any child could go to the study hall that hour and ask for any test from the library tests. He hurried and was one of the first to be in line. Only as many children could be taken as there were seats. He asked the teacher in charge for Language Arts test 51, 55 and 57. There was a limit of three tests at a time. He sat down and worked at them. They took about ten minutes to do. After he finished them, he brought them to Miss Inlay, who was in charge, and then obtained Math tests 32, 38, and 39. These took about 15 minutes to do. He brought these back to Miss Inlay and asked for Science test 58 and Social Science 90. These took him about ten minutes, and he just finished when the bell rang for the next period. He went to his locker, got his sneakers, tennis suit and racket, and went to the tennis court where Miss Daley gave instruction on how to lob. From there to the homeroom and then home.

Friday. In the homeroom, a mock trial was held. Miss Miller had given several days before a number of students instructions how to play various roles. Charlie Clark was the defendant, and Eli Meyerson was the prosecutor. Clark's lawyer was his sister Minnie. Arnie Schwartz was the judge and Irv Copi the policeman. On the jury was Stuart. The jury deliberated and found Charlie guilty. Following the roleplaying, which was to prepare them for a future visit to a court, Stuart went to his classes, and following lunch he spent two periods in rehearsal for the Shakespeare play *Midsummer's Night Dream* in which Stuart was to play the role of Puck.

On the last period of the week Stuart had a scheduled meeting with his teacher/counselor, Miss Miller. She looked over his progress chart (Figure 2) and below was the interchange between the two.

Miller: How are you doing, Stuart?
Stuart: Fine.
Miller: Enjoying school?
Stuart: Yes.
Miller: (Looking at her copy of the progress chart) Doesn't look like you are doing too well in math. This is the ninth week and you have passed only seven tests in math, but you sure are doing well in the others.
Stuart: I am doubling up on math, and I have been taking tutoring.
Miller: I got your tests that you took yesterday, and I am pleased to let you know you passed six of them: Math 38 and 39, Language Arts 51 and 57, and the one on Science, that's number 58 and the one on social science, number 90.
Stuart: You mean I failed Math 32 again?
Miller: I am afraid you did.
Stuart: I don't know if I'll ever understand that thing about dividing fractions.
Miller: I am sure you will some day. You are making very good progress. How's the play going?
Stuart: Fine. I am playing Puck.
Miller: That's good. I really want to see it. It is one of my favorite Shakespeare plays.

Following this conference, there was a short home room period to clean up and Stuart went home.

We have attempted to present what could be a typical week for a student. Notice that the first period every day, the small group at the sixth period on Thursday and the conference at the last hour of Friday are all part of the socialization program in Individual Education. The three morning periods were devoted to classroom activities, lectures etc., in Language Arts, Math, Science and Social Science. In the afternoons, Stuart had as part of the creative program tutoring, a class in cooking, one in guitar and in Spanish, a first aid course, tennis instruction and rehearsal for a play.

Essentially, every child goes to his homeroom for the first period of the day. The next three periods (depending on the school) may be devoted exclusively to academic subjects. The child now can go to any of these rooms or to the library or to the study hall. Every faculty member has the right to exclude any child, which she does ritualistically by pointing her finger at him as he enters the room or the area. This means GO!—which he must do in silence. A child after homeroom could go to the library and stay there all day. In the afternoon he can enter any of the creative classes (if the teacher will permit him, since in some cases, teachers will want students to register in advance) or he can be in the library or study hall, or he can go to the various tutoring classes. In short he has freedom of movement. If found wandering around, he is sent to the office for violating rule 2. If he does anything deemed dangerous or damaging, he is sent to the office for violating rule 1. If he should not leave a room immediately or in silence when pointed out he is sent for violating the GO signal—rule 3.

In short, children make up their own schedules and can change them at will. If they do not break the three rules, they pretty much can do what they want. However, they must attend homeroom, small groups and private interviews with their counselors. They have freedom with responsibility. *Violate the rules, suffer the consequences. Behave yourself and you can get a full education.* 99 percent of children in our schools get a full education.

PROSPECT

The writer believes that Individual Education is the system of the future, and will eventually replace the traditional system as the dominant modality of parent-child-faculty-administrator school relationships. This belief comes from three sources:

Theory

Individual Education is based on the theory of Individual Psychology which in the writer's opinion is the single best and most complete explanation for human nature and the most satisfactory guide for human behavior.

Reception

The second reason for this belief is the reaction of people who either have seen the system in action (such as teachers in Individual Education schools), or who have at arm's length studied the theory and the methodology. In every single case, experienced educators, such as professors of education, who have examined this system, and compared it with other systems, uniformly declare it to be superior and most probably the wave of the future.

Experience

The third reason has been the experience of the six schools using this method. Without exception all parents and all faculty members are convinced that children are happier, they learn more, they develop better as individuals, and that this system much better prepares them for living.

The reason for the success of this system, we are convinced, is that it is essentially more logical than other systems, it is simple to operate, it gives more education per dollar, and it neatly solves a number of problems that have plagued other systems, such as how to at the same time provide socialization experiences and how to permit children to grow at optimal rates. For example, systems based on "contracts" with children are illogical. What does one do if the child does not live up to the contract? Systems based on demands of the child in which the child has little guidance do not provide the structure that our Progress Charts provide. Lopsided systems that use one method of instruction are not universally applicable. Progressive systems that feature children doing what they want tend to fall apart since it is democracy rather than anarchy that is needed—especially in a democracy. In five of the six schools using Individual Education, the traditional system was replaced. Dramatic improvement changes were noted almost immediately in some cases. The reason is that the traditional system is nothing but a part time reformatory system. In Individual Education, choice is the central theme. If choices are one way, certain natural or logical consequences follow; if choices go differently, then other consequences follow.

In our schools, very dull children can operate in peace. They are not insulted with low grades, or criticised or made to feel inferior. Bright children can operate at their own pace. Bright or dull or average, children socialize with those of their own choosing. So it may be that two boys of the same age will socialize in the homeroom and in the small group but never be in the same classes if they differ in their intelligence, interest and abilities. Our system fosters at the same time individual growth and social interest—something that to our knowledge no other system does.

Moreover, in Individual Education, the faculty is permitted to grow. Teachers can learn during the school day in their creative courses. Parents play an entirely different role in our schools. They become the childrens' friends rather than their enemies. They give children space to be themselves, rather than serving as their wardens.

Those of us who are sponsoring Individual Education feel absolutely certain that we are the system of choice, and we know enough about the history of social changes to realize that the introduction of this system depends on courageous individuals who are not held back by the dead hand of the past, and that the growth of Individual Education is a function of time. We confidently expect a geometric growth in the number of schools and of students until some day, possibly still within this century, Individual Education will be the standard system in this country.

NOTES

1. By this time it should be clear to the reader that only for the sake of easy communication that we refer to students in the masculine person while faculty is referred to in the feminine person.

REFERENCES

Adler, A. The doctor as educator. In A. Adler & C. Furtmuller (Eds.) *Heilen und bilden.* Munchen: Reinhardt, 1914.

Adler, A. *The Individual Psychology of Alfred Adler.* H. L. Ansbacher & R. R. Ansbacher (Eds.) New York: Harper & Row, 1956.

Ansbacher, H. L. Individual psychology in its larger setting. In A. Adler, *The Individual Psychology of Alfred Adler,* H. L. & R. R. Ansbacher (Eds.) New York: Harper & Row, 1956.

Ansbacher, H. L. Individual Psychology. In R. J. Corsini (Ed.) *Current Personality Theories.* Itasca, Il: F. E. Peacock Co., 1977. (a)

Corsini, R. J. Individual Education. *Journal of Individual Psychology,* 1977, *33,* 295–349. (b)

Corsini, R. J. & Painter, G. *The practical parent.* New York: Harper & Row, 1975.

Dewey, J. *School and society.* New York: Macmillan, 1899.

Dewey, J. *Democracy and education.* New York: Macmillan, 1916.

Dewey, J. *Experience and education.* New York: Macmillan, 1938.

Havighurst, R. J. Review of Individual Education. *Journal of Individual Psychology,* 1977, 33, 402–403.

Hentoff, N. A. *Our children are dying.* New York: Harper & Row, 1969.

Holt, J. *How children fail.* New York: Pitman, 1964.

Ignas, E. Review of Individual Education, *Journal of Individual Psychology,* 1977, 33, 403–405.

Ignas, E. *Individual Education: an introduction.* Occasional paper 39, Industrial Relations Center, University of Chicago, 1978.

Illich, I. *Deschooling society.* New York: Harper & Row, 1970.

Kozuma, H. Summary of research on Individual Education. *Journal of Individual Psychology,* 1977, *33,* 371–379.

Kozol, J. *Death at an early age.* New York: Houghton Mifflin, 1967.

Madden, J. Staff training for Individual Education. *Journal of Individual Psychology,* 1977, *33,* 359–365.

Manaster, G. Editorial. *Journal of Individual Psychology*, 1977, *33*, 292–294.

Moran, P. The ability of Individual Education graduates to adapt to a change from Individual Education to a traditional high school environment. Unpublished Master's thesis. LaVerne College, 1976.

Muirhead, M. & Fong, J. An analysis of visitors' responses. *Journal of Individual Psychology*, 1977, *33*, 366–370.

Neill, A. S. *Summerhill*, New York: Hart, 1960.

Paresa, S. P. From the viewpoint of a parent. *Journal of Individual Psychology*, 1977, *33*, 350–352.

Parker, D. H. *Schooling for what?* New York: McGraw-Hill, 1970.

Pew, W. L. Review of Individual Education. *Journal of Individual Psychology*, 1977, *33*, 390–391.

Rogers, C. R. *Counseling and psychotherapy*. Boston: Houghton Mifflin, 1942.

Silberman, C. *Crisis in the class room*. New York: Random: 1970.

Whittington, R. Individual Education as an alternative school. *Journal of Individual Psychology*, 1977, *33*, 356–358.

CHAPTER 7

Psychotherapeutic

Models

RUSSELL GRIEGER, KAREN ANDERSSON, & FRANK CANINO

The purpose of this chapter is to acquaint the reader with some psycho-therapeutic models of education. Examples of these are numerous and include such diverse programs as those that aid students clarify their values (Simons, Howe, & Kirschenbaum, 1972), learn self-help and self-determination skills (Weinstein, 1973), and understand and accept culturally different people (Bruner, 1966). Indeed, there have been so many such programs that the *Personnel and Guidance Journal* devoted an entire issue to describing and discussing psychological educational programs (1973, Vol. 51, No. 9).

Among the more prominent programs of psychotherapeutic education currently in use are those based on client-centered psychotherapy (Rogers, 1975a), rational-emotive therapy (Ellis & Grieger, 1977) and reality therapy (Glasser, 1965). This chapter will describe each of these three models.

INTRODUCTION

Many perspectives concerning what children are to gain from education have prevailed over the centuries. Plato, for instance, wanted students to learn to think or to learn skills in asking and answering penetrating questions. The colonial Americans fostered the notion that the school's purpose was to inculcate Calvinist moral and religious principles. These principles were organized within *The New England Primer* (Ford, 1897), which became the teacher's bible. And, of course, there has consistently been an emphasis on teaching children content material and teaching them to read and write.

In the nineteenth century, however, some important changes in educational thinking came about. Johann Pestalozzi foreshadowed psychotherapeutic education by viewing the child as a potentially good being who could be perfected through education (Butts & Crenin, 1953). He recommended that this could best be done by making education enjoyable and stimulating, and suggested that the teacher's tasks were to use love rather than threat as motivation and to facilitate learning through doing. William James (1899) also argued for a non-aversive learning environment and revolutionarily suggested that the feelings a learner had about education would affect the learning that took place. And John Dewey, a contemporary of James, advocated that a primary function of education was to help students grow in their ability to actualize their basic values.

Following this leadership, a humanistic movement in education was in full swing at the beginning of the twentieth century and continues into the 1970s. Its aim is to focus on the total child, so that schools are not only concerned with teaching the "three R's," but also with helping children develop their unique potentialities and grasp the complexities of modern society. The field of psychology has done much to aid this movement by emphasizing areas outside the traditional cognitive sphere, including individual personality growth, coping skills, self-awareness and acceptance, and social sensitivity.

Today's educational attitude is certainly one of wide ranging flexibility and scope and a far cry from the days when schools offered a solely cognitive curriculum. As a result of this attitude, children are taught to combine relevant facts with interpersonal sensitivity in order to become intellectually critical and emotionally and interpersonally resourceful. Therefore, in its most sophisticated and complete form, psychotherapeutic education has the following objectives:

1. To help children develop their unique potentialities;
2. To help children explore and develop their ideas, values and attitudes;
3. To help children recognize, accept and constructively deal with their emotional reactions;
4. To help children understand and adjust to their world;
5. To foster children's skills in self-determination;
6. To teach children how to think critically and to learn how to learn;
7. To foster in children attitudes of self-worth and self-acceptance;
8. To increase children's ability to tolerate frustration.

Person-Centered Education

DEFINITION

"Person-centered education" (Holdstock & Rogers, 1977) derives from person-centered personality theory and client-centered psychotherapy. It views the individual as an organized whole that naturally moves toward an optimal level of development. Teachers are regarded as facilitators of a student's self-determined and self-initiated growth and quest for knowledge (Rogers, 1975d). Because behavior is believed to be a function of a person's unique perceptions, the person-centered educator best facilitates growth by becoming aware of the individual's internal frame of reference and consistently offering acceptance, understanding and empathy.

INTRODUCTION

Objectives of Education

The aim of American education is to prepare youth to become productive and independent members of society. Schools are instrumentally involved in the major developmental tasks, namely: increasing cognitive capacities and academic skills; challenging needs for achievement and mastery; facilitating peer group relationships; cultivating the process of socialization; crystallizing sex-role identification; and fostering awareness of ethical values and moral standards. In short, schools serve to transmit the knowledge, traditions, and beliefs underlying our cultural heritage.

Reasons for the Person-Centered System

Because the average child spends over a decade in the extrafamilial world of school, teachers are in a unique position to enhance societal and parental training. The accomplishment of this rests in the educator's ability to make learning meaningful, spontaneous, and personal. Without this, the discrepancy between what schools teach and what students need to learn as competent members of society will widen.

By creating and maintaining an educational environment that is dynamic and responsive to childrens' needs, interests, and personalities, the educational process fosters growth by encouraging children to develop more responsibility for their own thinking and behaving. Therefore, "education" implies a gradual progression from activities directed by others to self direction, and learners gradually become aware that they are acting rather than reacting to the environment. Such an awareness is foundational if children are to recognize that they are capable of controlling their destiny.

HISTORY

Beginnings

Person-centered education has its origins in early Jewish and Protestant religious principles and in the philosophic teachings of Zen and Yoga (Holdstock & Rogers, 1977). Each emphasizes the human capacity to control one's own fate and underscores the belief that effective living comes from within.

Other contributions to person-centered education come from phenomenological and existential philosophy. The predominant theme of existentialists such as Martin Buber, Karl Jaspers, SørenKierkegaard, and Jean-Paul Sartre is that one can: (a) become conscious of one's own existence; (b) realize that one has choices; and (c) recognize that being means evolving (Hamachek, 1977).

While Rogers was not influenced by a single psychological mentor, he acknowledges that his acquaintance with Otto Rank's work directly affected the development of person-centered concepts (Holdstock & Rogers, 1977). Rank's emphasis on people's responsibility for creating their own realities occupies central importance in person-centered theory. Person-centered theory contains features from an extremely diverse group of other psychological theorists as well, but the efforts of Kurt Goldstein, Andreas Angyal, Abraham Maslow and H. A. Murray, along with Rogers, particularly provided the impetus for extending the aims of psychology beyond the boundaries of behaviorism and traditional psychoanalytic theory. As founders of "The Association of Humanistic Psychology," this group represented a "third force" in psychology that sought to emphasize man's contemporary experience and conscious awareness.

There have been four major stages in the development of person-centered education. It originated with Rogers' development of "self theory" while he served as a clinical psychologist in Rochester, N.Y. There his therapeutic experiences and his knowledge of Rank's ideas shaped his belief in the human organism as self-directing (Holdstock & Rogers, 1977). His "non-directive" approach to psychotherapy emerged in 1942 with the publication of *Counseling and Psychotherapy* and underwent a process of rigorous formalization with the publication of *Client-Centered Therapy* (1951). During this time, Rogers emphasized that the helper facilitates client change by experiencing and communicating his own realness, caring and nonjudgmental understanding. Rogers identifies the next period as an "experiential stage" when the concept of organismic sensing became an important referent in guiding both the therapist's and person's behavior (Holdstock & Rogers, 1977). With the publication of *Freedom to Learn,* Rogers (1969) broadened person-centered therapy to education and other arenas. Person-centered education revolves around the concept of understanding the learner's internal frame of reference in an attempt to make learning more experiential and self-directed.

Current Status

Over the years, Rogerian personality theory has received extensive examination. Overall, the findings support Rogers' notion of the self as an important determiner of an individual's behavior. Exceedingly impressive evidence attests to the importance of the client's experiencing attitudes of genuineness, nonpossessive caring, and empathic understanding from the therapist (Aspy, 1975; Roebuck, 1975; Rogers 1975a, b). Moreover, client perception of attitudinal qualities of the therapist/teacher directly correlates with favorable results.

It should be emphasized that there is no school of person-centered education per se. Rather, it is regarded as a general philosophy of education designed to facilitate learning. Toward this end, Rogers' affiliation with the Institute for the Study of the Person at La Jolla, California has been concerned with expanding, refining and evaluating the premises upon which person-centered education is based. And, recent publications by Rogers (1974, 1975a, 1975c, 1975d), Hamachek (1977), Simpson and Gray (1976), Kolesnik (1975), and Ringness (1975) have addressed the issues of preparing educational personnel, designing humanistic curriculums and most importantly, involving students in the process of experiential learning to do this.

Aspy (1972), Hamachek (1977), Holdstock & Rogers (1977), Magoon & Garrison (1976), and Rogers (1969, 1974, 1975b & 1975c) review the evidence attesting the efficacy of person-centered ideas upon education. Their findings indicate that when teachers respond humanistically, students demonstrate: (1) increased school attendance; gains in both I.Q. and achievement; (2) expanded academic interests; (3) more involvement; (4) positive changes in self-concept, self-acceptance, self-evaluation and self-reliance; (5) deeper interpersonal relationships; (6) personal and social growth; and (7) psychological health. In addition, Simpson & Gray (1976) reviewed the extensive research regarding the effects of person-centered curriculum on students, teacher-training programs, and student and teacher attitudes. Their findings lend considerable validity to the premise that person-centered environments facilitate learning.

THEORY

The following concepts form the basis for understanding person-centered education.

Internal Frame of Reference. Rogers (1959) postulates that behavior is a function of the person's internal frame of reference. Reality is whatever is real to an individual at any given point in time. Behavior can therefore only be understood from the individual's point of view.

The Actualizing Tendency. The underlying human motive is to self actualize, that is, to develop one's capacities in ways that serve to maintain and enrich existence (Rogers, 1975a). Rogers' view is that people grow forever, and when free to operate they naturally mature and enrich their lives. The actualizing tendency is regulated by a phenomenon called the "organismic valuing process." According to Rogers (1959), experiences which are perceived as maintaining or enriching to the organism are positively valued, while those which are not so perceived are negatively valued. The human organism moves toward positively valued experiences and avoids those negatively valued.

Self-Concept. Perhaps the most significant idea in Rogerian theory is that of the self-concept. This is "the organized, consistent conceptual gestalt (whole) composed of perceptions of the characteristics of the I or me and the perceptions of the relationships of the I or me to others and to various aspects of life, together with the values attached to these perceptions" (Rogers, 1959, p. 200). The self-concept is a fluid, changing gestalt composed of a person's total collection of attitudes, judgments, values, and beliefs with respect to one's own body, behavior, worth and ability.

A basic need is for self-regard, or for the experience of acceptance, respect and love from self and significant others (Rogers, 1959). Since it is difficult for significant others to be totally accepting, conditions of worth develop. That is, children develop feelings of worth based on significant others' evaluations. The need to receive positive regard from others may become so important that it supercedes the organismic valuing process. When a person's behavior becomes significantly governed by conditions of worth, the individual is prevented from functioning freely on the basis of subjective experience. Thus, experiences are approached or avoided on the basis of the child's perception of positive regard from others. Positive self-regard is the hoped for end product of education and emerges when the individual can experience positive regard independently of attitudes shown by others.

Incongruence. The self is originally controlled by the organismic valuing process. As a person's need for positive self-regard develops, experiences and behaviors become differentially valued. For the individual whose self concept is congruent with his or her experience, psychological adjustment is maximal. Experiences contrary to the concept of self and conditions of worth result in anxiety. The degree to which experiences are incongruent influences a person's psychological adjustment (Rogers, 1959).

When an individual perceives a disagreement between some aspect of experience and his or her self concept, the person feels threatened by possible self-disorganization. Psychological defenses (e.g., denial, projection, obsessions, phobias) are attempts to maintain the sense of self worth. When an extremely high degree of incongruence exists, an individual's defenses may be so insufficient that acute psychotic behaviors may appear.

Therapy. Rogers (1959) postulates that it is possible to diminish incongruity by decreasing conditions of worth and increasing unconditional self-regard through person-centered therapy. When a person is exposed to the unconditional positive regard of a significant other (e.g., therapist, teacher, parent) who is genuine, empathic, and caring, conditions of worth diminish. Previously threatening experiences become accurately perceived and non-defensively integrated into the person's self structure.

Learning

The application of humanistic psychology to education lies not so much in its methodology but in its philosophy and goals. As a philosophy, it is concerned with designing and providing learning experiences that help individuals develop their unique potentialities. The major goals are: to develop the freedom to learn, rather than to teach content material; and to facilitate self-actualized growth, that is, to help students become aware of their internal dynamics, to help them recognize themselves as unique individuals, and to guide them in actualizing their potentials.

Accordingly, person-centered educators view learning on a continuum, with experiential and content learning representing polar opposites. They believe that people are naturally motivated to learn and that there is no need for rewards, punishments, programmed instruction, and the like within the context of a facilitative environment. They stress learning derived from experience that has personal meaning and relevance for the learner. In this atmosphere, they believe individuals will naturally explore and experiment to lend meaning to their world.

Teaching

Teaching from a person-centered perspective focuses on the attitudes of the teacher rather than on an educational methodology. The person-centered teacher: (1) keeps in mind that students bring their total selves to class; (2) recognizes that the teacher must have a thorough self understanding and make wise use of the self as an important teaching aid; (3)

emphasizes the here-and-now; (4) creates experiences that involve both thinking and feelings; (5) works at being an involved person who is actively caught up in the total education process; and (6) emphasizes being flexible.

While making use of instructional materials, the most important learning in person-centered education is that which occurs through the educator's personal qualities manifested in all dealings with students. The basic quality of the person-centered educator is genuineness or congruence. Such a facilitator is a person without shame or facade, having an awareness of his or her experiences and feelings at the moment of having them (Rogers, 1975a). The facilitator can be enthusiastic, sensitive, angry, bored or interested without appearing judgmental toward the students or relying on conditions of worth to maintain control.

The process of facilitation is further enhanced when the educator experiences and communicates sincere caring (i.e., prizing, acceptance, and trust) to the students. This requires that the facilitator exhibit non-possessive warmth, or caring which is not contaminated by judgments or evaluations. The facilitator unconditionally accepts each person because each is fundamentally trustworthy (Rogers, 1974).

Finally, the effective facilitator accurately and sensitively understands the way the processes of education and learning are experienced by the student. In essence, the person-centered educator understands the personal meanings of the individual's experiences as if he or she were "standing in the other's shoes" (Rogers, 1974 & 1975b).

APPLICATIONS

Curriculum, Academic

Rogers (1969) advocates informal, open, and non-graded classes. This does not mean that teachers do not prepare an educational event. Rather, he believes that there is no reason to adhere rigidly to preplanned schedules or modules. The task of the teacher is to be accepting, friendly and responsive. While seeing the importance of planned activities, the emphasis is on enriching learning environments that actively and experientially involve students in assuming responsibility for their own education and growth.

Having said this, it might be helpful to state what person-centered education is *not*. Nowhere is it suggested that "simply being a loving person" will enhance learning. Person-centered educators do not abdicate all responsibility for guiding a student's intellectual growth. There is a fine line between allowing students unconditional freedom and providing them with guided alternatives (Hamachek, 1977). Proponents of person-centered education object to rules and regulations (e.g., periods, bells, hall passes) which serve no useful educational purpose (Kolesnik, 1975).

In relation to educational beliefs, person-centered educators do not deny the importance of learning facts and skills necessary to enhance life. What they object to is the accumulation of facts instead of the understanding of principles. Memorization and regurgitation are not seen as learning (Rogers, 1969). Real learning means becoming aware of the interrelationship between events and ideas. Ultimately students are enriched as a result of thinking for themselves and are more capable of coping with a rapidly changing world.

Curriculum, Non-Academic

Since the main objective of person-centered education is to strengthen students' self-concepts so that they become self-actualized and self-reliant, person-centered educators emphasize helping students learn about themselves (i.e., their values, biases, prejudices, abilities). Any curriculum or exercise is examined from the prespective of how it facilitates the student's personal growth as opposed to how it teaches facts or skills. Consequently, emphasis is placed on exercises that attend to the following personally relevant areas:

1. *Clarification of values and beliefs:* exploring and evaluating the implicit and explicit assumptions which guide behavior.
2. *Emotions:* recognizing, understanding, and appropriately expressing feelings.
3. *Epistemology:* recognizing the different ways in which knowledge is acquired from the physical and social world, with a focus on experiencing one's own body.
4. *Socialization:* learning how to relate one's interests, values and knowledge to society as a whole.
5. *Needs:* becoming aware of, understanding, and appreciating one's own needs (e.g., physical, security, love, creative expression, knowledge, competency & self-worth) and finding out how one attempts to satisfy them.

Student Evaluation

Rogers (1959, 1969, 1975d & 1977) has repeatedly discussed the deleterious nature of guiding behavior by conditions of worth. He believes that external evaluation perpetuates fear of failure which then becomes the basic motivation for achievement. He suggests that grading only teaches students that learning means beating the system.

Person-centered educators believe that schools have the opportunity to enrich students' self-concept without subordinating or suppressing their values or integrity. This is in part accomplished without relying on grades and without the educators taking responsibility for evaluation. They do not assign readings or administer examinations unless requested by the students. The educators serve as guides helping students learn to be responsible and free (Rogers, 1969). Thus, the locus of education lies within the person, and the learners determine whether something meets their needs, eliminates an area of doubt or ignorance, or provides them with something they want to know.

Counseling

In the case of significantly distressed individuals, person-centered educators are expected to make referrals for person-centered therapy. At times, however, feelings of frustration, guilt, despair, anger, and inferiority may occupy and temporarily impair a normal student's functioning. In this case, Rogers (1969) advocates the use of an encounter group in which the objectives are to increase self understanding and independence, facilitate more direct communication of thoughts and feelings, and heighten the understanding and acceptance of others.

Rogers (1969) recommends that an encounter group consist of ten to fifteen students and a leader. It should be relatively unstructured, allowing the participants to decide what to do. The leader's role is to encourage honest and spontaneous communication and to clarify dynamic issues within the group. The leader does this by being genuine, understanding and caring, thereby creating an atmosphere which encourages students to reveal hidden aspects of themselves. Such risk-taking enables the individual to receive spontaneous feedback from group members which aids the person in recognizing self-defeating attitudes and testing more innovative, constructive behaviors.

Discipline

Discipline is the least discussed area in person-centered education. Rogers is opposed to teacher-imposed controls and limits to maintain classroom decorum. He views these as being inimical to active learning. Instead, he proposes that the genuine, authentic facilitator can arrive at rules of conduct in cooperation with the students.

ROLES

Administration

Rogers (1969) regards the traditional administrative structure (board member, superintendent, supervisor, principal) as a small, closed-minded community whose members rarely know each other as persons. If a climate of facilitative learning is to exist, he maintains that administrators must change by: (1) becoming less protective of traditional beliefs and more receptive to innovative ideas; (2) listening to community members and accepting their feedback; (3) communicating openly to each other and to their staffs without covert self-protection; and (4) establishing a democratic atmosphere.

The school principal is viewed by Rogers (1969) as being most important in establishing the school's direction. The task of the principal is to provide the necessary organizational conditions and methods of operation which will enable the individuals to use their potential freely. This requires that the administrator draw upon person-centered theory, particularly the belief in the inherent tendency of the human organism to learn and self fulfill. Moreover, the administrator serves as a coordinator of resources for staff members, students and teachers so that they can define and achieve their own educational goals.

Faculty

Person-centered theory regards teachers as facilitators and not disseminators of knowledge. Person-centered teachers are models who value interpersonal relationships in which individuals are free to be and open to experience. Their style must be genuine or authentic, respectful or prizing, and empathic. Person-centered teachers are genuinely concerned with the whole person as reflected by their attempts to foster their students' self-awareness, dignity, and autonomy. Taking this approach, effective teachers begin with the student's self-perception and helps him or her to develop new insights. This last point is perhaps most basic because it encapsulates the spirit of a person-centered learning environment. As a result of an environment based upon mutual trust and recognition, learning becomes spontaneous and personal.

Students

In keeping with the view of the human organism as self-actualizing, Rogers (1969, 1974, 1975a) has repeatedly emphasized that people are both active and reactive beings. In a climate where conditions of worth are paramount, behavior becomes externally controlled as opposed to organismically directed. More importantly, conditions of worth significantly determine behavior and self-concept, thus stultifying learning, as in the case of students who perceive themselves as failures. Rogers (1969) maintains that in a person-centered environment, where the conditions and qualities of genuineness, nonpossessive warmth, and understanding are present, students will readily display independent learning and take responsibility for self-evaluation.

Parents

The role of parents in fostering a child's self-concept has been extensively discussed by Rogers (1959 & 1975a). It is not possible in this space to review the literature regarding the contributions of these and other significant adults in a child's life, but the reader will note Byrne's (1974) review of the literature in which parental reactions correlated significantly with children's perception of themselves. Suffice it to say that parents are encouraged to provide the same conditions at home as the teachers do at school.

SYSTEM IN ACTION

The following components characterize a system of person-centered learning: (1) student freedom; (2) student-centered classrooms; (3) democratic practices; (4) focus on internal dynamics; (5) the fostering self-actualization and personal autonomy through experiences which promote individuality, self-discovery, and personal meaning; (6) an emphasis on the process of learning (i.e., learning how to learn); (7) educational flexibility and open, informal instruction; (8) reliance on personal interest and intrinsic motivation; (9) emphasis on enjoying learning; (10) focus on goal seeking; and (11) encouragement and support of self-expression.

Because of the flexibility of the person-centered classroom, it is difficult to describe a typical day. The reader is referred to anecdotal reports by students, teachers and administrators involved in person-centered learning experiences, presented in *Freedom to Learn* (Rogers, 1969), and in the entire Winter 1974 issue of *Education*. Several other texts provide excellent critiques of on- going person-centered programs devoted to the child, the adolescent, the college student, and the professional (Morgan, 1973; Patterson, 1973; Simpson & Gray, 1976; and Valett, 1977).

PROSPECT

As noted, the experimental literature attesting to the efficacy of person-centered concepts in therapy and education is quite positive. It can be concluded that when attitudes of realness, respect for the individual, and understanding for the person's private world are present, people become more understanding and caring for others and become better learners. The implications for education are several: (1) relevant learning combines the cognitive and effective-experiential; (2) in order for significant whole-person learning to occur, the teacher has to convey genuineness, non-possessive caring, and empathic understanding; (3) in order for teachers to maintain "humanistic" classrooms, they need to experience the same facilitative attitudes from administrators, supervisors, professors, and parents; (4) establishing a humanistic learning environment requires that those involved become open to new experiences and grow into individuals who can actually understand and genuinely accept very diverse views and feelings.

Given the impressive body of supportive data and the basic respect paid to person-centered concepts in our society, it can be predicted that person-centered education will thrive. Like most systems, however, wide spread acceptance will depend on the personalities of the people in authority in each school or system, as well as the prevailing political atmosphere of the community in question.

Rational-Emotive Education

DEFINITION

Rational-emotive education (REE) was developed by Albert Ellis, William Knaus and their colleagues at the Institute for Advanced Study in Rational Psychotherapy in New York City. This systematic position is based on the belief that people's emotional and behavioral reactions are caused by the unique ways in what they think about and evaluate their experiences rather than by the actual experiences themselves.

To prevent emotional and behavioral disturbances, which result from adopting and acting on irrational ideas, beliefs, or philosophies, REE teaches youngsters ideas that facilitate emotional and interpersonal adjustment and shows them how to apply these ideas on an ongoing basis.

INTRODUCTION

Objectives of Education

Basic to psychological education is the assumption that all people have two inherent and primary motivations. One is to remain alive and a second is to maximize happiness, pleasure and contentedness. Experiences that promote happiness are valued and sought, and experiences that inhibit happiness or lead to pain are devalued and avoided. While people uniquely and individually define for themselves what will make them happy, they usually determine that one or more of the following will do so: being loved and approved; belonging to a primary group and community;

achieving social and academic-occupational competence; attaining self-confidence and self-acceptance; and finding physical comfort and pleasurable leisure time activities.

Sound psychological education endeavors to provide people with information and experiences that allows them to think, act and emote in ways that are helpful to reaching their goals and thereby to actualizing happiness. It does this by: (1) teaching healthy values, beliefs and attitudes; (2) showing ways to recognize, accept and appropriately express thoughts and feelings; (3) teaching the process of sound problem solving, critical thinking and decision making; (4) imparting skills in making and maintaining intimate interpersonal relations; as well as by (5) teaching core academic skills.

Reasons for Rational-emotive Education

Rational-emotive education views people as living in three main arenas: the cognitive, the emotive, and the behavioral. Moreover, people are seen as cognizing, emoting and acting transactionally and interactively, so that it is rare if ever that they think, emote, or act in a pure way. Thus, for example, a person playing golf will not only act to swing the golf club, but will also think about the act ("I want to keep my head down." "I really loused up that shot.") and emote about the act (feel pleased, frustrated, angry).

For these reasons, REE is a comprehensive system of psychological education that while stressing the cognitive mode, focuses on all three arenas. It believes that the most effective, complete and enduring learning takes place when students begin to act differently and particularly when they think in some way different than before. The most effective learning takes place when philosophic, value, or attitudinal gains or changes lead to happiness. Effective teaching capitalizes on providing experiences that encourage students to concurrently think, act and emote in order to bring about basic philosophic change.

HISTORY

Beginnings

Rational-emotive education is a direct offspring of rational-emotive therapy (RET) and shares RET's beginnings. Both RET and REE trace their roots to the ancient stoic philosophers, particularly Epictetus and Marcus Aurelius, whose major premise was that "Men are disturbed not by things, but by the view they take of them." Spinoza and Bertrand Russell were prominent among latter day philosophers who introduced this idea to western civilization, and Shakespeare, in *Hamlet*, poignantly paraphrased

Epictetus by saying, "There's nothing either good or bad but thinking makes it so."

Rational-emotive education is also well rooted in psychological thought. Perhaps the most significant modern psychotherapist to set its stage was Alfred Adler. In his various writings he echoed both Epictetus' and RET's A-B-C theory of personality by stating: "No experience is a cause of success or failure. We do not suffer from the shock of our experiences—the so-called trauma—but we make out of them just what suits our purposes. We are self-determined by the meaning we give our experiences; and there is probably something of a mistake always involved when we take particular experiences as the basis of our future life. Meanings are not determined by situations, but we determine ourselves by the meanings we give to situations" (1931). Further: "I am convinced that a person's behavior springs from his ideas" (1964a). And: "The individual ... does not relate himself to the outside world in a predetermined manner, as is often assumed. He relates himself always according to his own interpretations of himself and of his present problem. It is his attitude toward life which determines his relationship to the outside world" (1964b).

It was Albert Ellis (1962, 1971, 1973a), however, who founded and primarily developed RET and who directly paved the way for rational-emotive education. Ellis was practicing classical analysis and similar forms of therapy in the late 1940s and early 1950s when he noticed that his clients rarely demonstrated elegant or long-lasting benefits from the insights they gained into their early childhood experiences, the supposed locus of emotional disturbance. For, even when his clients' painful memories were brought to light and exorcised through the traditional methods of free association, dream analysis, and the exploration of the therapist-client relationship, Ellis found that patients did not entirely get over their symptoms and tended to create similar problems about other memories and even about current experiences.

The more Ellis observed his clients, the more clearly he saw that Epictetus and Adler were correct. He realized that all people, not just scientists, develop and operate on theories (i.e., ideas, philosophies) about themselves and life; that people, rather than being victimized by their past experiences, become wedded to ideas about what should and should not be; and that people energetically and religiously evaluate themselves and their experiences in light of these ideas and then act on them. He further realized that emotional disturbance does not result from conflict or tension over repressed memories, but from holding absolute, dogmatic ideas that are non-sensible and self-defeating. In particular, Ellis observed that people tend to take quite sensible, appropriate preferences—for affection, accomplishment, fair treatment and comfort—and illogically demand to have them, so that without them life and themselves become unbearable.

He also realized that people actively perpetrate their own disturbances by reindoctrinating themselves over and over with their non-sensible ideas and stubbornly resist giving them up despite overwhelming evidence of their lunacy.

Armed with these discoveries, Ellis developed rational-emotive therapy. RET is uniquely oriented toward philosophic-ideational re-education and is largely, though not exclusively, a highly cognitive, experiential, didactic methodology.

The most immediate precurser of rational-emotive education was the Living School (Ellis, 1973b), a private school for the normal child run by the Institute for Advanced Study in Rational Psychotherapy. The purpose of this school was to teach students, alongside traditional academics, the principles of rational living on which rational-emotive therapy is based. Regular classroom teachers were extensively trained and supervised in RET so that they could facilitate this learning through a variety of methods, including (1) group discussions and group counseling, (2) individual discussions concerning day to day problems, (3) games and the use of stories, (4) audio-visual methods, and (5) workshops for parents. It was at the Living School that William Knaus and his colleagues developed the program of rational-emotive education. It is presented in a manual titled *Rational-Emotive Education* (Knaus, 1974) and is a planned sequence of emotional lessons following the themes of rational-emotive psychology. The Institute for Advanced Study in Rational Psychotherapy has also published a series of 10 videotapes demonstrating how rational-emotive principles are taught in regular school classrooms (Eyman and Gerald, 1977).

Current Status

The status of rational-emotive therapy and rational-emotive education are intimately intertwined since they share the same premises about human nature. The Institute for Advanced Study in Rational Psychotherapy has a register of several hundred psychotherapists who claim to practice RET predominantly, while hundreds more apparently follow at least some of the major principles and practices of RET. In addition, there are now RET affiliate branches in San Francisco, Chicago, Cleveland, Clearwater, Florida, and the Netherlands, and several others are being considered for affiliation at the present time.

RET fares quite well in the experimental literature. Findings with regard to the major premises behind RET (see THEORY section) are legion and overwhelmingly supportive (Ellis, 1977). The research comparing RET with control groups or other forms of therapy is also plentiful and again generally supportive of RET's comparative effectiveness (DiGiuseppe and Miller, 1977).

Evidence of the effectiveness of REE falls into two types, testimonials to its success, and controlled experimental studies. Among those who testify to the effectiveness of REE are Daly (1971), DiGiuseppe (1975), DiNublie and Wessler (1974), Hauck (1967), Knaus (1970), and Wolfe (1970).

The experimental evidence surrounding REE is scant at this time but is entirely supportive of its effectiveness. Two researchers have compared the effects of REE with those of an attention-placebo group. Albert (1971) studied two groups of fifth grade inner city children, one group with a variety of signs of emotional disturbance but receiving REE, and the other group relatively free of such signs, but also receiving REE; both groups were compared with counterparts given attention-placebo treatment. All children met an hour a day for four days a week over a five week period. He found that those children who experienced REE showed less test anxiety and more positive classroom behavior than the control children. Likewise, Brody (1974) compared fifth grade children from a middle income school district who received REE with a similar group who received placebo treatment and found that the REE group demonstrated significantly higher self esteem, less test anxiety, and greater tolerance for frustration.

The remaining studies compare REE with other forms of emotional education. Katz (1974) compared REE with a program grounded on psychoanalytic concepts and found that the children receiving REE scored significantly higher on the Coopersmith Self-Esteem Behavior Rating Form than the children receiving the analytic regimen. Knaus and Block (1976) assessed the relative effectiveness of REE with a non-directive condition and a no-treatment control group in a population of inner city 17 and 18 year olds with high absenteeism and academic failure rates. They found that in comparision with the others, the REE condition effectively cut into absenteeism and failure rate and increased both self-concept and social and ethical awareness. And, Knaus and Bokor (1975) compared REE with a Self-Esteem Enhancement Group (SEEG) and a no-treatment control group in three intact eighth grade classes in a low income school district on test anxiety and self-esteem. Both emotional education groups showed significantly more gains than the control group, but the REE group significantly outstripped the SEEG group on both measures.

THEORY

Rational-emotive education directly derives from rational-emotive therapy and follows RET's major propositions (Ellis, 1962, 1971, 1973a; Ellis & Grieger, 1977). These are as follows:

Primacy of Thought. People are unique in their ability to think, particularly in their ability to think abstractly. Moreover, people find it virtually impossible to not think and are chronic constructors of theories about the way the world and themselves are and should be. Hence, they rarely if ever act without also thinking, for their acts are usually grounded in a whole set of assumptions based on prior experiences; and they also rarely feel without thinking, for their feelings are usually accompanied by some evaluation of the goodness or badness of the experienced situation.

People also have powerful tendencies to think sensibly, rationally and logically and to consequently carve out pleasures, to attain their goals, be creative and joyful, actualize their individual potentials and facilitate their interpersonal relationships. At the same time, people have powerful tendencies to think irrationally, or unempirically and nonsensibly, and therefore to repeatedly make mistakes, prohibit the attainment of their goals and potentials, create all sorts of unhappiness, and interrupt and even destroy their relationship with important others. Both the human proclivity for straight as well as for crooked thinking have powerful innate, biological components which are strongly reinforced by cultural and family teaching processes.

Thinking Creates Feelings. Human thinking, feeling and behaving are not separate processes but significantly overlap. Thinking meditates between experiences and responses so that people's emotional and behavioral reactions reflect not so much a direct response to their experiences but one to their thoughts about the experiences. Moreover, people develop beliefs and philosophies about how the world and themselves should and should not be and they regularly and consistently evaluate their experiences in these lights and act accordingly.

This proposition is captured in RET's *A-B-C* theory of personality, whereby: *A*, an activating event or experience, does not directly cause *C*, an emotional and/or behavioral consequence; rather, *B*, the person's belief, attitude or idea about *A*, more directly and significantly causes *C*. Take, for example, an eighth grader who is called upon to read his book report in front of the class (an *A*, or event). He would variously respond (a *C*, or consequence) depending on what his evaluative thoughts (a *B*) about the event are: He could, for instance, think something like: "Gee, I can't wait to get up and show my stuff," and he would then react at *C* with enthusiasm. Or, he might take the attitude: "What a stupid thing to do; that's a dumb thing to ask me to do," And he would probably feel some degree of resentment and act in some uncooperative manner. Or, he might, again at *B*, evaluate the event thus: "I'll probably mess up; what if they think I'm dumb; that would be terrible; I'll never be able to face them again." And, thinking this, he would probably read with apprehension or try to avoid doing it.

The Cognitive Base of Emotional/Behavioral Disturbance. Since almost all emotional and behavioral reactions have a cognitive base, emotional disturbance results largely from the ideas or beliefs people hold. The main reason why people become chronically and/or frequently anxious, self-downing, depressed, angry, procrastinating, and a hundred other symptomatic ways of behaving, is that they adopt and regularly act on ideas that logically lead to these symptoms.

Most forms of emotional disturbance involve clinging to dogmatic, unsupportable, magical and superstitious beliefs. More specifically, emotional disturbance results when people firmly believe that they absolutely *must* have some state of affairs and *must not* have its reverse. or else it would be too *awful, horrible* and *terrible to endure.* Most people firmly, yet erroneously, believe that they *must* do well and get the approval of people for whom they care, that others *must* treat them fairly and considerately, and that the world *must* be an easy place for them to live. Believing in these "musts," they desperately seek after, cling to, and worry about getting, keeping and loosing things which are only better to have, but not utterly necessary. And such persons become despondent when they do not get what they believe they must have.

Furthermore, most forms of emotional disturbance involve people's evaluation of themselves or of other persons as totally good or bad. Thus, when they do something seen as good by themselves or others, they deify themselves as wonderful and worthwhile. They then feel good, but for a price, for they also tend to suffer profound anxieties about maintaining the performance or the approval lest they lose their worth. When they fail in their performance or in obtaining the approval of valued people, they vilify themselves as rotten or worthless, and they suffer guilt, depression and despair.

Take again the eighth grader mentioned above who anticipates being called upon to perform in class. If he only thinks, "I hope I do well if he calls on me, but if I don't, it's ok and I'm ok," he will at worst be slightly apprehensive and will probably perform well if called upon. But, if he thinks something like, "I must, I just have to do well," he becomes over-concerned and experiences anxiety. And, when he proceeds to thinking: "If I don't do well, it will be horrible; I'll be a real dummy and everyone will laugh at me," he really cooks his goose. He becomes devastated with anxiety, probably performs poorly, and feels rotten about himself as a result.

Therapy as Cognitive-Emotive-Behavioral Change. To understand people's emotional and behavioral reactions, and to understand their emotional disturbances and self-defeating conduct, it is important to understand how they habitually think and what are their ideas, beliefs and philosophies about the world and themselves. To improve significantly the maladaptive way people respond, people must change the ways they think and believe. Rational-emotive therapy employs a variety of behavioral, emotive and especially cognitive techniques to help people identify, acknowledge, examine and change their irrational ideas, beliefs and philosophies. In its most elegant form, rational-emotive therapy helps people find and relinquish their "musts," helps them accept the grimmest of realities as non-horrible and endurable, and teaches them to stubbornly refuse to rate themselves or others. To do this, it is highly active-directive, educational, and philosophic, and it employs the logico-empirical method of scientific investigation.

Learning

The learning that takes place in rational-emotive education is twofold. First, since most people tend to be sloppy thinkers, and are especially prone to think dogmatically, absolutely and non-sequentially, students are taught how to think objectively, empirically and scientifically. REE teaches them to be aware that they are thinking and to detect the thoughts which lead to unwanted feelings and actions. Perhaps most important, REE teaches the logico-empirical method of scientific questioning and disputing. It teaches students to take ideas or philosophies arrived at during the detection process and to rigorously: (1) debate their validity by raising rhetorical questions about them; (2) discriminate between hypothetical needs and real wants, between undesirable consequences and assumed "horrors," and between poor performances and so-called bad people; and (3) define terms precisely in order to avoid evocative overgeneralizations and overdramatizations.

The second type of learning in REE is the development of ideas or philosophies that promote emotional well-being. REE particularly teaches, but does not limit itself to, the following ideas. One: I can realistically and appropriately want anything, but there is hardly anything that I must have in order to survive or to survive happily; and I particularly do not need to always do well, to always be approved, or to always have things go easy and well for me. Two: there is little of anything awful, horrible or terrible in this world, although there are frequent frustrations, discomforts, and annoyances that I would be better off not having; and I can certainly stand the various frustrations that I will inevitably face. Three: I am a fallible human being who is and always will be a talented mistake maker and, while it would be good for me to sometimes evaluate how well I behave and to change those poor or self-defeating performances or traits, I never have to down or degrade myself for my mistakes; I can accept me no matter what, while not accepting some of my traits. And, four: if I work hard and diligently, I can make substantial inroads into the frequency, intensity and duration of my unhappiness and I can function happily and productively a significantly higher proportion of the time than I would otherwise.

Teaching

The teaching of rational-emotive education begins with the attitudes held by the teacher. Rational-emotive teachers are fully accepting of each child. They recognize that each child is eminently fallible and they therefore expect each child to make mistakes regularly. When the child performs poorly or misbehaves, he or she is accepted and not judged as unworthy. Self-defeating behaviors and stupid actions are open to feedback and change efforts, but these poor performances are not generalized to viewing the child as bad. Moreover, rational-emotive educators recognize that most children use only limited amounts of their cognitive, emotive and behavioral rsources. Believing that each youngster has the potential to control his or her destiny by acting on rational premises, these educators patiently provide growth opportunities that will help children develop the skill of thinking and a sensible philosophic base.

Through such behavior, rational-emotive educators model rational living. They fully and genuinely acknowledge their feelings and actions, they take responsibility for creating their own feelings and actions, and they energetically act to challenge scientifically the premises on which they operate. They openly demonstrate how to exist without demanding perfection from themselves, absolute love and approval from others, or uninterrupted comfort from their world. They also show students how to face frustrations gracefully, without "catastrophizing." And they demonstrate that it is possible and desirable to evaluate how well they act while always accepting themselves.

With regard to more formal efforts, rational-emotive educators present to the students both individual and group learning experiences. They also capitalize on opportunities for learning through events that spontaneously occur during the course of the regular school day. They also present specially constructed exercises and games, use student-created stories as well as published books and films, and employ various experiential techniques, such as role playing, psychodramas, risk exercises and the like, to help students adopt rational attitudes. Throughout, they reinforce and support children while maintaining a Socratic posture.

APPLICATIONS

Curriculum, Academic

Rational-emotive education provides no academic curriculum and limits itself in the format sense to the programs described in the next section of this chapter. Nevertheless, REE presumes that the teacher is well-grounded in rational-emotive theory and a good many of the techniques of RET so that he or she can take advantage of the many opportunities that spontaneously arise during the school day to teach to the children rational ideas and behaviors. Thus, REE becomes part of the total school experience for the child and is interwoven in formal instruction, teacher counseling, discipline and the like.

APPLICATIONS

Curriculum, Non-Academic

The curriculum of REE is a systematic approach for teaching children to use rational-emotive concepts in their everyday lives. While it can be done as a whole or in parts, the curriculum is designed to be taught over 20 to 30 sessions, three to five times a week, for a six to nine month period. It consists of six lessons which help children: (1) learn about feelings and how they develop; (2) discover how to identify and challenge their irrational beliefs; (3) develop skills in changing feelings of inferiority; (4) accept themselves as fallible mistake-makers whose worth is not determined by their actions; (5) learn not to overreact when their desires are frustrated; and (6) develop perspective-taking and frustration tolerance, among other specialized skills. Each chapter contains a brief introduction for the teacher and three or four detailed experiential student activities.

The lesson on "Challenging Feelings of Inferiority" illustrates how REE is used. This chapter focuses on the tendency of children to rate themselves as inferior if they do something poorly. This chapter's first activity shows that people are composed of thousands of traits or characteristics and are therefore complex rather than simple. The teacher generates a discussion by asking a series of provocative questions: *Are people simple or complex? What are some of the characteristics people have? Do all people have all the same characteristics? If all people are complex, why is it inaccurate to call a person a "nerd"?* At the end of this discussion, an assignment is given to each student to write as many "doing" (e.g., playing ball), "personal" (e.g., honesty) and "feeling" things (e.g., happy) about themselves that they can.

The second activity capitalizes on this homework. Each child draws a huge circle with many smaller circles inside it, and then fills the smaller circles with the "doing," "personal" and "feeling" things he has generated about himself. The teacher than initiates a discussion about why no one equals any one of these things and why no one is either all good or bad because one of the smaller circles is good or bad.

Student activity three is a game to teach students how to overcome the idea that they may be a "bad" person. The children first write several derogatory names (e.g., idiot, fool) on separate sheets of paper which are then folded. They also write various things about themselves (e.g., good friend, poor speller) on still other sheets of paper. The teacher then calls on a child to select both a derogatory name (e.g., fool) and a trait (e.g., poor speller), and then has the child, assisted by the rest of the class, determine why being a poor speller does not make the child a fool. This activity continues as several children take turns, with the teacher assisting in disputing feelings of inferiority and in producing rational arguments for not feeling inferior.

Student Evaluation

There are various ways to evaluate the children's knowledge and application of REE concepts. Two more formal ones are teacher-designed content acquisition tests and the *Children's Survey of Rational Concepts* (CSRC) (Knaus, 1974). These provide information about those concepts that may need clarification or modification for individual students. Less formal methods for evaluating student acquisition of REE are observing students' responses during lessons and following homework assignments.

Ultimately, however, the best indication of whether students have acquired the concepts and learned how to implement them is their handling of spontaneous or unplanned classroom occurrances. For instance, one youngster may call a second youngster a name and the way the second responds will indicate how well he or she has learned the concepts in the "challenging feelings of inferiority" lesson.

Counseling

Psychotherapy or counseling is not the role of the rational-emotive teacher. When a child shows frequent, particularly intense and/or prolonged maladaptive emotional or behavioral reactions, the teacher can refer the youngster to a psychotherapist who will help the child explore and change the irrational thinking behind the problem.

Nevertheless, the astute teacher can find numerous opportunities to teach rational-emotive psychology during the school day that will tend to have positive effects. In fact, the most far reaching personal learning often takes place through dramatic experiences that spontaneously arise. When Johnnie becomes upset for failing a spelling test, for instance, the teacher has an excellent opportunity to help him understand that it is merely regretful, not terrible, and that he is not a failure for failing the test. When Susie cries because Sally and Billy refused to play with her, the teacher can help her see that, while it might be nice to be their friend, it is not absolutely necessary and that she is an acceptable person despite their preference not to be her friend. Through encounters such as these, the teacher can undercut tendencies to react in maladaptive ways and promote emotionally healthy ways of functioning.

Discipline

Rational-emotive education embodies no disciplinary system. Rather, necessary disciplinary actions are conducted in a spirit consistent with rational-emotive psychology in general. Specifically, the rational teacher will realize that all children regularly make mistakes and, while taking steps to correct them, does not condemn the child for the mistake. The teacher recognizes that he or she is likewise fallible and hence does not take the authoritarian attitude that "I am always right no matter what." Furthermore, the teacher consistently "anti-awfulizes," thereby viewing every misbehavior or academic frailty as merely inappropriate, and stubbornly refuses to demand that things always turn out in predetermined ways. Thus, discipline is conducted firmly, but also with a spirit of acceptance.

ROLES

Administration

Rational-emotive education defines no special role for the school administrator. It is well-known, however, that administrative philosophy and policy will affect tremendously the philosophies conveyed to children and will shape the psychological educational efforts of teachers. Administrators who are familiar with rational-emotive psychology, who are open to new ideas, and who are by nature willing to challenge traditional values will be most likely to encourage and support rational-emotive efforts.

Beyond this, administrators can be most helpful in a number of practical areas. Because of the special concepts involved, workshops and seminars need to be conducted to orient teachers to REE; because of the advisability of working simultaneously with parents and children, coordination among several school people and a public relations type "selling job" to parents is often necessary; and because after-school time is often needed to develop parental programs, special building arrangements are often necessary. These and other things can best be facilitated by the interested administrator.

Faculty

The primary responsibility for transmitting rational-emotive psychology to the students rests with the teacher. Flexibly following the program

(Knaus, 1974), the teacher implements and administers REE as a part of the regular school curriculum. He or she acts to teach a rational philosophy by asking evocative questions, drawing out ideas, structuring activities and exercises, clarifying and reflecting student statements, and assigning relevant homework.

This offers a glimpse of the teacher's role, yet it does not adequately convey the breadth of tasks involved in rational-emotive education. The rational-emotive teacher will also: (1) teach the A-B-C formula of emotional reactions, since it permeates all pedagogical efforts and is a building block to all rational ideas; (2) energetically stimulates open-minded probing, thinking about, and questioning of any and all student assumptions about life and themselves; (3) recognize when children are upset, identify the irrational ideas causing their upsets, and help them become aware of these ideas; (4) teach the children how to question, challenge, and dispute their ideas and particularly encourage them to dispute the faulty ideas that cause them to be upset; (5) structure as many situations as possible to teach and reinforce rational beliefs; and (6) serve as a model of rational thinking and behaving. All in all, the teacher acts in both a pre-planned and opportunistic way to train students to think in a logico-empirical fashion and to facilitate the acquisition of rational ideas.

Students

The role of the students in REE is not unlike their role in their general education. In rational-emotive education, however, it is recognized that students, like almost everyone else, generally have the worst of two worlds. On the one hand, they have probably acquired a series of irrational ideas on which they frequently act; on the other hand, they tend to be sloppy, lazy thinkers who unquestioningly accept as truth that which they already believe to be true. Accordingly, they tend to believe more and more in their irrational ideas as time goes by and to thus become more and more susceptable to neurotic ways of responding.

The primary aim of students, then, is to learn to think empirically and to develop sound habits of questioning basic ideas or beliefs. Specifically, their job is to doggedly search for, recognize and acknowledge their irrational ideas, to actively and rigorously question the validity of these ideas, and to energetically act on the rational alternatives to their irrational ideas. They must become genuinely involved in the REE exercises and willingly cooperate with the teacher and their peers in using the various classroom incidents that regularly occur to promote rational thinking.

Parents

Parents play an extremely crucial role in rational-emotive education, particularly with younger children who are less able to think critically and who are more dependent on their parents for "truth." The most energetic and capable efforts of teachers to promote rational ideas will be hopelessly undercut by parents who propagandize their children with conflicting notions. Alternatively, a complementary effort by the teacher and the parents will have the best chance of succeeding.

The most effective REE efforts with children will therefore teach parents rational-emotive psychology and show them how to guide their children according to rational-emotive principles. While there is no specific parent training program, this entails teaching parents the ABC's or RET, helping them eliminate self-blaming ideas that lead to feelings of parental and personal inferiority (Ellis, 1978), and facilitating the exploration of their pet child management notions, including a number of irrational ones uncovered by Hauck (1967). This can be done through individual guidance sessions or, more appropriately, through parent education groups. Efforts with parents also include showing them how to systematically reinforce the rational ideas being conveyed to their children at school, and sensitizing them to both the issues behind and the techniques to deal with a variety of childhood emotional problems, including fears of failure, worry and depression, and lack of discipline. Armed with all this, the parents can be a tremendous asset to the school's REE program.

SYSTEM IN ACTION

A portion of a typical day in a REE-oriented classroom would go something like the following.

8:30–9:15. Mrs. Smith conducts a math test which the children themselves correct. Near the end she hears Bobby taunting Sammy for failing the test and Sammy responds with embarrassment and despondency. She decides to use rational-emotive concepts with him and the following conversation takes place.

Mrs. Smith: Sammy, you look down in the dumps.

Sammy: (Silence)

Mrs. Smith: I guess you feel bad about the test, particularly with Bobby taunting you.

Sammy: (Silence)

Mrs. Smith: I bet you're feeling bad has something to do with the name calling game we played a couple of days ago.

Sammy: What do you mean?

Mrs. Smith: Well, can you remember how we discussed reasons why you are *not* a rat because you struck out in the softball game?

Sammy: Cause I'm good at building things and basketball.

Mrs. Smith: Right! So, you're not a rat for doing anything poorly. And, another reason, remember, is that this is only one performance and its only disappointing and not terrible . . . So tell me, and think before you answer, are you a rat for failing this test?

Sammy: No!

Mrs. Smith: Can you tell me why you are not a rat now?

Sammy: Because it was only one thing, and I'm good at lots of thing, and nobody's ever a rat. They only do wrong things sometimes.

Mrs. Smith: Wow! You've got it. You'll feel much better if you continue to think that straight. And, you can now study for the next test instead of moping.

9:20–10:00. Mrs. Smith conducts the regularly scheduled REE lesson. Because of the incident with Sammy, she reviews the ideas behind feelings of inferiority. With Bobby's taunting of Sammy in mind, she then helps the class think about why it is just as unreasonable to evaluate others as to evaluate themselves.

10:05–10:45. The class breaks into small groups to work on special geography projects. Mrs. Smith overhears two students arguing about the next step in their project when a third student, Gwen, says: "There is probably no one way to do it. Let's talk about which ways may be better than others." After letting the students talk about this idea, Mrs. Smith quietly praises them for their problem solving efforts and helps them further explore the idea that there often is no single best solution to a problem.

PROSPECT

As previously discussed, the theory and practice of rational-emotive education and its parent system, rational-emotive therapy, is supported by a great deal of experimental literature. Also, more and more clinicians predominantly or in large part practice cognitive forms of psychotherapy. Moreover, most of the major philosophical underpinings of rational-emotive education are in tune with the *Zeitgeist* of the times, including viewing people on basically responsible for their own actions, accepting people regardless of their poor actions, seeking realistic goals and vividly pursuing them, and the like.

For these reasons, rational-emotive therapy and rational-emotive education can be predicted to play a growing role in the psychological and educational endeavors of more and more people. It will be limited only by the enthusiasm, energy, charm and skill of its proponents in making it further known to and valued by both the professional and lay public.

Reality Education

DEFINITION

William Glasser's educational ideology derives from Reality Therapy (RT). This system of psychotherapy implies that people become unhappy because they fail to meet their basic needs effectively. RT teaches its clients to alter their behavior in order better to satisfy their needs. The principles of reality therapy are used within the classroom to teach children how to set appropriate goals, to take responsibility for their actions, to learn how to evaluate the way their actions interfere with goal attainment, and to learn to select ways best to meet their needs.

INTRODUCTION

Objectives

Education in the United States today should encompass a wide variety of activities aimed at enhancing the child's social and emotional, as well as academic, growth. Most generally, education should concentrate on fostering the development of curious, eager minds able to critically analyze the knowledge offered and minds that are able to utilize that knowledge constructively within the larger world.

Within this framework, attitudinal components are of foremost concern. Motivation and academic flexibility are particularly key constructs which must permeate the educational system if schools are to produce a generation of knowledgeable and conscientious citizens. Children need to understand and relate to the purpose of education if they are to expend the energy necessary to excel. If confronted with a boring, dull routine, children will learn unconstructive ways to avoid the system, which will in turn label them failures.

Reasons for Reality Education

Based on the principles of Glasser's reality therapy, reality education focuses on creating a "successful identity," or an identity that is free to explore and learn to its fullest. Such an identity must be carefully nurtured within an atmosphere of mutual respect and involvement. Thus, the reality education approach attempts to make education relevant and rewarding by providing ample opportunity for individual success. Children are encouraged to explore and create, to develop opinions, and to evaluate their ideas and actions. Through interaction with faculty and peers, they learn responsibility and commitment which serve to motivate them towards attaining greater academic achievement. By becoming active participants in the educational process children become interested in learning and discover the self rewarding properties of knowledge. They become increasingly aware of their responsibilities to themselves and others, and are capable of fulfilling those responsibilities.

Thus, using the context of the classroom, reality education provides a model for living which extends outside of school. The skills a child acquires within this system are those that permit him to think constructively, and act responsibly. Simply put, reality education tries to teach children how to succeed.

HISTORY

Beginnings •

Glasser began conceptualizing the principles of reality therapy during his psychiatric residency at UCLA in 1957. Under the guidance of G. L. Harrington, he began to appreciate the greater value of attending to clients' conscious ways of dealing with their present realities rather than delving into the unconscious antecedents of their behaviors. He began to view therapy as a vehicle to teach people better ways currently to fulfill their needs.

It was not until later that reality therapy became a rounded system of intervention. Shortly after opening a private practice in Brentwood, California, Glasser accepted a position as head psychiatrist at the Ventura School, a home for delinquent adolescent girls. In this closed community, he applied his ideas about therapy to all areas of the young women's lives—education, daily living and psychotherapy. Rejecting the notion that his patients were emotionally disturbed, Glasser treated them as people choosing to behave irresponsibly. He and his staff taught the residents how to behave in a realistic, mature fashion with firm yet fair discipline. All the girls were aware of the rules and the penalties for breaking them. Through a reality-oriented approach, the girls began to discover new ways to meet their needs and to realize that they themselves were responsible for the consequences they suffered.

While Glasser's 12 years at Ventura helped to solidify his ideas, the publication of *Reality Therapy* in 1965 served to inform the therapeutic community that a new approach to intervention was indeed working. Despite the fact that Glasser maintains he was not influenced by prior theorists, reality therapy incorporates many ideas presented by earlier theorists. One can trace the essence of reality therapy back to the early 1900s when the Swiss physician, Paul Dubois (1909), promoted a "common sense" approach to treatment in which he urged doctors to deal with their patients as friends. Prior to World War II, Alfred Adler (1927) developed the theory of Individual Psychology, and Adolf Meyer (1948) later developed an empirical approach to therapy. The self-actualization concepts developed by Abraham Maslow (1954) and the notion of individual behavior promoted by Allen Wheelis (1956) also preceeded reality therapy. Thus, while Glasser does not formally recognize the influence of earlier theorists, the therapeutic community was well prepared for the emergence of reality therapy.

Shortly after *Reality Therapy* (1965) was published, Glasser named his office in Brentwood the *Institute for Reality Therapy*. As RT became popular, he traveled across the country to lecture to clinicians of almost every theoretical orientation. The Institute served as an information and training center designed to promote further Glasser's theory and techniques.

Simultaneously, Glasser began to implement his ideas in the public school system of Watts, California. The success of his model in that system prompted Glasser to write *Schools Without Failure* in 1969. In response to the book's rapid acclaim, The Educator Training Center (ETC) was soon established in Los Angeles. The ETC provided school personnel with the opportunity to attend seminars and participate in workshops conducted by Glasser and his affiliates concerning the application of reality therapy in the classroom. The principles of psychological education as proposed in *Schools Without Failure* were further promoted when the William Glasser - LaVerne College Center was founded in 1970 at LaVerne College in Southern California. Offering graduate and inservice credits, this facility was created to provide teachers the opportunity to learn the theory and techniques articulated in *Schools Without Failure* while actively and immediately trying what they learned in their classrooms.

Current Status

In recent years, Glasser has focused his attention on areas outside education. Yet, the Educator Training Center remains a prosperous, active enterprise. Expanding beyond its Californian roots, the ETC's numerous branches provide a wide system of communication that facilitates the refinement of reality therapy's educational techniques.

Formal analysis of Glasser's approach has proven it to be an effective alternative to more traditional systems of education (English, 1970). Numerous studies have shown that the principles of Reality Therapy applied to the classroom are successful in reducing "disciplinary problems, increasing school performance, and enhancing teacher involvement with each other, with students, and with the school system" (Glasser and Zunin, 1973, p. 308).

Other studies have focused on specific areas within the classroom environment. Several recent studies have empirically shown the *Schools Without Failure* approach to be useful in eliminating problem behavior in the classroom (Rudner, 1973, Gang, 1975, Palmatier, 1976, Cates and Gang, 1976). Also, Hawes (1971) demonstrated the program's effect on increasing self responsibility, and Butterworth (1973) utilized Glasser's principles to help promote responsible decision making.

THEORY

To understand how Glasser conceptualizes psychological education, it is necessary to understand reality therapy. Intrinsic to RT is the concept of identity. Throughout life, one strives to discover and develop an identity. The strength of one's identity is dependent upon the view one holds of oneself in terms of personal success or failure and tends to direct one's future actions.

People's identities are directly related to the manner in which their needs are met. In developing his theoretical orientation, Glasser identifies two basic and universal needs: 1) The need to love and be loved; 2) The need to feel worthwhile to oneself and to others. If these are not fulfilled, individuals experience an empty, meaningless existence that perpetrates a negative self-concept. They are then prone to behave in unrealistic ways to meet their needs and fail to recognize the impact that their behavior has on their subjective feelings and others. Thus immersed in their own emotionality, they are unable to evaluate their behavior realistically and alter it in order to exert a positive effect on their self-image and receive positive responses from others. The key to happiness is for people to make appropriate decisions and to act upon them realistically. It is upon this premise that reality therapy revolves.

The process of reality therapy teaches people to evaluate their behaviors and alter them to better and more appropriately meet their basic needs. Beginning from a here-and-now approach, reality therapy focuses on present behavior and insists that clients take an active role in altering their undesirable behaviors. By altering their behaviors, clients are in a better position to satisfy their needs simultaneously, but indirectly altering the components of the problem situation.

Because close involvement with others is deemed to be necessary for personal adjustment, reality therapy begins with the development of a strong personal relationship between client and therapist. As Bassin (1976) states, "Learning how to become involved is both the most important and most difficult assignment in conducting reality therapy" (p. 286). The therapist becomes a friend who cares about all aspects of the client's life and is genuinely interested in helping the client discover new ways to satisfy basic needs.

After a solid interpersonal foundation has been established, the reality therapist teaches clients to evaluate their behavior and take responsibility for it. It is Glasser's contention that one cannot feel worthwhile if one is not capable of self-evaluation. The role of the therapist in the self-evaluative process is to reject unrealistic behavior and to help clients develop alternative modes of interaction that will prove more beneficial. The skill of therapy is to induce the client to take responsibility for poor behavior and the unhappiness it causes in order to provide incentive for change.

Once clients accept responsibility for their actions, they are in a position to define specific goals and to develop plans to meet these goals. Because therapeutic success is dependent upon establishing goals that have a reasonable chance of success, the therapist spends much time helping clients decide how to set and meet their goals. The pros and cons of each suggested alternative are judiciously weighed, and when both parties are satisfied, they sign a contract committing themselves to the plan of action. Should the client fail to meet the requirements of the contract, an alternative course of action is immediately outlined and implemented.

Learning

Reality education focuses on helping children realistically meet their basic needs, an accomplishment which theoretically leads to academic success. Academic learning is the end product of more global learning which involves the development of a successful identity.

Using methods similar to those in therapeutic encounter, teachers encourage children to evaluate their behaviors and to act in a manner that is both responsible and best suited to need attainment. A casual verbal reminder by the teacher will often help children investigate their behavior to determine whether or not they are acting in a manner most likely to obtain their objectives. Children are also taught to behave responsibly through active participation in problem solving exercises. Through the use of both academic and non-academic exercises, children learn to analyze problems and to cooperate with each other to develop and act upon solutions. Learning does not involve intense memorization of facts, but the constructive and creative application of facts. Emphasis is on the generation of ideas, opinions, and alternatives rather than on getting right or wrong answers. In this way, children learn that what they *think* is important, and that they as *thinkers* are valuable. Thus, the child's exposure to academics provides experience in evaluation, problem solving and commitment, all elements considered essential for the development of a successful identity.

Teaching

Within Glasser's system teaching extends beyond academia. While subject matter is hardly ignored, it is presented within a larger conceptual framework designed to promote a successful identity. Education begins with the development of a supportive relationship between teacher and student. Regardless of a student's attitude or behavior, the teacher is accepting and affectionate in order to help the child recognize options and direct actions to meet appropriate goals. The teacher who becomes a reality therapist is committed to helping students experience personal and academic success in the classroom.

As in RT, the primary goal of reality education is to teach children responsibility. This is best achieved when students are intrinsically motivated to learn and enthusiastic about what they have learned. Through the use of open-ended questions and class discussion, teachers help children actively discover that what they study has relevance for their lives in general. Once children understand how the knowledge gained in the classroom affects their personal lives, they are better prepared to accept responsibility for learning and are able to direct their actions accordingly.

It is the teacher's responsibility to create an environment that practices and requires self-discipline and commitment. When exposed to these principles, children discover the rewards inherent in these ideals and incorporate them into their personal repertoires. The classroom therefore becomes a model in which the teacher provides the guidelines for personal growth.

APPLICATIONS

Curriculum, Academic

The academic curriculum of RT focuses on using relevant facts to facilitate creative, constructive thought. While emphasis in the early grades is placed on acquiring "basic" skills, the program must be flexible enough to also permit students to pursue personal interests. Subject matter must provide practice in applying the knowledge gained in the classroom to other areas of living. The flexibility of the curriculum should increase as children mature and are better able to take active responsibility for their academic pursuits.

Glasser strongly opposes segregating children into special ability classes, which induce feelings of inferiority and thwart the development of a successful identity. The only exception is reading instruction, because reading plays such a vital role in all of education. In a setting in which all students read on the same level, the child who is having difficulty is less likely to feel inferior and more apt to concentrate on the learning process.

If children are to take an interest in reading, the material must be enjoyable. The teacher is responsible for discovering where the student's interests lie and using materials other than basic texts such as comics and magazines.

The remaining subject areas should be taught in a manner appropriate to the needs of each child in the class. Glasser suggests the use of individualized or small group instruction to permit the children to progress at their own pace. This method is particularly useful for mathematics and writing. More complex areas, such as social studies or science, are better suited to class discussion. Material should be presented orally and the students should be encouraged to discuss the areas they are studying.

After the basic facts within a particular lesson have been covered, "open-ended meetings" can be utilized to discuss the issues in the topic. Such meetings are an essential aspect of Glasser's model and help the students creatively apply to their lives their newly acquired factual knowledge. Through "brain-storming" they discover how a particular subject is personally relevant. They thus become aware of the purpose behind their study and become intrinsically motivated to increase their knowledge. By placing the emphasis on application rather than on memorization, failure becomes less threatening and children gain confidence in their ability to deal with academic material.

Curriculum, Non-Academic

Glasser's system is particularly relevant to exploration of areas outside the academic realm. Children of all ages are encouraged to develop extra curricular interests and pursue them. For this reason, Glasser disapproves of excessive homework. The time spent away from school should be used to explore areas not covered in the academic framework.

Within the classroom, Glasser's model utilizes traditional extra-curricular activities, such as music, drama and physical education. Glasser also advocates the use of seminars conducted by teachers, administrators and parents which make use of the special skills and interests and provide students with exposure to ideas and skills not usually available within the typical school day.

Another essential aspect of the non-academic curriculum is the development of moral attitudes. It is Glasser's contention that many children progress through school without exposure to the moral and ethical premises upon which society rests. Glasser relies on the use of the open-ended discussions to pursue the issues of lying, cheating, stealing, and so on. Amidst a non-threatening and non-punitive atmosphere, children are encouraged to discuss such critical issues and if necessary to develop alternative behaviors that meet the desired ends but do not rely on immoral actions. By exploring problems together, children learn to help each other work through conflicts and experience the value of morality. The classroom serves as an environment in which ethical behavior is practiced, thereby providing a model for generalized attitudes and actions.

Student Evaluation

Glasser criticizes traditional education for the emphasis it places on grades. When education revolves around a grading system, the child soon learns that grades are the single most important factor of the school experience. Self-esteem becomes based on the relatively meaningless marks brought home. Thus, good students work primarily to earn the approval of their teachers and parents and fail to recognize the personal value of their efforts, while poor students become unalterably convinced that they are failures and lose interest in school altogether.

Glasser recommends abolishing grading. Within his system all students in the elementary grades are promoted at the end of the academic year. Report cards are replaced with written progress reports that provide a description of the child's performance in each subject area. Strengths and weaknesses are discussed in depth along with the teacher's future plans for the child.

Student evaluation is measured through oral and written assignments that emphasize thinking. Objective tests are useless in that they indicate how well a child has memorized material and not the degree of understanding and mastery achieved.

Secondary schools are encouraged to employ the same evaluative principles as elementary schools, but Glasser has adapted them to fit the traditional structure of higher education. Each teacher sets specific standards and informs the class of these standards at the beginning of the semester. Only those students who meet the standards receive credit for the course. Those who are unable to do so are encouraged to repeat the course but receive no penalty for failing to earn credit. No grades are given and transcripts are replaced with individualized reports. When applying to college, students are encouraged to submit samples of their work for which they have received superior recognition.

Counseling

Behavioral and attitudinal problems are dealt with directly in the classroom through social problem solving meetings. The purpose of these meetings is to deal with the individual and group problems that confront the class. A teacher may call such a meeting any time that the need arises, but usually specific times are set aside each week.

During the social problem solving meeting, the children meet as a unit and are encouraged to raise issues about specific individuals and about procedures that affect the whole class. Each child learns to recognize that he or she has individual and group responsibilities and that he or she is obligated to help discover solutions. Operating within a non-judgmental framework, children confront their peers and attempt to work out personal conflicts. The reasons behind inappropriate behavior are explored and the children are given opportunities to express their feelings. The entire class then attempts to develop reasonable alternatives to inappropriate actions. Although the teacher may be called upon to answer questions or offer suggestions, it is important to note that the class itself reaches the final decision. Furthermore, the solution never includes punishment or fault finding.

Through these meetings children experiencing difficulty learn that their peers care about them. This is further emphasized when they realize that the class has committed itself to helping them deal with their problems and that they actively participate in a solution that includes the efforts of their classmates. As in reality therapy, the social problem solving meeting creates a supportive and caring atmosphere that encourages self-evaluation and promotes commitment to action.

Discipline

In no other realm is Glasser's orientation as dramatic as this. Teachers and students have specific responsibilities that cannot be sacrificed if education is to be productive. Glasser's basic disciplinary paradigm is that the teacher is responsible for making education relevant and interesting and that students are responsible for attending class, studying, and learning to the best of their abilities.

The teacher promotes discipline by informing the students that they are responsible for making their own decisions and meeting their responsibilities. The teacher needs to remind the younger pupils of their responsibilities and express an active interest in their ability to meet the demands imposed upon them. The teacher confronts youngsters who are behavior problems and asks them if their actions are helping them complete their assignments. Children are thereby forced to evaluate their own behavior. The teacher recommends alternatives and children are given the opportunity to choose to behave in a manner appropriate to the studies. Severe problems are dealt with in the social problem solving meetings discussed before.

When a student's classroom behavior becomes intolerable, the student must be removed to the principal's office where he or she is encouraged to discuss the reasons for being asked to leave. The principal's role is to solve problems. The principal helps the child develop a plan which will permit re-entry into the class. Once the plan has developed, the child returns to participate in a social problem solving meeting where the plan is presented to the classmates. If the class finds the plan acceptable, they reinstate the child. If not, the principal may be asked to join the group to discuss the issue further and to help develop a new plan.

ROLES

Administration

The primary role of the administration is to facilitate the necessary bureaucratic changes in order to implement reality therapy effectively. The principal and the superintendent are first responsible for obtaining the knowledge necessary for reorganizing the present system along the lines described above. This process involves a cohesive effort to infiltrate new ideas and techniques to all key personnel. Faculty meetings and workshops need to be arranged to introduce teachers to Glasser's ideology and to train them to conduct the various kinds of class meetings.

As change occurs, the administration must remain alert for problems and correct them before they destroy the system. It is therefore imperative that the administration remain involved by visiting classrooms, participating in class meetings, and conducting feedback sessions with teachers and parents.

Faculty

The success of Glasser's system depends on the teachers. The faculty must work together as a community dedicated to each other, the students and the system. No longer are classrooms isolated units, but environments that welcome outside input and constructive criticism. Through faculty meetings and workshops, a strong system of communication must be established whereby teachers can work through professional problems and practice new techniques. Team teaching is strongly recommended, especially when teachers are first learning to conduct class meetings. Each faculty member must be responsible for evaluating his or her own progress as well as that of colleagues.

It is the teacher's responsibility to make education relevant to students. Thus teachers must rely on imagination and creativity rather than structured textbooks, create the supportive environment necessary for the development of responsible, committed minds, and act as models for personal growth.

Students

Students in Glasser's system must take active responsibility for their own education and for that of their classmates. They need to police their own actions and those of their peers to help maintain a cooperative atmosphere conducive to learning. When problems arise, the students must commit themselves to discovering solutions and acting upon them in a constructive fashion.

Parents

Parental input and cooperation is not an essential feature of Glasser's model. When developing his educational constructs, Glasser's intent was to create a system that would help children to satisfy their basic needs. Cognizant of the fact that too many children enter school deprived of the family environment necessary for satisfactory personal development and academic success, he constructed a system that would provide children with the emotional support and involvement missing from their life outside school. While parents are welcome to contribute their ideas and skills, their failure to do so does not adversely affect the educational process.

SYSTEM IN ACTION

The following will help the reader see how the various components within Glasser's system work to form an integrated model.

8:30–9:15. The children in Mrs. Jones' fourth grade class break into their reading groups. Several children collect materials to bring to the resource room where they will meet with children from other classes. The remaining children are scattered in various corners of the room. One group, working with Mrs. Jones, is discussing the issues within a story they have just finished reading. Another is working on a special poetry project under the guidance of a 6th grade student who is attempting to receive a "superior recognition" in language studies. A third is working independently on increasing their sight vocabulary by paging through magazines to discover new words.

9:20–10:00. The children have returned to their seats to work on math. Mrs. Jones is assisting individual students while several children ahead of the rest of the class are working with classmates who are having difficulty.

10:05–10:45. Mr. Smith, who teaches 5th grade, comes to the class to conduct a special seminar on space exploration. He has brought life-like models of various spacecraft and color slides to capture and maintain the children's interest. Mrs. Jones is supervising Mr. Smith's class, where the children are working on individual art projects.

10:50–11:30. Mrs. Jones returns and conducts a special problem solving meeting. Someone in the class has been taking money from the pockets of other children's coats. The victims are given an opportunity to express their feelings. The class then decides how best to handle the problem. Several children are anxious to discover who the "thief" is, but one child is quick to point out that no one will confess if they fear reproach. The children then decide to discuss some reasons people steal and offer alternative solutions for obtaining money. They then decide that the best possible solution is to give their money to Mrs. Jones for safekeeping. The discussion ends with the children urging the person taking the money to confess so that the class can help him or her deal with the problem.

11:30–13:00. Social studies begins. Mrs. Jones reads aloud from the textbook while the children follow at their desks. The class is working on a unit involving ancient Egypt. They are devising their own hieroglyphic system which leads to an open-ended meeting concerning the necessity for a system of written communication.

PROSPECT

In reviewing Glasser's system, one becomes excited, yet a bit sceptical. The philosophical and structural changes inherent to its application would require an enormous amount of initiative and dedication. Yet when one seriously considers the rewards inherent to this system in terms of personal and academic growth, it seems that it deserves considerable attention. At a time when the country faces a serious drop-out problem coupled with an apathetic striving towards meaningless grades, it seems appropriate to investigate alternatives that may serve to alter the situation.

By attacking the problem from its roots, Glasser's approach affects the entire system. It forces educators to confront their values, their purposes for teaching, and their interest in young people. The questions and principles implied within this approach concern themselves with preparing citizens who are emotionally and intellectually equipped to face the problems of living in a larger world now and in the future. William Glasser's guidelines serve as a source of inspiration and provide a concrete approach to the serious re-evaluation of the present academic system.

PROSPECT FOR PSYCHOTHERAPEUTIC MODELS

This chapter has presented the psychotherapeutic models of education of Carl Rogers, Albert Ellis and William Glasser. The experimental literature attesting to their benefits is both extensive and positive. While all three derive from different theoretical positions and have unique things to offer, each has been shown to increase student self-esteem and self-acceptance, expand student interest and involvement, increase academic performance, reduce "discipline" problems, increase school attendance and promote psychological well-being.

Given all this, it would seem reasonable to expect that more and more educational systems are incorporating the ideas from these and other psychotherapeutic models into their philosophy and curriculum. Unfortunately, this does not seem to be the case. The political and social liberalism of the 1960s, which spawned such educational concepts as open classes, freedom of expression, total child development and social promotion, has given way in the 1970s to a more conservative posture. We thus see a renewed emphasis on the three R's, a reinvigorated respect for classroom structure and discipline, a pronounced demand that students master content material, and a strong push for college education. As a consequence a trend seems to be developing to minimize psychological educational efforts and to concentrate on traditional educational goals.

Does this mean that psychotherapeutic education is dead? Not at all. The belief in the basic value of the individual human being remains a philosophical pillar of our society, and many significant consciousness-raising issues, including women's and children's rights, are still a strong part of our zeitgeist. It can thus be predicted that a good many teachers and systems will integrate psychological education into the school day, while some others will not, depending on the individual personalities involved, the values of the particular community in question and the current political atmosphere of the country at large. And, as the socio-political climate gradually swings again to a more liberal and optimistic posture, psychological education will predictably increase in stature.

REFERENCES

Adler, A. *The practice and theory of individual psychology.* New York: Harcourt, Brace & World, 1927.

Adler, A. *What life should mean to you.* New York: Blue Ribbon Books, 1931.

Adler, A. *Superiority and social interest.* In H. L. Ansbacher & R. R. Ansbacker (Eds.), Evanston, Ill: Northwestern University Press, 1964. (a)

Adler, A. *Social interest: A challenge to mankind.* New York: Capricorn Books, 1964. (b)

Albert, S. *A study to determine the effectiveness of affective education with fifth grade students.* Unpublished masters thesis, Queens College, 1971.

Aspy, D. *Toward a technology for humanizing education.* Champaign, Illinois: Research Press, 1972.

Aspy, D. The humane implications of a human technology. *Peabody Journal of Education,* 1975, *53,* 3–9.

Bassin, A. The reality therapy paradigm. In A. Baccin, T. E. Brattler, & R. L. Rachlin (Eds.), *The reality therapy reader.* New York: Harper and Row, 1976.

Brody, M. *The effect of the rational-emotive affective education approach on anxiety, frustration tolerance, and self-esteem with fifth grade students.* Unpublished doctoral dissertation, Temple University, 1974.

Bruner, J. S. Man: A course of study. *E. S. T. Quarterly Report,* 1966 (Spring/Summer),

2–13.

Butterworth, B. Helping children make responsible decisions. *Educational Horizons,* 1973, *31,* 9–14.

Byrne, D. *An introduction to personality: Research, theory, and applications* (2nd ed.). Englewood Cliffs, New Jersey: Prentice Hall, 1974.

Cates, J. T., and Gang, M. J. Classroom discipline problems and reality therapy: Research support. *Elementary School Guidance and Counseling,* 1976, *11,* 131–137.

Daly, S. Using reason with deprived pre-school children. *Rational Living,* 1971, *5,* 12–19.

DiGiuseppe, R. The use of behavioral modification to establish rational self-statements in children. *Rational Living,* 1975, *10,* 18–20.

DiGiuseppe, R. A., and Miller N. J. A review of outcome studies on rational-emotive therapy. In A. Ellis and R. Grieger (Eds.), *Handbook of rational-emotive therapy.* New York: Springer Publishing Co., 1977.

DiNublie, L., and Wessler, R. Lessons from the Living School. *Rational Living,* 1974, *9,* 29–32.

DuBois, P. *The psychic treatment of mental disorders.* New York: Funk and Wagnalls, 1909.

Education, 1974, *95,* (2) (whole number).

Ellis, A. *Reason and emotion in psychotherapy.* New York: Lyle Stuart, 1962.

Ellis, A. *Growth through reason.* Palo Alto, Calif.: Science and Behavior Books, Inc., 1971.

Ellis, A. *Humanistic psychotherapy: The rational-emotive approach.* New York: Julian Press, 1973.(a) New York: McGraw-Hill Paperbacks, 1974.

Ellis, A. Emotional education at the living school. In M. M. Ohlsen (Ed.), *Counseling children in groups.* New York: Holt, Rinehart & Winston, 1973, pp. 79–94. (b)

Ellis, A. Rational-emotive therapy: Research data that supports the clinical and personality hypothesis of RET and other modes of cognitive-behavior therapy. *The Counseling Psychologist,* 1977, *7,* 2–42.

Ellis, A. Rational-emotive guidance. In L. E. Arnold (Ed.), *Helping parents help their children.* New York: Bruner/Mazel, 1978, pp. 91–101.

Ellis, A., & Grieger, R. *Handbook of rational-emotive therapy.* New York: Springer Publishing Co., 1977.

English, J. The effects of reality therapy on elementary age children. Paper presented at the California Association of School Psychologists and Psychometrists, Los Angeles, California, March, 1970.

Epictetus. *The works of Epictetus.* Boston: Little, Brown and Co., 1899.

Eyman, B., and Gerald, M. *Teaching rational-emotive education to children.* New York: Institute for Advanced Study in Rational Psychotherapy, 1977 (Videotape).

Gang, M. J. Empirical validation of a reality therapy intervention program in an elementary school classroom (doctoral dissertation, University of Tennessee, 1974). *Dissertation Abstracts International,* 1975, 4216-B. (University Microfilms No. 75-3592, 76).

Glasser, W. *Reality therapy.* New York: Harper and Row, 1965.

Glasser, W. *Schools without failure.* New York: Harper and Row, 1969.

Glasser, W., and Zunin, L. M. Reality therapy. In R. Corsini (Ed.), *Current psychother-*

apies. Itasca, Illinois: F. E. Peacock Publishers, 1973.

Hamachek, D. Humanistic psychology: Theoretical-philosophical framework and implications for teaching. In D. Treffinger, J. Davis, & R. Ripple (Eds.), *Handbook on teaching educational psychology.* New York: Academic Press, 1977, pp. 139–160.

Hauck, P. A. The rational management of children. New York: Libra Publishers, Inc., 1967.

Hawes, R. M. Reality therapy in the classroom (Doctoral dissertation, University of the Pacific, 1970). *Dissertation Abstracts International,* 1971, *32,* 2483-A. (University Microfilms No. 71-28,083, 200).

Holdstock, T., and Rogers, C. Person-centered theory. In R. J. Corsini (Ed.), *Current personality theories.* Itasca, Illinois: F. E. Peacock, 1977, pp. 125–151.

Katz, S. *The effect of emotional education on locus of control and self concept.* Unpublished doctoral dissertation, Hofstra University, 1974.

Knaus, W. Innovative use of parents and teachers as behavior modifiers. Paper presented at combined Seventh Annual School Psychology Conference and Second Annual Special Education Conference. New York: Queens College Publications, January, 1970.

Knaus, W. J. *Rational-emotive education.* New York: Institute for Rational Living, Inc., 1974.

Knaus, W., and Block, J. Rational-emotive education with economically disadvantaged inner city high school students: A demonstration study. Unpublished manuscript, 1976.

Knaus, W., and Bokor, S. Teaching rational-emotive education to sixth grade economically disadvantaged children. Unpublished research report, 1975.

Kolesnik, W. *Humanism and/or behaviorism in education.* Boston: Allyn & Bacon, 1975.

Magoon, R., and Garrison, K. *Educational psychology: an integrated view.* Columbus, Ohio: Charles E. Merrill, 1976.

Maslow, A. H. *Motivation and personality.* New York: Harper and Row, 1954.

Meyer, A. *The common sense psychiatry of Dr. Adolf Meyer.* A. Lief (Ed.), New York: McGraw-Hill, 1948.

Morgan, H. *The learning community: A humanistic casebook for teachers.* Columbus, Ohio: Charles E. Merrill, 1973.

Palmatier, L. L. Can the counselor improve school discipline? *School Guidance Worker,* 1976, *31,* 41–50.

Personnel & Guidance Journal, 1973, *51,* (9) (whole number).

Patterson, C. *Humanistic education.* Englewood Cliffs, New Jersey: Prentice-Hall, 1973.

Ringness, T. *The affective domain in education.* Boston: Little, Brown & Company, 1975.

Roebuck, F. Human thoughts and humane procedures—effective behaviors. *Peabody Journal of Education,* 1975, *53,* 9–14.

Rogers, C. *Counseling and psychotherapy.* Boston: Houghton Mifflin, 1942.

Rogers, C. *Client-centered therapy.* Boston: Houghton Mifflin, 1951.

Rogers, C. *Freedom to Learn.* Columbus, Ohio: Charles E. Merrill, 1969.

Rogers, C. A theory of therapy, personality, and interpersonal relationships, as developed in the client-centered framework. In S. Koch (Ed.), *Psychology: A study of a science* (Vol. 3, *Formulations of the person and the social context)*. New York: McGraw-Hill, 1959.

Rogers, C. Can learning encompass both ideas and feelings? *Education,* 1974, *95,* 103–114.

Rogers, C. Client-centered psychotherapy. In A. Freedman, H. Kaplan, & B. Sadock (Eds.), *Comprehensive textbook of psychiatry/II.* Baltimore: Williams & Wilkins, 1975, pp. 1831–1843. (a)

Rogers, C. Empathic: An unappreciated way of being. *The Counseling Psychologist,* 1975, *5,* 2–10. (b)

Rogers, C. New directions for humanistic education: An introduction to NCHE. *Peabody Journal of Education,* 1975, *53,*1–2. (c)

Rogers, C. On the facilitation of learning. In D. Read & S. Simon (Eds.), *Humanistic education sourcebook.* Englewood Cliffs, New Jersey: Prentice Hall, 1975, pp. 3–22. (d)

Rogers, C. *Carl Rogers on Personal Power.* New York: Delacorte, 1977.

Rudner, H. L. A practical model for controlling a group of behavior problems in the classroom. *Canadian Counselor,* 1973, *7,* 119–125.

Simons, S. G., Howe, L. W., and Kirschenbaum, H. *Values clarification: A handbook of practical strategies for teachers and students.* New York: Hart, 1972.

Simpson, E., and Gray, M. *Humanistic education: An interpretation.* Cambridge, Massachusetts: Ballinger Pub. Co., 1976.

Valett, R. *Humanistic education: Developing the total person.* Saint Louis, Mo.: C. V. Mosby, 1977.

Weinstein, G. Self-Science Education: The trumpet. *Personnel and Guidance Journal,* 1973, *51,* 600–606.

Wheelis, A. The vocational hazards of psychoanalysis. *The International Journal of Psychoanalysis,* 1956, *37,* 171.

Wolfe, J. Emotional education in the classroom. *Rational Living,* 1970, *4,* 23–25.

CHAPTER 8

Behaviorism
in Education

SCOTT MACDONALD

DEFINITION

Behaviorism begins with the belief that behavior can be best understood when individual meaningful acts (those which lead to a certain identifyable outcome) are examined regarding the environmental conditions that evoke and maintain them. Consider the behaviorist as a careful TV cameraman: as the behavior of interest is made, the cameraman "freezes" the action, and examines prior and subsequent events, as well as the situation in which the behavior occurred. This analysis of a person's activity into functional acts, along with evoking situations and subsequent "rewarding" events is what comprises behaviorism.

In the educational setting, behaviorism focuses on three major areas. First, the student: what the student can do at this point, and what is desirable for the student to learn to do. Second, the teacher becomes the focus of attention, because the teacher directs actions of students, and represents a major source of rewards which can be made contingent on student behaviors. Third, the classroom environment is important especially the curriculum materials which can vary widely in level of difficulty, intrinsic interest and continuity.

Behaviorism in education focuses on an analysis of the situation in which students display new behavior (called learning). The analysis includes student behaviors, contingent teacher acts, and relevant aspects of the environment in which the new (learned) behaviors occur.

INTRODUCTION

Objectives of Education

The only thing all educators appear to agree on is that education should be a public effort. What should be taught, how it should be taught, and for what purposes are all topics of controversy.

The problems raised by the diversity of opinions regarding educational goals is not a function of inadequate exploration of the issue. Rather, the variety stems from the contributions of many great educators who have provided persuasive, though divergent, arguments regarding the issues attendant to education. Diversity also stems from the nature of the educational process itself. A close examination of education reveals the intermixing of philosophy of education with such practical matters of room and class size, selection of texts, and the approach to classroom management. Henderson (1947) discusses the opposite pulls of preserving social values and enhancing individual progress at several levels of analysis. While there are some points at which individual development may seem contradictory to preservation of social order, there are clear cut differences among educators regarding which aspects of the social order should preserved, and which parts should be manipulated so that our social order can maintain pace with the demands made upon it by our modern world.

Baier (1973) discusses in detail the goal of education as the moral autonomy of society's citizens. But the idea of autonomous citizens is itself controversial. One of the problems centers on whether it is an individual's obligation to live by the established social order, or to take steps to get society to adopt or change those laws which would be most advantageous to society.

Educational objectives, of course, are not the sole provence of philosophers of education. The world situation often has a way of rudely intruding practical issues into an ethical argument. The advent of Sputnik, for example, caused the disparate rays of various educational arguments to suddenly focus on advancing technology through the lens of perceived national crisis. For several years there was a period of national harmony regarding the goals of education. However, as the threat of Russian space technology waned, another national crisis appeared on the scene: unequal educational achievement by some racial minority groups. A period of educational soul-searching followed, focusing on the relationship between educational achievement and status advantages in the social order. And, most recently, an overall decline in educational achievement has fomented a general reforming on the basic questions: *education for what?*

While the mainstream of American education has struggled with problems of the relative priorities of objectives, education of students with lesser academic talents has continued on a more stable path of preparing students for vocational entry. Federal and state governments have sponsored several types of educational programs which offer job training. The central focus of these "trade" or "vocational training" schools is the training of students for specific trade skill levels. While some of the training involves academic courses, the objectives of such courses is remedial and is offered to provide ancillary skills to the job seeker, or a high school diploma for the specific reason of meeting job-entry requirements. In the designing of curriculum and teaching programs, trade and vocational schools consider enhancing job preparedness above all other objectives.

Educational objectives vary according to time, place and students. There are always the tugs and pulls of society's practical demands balanced against the philosophies of those who shape educational programs. At any given time, whether in the midst of a fundamentalist swing to enhance basic academic skills or a liberalization to enhance individual freedom, a broad spectrum of educational goals is reflected in our colleges and educational institutions. While for some, the educational choice is more limited, for many American students, regardless of the *Zeitgeist,* there is a choice of educational goals available from strict vocational development to very liberal goals of general preparation for life in structured or unstructured curricula depending on schools and subjects to be studied.

We may, indeed, see a return to *both* fundamental curriculum and discipline imposed by the school, in some schools; and an emphasis on individuality and diversity in yet other schools. The emphasis on diversity in educational goals reflects our current concerns for individual diversity and may be education's response to the diversity of needs found in our student population.

Reasons for this System

One need only review the curriculum of a College of Education to begin to appreciate the position of a new teacher. One would gain further understanding by attending sessions during which teachers-to-be were actually undergoing training in leading a classroom, designing a lesson, or establishing learning goals. The most poignant time in the teacher's metamorphosis comes when an education major is awarded the degree, and then walks into class on the first day. From that time on, the teacher has a cluster of demands to deal with for which specific training is lacking to some degree. The teacher may perceive some of the demands and not others: the teacher may be able to cope with some and not others.

The teacher must assess where students are at in respect to academic achievement. For it is at that point that teaching most effectively begins.

The teacher may start out depending on achievement or mastery tests. But the teacher may still want to know who has trouble manipulating certain concepts, who works well alone, and who works well without assistance. Each of these requires individual assessment.

Once the teacher knows where each student is, the teacher may need to present different material to various students because they each differ in readiness. Now the teaching task is to formulate learning experiences to provide the necessary skills: does the teacher know how to develop experiences whose outcome is specific skill development? A second part of readiness concerns characteristics of student learning behaviors. How does a teacher stimulate one student to study rather than talking to a neighbor, or three students to work on a team rather than sitting silently while one student dominates a group? By what strategies does the teacher guide the activities of various students to maximize their native talents?

Suppose an otherwise capable student displays an academic deficiency which should have been developed at an earlier time. How is the deficiency pinpointed and what remedial measures may be taken?

Some skills are the end products of a sequence of prerequisite skills. By what strategies are students taught such chains of skills, and how are the sequential skills tracked?

The teacher may enter the classroom without much exposure to younger children. How is the teacher to understand the simple principles of classroom management: how is the teacher to grasp the hundreds of interrelated behaviors which must be directed to optimize the classroom as an environment for learning? By the same principle, how does the teacher foster non-academic behaviors such as student initiative, curiosity and self-reliance? Can the teacher develop creativity in students?

Finally, the teacher will ask questions about materials. How is the teacher to select from among the various teaching materials, texts and audio-visual devices. When is a regular text indicated: when is a programmed text indicated?

Behaviorism was introduced into education, as it was into other human services, to respond to some educational problems which plagued teachers. At first, behaviorism was introduced to help correct classroom misbehavior of some problem students, and to help students who otherwise were having learning problems (i.e., culturally deviant students and students with one type learning disability or another). The effectiveness of the method soon spread so that the method was extended into normal classrooms to enhance the teaching skills of teachers. Counselors and teachers alike discovered that routine problems were resolved favorably by the techniques of behaviorism. Since these principles assisted in influencing control problems and leading to "on task" performance, teachers explored the techniques as solutions to more academically sophisticated problems.

One off-shoot of the principles was the development of programmed texts and other subject materials. For example, it was found to be valuable in some rote learning tasks to follow questions by the learner's response and then with feedback about the learner's performance. This could be done simply with a mechanical device or even by proper sequencing of materials in a book. Thus, the technology could supply teaching aides which would free teachers to do other tasks while simple presentation could be done programatically by book or machine. The hardware and know-how in this area has greatly proliferated so that computor assisted learning is common in many schools.

Finally, behaviorism has been able to untangle some of the knotty questions regarding what a good teacher does. Behaviorism assures us that part of good teaching is establishing signals for students to change from one activity to another. Good teaching applauds behavior directed toward responsible acts and those activities which lead to learning. Good teaching ignores minor disruptive acts and those which bid for attention. Behaviorism has begun to establish the links between teacher behavior and the desired outcomes of teaching.

Behaviorism is not a static set of rules or procedures by which teaching should procede. It is a practical application of principles shown to influence human behavior. Behaviorism, then, is a technology which actively seeks to help solve those problems brought to light by teachers and educators as they practice their art in the classroom.

HISTORY

Beginnings

The experimental foundations underlying what became later known as behaviorism began at the turn of the century. Milhollan & Forisha (1972) credit Thorndike (beginning about 1898) and Pavlov (whose work began a few years earlier but not translated into English for over two decades) as setting the stage for behaviorism. Thorndike's contributions to American education were twofold. First, he focused attention of experimentalists on the link between a learned behavior and its subsequent reinforcement. Second, it was his mounting prestige as a scientist which permitted him to effectively oppose two educational theories which had become popular by the time Thorndike had become a psychologist of national repute in the 1920's. Thorndike opposed the notion, taken from evolution, that learning material should be carefully sequenced to learners at a stage when they were "ready" for it. Thorndike also weakened the position that learning formal subjects such as Latin and Greek strengthen other mental faculties such as reasoning and memory. Pavlov, meanwhile, working with his dogs, had established the "conditioning" process by which dogs learn to salivate to a previously neutral cue by association of the cue to the presentation of meat powder.

Even while Thorndike continued his animal experiments, it was popular among American psychologists to consider thoughts, images and other *mental* phenomena as *the* realm of psychology. About this time, in 1913, John B. Watson published *Psychology as the Behaviorist Views It*. Mowrer (1976) considers this publication the beginning of the first phase of behaviorism. Mowrer considers the second phase, occuring when Freud's popularity and animal experimentation had reduced the influence of behaviorism to have begun in 1938 as Skinner's influence began to take hold following the publication of his *Behavior of Organisms*.

During the first phase of Behaviorism, Watson popularized the position that mental events such as thoughts and images are private experience and not public knowledge, hence, lie outside the realm of science. Watson asserted that scientists concern themselves with that which is publically verifiable. That which can be seen, in Watsonian psychology, is behavior. Watson considered muscular movements and activities of glands the proper realm of psychology. Thoughts, for example, were considered by Watson to be no more than movements of the throat; subvocal speech. Watson took the position that human behavior occurred in relationship to the environment, the result of learning, not the result of traits, instincts or other "internal" events. Watson accepted fear, anger and love as innate emotional reactions which occur in response to environment events. The conditioning of fear in Albert, an eleven month old child, served as subject matter for the famous Watson and Raynor (1920) experiment which served as a prototype for later behaviorists to apply their principles to human problems.

Watson was not a thorough theoretician and supplied little data to support his position. He was interested in other things such as applied psychology and, soon after he left academic psychology and went into industrial work. After Watson, Clark Hull followed with a thorough theoretical framework based on animal experiments. In the 30's and 40's, Freudian psychology was embraced by American psychology and the application of behaviorism to social problems waned. (Mowrer, 1976).

Skinner ushered in the second phase of behaviorism. Although the scientific community was slow to react to his *Behavior of Organisms* published in 1938, and to his systematic scientific theorizing, his influence gradually mounted until, in the mid-60's, he was one of the most prominent social scientists in the country and probably, the world. Like Thorndike and Pavlov, Skinner restricted himself to the study of overt actions. His data were the actions of organisms, most often rats and pigeons, and often times those actions as measured by the operation of levers in such devices as his "Skinner boxes", recorded on rolls of paper. It appears that his success with devices maintained his interest in mechanical apparatus which led to his development of "teaching machines" which have found themselves in the standard armamentarium of classroom equipment.

The demonstration by Skinner and his co-workers that animals were influenced by the contingent delivery of rewards (called reinforcers) was the basis for a flood of activity by behaviorists in applying their principles to human subjects. Greenspoon (1950) was one of the first researchers to demonstrate that human verbal behavior could be influenced by conditioned social reward. Other researchers began to apply the principles of behaviorism to human problems: Lindsley (1956) for example, demonstrated the utility of the behaviorists' principles in treating mental patients. As the behaviorists began to apply their ideas to human problems, the promise to educational settings was soon realized. Staats was one of the first and one of the most productive researchers applying behavioral principles in the educational setting (e.g. Staats, Staats, Schutz and Wolf, 1962).

The rapid growth of theory and research in behaviorism is indicated by the birth of two journals. First, the more theoretically oriented *Journal of Experimental Analysis of Behavior* was begun in 1958, and then the rapid growth of applied behaviorism gave rise to the *Journal of Applied Behavior Analysis* in 1968. While earlier research stressed theory and reported work done mostly with rats and pigeons as in the former journal and others, the rapid growth of applied research emphasized applications to human problems in the latter named journal and others. From its beginning but a decade and a half ago, behaviorism in education has moved from concern with controlling misbehavior in classroom and enhancing rather simple responses to helping students enjoy reading by strengthening encoding behavior, encouraging novel and creative behavior and most other specifically identifyable behaviors. In addition, behaviorism has helped clarify some traditionally sticky problems such as identifying what is "good teaching", assessment of learning goals, developing a rationale for presentation of subject matter and sequencing learning experiences. The history of behaviorism to date, with few exceptions which will be mentioned later, has been to influence some of the operations of the educational enterprise, rather than develop a given type of school or philosophy of education.

Current Status

Skinner's statement in 1954 is an apt comment regarding a part of a seemingly perplexing situation regarding the current status of behaviorism in education today (Skinner, 1954). In that article, he said that the science of behaviorism consists of improving teaching and learning. He went on to enumerate that the art of teaching included careful rewarding of student behavior such that guiding behavioral development and building academic skills results. Naturally, as the inventor of teaching machines, he clearly stated (some educators feel he has *over*-stated) the promise offered to both teachers and learners by the precision and flexibility of teaching machines and related equipment. Thus, as Skinner predicted, behaviorism has found advocates in education regarding manipulation of student behavior in classrooms, involvement in developing academic skills, defining teaching skills, development and sequencing educational materials, assessing student needs and achievements, and desiderata of learning environment. This first part of the enigma of why behaviorism works but is unpopular with many teachers will be expanded before getting to the second part.

Scarcely a large school district in the country has gone untouched by what has become two traditional aspects of behaviorism in education: manipulation of environmental contingencies available to teachers to elicit pro-school behaviors, and one or more of the various forms of programmed materials. While it was more typical a decade ago for behaviorists to work with experienced teachers in school settings, the spread of behavioral principles has extended into school of education curricula, so that students, in the process of obtaining teaching credentials, become exposed to its principles even before setting foot in the classroom. Use of the terms, "time-out", "reinforcer", and "behavioral repertoire" no longer mark the speaker as an applied social scientist, but are heard in teachers' lounges and the offices of principals during the transactions of everyday business. The technology of behaviorism, itself, was turned to the task of altering *teachers'* behavior so that they, in turn, then applied behavioral principles to influence the behavior of students. A flood of teachers' manuals came off the presses as the 60's gave way to the 70's (see, for example, the typical volume by Fargo, Behrns & Nolen, 70). The increasing availability of consultants to schools, however, didn't result in an alleviation of the sorts of problems that were most obviously amenable to resolution through the techniques practiced by the consultants. But behaviorism is a technology on the march: direct observation of teachers in classrooms gave way to the new electronics. Microteaching arose as a possible answer to some of the problems of getting teachers to actually apply the principles of the technology in classrooms (Webster & Mendro, 1974).

The present state of the art is marked by the presence of three classes of professionals who utilize behaviorism in education. The first group may be called the "hard liners", those who adhere to the more classic formulations of behaviorism according to the traditions of Watson and

Skinner. Their contribution to education continues through their continued pressing the basic conceptualizations further into educational problems. Their continued interest may be demonstrated by comparing the articles in the journal which reflects their standards, *Journal of Applied Behavioral Analysis* (JABA). In counting articles in the 1968 (Volume 1) publications as compared to the 1977 (Volume 9) which include in the "procedure" portion of the articles the key terms: students, teachers and classrooms, a cursory count reveals 14 such articles in the earlier year and 15 in the latter year. Further, eight of the 14 articles in the earlier publications were concerned with control or/and pro-academic behaviors (attending, etc.) compared to 8 of the 15 in the latter publications with a similar area of interest. The later articles, of course, show the increased sophistication of nine years of shaping and honing. The core of dedicated scientists who stimulated the rise in interest in "behavior modification" are still at work, though that particular term has all but fallen into disuse.

Those adhering closely to the principles of behaviorism have had a pronounced impact on education of children with learning problems. Whether the problems have been identified as having definite organic basis or not, as in the case of brain-damaged children or those rendered deaf by an early or prenatal disease, programs based on behavioral principles have become treatment modalities of choice because of consistent positive results. The frustrations and feelings of hopelessness found in settings where children with serious learning problems are found can well be understood by those who have come in contact with the struggles of teacher and student. The behavioristic formulation has provided an effective way in which such problems can be perceived (attending to the specific behaviors known to be deficient to the learner) and thereby provide a framework for remedial exercises (developing strategies to increase either those deficiencies which are weak, inadequate or absent) or for conceptualizing the problem so that alternative capabilities of the learner can serve as substitute for the missing abilities. Once this is done, the methodology for the learning paradigm is laid out. Hall and Broden (1967) for example, have demonstrated that reinforcement principles have resulted in behavioral changes in brain-injured children with developmental deficits which were not amenable to previous efforts at modification.

While the greatest thrust of the efforts of those most directly involved in behaviorism in education have involved themselves in public elementary schools and in the education of handicapped, Kellar (1974) is a notable exception by the fact that he applied the principles to college teaching. Convinced on the basis of behavioristic principles that college lecture system results in minimum changes in students, he developed a "Kellar Plan" using principles to which he was committed to evoke maximum changes in his students. His plan has resulted in a minor revolution in presentation of college courses.

The "hard nosed" behaviorists have made two other inroads into educational practices which should be mentioned in an update section, both of which involve delivery of learning services to group audiences. The first is the demonstration that behavioristic principles can be organized so that a group of students become involved in a system which delivers secondary reinforcers (rewards) for their pro-academic behaviors. This system has been reported for a group of boys who were high risk to drop out of school by Phillips (1968) and has been duplicated in many similar projects elsewhere. The success in training teachers individually has led to use of group techniques in equipping teachers to use behavioral principles in classrooms. After the long and extensive series of demonstrations of the appropriateness of behavioristic principles being applied to various classroom problems, the next step was to pass on to teachers the methods which had been proven useful. Hosford (1969) demonstrated a successful method of teaching teachers to reinforce desired student behavior by encouraging teachers to do so. Hosford indicated that the success of the methods itself is enough to maintain the teacher behavior taught. This central issue will receive more detailed discussion later.

The state of the art includes a large number of social scientists who have been influenced by behavioristic principles and include them in another, often related, discipline. Krumboltz (1969), for example, uses behavioristic principles in his demonstration of the usefulness of this technology in combination with vocational problem solving skills. The learning package contains units to develop cognitive skills related to job seeking and holding. The careful integration of several strategies including behavioral ones in a reading program are reported (Smith, Hamil, Frase & Poston, 1975) in which several disciplines combine to produce learning environments and materials appropriate to student needs. Any discussion considering the state of the art influenced by behaviorism would be incomplete without mentioning the efforts of Herbert Klausmeier and his associates who have assembled their system of Individually Guided Education (IGE) including teaching strategies, materials development, personnel and delivery organization, community base and other aspects of education in a well-integrated educational program in which behavioristic principles are deeply imbedded (Klausmeier, Rossmiller & Saily, 1977).

The state of the art seems to reflect a massive effort whose conclusion must be an overwhelming demonstration that those behaviorists and others who include behavioristic principles among their basic concepts and tools, have had significant and salutary effect on the educational enterprise. But this is the enigma. It is to be expected that any new procedure would bring with it thoughtful criticism.

Behaviorism has certainly been the focus of professional review. Palardy (1970), for example, has raised questions regarding short and long term effects of behavior modification: does the teaching of conformity, for example, only hide classroom problems which might need deeper resolutions? Cote (1973) has wondered whether behavior modification doesn't indeed crush creativity in children. The criticism may seem well taken in view of the plethora of studies in which conformity is the object of the techniques, even though other authors have demonstrated the use of the same techniques in developing creativity (Glover and Gary, 1975). It is possible to take the position that behavioral principles are compatible with more "humanistic" procedures (Fitt, 1976), and some teachers have actually included behaviorist techniques in open classrooms (e.g., Winett, 1973). Further, studies show that teachers who have been exposed to behavioral training demonstrate altered behaviors after such training (e.g., Bowles & Nelson, 1976). But regardless of the viewpoint one assumes, it is enigmatic that a system which has proven over and over again to help teachers resolve many problems in a variety of classrooms that teachers, as a profession, look upon behaviorism with disdain. The many articles appearing in the educational journals critical of behavioral practices are summarized by an article by MacDonald (1973) in which a group of 31 teachers, one year after they learned principles of and expressed positive feelings for behavioral training, admitted that they had not used behavioral principles in teaching the last six months, or had used them on only trivial issues, and that they were completely opposed to further use of behavioral principles in classroom problems.

Thus, the current status of behaviorism seems to be, to modify an old saw, a technology without a classroom to change in. A core of dedicated and talented psychologists continue to develop new applications to the educational scenes. Old friends have taken bits and pieces of the technology and have built new technologies, always with new names and often without leaving behind traces of credits. Books and other literature designed by behaviorists are within the reach of most teachers, yet the teaching profession seems, in spite of the apparent counterproductiveness of the stand, to keep behaviorism at the door and become progressively less hospitable a host.

It would seem that the strategy of behaviorists to use a model of behavioral change with teachers that has proven successful with students has largely failed. It is easy enough to understand why the similar model of prompting teachers to use behavioral strategies and then reinforce them was adopted in the first place. One generally uses that which has proven successful. What is difficult to understand is why behaviorists continue to use the same paradigm after continued failure. Tanaka-Matsumi & Tharp (1977), for example, propose a model of consultation to schools in which the consultant (behaviorist) maintains a relationship with the mediator (teacher) during the intervention. This model for effecting the behavior of the teacher, however, is not feasible for the typical educational setting. Teachers have proven capable of implementing programs based on behavioral principles. The problem seems to be one of conceptualizing the teacher as a person, and teachers as professionals. There are many differences between children attending classes and teachers engaged in their classroom activities. To apply the same simple reinforcement model to both may be inappropriate. Are behaviorists acting like subjects who have been strongly shocked, or who find themselves in insoluable problem situations and suffer from response fixation? It would not be surprising to see those concerned with furthering behaviorism working in other ways to influence the profession of teaching through professional organizations, Boards of Education, and through legislation to alter the institutions of education to be more amenable to behavioristic principles.

THEORY

Learning

Behaviorism, itself, is at once the philosophy behind, and the product of, what is called learning theory. To the behaviorist, learning simply refers to observed or demonstrable change in behavior. To infer that learning has taken place in a student, the behaviorist must first know what response the learner makes under given conditions at time #1, and then what response the learner makes under similar conditions at time #2. If there is a difference, learning is said to have occurred. This is not to say that maturation of the young child and that the inherited characteristics of the child are ignored as sources of behavioral determination. Rather, the child is considered a "fantastically capable learning mechanism . . . " which at birth is devoid of input, and that, while biological structure of the child provides input, the child's early responses, before learning takes place, are random and haphazard (Staats, 1971).

By the time the child reaches the classroom, essentially all behaviors of interest to the teacher have come under the influence of learning. Certainly such biologically determined limits as intelligence, reactivity and size take part in shaping and limiting what is learned by the child. But the shape of behavior, that to which the child responds, the specific nature of the response, and the development of skills are all largely determined by learning. It is the learning aspect of student behavior which occupies the focus of attention of this chapter. Further, while learning theory is the subject matter of the behaviorists and concerns range into a variety of theoretical areas and issues, only those aspects of learning theory which apply directly to selected classroom topics will be discussed here.

An operant behavior occurs as a function of its consequences

Perhaps one of Skinner's greatest contributions was his recognition of the importance of the fact that when a rat was placed in a box in which there was a lever which, when first accidentally pressed, delivered a food pellet, that the lever pressing response rapidly increased (Skinner, 1932). It was Skinner's recognition of the importance of this "reinforcement" principal as fundamental to a majority of our waking behavior that gave behaviorism such a boost in dealing with the explanation and control of behavior. This is known as operant conditioning.

If a teacher wishes to increase the frequency of a behavior which already occurs in the repertoire of a student (an *operant* is a behavior which acts on the environment, not as a reflex to a stimulus, but as a function of the reinforcement history of the act) the teacher rewards the student as immediately after the act as possible. This contingent rewarding (called *reinforcing* by learning theorists) of a desired behavior (operant conditioning) raises the probability that the rewarded behavior will re-occur. Bucher and Okovita (1977) are two researchers out of literally hundreds who have demonstrated the relationship between student behaviors and subsequent reinforcement. The conditioning is most basic: reward on act soon after it occurs, and the student will engage frequently in that rewarded behavior.

Behaviors which have proven to be influenced by subsequent reward include (a) sitting quietly, (b) attending to teacher or academic materials, (c) raising a hand when students wish to address the teacher, (d) cooperating with other children on a task, (e) giving the correct numbers when shown an addition problem, and (f) including relevant references to support arguments in verbal debate. The operant may be conceived as a class of responses demanding skeletal muscles in movement and those involved in verbal replies. Traditional behaviorists prefer to deal with the actual verbal behavior, though those with other leanings may deal with the inferred thought process theorized to lie behind the verbal activity.

Operant conditioning is certainly a powerful tool in teaching, but its use requires discipline on the part of the teacher. For, if rewarding a student for behavior desired by the teacher strengthens that response (it occurs more frequently), wouldn't rewarding behaviors not desired by the teachers also strengthen them? Most teachers have found the answer to this themselves. With students who misbehave and then receive attention (positive social reward), misbehavior is all the more likely to occur. The problem occurs when teachers act in such a way that they believe they are delivering a punishment but the effect is that of a reinforcer. This is frequently demonstrated when students display increased frequency of an

undesirable behavior when the teacher follows their behavior with a verbal "punishment" only to find, paradoxically, that the behavior increases.

Breaking contingencies between behavior and rewards extinguishes the behavior

It has been observed often that the most rewarding aspects of a child's
environment are the plaudits gained from peers. Thus, a teacher confronted with a student whose misbehavior is followed by titters from
peers may seem helpless to control the contingency between misbehavior
and subsequent reward by peers. The principle, however, is clear. The
child's misbehavior, if separated from a following reward, will decrease.
The same principle holds when a teacher discovers that it is the teacher's
own attention to misbehavior which raises it to such troublesome frequency. Thus, it is often suggested that an effective way to reduce misbehavior in a classroom is simply to reward positive behavior, and ignore
all else. This is not to say that all horseplay, etc., will disappear. It will,
however, avoid the problems engendered by rewarding such undesired
behavior by attending to it and thereby increasing it.

Careful punishment, in an environment rich with reward opportunities, will extinguish behaviors

Some behaviorists assert that all undesired behaviors will not extin-
guish even with teacher controlled contingencies. In such situations, it has
been demonstrated that students may be provided a variety of alternatives
which bring rewards, and informed that undesirable behaviors will be
followed by punishment. In such situations, the undesirable behavior will
tend to be suppressed by the punishment, and will tend to disappear
because of the easy availability of rewards for more desirable behaviors
within the student's capabilities of performing (Clarizio, 1971). It should
be noted that this strategy is not accepted by all behaviorists, some of
whom assert that rewarding positive behaviors, alone, is sufficient to
establish behavioral control. This is based on the assumption that if students are doing desired things and being rewarded properly, then the
concern with suppressing non-desired behavior is not needed. In the normal classroom, this is probably true. However, with some types of learners
more heroic methods may be justified (Lovaas & Simmons, 1969).

Students can learn new responses by oberving others

Bandura (1965) pioneered a new approach to learning in which learning
occurred without the student actually engaging in the behavior. Called
"observational learning", this method asserts that students learn by
watching "models" engage in certain behavior, the efficiency of learning

depending on the exact nature of what is observed. In those cases where the model engages in behavior leading to reward, and when socially encouraged, the observers are likely to engage in similar acts especially in similar situations.

Modeling is a powerful teaching tool when new responses are desired. Behaviors which can be influenced range from learning aggressive responses in free-play situation to moral judgements. However, learning through modeling is not a process which can be turned off and on at the whim of educators or public officials. There is no reason why children observing teachers engaging in behavior prohibited to the children shouldn't learn to engage in the prohibited behavior and then go to the classroom and suddenly learn certain desirable behaviors selected by the teacher. This principle is one of the reasons for the concern for violence on TV (children will model rewarded aggressors) or for the concern over spectacles public officials make of themselves.

New behavior can be developed by careful presentation of rewards

Modeling, however, is not the only process by which new behaviors can be developed in the learner. One well studied method is called "shaping" which refers to the process by which a teacher may establish a reward contingency to a desired behavior, such as well-articulated speech. When the contingency is well established, the teacher waits until a particularly fine example of the behavior is displayed and then rewards it quickly. As the learner fluctuates in behavioral output from satisfactory to exemplary, the teacher rewards only the "top part" of the behavior, and the learner's output gradually becomes more like that desired by the teacher. Soon what was exemplary becomes common, and the teacher again waits for outstanding behavior relative to the new standard. In this way, highly skilled behavior can be developed from what was previously mediocre behavior.

The shaping of behavior, however, can go two ways. Shaping depends on response variability. That is, each time we respond, we respond somewhat *differently*. If we hop on one foot, we may hop at heights of 6, 7, 8, 6, 7, 5, and 9 inches off the ground. We could shape hopping by rewarding only those "top part" hops of 8 and 9 inches. This would call for careful attention to reward only superior performances. What can happen in the classroom is just the reverse. Some students under contingency management try to elicit rewards from teachers when their behavior gets near the criterion previously established. If rewarded, the student has begun a process of decrement learning, in which the standards are lowered, rather than raised. While this is also a process of *shaping*, it is really the teacher who is being shaped, rather than the student.

In a practical demonstration of this principle, Azrin and Lindsley (1967) demonstrated that cooperative behavior could be developed without the specific use of instructions. Rewarding cooperation alone, was the active agent in the bringing about cooperative behavior. While this study was a "laboratory demonstration", the elements of the study are instructive to the teacher whose classroom suggests many opportunities to apply the principles.

Behavior can be conditioned to occur in the presence of
certain stimuli

A student who stomps his feet and cheers at a basketball game is likely to go unnoticed. Should the student stomp and cheer in class he will become the focus of attention. One of the tasks of living is to learn to produce differential behavior appropriate to the situation (stimulus condition, to the behaviorist). Differential responses to specific situations is essential to the orderly conduct of social process. The skills of the learner, however, demand more sophistication in learning stimulus control of behavior than those mentioned above. It is possible for students to learn to study only under certain teachers, or under specific conditions, whether the learning is consciously monitored or not. If students are only rewarded for work done in the presence of the teacher, students will learn that the presence of the teacher is essential part of the learning. Thereafter, students will not work when the teacher leaves the room, and perhaps learn that homework is to be done only in the classroom. Such stimulus control was demonstrated by Marholin and Steinman (1977). The authors rewarded students when they worked both with teacher present and with teacher absent. Thus, it was work behavior which became the critical element of the stimuli, not any behavior occurring in the presence of the teacher. This was demonstrated by the consistent work of the students regardless of surrounding conditions.

Neutral stimuli can become rewards and stimuli for
other behaviors

Staats (1975) has argued that previously neutral stimuli can take on rewarding properties through classical conditioning. He then argues that the conditioned reinforcing stimulus becomes capable of eliciting specific reactions (becomes a directive stimulus). This formulation becomes useful in understanding the complex learning seen in language, where chains of words seem to flow endlessly without apparent direction or reward. Staats' formulation, however, provides a key to the problem. Words, phrases, song lyrics or preambles can become conditioned to elicit certain emotional states, and can come to elicit certain other behaviors, especially words. Further, words can come to have certain values when spoken by one person or another. The words of a teacher, then, can be conditioned to evoke specific reactions in some students (perhaps other reactions in other students!). The word "test" produces nearly debilitating anxiety in some students. "Let's go to work, class" seems to be a cue to some students to get sleepy and talk to neighbors. If words are the tools of the teacher, great effort should be made to keep them meaningful by the rewards which are established in their proximal occurrence.

*The frequency of reinforcement influences
characteristics of responses*

A great deal of research shows the efficacy of rewarding desired behaviors. There is also a strong literature which supports the notion that conditions in which reinforcers are selected and how they are presented to the learner determines the rate of learning, and how long the learning will be sustained in the face of "thin" reward situations. The principles are well known: to enhance learning, reward immediately after the desired response is made. To enhance rapid learning, reward every correct response. As the response begins to occur frequently, require more responses to gain a reward (fading). When quality of response is a part of the situation, demand gradually improving quality to gain the reward (Becker, 1971). An application of this has been developed in which a student agrees to perform certain behavior which hasn't yet become desirable, in return for which the student is permitted to engage in one which has become more desirable (Premack, 1965). Reinforcement of groups has also been established as a viable form of classroom management (Wolf & Risley, 1967).

Careful management of reinforcement schedules permits the teacher to maximize the rate of learning, and to minimize the degree of "control" implied by the necessary acts of reinforcement. The issues to be considered are the schedules of reward as discussed above, reinforcing characteristics of the reward (does frequent presentation of fudge tend to satiate the learner, or does the sweet smile of the teacher lose its potency?), and the potency of the reward in regard to the learner. Each of these aspects vary from learner to learner. At the one extreme, there are learners who have come to be reinforced by the learning itself, and at the other extreme are students who have learned an aversion of the teacher, the school, the texts, and/or the classroom. Each presents different problems in terms of arranging the classroom contingencies to the teacher.

Eventually, the teacher wishes to reduce the role of the reinforcer in the maintenance of the desired behavior. The strategy consists more than simply thinning the ratio of reward to desired behavior (fading). The teacher attempts, through encouragement and verbal conditioning, to associate the learner's own verbalizations (goal statements, statements of interests, etc.) to become rewards for study, curiosity, and other academic skills. The thinning process depends on the teacher maintaining an irregular ratio of rewards to the behavior. It is as if the teacher is attempting to prevent the student from knowing when the next reinforcer is occurring: will it be on the 9th or 29th repetition of the desired behavior. It has been demonstrated that if the pattern is regular, the response rate of the student will drop, again as if the student "waits" for the likelihood of the reward in occurring, assuming that the student has a good idea when it will occur.

The relationship between behavior and rewards may
be very complex

At the simplest level of analysis, a given reward might lose its reinforcement value simply because the student becomes satiated with the consumable reward. The relationship between reward and behavior, however, is often far more complex. In the case of a student who is beginning to learn addition facts, the reward may need to be monumental to get the student to attend to the somewhat aversive task. As the student develops competence in the task, however, addition no longer evokes in the student an unpleasant emotional reaction, and, in fact, the student begins to enjoy the competency achieved through learning. Eventually, the skill will come under the reinforcements which are available to all of us, such as good grades, complements from parents, or simply success itself!

When the classroom serves as a generalized aversive stimulus, rewards are useful in gaining constructive behavior of students. As the teacher is able to teach students the positive reward value of teacher's presence, the reward necessary to evoke *any* behavior lessens. Further, as the student begins to gain rewards from attending behavior and from the beginnings of competence, other sources of reward become available to the student. The generalized reward properties of the classroom do not necessarily remain constant to the student through the course of the students' lifetime, nor even through the course of the year. Certainly the discussions of making the classroom more "open" can be considered in terms of drastically altering the reward properties of the classroom environment as well as the flow of activities within it. Obviously, unlimited space will not make classrooms pleasant places in which people may engage in self-development. Critical is the gradual enhancement of the positive aspects of those acts which lead to self-enhancement. Through conditioning and operant management, schools, classrooms, teachers and learning materials can become more or less aversive as stimuli to students. The relationships are not static. Students are always in process of learning, and learning involves the alterations in reward properties of the learning situations, as well as relationships between behavior and situations in which they occur.

Teaching

Gage and Winne (1975) have stated that the dominant thrust in teacher education during the last decade has been performance-based teacher education (PBTE). While they indicate the difficulty of defining PBTE, they do offer a terse definition which contains the elements of teacher training: *emphasis on student achievement of educational objectives and teacher behaviors both verbal and non-verbal that will enhance teacher goals.* Behaviorists would generally agree that this is what teaching should be concerned about. Each aspect shall be discussed separately.

Use of behavioral objectives enhances teaching

A behavioral objective is a statement of a concrete, specific, measurable goal which provides clear, precise explanation of what the learner is to do (Plowman, 1971). The behavioral objective, a unit with which the teacher plans lessons and focuses student talents, is a behavior to be exhibited by the student to indicate that the learning objective has been completed. From the standpoint of insuring whether the student has achieved the object of the lesson, then, the behavioral objective simplifies and clarifies the task of teacher and student alike.

But where do behavioral objectives come from? They must derive from the teacher's organization and conceptualization of the development of the students through academic achievement. Objectives come from cultural, societal and experiential sources which reflect the values as acquired over time. The objectives stem from an organization of objectives which, when considered as a sequence, move the student from one point in academic, social and personal development to a point further along in the development of that person as the student moves toward eventual adulthood and toward a more complete fulfillment of skills and talents. Those influenced by behaviorism are not loath to bring into the educational planning non-behavioral concepts, generalizations and values, but are free to recognize that educational planning and implementation is enhanced when behavioral objectives become the end point in such planning.

Behavioral objectives, when they are a part of a conceptual organization including developmental plan and cultural values, are enmeshed in a sequence of behavioral objectives that move coherently from a point of relatively little skill onto a point of high skill through a path of desired learning. The strength of the behavioral objective, when it is a part of a well integrated sequence of behavioral objectives, is that it identifies for teacher and student alike, what is expected of student in terms of learning, and what is expected of teacher regarding the focus of her efforts. The behavioral objective coordinates their joint efforts. The behavioral objective also simplifies the task of measuring the learning achieved by the student. With ambiguous objectives, the final performance of the student is ambiguously defined. When rigorously defined, the measuring of success is simple and straightforward.

Specific teacher acts (reinforcement) enhance student performance

The behaviorist regards the teacher as one of the critical sources of reward in the classroom. While peers often serve as informal reinforcers for undesirable behavior, it is the teacher's encouragement of students, and the teacher's smiles, encouragement, and pats on the back that serve as a major reward for student learning behavior.

While punishment or aversive training may play a part in student training, it is the position of this writer that punishment is needed only in extraordinary cases and not in the regular classroom. Hence, this discussion will focus on teacher reward behavior. Some authors assert that withholding rewards is, in fact, punishment, but this writer takes the position that student and teacher have an explicit or at least, a tacit, contract that when the student does that which the teacher considers productive of learning, the teacher rewards the student. While the teacher doesn't reward every student act, this doesn't imply teacher punishment. This will be discussed below in discussing schedules of reinforcement.

Walker and Hops (1976) are one set of authors among hundreds who have shown that teachers who direct social approval contingent on approved performance or on pro-academic behavior contribute to student achievement of learning goals. They found that teachers who rewarded either students who actually achieved, or those who displayed pro-academic behaviors outperformed students not so rewarded. There are differences in opinion among researchers regarding the details of how, when and what should constitute most efficacious rewarding, but teachers are assured by their own experience that rewarding students does pay off in enhanced performance.

The previous discussion of learning principles also provides some clues regarding when teachers should apply rewards to learners. First, the teacher must determine what is a reward. Generally, teacher smiles and approval are powerful rewards, but with some students, teachers find that cookies or other consumables early in the relationship may serve to establish the teacher as a positive, rather than a negative value in the classroom. The teacher directs students to engage in productive activity and signals by careful use of smiles, point or token awards when the students are doing just what teacher wants them to do. Finally, the behaviorist teacher rewards students for portions of completed work. In the "early" phase of response acquisition, the teacher consistently rewards. When a student first tries a behavior, for example, the teacher will reward each successful response. Then, after the student begins to "get" what is expected, the teacher may change the requirements for a reward. The teacher may ask for neater work, or more of it. Further, the teacher may let students know that they are doing well, and the students should begin rewarding themselves (a teacher remark like, "this is excellent work" may stimulate students to so describe their work to themselves, thus becoming self-rewarding). The wise teacher does not criticize the student or the student's work. The teacher will indicate what is desired (gain reward) and that which is not (teacher ignores).

Teaching is a fine art. Even in the management of reinforcers, it should be clear that the process is anything but mechanical. At some point, the teacher decides to ask for enhanced performance for reward (shaping). Likewise, the teacher, when a student is beginning to achieve regular success on a particular learning task, may begin to "thin" the rewards. That is, the teacher may begin a student on a new task by rewarding every problem with a smile and "good job". But when the student begins to show interest in the task, and some ability to proceed without it, the teacher may wait for a group of problems before saying "good job". Finally, the teacher may wait for an entire day's lesson before making this encouraging statement. Teachers may also demonstrate a variety of rewards ranging from a brief nod of the head to a brief grasping of the shoulder to show extreme delight.

As the teacher may reward, so also may she ignore. In nearly every classroom some students choose to engage in various forms of undesired behavior. If one were to observe any student for an entire period, one would discover that every child engages in some pencil chewing, looking at the ceiling, rustling through a desk, and so on. Most of this behavior is ignored by the teacher. It is only when students either engage in a great deal of such non-productive behavior, or actually engage in disruptive behavior, that the teacher becomes concerned. Teachers are tempted to direct remarks at such students on the assumption that statements which direct students in how to behave will, indeed, get them to behave accordingly. However, in some cases, the teachers' directional remarks, or even desist remarks, act as rewards, and have the exact opposite effect of what was intended. In such cases, teachers are advised to ignore disruptive behavior, and take special care to reward such students when their behavior warrants it.

Priming students often elicits desired behavior

One of the problems teachers may encounter is a high frequency of restlessness, or other behavior in students who show little desirable target behavior. This makes it difficult for the teacher to reward the student. Several methods have been discovered to "prime" the student, which seem unobtrusive and which avoid direct confrontation which so often proves counterproductive. The teacher may observe a student next to the one of concern, and reward *him* for a desired behavior. This often results in the student of concern imitating the rewarded student, which now gives the teacher an opportunity to reward the desired student. Some teachers will walk over by the student of concern and look elsewhere while talking. When the target student displays the desired behavior, the teacher stops talking, and rewards the student. The teacher may also "lie": that is, suddenly look at the target student, smile, and reward him for a desired behavior, even though the target student had not displayed that behavior. This has often resulted in the target student displaying the desired behavior for a short time, enough to gain reward.

These teacher "priming" behaviors are used to elicit from the student a behavior which will permit the teacher to reward the student. When a student engages in behaviors approximating those desired, the teacher may engage in "shaping" the student's behavior into that which is more productive for the student, by means of rewarding.

Students will copy teacher behaviors which lead to
rewards

Bandura's (1965) research on modeling behavior has had profound impact on the behavioristic approach to teaching. This approach establishes a means to teach students new-for-them behavior. A teacher may stand up in front of a class and demonstrate how to react to an upset child. A teacher may model a chemistry experiment, including a variety of skilled acts. A teacher may select a difficult word, and model for a class how to look up the word in the dictionary. In each case the teacher engages in desired behaviors which students may have never, themselves, engaged in. Such behaviors would belong in development through shaping, but take only a short time to develop through modeling. In each case, the teacher insures that success will result from imitating the displayed teacher behavior. After such displays, students will tend to "copy" the teacher, or engage in behaviors the student thinks are similar to those of the teacher. When the student begins to display approximate behaviors, the teacher can engage in finer-grain teaching to produce the skilled acts desired.

Teachers have, for a long time, practiced modeling. Teachers usually dress well, speak well and conduct themselves with decorum to set a proper example for students. But it is not enough to set an example. The teacher who dresses well and then becomes a source of pain to students through criticism, etc., becomes a negative example. Students could actually begin dressing poorly, to demonstrate the distinction between themselves and an unpopular teacher. To serve as a model, the teacher must display distinctive qualities, be successful in attaining desirable outcomes, and retain favorable interpersonal attraction to be a positive model.

Group seating and rewarding can enhance student performance

While the teacher maintains the responsibility to determine exact contingencies between behavior and rewards, organization of classrooms can be used to maximize behaviors and their contingencies. Some instruction must be done on an individual-to-individual basis, and other instruction may be done by individual or group instruction. Many teachers have demonstrated the effectiveness of organizing classrooms into task groups in which the group is rewarded when all members of the group have completed certain tasks (e.g., Simmons & Wasik, 1976).

Organization of the classroom takes deliberation and some thought. Simmons and Wasik found that student seating arrangement based on sociometric choice became more disruptive than constructive. However, when the classroom was restructured into work groups, and the rewards were based on task completion by all members of the groups, the students became far more work-oriented, peers helped slower students in acceptable ways and work output greatly increased. The exact structure of the group depends on the desired end of the teacher. If "responsibility" is one of the desired outcomes, the teacher may choose to select as a behavior the handling of materials, and make such behavior one of the requisites of the group being rewarded. Compliance is another outcome that could be selected, and reward made contingent on it. In such a case, the peers become sources to quiet fellow group members.

Other forms of classroom organizations are, of course, available. Student groups may range from diads to combinations of several classes for the purposes of showing movies, or delivering lectures. Groups of students sit in groups, stand during competitions, and lay on the floor during exercises or some forms of art work. Chairs may be realigned to demark "boundaries" or areas can be "marked" by use of bookshelves, aquariums or hanging art. "Work stations" may be used when several tasks are to be done: students group about one work station to complete task one, while others are at station two, doing another task. In such classroom organization, the teacher circulates and encourages students as they get into the swing of what is the intended purpose of each activity. Soon, peer interaction becomes an important source of reward.

Curriculum materials vary greatly in their inherent
rewarding values

Some stories are "fun" to read, and some are not. Those that are fun to read need no other reward to the reader than to be within reach of the reader: the material takes it from there. But some books are difficult to wade through and are almost aversive in the reaction they evoke in the reader. A comparison of such a differential in extent materials was made by Cook and White (1977). The attempt to use the reward properties of books, themselves, as a means to get students to improve their reading skills was popularized by the *Hooked on Books* (Feder & McNiel, 1968) volume.

From a theoretical as well as practical point of view, teachers are well advised to select attractive reading material. Especially in the early stages of learning a skill, it is important to prepare inherently rewarding tasks for learners to engage in. This tends to make learning that task "fun" and no encouragement is needed to gain student participation. Once the student achieves some skill at a task, more difficult material is appropriate.

There are several areas in which subject matter may differ, each which may have some influence regarding its attractiveness or non-attractiveness. Vocabulary, obviously, is one of the variables in subject matter. Most teachers are careful to select material which does not have too many words. On the other hand, some students like the challenge of *some* new words; selection of material with no new words is a poor procedure. Writing style is an important factor in the attractiveness of curriculum material. Some writers have wit expressed in the material, while others have none. Students, like everyone else, like to laugh. Illustrations for beginning readers are important because they not only give a pictoral idea about which the story is written, but give the student a favorable impression of the story before and during the reading. But this effect should not be considered only applicable to children: publishers of college texts have come to include considerable pictoral and graphic materials in their publications in recent years because of the positive response of college students. Perhaps the last point to consider is the organization of the material. Behaviorists follow the discoveries of learning experiments which show that when many things are to be learned, learning is most facilitated by lumping things into meaningful or discriminable chunks. One would conclude from this that long discussions in books would be easiest to learn if broken into sub units. Long lectures would be most remembered if thoughts were set apart by meaningful cues or acts on the part of the speaker. Long lessons would best be broken into chunks so that the learner can first deal with the number of elements in the lesson, then the details in each element, or chunk. Materials with plenty of headings, special displays and short discussions are those likely to be best remembered.

APPLICATIONS

Curriculum, Academic

Behaviorists have not addressed the issue of curriculum with the detail of other educators. This is perhaps because behaviorists have really been adjunctive rather than centrally involved in educational matters. Except for those who have skills and interest central to education, behaviorists have been concerned with the problems of assisting the learner to deal effectively with that which the curriculum specialists (some one other than the behaviorist) have selected for study.

The educational behaviorist actually has two areas of interest. The first is arranging the curriculum so that it is more learnable. Keller (1974) has popularized the "unit Mastery" system in the presentation of college level courses. His curriculum was based on breaking a given subject matter into lesson-sized chunks. Students were encouraged to read the material in the basic lesson, as well as engage in ancillary learning experiences prepared by the instructor which might include experiments, film-strips and learning through other sensory modalities. Then, when the student is ready, an examination is taken. A pre-established criterion for "passing" each unit is announced before the course is offered, and each student must pass each unit at that level to receive credit for that unit. Students may take exams on each unit as many times as they wish: theoretically, each unit has countless exams, so that the student may take the exam as many times as the student chooses. Each exam is constructed from a pool of items so that no two exams are the same. While some have criticized the testing method as encouraging students to take exams before they are prepared, experience has shown that most students actually take only one exam per learning module. Since the criterion for each exam is pre-selected, this means that students seem to learn how much to study to pass each exam. The level selected is usually that which is demanded by "A" performance. This means that a large proportion of students earn "A's" using this teaching methodology.

In taking a course by this unit mastery method, students find themselves working at their own speed, and attending those ancillary activities which they want to, and not attending those which for them, individually, there is no appeal. The method depends on a great deal of preparation on the part of the teacher, because the testing pool, the ancillary activities and the presentation of materials all must be coordinated. In some places, the course is student-paced. That is, the student moves as quickly or as slowly as the student chooses, some finishing a course in two or three weeks. In other presentations, the course is offered at the same rate as any other course, being coordinated to end with the semester.

Behaviorists have been involved more closely with curriculum of retarded learners because the curriculum of the retarded tends to be more concrete and circumscribed than that of normal students. It is with such a well-defined objective that the behaviorist can best deal with the tools of the technology. Thus, the behaviorist can deal with sequencing the learning tasks of a retarded learner because they are better specified by the educational curriculum builder. The behaviorist can sequence that which is known, and gain an idea of what is needed to be added to the curriculum by observing the performance of the retarded. All too often, in the eyes of the behaviorist, the traditional curriculum builder doesn't know specifically what should follow what, and has little idea of the chunks which are missing in order to achieve real mastery of a stated skill.

Curriculum, Non-Academic

The behaviorist has difficulty separating that which is part of the academic curriculum and that which is not than most educators. First, the behaviorist sees that each behavior is related to other behaviors in the repertoire of the learners in sequences and hierarchies, linked together by communalities of response and stimulus similarities. Further, the behaviorist is aware that one learns many things when learning to read: the student learns to *like* to read or perhaps develops an aversion for reading. To the behaviorist, the likelihood with which the student will actually read in the future cannot be separated with the skill in reading can potentially be done (though won't, because of the aversion). The skill, and the frequency with which it will be displayed are part of learning. Therefore, the teacher who is confronted with one pupil who doesn't have the skills to read, and one who has the skills but who won't, has the task of teaching two students to read. In one case, the learning may be that of basic skills, and in the other, attitude modification. But in both cases, the teacher confronts the issue of getting the student to engage in specified behaviors which should lead to the student actively engaging in reading behavior.

It might seem that behaviorism is aptly suited for training students to engage in those skills requiring skeletal musculature. Athletics, manual training and motor learning are *behaviors* which seem more adaptable to training. This is really not the case. It might appear easier to focus on those gross physical behaviors as targets to be developed. *All learning,* for the behaviorist, involves discernable change in behavior. Thus, the behaviorist would ask what behavior has changed in determining if a person had learned something. Academic learning involves behavior (vocal responding, writing answers) as well as those displayed by the athletic squad. It is a matter of careful specification for the behaviorist.

For the behaviorist, the teaching of self-care skills are important. With the assumption that behaviors occur in relation to the probabilities of reward, the learner is dependent on other persons as long as they are the major director of activities and source of rewards. Students are enhanced, then, when they learn to direct their own behavior toward meaningful goals. The term *meaningful* is used in the sense here to indicate that some goals of the learner result in desirable outcomes which may not be immediately rewarding (study behaviors) but may, in the long run, promise payoffs for the learner: such would be a "meaningful" goal. The learner may develop self-directive activity by learning to become an accurate self-monitor (Thoresen & Mahoney, 1974). The behaviorist sees the development of self-monotoring and self-rewarding a part of learning as much as learning to say "four" when the teacher says, "how much is two and two?"

Behaviorists are often criticized for "bribing" students by making a contingency between desired behavior and a reward. Many critics state that students *should* learn because they are obligated to, and that teachers *should* not "pay" them for behavior which society expects of them. This ethical issue is often raised, because it is assumed that students learn, from behaviorists, not to perform responsibilities without being paid. Nothing could be farther from the truth.

It might first be useful to state that "bribes" is a term normally used to indicate that a person pays money to get someone else to do something which is either illegal or at least disadvantageous to a person who is not in position to protect his/her own best interests. Thus, the briber is taking advantage of someone else. In the case of rewarding students, no one is the loser: indeed, everyone gains.

But taking this ethical issue a step further, it will become clear that the similarities between bribes, and rewarding desired behavior disappear altogether. In rewarding a student, the teacher uses the thinnest reward schedule possible, and uses the reward to lead to the highest level of skill. In our discussion of teacher skill, it was noted that the teacher eventually "thins" the reward, and eventually attempts to turn the responsibility of "rewarding" over to the natural environment (having skills should be rewarding). Thus, the use of rewards by the teacher is *a temporary device* to get students to do that which they wouldn't do without the reward. This can be put another way. Suppose a teacher would like a student to learn to spell "cat". Suppose the student is reluctant to act in any way which would foster that learning. The teacher can scold, force or reward the student, or ignore the student altogether. It is the behaviorist's position that the teacher should use the most attractive means available to get the student to engage in the desired behavior. Scolding or other forms of punishment generally lead to undesirable side effects, unless there are rewarding alternatives to the student. Ignoring the child may well teach the child that the teacher, hence the adult world, really doesn't care what the child does. So, from a behavioristic view point, it is ethically irresponsible *not* to take that course of action which provides the student with the most salutary outcome, reward for the behavior, when it is understood that by "rewarding" the behaviorist means using the "lightest" reward practicable.

Student Evaluation

Student evaluation means something different to the behaviorist than to the traditional educator. At the simplest analysis, the learning task itself provides the evaluation. The student, of course, knows what he/she can do. Student evaluation demands that the student and educator agree on specific goals. The behaviorist does not recognize the legitimacy of statements like, "some skills cannot be measured", or "learning is too subtle to be measured". Rather, the behaviorist asserts that if one human can detect the learning of another, it can be measured, otherwise it falls outside the realm of concern of the behaviorist.

The linkage of the behavioral objective and the evaluation of students can be readily seen. The emphasis of the behaviorist that the educator know the behaviors desired as end products of the learning experience makes the evaluation a matter of detection of the quality of the target response, the conditions in which it was made, and the frequency with which it is made.

Grades are given periodically to reward behavior. Daily report cards help the student focus on behavioral expectations, and understand the pace expected. Students with poor study habits are often benefitted by this "focusing" activity during that period required to enhance the length of time during which the student can attend to work. Grades don't have the same evaluative meaning for the behaviorist that they do for traditional teachers, because of the emphasis on specified skills. Grades can be quantified in terms of number of skills acquired in a stated time. Normally, however, as in the unit mastery system, most students have access to achieving all the skills required, so that the "A" grade becomes the one expected of students who apply themselves.

Behaviorism has moved into the area referred to as "thought" only recently. Behaviorists who have other disciplinary concerns may well reflect concerns in this academic area. While at the present time behaviorally oriented educators are satisfied to deal with verbal manifestations of thought, and infer as little as possible about the "internal activity" of the student, there are two notable exceptions. Psychologists with behavioral interests have begun working with students to give themselves self-instructions (how does anyone know whether the instructions were given?) and have been satisfied with the results. "Images" have been used by behaviorists for years who have apparently assumed that verbal reports about these mental events accurately reflect that which is reported.

Counseling

Behavioral counseling appears on the surface to be a simple procedure. Actually, it is extremely complex, though the simplification of the client's problems conceptually is one of the useful steps in behaviorally oriented counseling. Whether the problem is brought to the counselor by the teacher, or the student, the counselor must first listen empathically. The behavioral counselor needs to formulate the nature of the problem, and often this is a process of disentangling a confusion of thoughts and feelings, and often a misplacement of the problem itself. In teacher referred problems, the counselor may agree with the teacher that the target is the student. The exact nature of the problem, however, is another matter. Some teachers refer to students as problems when it is their own perception, alone, of which the problem consists. Assessment of student behaviors and discussion with teachers often relieves the problem. More likely, there are behaviors exhibited by the student which obstruct the student from achieving objectives which are the problem. Obviously, a thorough assessment is required which may include observation of the classroom, talks with the teacher, student, parents and some times others. The counselor, after the assessment phase, discusses with the teacher the goals established for the student. Again, this can be difficult, if the counselor, teacher, or student disagree on the goals to be established for the student. Often a conference with all interested persons can establish goals acceptable by all. The solution to the problem, then, becomes a program including specification of step-wise sequence of behaviors expected of the student, and those rewards which will be contingent upon performance of agreed upon behavior. Usually, the counselor will not see the student in private sessions except in those cases in which goals need final specification, or when sessions are required to finalize agreements regarding the establishment of the program. Such a program will usually require monitoring and even some "fine tuning" so that the little details demanded by any behavioral program will, in fact, be taken care of.

It is the teacher in the school setting who makes behavior counseling simple. This is because the teacher establishes the goal of the counseling, or at least precipitates discussion of specific goals. It is when the student comes for help that behavioral counseling can become complex. The problems of students can include difficulties in formulating goals, identifying someone else as the problem, identifying the problem as a *feeling* (rather than behavior of the student), or refusing to accept the goals set by others (Krumboltz & Thoresen, 1969). The skilled behavioral counselor will help the student to rephrase or reconceptualize the problem into behaviors (they may be actions, feelings in reaction to something, thoughts) over which the student has control, and then work out a plan to acquire those behaviors the student lacks, or drop those undesirable behaviors which are troublesome, or alter those attitudinal or emotional reactions which are troublesome. (Identification may take several sessions.) This identification is often the most critical step of the counseling (and may take the most skill). Then a program for behavioral change is developed and implemented. Again, the counselor would not necessarily meet regularly with the student, except to monitor the progress of the behavioral change problem.

Group counseling has not attained great popularity among behaviorists. To the degree to which it is an individual matter to identify the client's problems in terms of behaviors, a process that often takes hours of clarification, focusing, and even educating the student, the group setting is awkward. Some assert, of course, that many students have similar problems, and that a group of students with common problems can benefit from sharing problems in several ways. Students can learn that others share their problem. Students can be reinforced for attempts to acquire new behaviors, and in fact, can reinforce each other in a way that a single counselor could not do. Finally, it seems as valuable for students to value themselves by making positive self-statements (Hansen, Niland, & Zani, 1969).

It is easy and perhaps tempting to think of behavioral counseling as mechanical and easy. It is tempting for inexperienced behavioral counselors, as it is with any young professional in training, to overestimate one's own capabilities. But effective and professional behavioral counseling takes supervised training, and a high degree of skills which must be attained with supervised sessions in which the student has opportunity to review skills with a seasoned practitioner and to model difficult behaviors. In a comparison of Master's level and Doctoral level behavioral counselors, Abidin found that the less experienced counselors were less careful not only in the assessment phase of counseling, but in every phase of behavioral counseling (Abidin, 1977).

Discipline

Discipline is now, as it has been for decades, one of the most talked about issues in education. For some, discipline is simply getting students to do what faculty wants them to do. For others, it is having students follow laws, whether established by society, school faculty, or the students themselves.

If discipline is something which comes from without the individual, then it is a matter of someone establishing sets of behaviors which are desirable, setting rewards, establishing a set of behaviors which are forbidden, and setting aversive conditions contingent upon them. That perhaps sounds mechanical: actually, it describes the situation in which we all find ourselves. When anyone in society does something laudable, he receives praise and acclaim: when somebody does something forbidden, (provided he is caught) he is put in jail, or fined, or otherwise punished. But that is not the kind of discipline the behaviorist wants to talk about in the school setting.

Discipline can be seen from an individual's point of view. Each student has a distinctive behavior pattern, and this is to be encouraged, as long as those behaviors meet certain minimum criteria, such as being lawful. We may refer to a person's behaviors as his/her repertoire of behavior. A person's repertoire of behavior develops from experiences which cannot be retrieved. Those conditions which maintain the behaviors in a repertoire, however, can be discovered. Simply, rewarded behaviors tend to persist. A set of rules consistently disobeyed raise questions about the school's discipline policy. For any discipline or set of rules to succeed, the total environment of the school needs to support the policy.

The school can take the position that discipline should be established in students at home. But discipline is a life-long struggle each person has in maintaining some balance of self-reward of various kinds. Indulgence in consumables is contrary to self-statements about maintaining health, bodily attraction and so on. This battle of the waist-line, battle of smoking, drinking and self-conditioning is a national problem. We all have problems with self-discipline, and the school is a place which can contribute to improved self-discipline, or it can actually be detrimental to such individual self-control.

Discipline can be defined as the setting of personal goals for behaviors and maximizing adherence to social guidelines for behavior. That which helps maximize adherence to the behaviors, then, helps the person become "disciplined". School discipline, then, means that there are certain behaviors the school wants students to observe. Suppose a principal asks how school discipline could be maximized. The request really concerns the question of how students could be encouraged to engage in certain behaviors, presumably pro-academic with a reduction of vandalism, truancy, etc. The first point is that the more school-desired behaviors matches those of individuals, the more likely they will be observed. This principle underlies the practice of involving students in the establishment of various school regulations. But the problem goes deeper. The question becomes, how can students be led to engage in the behaviors defined by the school? In some respects it is a developmental problem. How do we get students to do *anything?* Some things we don't have to get them to do. Other things are different. When we want to influence student behavior, every point of contact between the school and the student is an instance of strengthening or weakening various behaviors. Of course it is ludicrous to attempt to make an analysis of each contact each student has with the school. However, a simple principle emerges which may serve as a guideline for the maker of school policy. Discipline for an individual is a combination of internalized self-statements of the student, and the reward properties of each situation. Schools can manipulate the reward properties of each situation in the absense of students. Schools can also tend to influence the self-statements of students but not by threats, punishments or other aversive means. It is a close, cooperative enterprise which tends to alter self-statements of students in the direction of mutually acceptable behavioral goals.

ROLES

Administration

School administrators are important to the overall functioning of the school. The responsibilities of the administration are interlocking, each influencing and in turn being influenced by the various functions. Separate functions will be discussed, although we know in advance such functions cannot, in reality, be separated.

Administrators select and train teachers. These are two of the key responsibilities of administration. A behaviorist, as an administrator, would hire carefully, insuring that each teacher hired was amenable to achieving clear identification of student goals and learning objectives, appreciated participating in out-of-class activities, and would consider him/her self a part of a team. With basic appreciation of these ends, the teacher is already a behaviorist, whether or not trained as such. Anyone can learn behavioristic principles: the point is that the administration would want teachers to reflect, among themselves, some common basic ideal regarding what education is about.

Next, the behaviorist principal or administrator would set up school incentives which rewarded teacher initiative, cooperative behavior and other desirable professional objectives. The administrator would probably meet with teachers to establish the goals of the school, and ask cooperation in establishing a situation which would be conducive in achieving them. The administrator would be interested in establishing teacher-supported programs in teacher evaluation, teacher development and student development. The administrator would need policy freedom and funds to achieve an essentially developmental orientation. Concern with these matters actually underlies the operation of any classroom. While the operation of the classroom is largely the sphere of the teacher, the conditions in which the teacher works can have profound influence on how the teacher acts. And that is the concern of the administrators.

The administrator would do that in his/her power to make the school a pleasant place to be and work. Also, the administrator would continually think of ways to get teachers, pupils, administrators and community members to interact in ways which would lead to solution of problems. This in itself wouldn't solve classroom or counseling problems, but would establish a base for such solution, and would model for teachers the basic operations related to effective school operation.

Administrators have a strong influence over the relationship of students to the school through establishing goals for teachers and other school personnel. The principal is perhaps the major social model in the school and can exert influence on all others by demeanor, style of interaction, effort extended on behalf of school and faculty, and concern for those around the school. Some principals never go into classrooms; some go only in those that are disruptive; some principals visit classrooms which have completed a good job at something. These differential acts, create different atmospheres among schools.

The principal influences a wide range of school operations from discipline to whether or not faculty cooperate to achieve goals. The principal's influence in these matters can be by default: the principal can leave these matters to others, or can have a strong hand. The behavioral principal would be concerned with the establishment of behavioral goals for in-class and out-of-class behavior, and would support rules and goals set by teachers and students. The principal would work to have all persons in the school be a part of such goal-setting.

Finally, the principal or school administrators would be involved in community affairs with the parents. The principal would work to minimize the gulf which often exists between school and home. Behaviorists, whether they are counselors or administrators, view students as adapting first to home then to the school. Thus, behaviorists would minimize potential conflicts between the two in terms of goal setting. The school should know the expectations the community has for the school and vice versa. When differences arise, conferences should be held, and this is usually the province of the administrators. The principal wouldn't try to interact with each parent of each child in the school unless, perhaps, it was a small school. The administrator would try to make it possible for teachers and parents to get together.

Faculty

The central task of each teacher on the faculty is to help each student in the class select reasonable learning goals and then assist in achieving them. Behaviorists emphasize "learning", since that is the change with which the behaviorist is concerned. Teachers assist students in learning in a number of ways which may not be obvious to them. First, before students show up at class, the teacher has already set the stage for learning situation. The teacher has selected materials, arranged the room, and perhaps prepared a presentation on a subject. The teacher has thought about the material of the course: what behavioral objectives should precede, which ones should follow, what objectives are easiest read about, and which ones can be demonstrated. The teacher, by the time students arrive, has selected a good deal of the stimuli to which the students will respond. This is a large portion of teaching, and it occurs before the bell has rung!

Faculty are, of course, the major guide to students in the classroom environment. The teacher either intentionally or unintentionally selects a teaching style. Will students be directed to materials on their own, or will the teacher make presentations? will the class be a combination of the two, plus other methods of presentation? Fundamental to any teaching style is the ability of the teacher to lead students to selecting learning goals. By some, this is done before meeting with the students by simply deciding on the lecture topic, book to be used, the exam questions to comprise the test. Other teachers provide a "menu" of learning experiences and ask students to decide, and yet others encourage students to select their own.

Teachers also create the atmosphere in the classroom. Some teachers are strict, others lenient. The teacher sets the style of the classroom in terms of its organization, behaviors expected, and how rewards will be distributed. Loos, Williams and Bailey (1977) have emphasized the importance of teaching style and teacher(s) as reward givers in the elementary classroom. These components of atmosphere, the operation of the classroom and degree of rewardingness on the part of the teacher, are established by teacher choice. To some degree, the behaviorally-oriented teacher would have such choices to make as when to work in groups, when to use other students as rewarders, what would constitute approved behavior in the classroom, and so forth.

Behaviorally oriented teachers vary a good deal on out-of-class concerns. Some consider behavior outside the classroom as important as that which occurs in it. The rationale is that eventually students will leave the classroom and they will enter into "real life". It is at that point that schooling should be of use to the student. Such teachers are concerned with integrating students' repertoire of social and academic skills which are to be evoked under appropriate circumstances. Behavioral teachers will

334 / *Alternative Educational Systems*

sponsor clubs, and so forth, so that they can have opportunity to work with students under more "life-like" situations. At such time, the behavioral teacher is much more the model for students than in the classroom where academic behaviors are artificially emphasized.

The teacher knows that life is comprised of an infinite variety of different situations, and that students learn skills under certain, limited, circumstances. To provide students opportunity to make the proper discriminations and generalizations (that is, learn which behaviors should be displayed under what conditions) the behavioral teacher may "mix" situations and have students roleplay in the classroom, or may ask for academic skills in social situations. The aim is the most appropriate display of skills in view of the situation, and the skill of selecting appropriate behaviors takes practice on the part of all of us.

Students

Students who find themselves in a classroom are affected by the friendliness and warmth of the teacher who should be approachable and eager to encourage students. Students in an "upper" class might find it hard to really discern any difference between this class and others taken previously because the behavioral teacher would give each student a lot of choice and use mainly social rewards. Students would usually react positively to teacher challenges to "go and do"; and to select their own activities. The teacher might suggest activities but would encourage students to guide their own learning. In those classrooms where students have already acquired skills in self regulation, goal selection, social behaviors and use of teachers, the teacher would work on further development of these skills in a setting in which social rewards (teacher approval, excitement, spontaneity) were used. In classes where those skills are absent, students would become aware that the teacher wanted behaviors associated with individual selection of goals, learning oriented activities and social skills developed, and the students would notice that the teacher would lay emphasis on those goals by the use of praise, distribution of free time, permitting desired activities and so on. At whatever level of skill, students would learn that the teacher expected the student to identify useful personal goals, and to work for such goals in any of a number of ways, depending on which seemed best suited to the student.

Students would be expected to participate in classroom activities for a number of reasons. The student becomes skillful only in active display of skills. Also, students learn to evaluate themselves better when they are active responders. It is easy to convince oneself that facts are known or concepts understood when actual performance may reveal something less than that truly exists. Actual performance displays not only deficiencies in learning, but also tends to build competence in active roles. Even when a student fails to achieve a given level of competence a good deal is learned in failure. In addition, subsequent performance is always enhanced by the previous "error". The student will notice that the teacher encourages the student in the behavioral classroom to display skills so the student and the teacher can see accurately what the student is capable of, and what is needed for the next skill. Such performance gives the teacher an opportunity to assess the student's progress (or lack of it) and material for subsequent review of the student's progress.

Some students will be perplexed by the "stupidity" of the behaviorally oriented teacher. Students who appeal to the teacher that they *know* something in their head but just cannot verbalize it will find the teacher sympathetic but recalcitrant in not awarding the "knowing". Students will notice that attempts to get the teacher to accept incomplete work, or to infer from presented data or gestures that the student "really knows" something but cannot express it seems to fall on deaf ears. The teacher is interested, but terribly concrete. The teacher asks for complete answers, and asks for definitions. Replies filled with faddish words and slang are met with quizzical looks and requests to explain. When the students learn to present ideas simply and in plain English, they find the teacher to be reasonable, and even enthusiastic.

It would be difficult to say whether the teacher would be for or against women's lib, capital punishment or right to work. But the teacher would be a likely candidate to help students in after-school activities, and the students would find the teacher warm, interested in a variety of things and eager to join into activities which were exciting, timely and fun. In short, the ideal behaviorist teacher would seem to be a warm person in whom the student would find admirable qualities and a person after whom one could model her/him self (Yussen and Levy, 1975).

Students would also find that the teacher would be concerned with student government. While the teacher would be concerned about those who disregarded existing rules, the teacher would support student efforts to handle student affairs. And, the teacher would be ready to call upon the principal for money and supplies to support student projects which showed planning, thought, and an effort to acquire new skills.

Parents

Parents in a behavioral setting would be expected to work with teachers toward the growth of students. This would mean at some points that they would help set learning objectives along with the teachers. With more capable students, or with older ones, parents would be expected to refuse to help students arrive at such goals which teacher and parent felt the student was fully capable of establishing. Some parents would never hear from teacher or faculty, because their children would be manageable using the skills and resources available to the teacher and school, and the student would show steady growth in acquiring self-directive and self-evaluative skills.

Other parents would be asked to confer with teachers and school officials to work out problems with students for whom agreements had proven unsuccessful. Generally, parents would find that one or two conferences would be sufficient to straighten out problems in communications between teacher and parent and student. When simple clarification of expectations and goals fail to clear up a problem, a subsequent contact might be made. The conference might concern clarification of communications (the most common problem), or it might extend to assessing the skills of the student, behavioral objectives or a plan to achieve such objectives. Normally, the development of objectives and plans to achieve them procede smoothly and can be established in one meeting of an hour. Following the agreement, follow-up contacts are useful to insure that the plan is being carried out. Communication can be by daily phone call, and would only rarely require a visit by parents. Letters or notes are sometimes used, though they are subject to interception by spirited students, and the thwarted plan may be an unfortunate learning experience for a resourceful but badly directed student.

Some parents may volunteer for classroom duty or have other contact with students in school activities. The parent and the behaviorally oriented teacher will find themselves discussing just what is expected of the students, and hence, what the parent should do to contribute to the behavioral objective of the school. As an assistant to the teacher in the classroom, the parent is expected to be spontaneous, though within the guidelines of the learning objectives. The parent can often times supply social rewards unavailable to the teacher, and can accurately assess student progress in areas unknown to the teacher.

Teachers often enjoy informal contacts with parents because such contacts let the teacher know the background of the student in terms of family background, community interests and problems.

The parent, in the behavioral environment, is a potential rewarder, an assessor of progress and needs, and a model for student behavior. The parent helps the student identify and establish short and long term goals. The reader will note that these are the basic characteristics of the good teacher. The behavioral teacher is aware of the basic similarities of parent and teacher vis-a-vis the student and tries to communicate this in every action.

SYSTEM IN ACTION

Systems of education based on behavioral concepts vary as widely as the needs of the students. In the average school in which students are study-oriented and the value of education is recognized by students, the system would work similarly to traditional education, at least to outward appearances. That is, there would be one teacher per classroom, and the school may well have set periods during which students were expected to concentrate on specified learning tasks. There might be a math teacher, and one responsible for English.

Teachers in this situation would assess students as they began the course. In many classes, students might have similar entry skills, so the teacher would have the simplified task of preparing one general course of study. If the class were large, the teacher would conceive of his/her job as that of presenting material of the widest variety possible, using all sensory modalities. That is, in classes, say, exceeding sixty students, the teacher would work on providing materials for students. A Keller type plan might be developed. Student discipline problems would be considered with the principal. In large classes, the teacher cannot become the teacher of social skills and so large classes require organization and cooperation among students. Therefore, students would have to meet certain minimum behavioral standards to remain enrolled in the class. The teacher would be concerned with regular (weekly, bi-weekly) assessing of student progress, and filling in where weaknesses in the curriculum showed up. In this situation, the teacher really becomes a manager and facilitator, and the rest of the school becomes a source for support services.

Where the enrollment is smaller, the teacher can assume more functions than the manager of resource materials and formal assessor of student progress. The teacher becomes a model for complex behaviors, personal guide for individual learning goal selection, and organizer of the social context. Smaller ratios of students to teacher permit a social mix with the exposure of academic material. The paths of students can become more diverse. Teacher lecture becomes less important, because teachers can ask students to engage in individual or small group activities and be prepared to guide such activities into the most rewarding directions. The teacher is free to contact other faculty and parents in special circumstances and regulates rewards more precisely with activities, so a wider variety of behavioral goals is possible (MacDonald, 1971).

At the school level, the faculty with the guidance of administrators consider skill paths for students, and offer the widest variety of course offerings and ancillary learning opportunities through mini-courses, extracurricular experiences and athletics. Some faculty would work with community groups to extend the school experiences into occupational and special activity opportunities so that students can learn actively after school hours, during summers, but more importantly, in activities which closely resemble "real life" situations. The faculty and students would spend time together discussing within school problems such as deportment and what students should be focussing on to achieve certain long-range goals. They would spend time talking about extra-curricular activities related to vocational skills and those skills not trainable on campus. The behavioral principles in the normal school, then, would be concerned with straightforward tasks of assessing current talents, examining student learning objectives in view of long range goals, helping the student select most desirable paths to achieve both goals and objectives, and to help develop other interests, talents and skills in the student. These would all be achieved in the framework of identifying learning objectives, and finding activities requiring behaviors which would develop the requisite skills. In the normal class situation, the management of such learning activities is relatively simple and needs no further elaboration.

It is more typical to encounter learning based education where these are more serious learning problems. This is probably the case because good teachers in normal classrooms *are* influenced by learning theory, and are good (but perhaps without notable) examples that drew attention. Thus, it is in more difficult situations that discussions of behavioral approaches to education often take place.

In a difficult classroom, one would note several characteristics of the behaviorally oriented education. Clear structure would be most evident as the teacher made clear, and would not hesitate to redefine, the immediate goals of those present. Behavioral expectations would be noted frequently, and the teacher would often comment on those exhibiting the desired behaviors. As Shumaker, Hovel and Sherman (1977) have shown, the teacher may well use parents or other adults to help structure the classrooms, pass out social rewards, and help manage the considerable clerical work involved in the necessary task of making out frequent (daily, weekly) report cards. In many instances, the teacher or other adult helper in the classroom will be working individually with students, or groups of them. It is not unusual for a classroom with difficult students to operate on a "token economy" which is a carefully planned program of awarding tokens or points for certain desired behaviors (completing lessons, getting to class on time, bringing pencil, etc) and permitting earned points to be "spent" for privileges (playing high interest game during school hours, first in line for lunch, get to pick next activity, etc.). Such special classroom organizations, however, take a great deal of work to handle correctly (Drabman & Tucker, 1974) and a teacher really needs help to make it work. Most successful token economies have more personnel than a single assigned teacher. Volunteers can be used to fill in the necessary gaps in coverage not possible by the only teacher in the classroom. Token economy classrooms vary a great deal in the type of student accomodated. In some cases, it is necessary to restrict the population in a token economy because not all types of students "mix" in such a setting. Very aggressive students, for example, may not mix well with retarded ones, or with those with truancy problems. Some schools will operate several such classrooms to accomodate different types of students. One, for example, had one such room for unmarried mothers, and another for low ability students who were drop-outs.

While organization of a classroom into groups serves many purposes, several are related to management problems of difficult students. Young students can be difficult to manage and present problems in attaining academic improvement. It is often surprisingly effective to organize a classroom of young students into groups, and make rewards contingent on group performance. Among students with attention problems, or behavioral problems, the teacher gains the assistance of those group members who are interested in gaining the rewards. Group contingencies have been shown effective not only in influencing social behaviors, but also academic ones, even after considerable time delay (Wilson & Williams, 1973).

The methods of the behaviorally oriented educator do not take specific forms, however, because problems seem to vary from student to student and from area to area. Students who have strong aversion to the physical plant of a school may be approached at a park or neighborhood gathering place. Learning materials might be delivered there, or a process of "learning to like school" may be instigated to lessen the aversive properties of the school. In one case a group of pregnant unmarried students wanted to complete their high school educations but were embarrassed to attend classes. A teacher intervened with a principal who had insisted that they attend school, and set up a program off campus where constant embarrassment was not a constant stimulus to detract minds from academics.

With the pressure to achieve in school exacerbated by the competition to gain entrance into preferred colleges, some students develop debilitating anxiety under test conditions. The behaviorally oriented educator is especially useful in such situations because of the success of learning theory in conceptualizing the problem and treatment regime. Through relaxation, or manipulation of the testing conditions, or use of "small" tests, the behavioral educator can work with nervous or anxious students to attain maximum performance from them. Many students react strongly to various aspects of the educational setting, and behavioral education is most capable of working for solutions to such problems.

One last note in the discussion of how behaviorally oriented educators would operate classrooms and educational settings. The country is still entangled in reaching its goal of equal education for all. This means, in one form or another, integrating schools. This means that educators must face the problems of creating educational settings in which cooperative behaviors of all classroom members is achieved. In the behaviorally oriented classroom, experiences would be structured in which black and white students would be led to cooperate with each other, and a reward for such cooperation would be forthcoming. While the approach may seem "canned", it has proven useful (Best, Smith, Graves & Williams, 1975). The form in which the activities would be presented would vary depending on the age of the children. One of the most widely used methods, whether or not integration is the intention is to include both black and white members on athletic teams. The rewards are so strong for team efforts that only a brief time is normally required before cooperation among players is complete. Problem solving groups report similar findings when intellectual, rather than physical, activities are the focus of activities.

PROSPECT

The behavioral influence on education has been powerful, but has not had the wide appeal proportional to its demonstrated effectiveness. Many educators are personally and professionally opposed to behavioral technology, and with good reason. There have been many instances in which poorly or incompletely trained behaviorally trained consultants have provided teachers and administrators with poor advice, or delivered the advice in an unprofessional fashion. To the student learning behavioral theory and technology, the system may be alluring and the temptation to offer advice which seems so badly needed and easy to offer may overcome good judgment. The easiest mistake is to fail to assess the problem situation thoroughly which may result in identifying the wrong problem, and perhaps even the wrong person as the target of an intervention. Training institutions must show great care in providing students with adequate supervision.

Behavioral scientists generally are not educators, so that behavioral technology is infused into education through consultation, workshops, and teacher training. Typical teacher training consists of a course or two in "behavior modification" or similarly named courses which provide the student studying to become a teacher with an incomplete preparation to infuse the ideas basic to behaviorism with others in the teaching profession. Many teachers have been exposed to behavioral technology during the summer, or during an afternoon or evening course as a part of professional training. Such an exposure seems to "tack on" to those skills of the teacher a few behavioral tricks. The heavy demands on a teacher's time and energy preclude an integration of ideas, especially if further deep study is required. This is the case with behaviorism's partial success in education. Teachers have received incomplete preparation, and grasp only those few aspects which fit outstanding problems.

It might be "the nature of the beast" that this should be true. For, those who are strongly behaviorist in orientation seem to find themselves in the minority. Other social scientists have studied the principles, embrace them, and move on to new concepts and viewpoints, retaining that from behaviorism which is useful but adding to the principles that which is needed to continue to respond to new challenges. There are many consultants and educators who have "borrowed" behavioral principles and added them to the existing skills or have later added on other skills so that many are what have been called in this article "influence by behaviorism". It is this group who may well have an impact on education in the future, but it won't be called "behavioral" in all likelihood. Many people have aversive reactions to the name "behaviorism" and the person who wishes to influence others is well advised to pick appealing words for names and slogans. Behavior modification, behaviorism and learning theory are not highly attractive names and would be at the bottom of the list to be included to describe anything.

There will continue to be behavioral influence on education. Contributions will continue to be made by those with behavioral training. But more and more behavioral research will move into the "internal" arena: behaviorists will be investigating emotional reactions and thought processes and the interactions of the two. The behaviorist will be asking the respondent what he/she is feeling and thinking, and will be taking the reply seriously. Complex words and sentences will serve as data from which inferences about "thoughts" will be made. And then we may ask, "Is this behaviorism?" Behaviorism is not a doctrine or belief system. It is an area of study which is constantly undergoing change and shifts in methodology, area of interest and procedures.

There are already some who are saying "this is behaviorism; that isn't". Behaviorism will probably never be fully embraced by educators. And that is the way it should be. Behaviorism is quicksilver: it is a set of ideas and ways of doing things that, as soon as identified, changes and becomes something else. Behaviorism is useful in stimulating useful thought and research. But its nothing you'd want to build a school upon.

REFERENCES

Abidin, R. R. Operant behavior consultations as conducted by masters' and doctoral level psychologists in Virginia. *Journal of School Psychology*, 1977, *15*, 225–229.

Baier, K. Moral autonomy as an aim of moral education. In G. Langford and D.

J. O'Connor (Eds.), *New essays in the philosophy of education.* London: Routledge & Kegan Paul, 1973.

Bandura, A. Vicarious processes: a case of no-trial learning. In L. Berdowitz (Ed.), *Advance in experimental social psychology.* New York: Academic Press, 1965.

Becker, W. *Parents are Teachers: a child management program.* Champaign, Ill.: Research Press, 1971.

Best, D. L., Smith. S. C., Graves, D. J. & Williams, J. E. The Modification of racial bias in preschool children. *Journal of Experimental Child Psychology, 20,* 193–205.

Bowles, E. P. & Nelson, R. O. Training teachers as mediators: efficacy of a workshop versus the but-in-the-ear technique. *Journal of School Psychology, 1976, 14,* 15–19.

Bucher, B. & Okovita, H. Effects of differential reinforcement and task difficulty on preschoolers' compliance with teacher instructions. *Journal of Experimental Child Psychology, 1977, 23,* 226–236.

Clarizio, H. F. Toward positive classroom discipline. New York: John Wiley & Sons, 1971.

Cook, V. J. & White, M. A. Reinforcement potency of children's reading materials. *Journal of Educational Psychology, 1977, 69,* 231–236.

Cote, R. W. Behavior modification: some questions. *The Elementary School Journal,* 1973, *74,* 44–49.

Drabman, R. S. & Tucker, R. D. Why classroom token economies fail. *Journal of School Psychology, 1974, 12,* 178–188.

Fargo, G. A., Behrns, C. & Nolen, P. (Eds.) *Behavior modification in the classroom.* Belmont, Calif.: Wadsworth Publishing Company, Inc., 1970.

Feder, Daniel N. & McNiel, Elton B. *Hooked on Books: Program and Proof.* New York: Berkley Publishing Corp., 1968.

Fitt, S. Bridging the gap between humanism and behaviorism. *The Elementary School Journal.* 1976, *77,* 12–17.

Flanders, N. A. *Analyzing teaching behavior.* Reading, Mass.: Addison-Wesley Publishing Co., 1970.

Gage, N. L. & Winne, P. H. Performance-based teacher education. In Ryan, K. (Ed.) *Teacher education, the Seventy-Fourth Yearbook of the National Society for the study of education, part II.* Chicago, University of Chicago Press, 1975.

Glover, J. A. & Gary, A. L. *Behavior modification: enhancing creativity and other good behaviors.* Pacific Grove, Calif.: The Boxwood Press, 1975.

Greenspoon, J. *The effect of verbal and nonverbal stimuli on the frequency of members of two verbal response classes.* Unpublished doctoral dissertation, Indiana University, 1950.

Hall, R. V. & Broden, M. Behavior changes in brain-injured children through social reinforcement. *Journal of Experimental Child Psychology, 1967, 5,* 463–479.

Hansen, J. C., Niland, T.M. & Zani, L. P. Model reinforcement in group counseling with elementary school children. *Personnel and Guidance Journal, 1969, 47,* 741–744.

Henderson, S. Van Petten. *Introduction to philosophy of education.* Chicago: University of Chicago Press, 1947.

Hosford, R. E. Teaching teachers to reinforce student participation. In Krumboltz,

J. D. & Thoresen, C. E. (Eds.) *Behavioral counseling: cases and techniques.* New York: Holt, Rinehart and Winston, Inc., 1969.

Keller, F., Sherman, S. & Gilmour, J. *The Keller plan handbook.* Menlo Park, Calif.: W. A. Benjamin Company, 1974.

Klausmeier, H. J., Rossmiller, R. A. & Saily, M. *Individually guided elementary education: concepts and practices.* New York, Academic Press, 1977.

Kolesnik, W. B. *Humanism and/or behaviorism in education.* Boston: Allyn and Bacon, Inc., 1975.

Krumboltz, J. D. Vocational problem-solving experiences. In Krumboltz, J. D. & Thoresen, C. E. *Behavioral counseling: cases and techniques.* New York: Holt, Rinehart and Winston, Inc., 1969.

Loos, F. M., Williams, K. P. & Bailey, J. S. A multi-element analysis of the effect of teacher aides in an "open" style classroom. *Journal of Applied Behavior Analysis,* 1977, *10,* 437–448.

Lovass, O. I. & Simmons, J. Q. Manipulation of self-destruction in three retarded children. *Journal of Applied Behavior Analysis,* 1969, *2,* 143–157.

MacDonald, W. S. Battle in the classroom. Scranton: Intext Educational Publishers, 1971.

MacDonald, W. S. Teacher consultation and Boyle's Law: studies in hot air. In MacDonald, W. S. & Tanabe, G. *Focus on classroom behavior.* Springfield, Ill.: Charles C Thomas, 1973.

Marholin, D. & Steinman W. M. Stimulus control in the classroom as a function of the behavior reinforced. *Journal of Applied Behavior Analysis,* 1977, *10,* 465–478.

Milhollan, F. & Forisha, B. I. From Skinner to Rogers: contrasting approaches to education. Lincoln, Nebraska: Professional Educators Publications, Inc., 1972.

Mowrer, H. O. The present state of behaviorism. *Education, 97,* 4–23.

Palardy, J. M. Classroom management: more than conditioning. *The Elementary School Journal,* 1970, *71,* 162–165.

Phillips, E. L. Achievement Place: token reinforcement procedures in a home-style rehabilitation setting for "pre-delinquent" boys. *Journal of Applied Behavior Analysis,* 1968, *1,* 213–223.

Plowman, P. D. Behavioral objectives: teacher success through student performance. Chicago: Science Research Associates, Inc., 1971.

Premack, D. Reinforcement theory. In Levine, D. (Ed.) Nebraska symposium on motivation. Lincoln: University of Nebraska Press, 1965.

Schumaker, J. B., Hovell, M. F. & Sherman, J. A. An analysis of daily report cards and parent-managed privileges in the improvement of adolescents' classroom performance. *Journal of Applied Behavior Analysis,* 1977, *10,* 110–117.

Simmons, J. T. & Wasik, B. H. Grouping strategies, peer influence, and free time as classroom management techniques with first and third-grade children. *Journal of School Psychology,* 1976, *14,* 322–332.

Skinner, B. F. On the rate of formation of a conditioned reflex. *Journal of General Psychology,* 1932, *7,* 274–285.

Skinner, B. F. The science of learning and the art of teaching. Reprinted in Hohan,

M. and Hull, R. E. Individualized instruction and learning. Chicago: Nelson-Hall Co., 1974.

Smith, P. J., Hamil, R. G., Frase, L. E. & Poston, W. K. The Flowing Wells Public Schools reading support system. Tucson: Flowing Wells Public Schools System, 1975.

Staats, A. W., Staats, C. K., Schutz, R. F. & Wolf, M. The conditioning of textual responses using "extrinsic" reinforcers. *Journal of the experimental analysis of behavior,* 1962, *5,* 33–40.

Staats, A. W. Social behaviorism. Homewood, Ill.: The Dorsey Press, 1975.

Thoresen, C. E. & Mahoney, M. J. Behavioral self-control. New York: Holt Rinehart & Winston, 1974.

Walker, H. M. & Hops, H. Increasing academic achievement by reinforcing direct academic performance and/or facilitative nonacademic responses. *Journal of Educational Psychology,* 1976, *68,* 218–225.

Watson, J. B. & Raynor, R. Conditioned emotional reactions. *Journal of Experimental Psychology,* 1920, *3,* 1–14.

Webster, W. J. & Mendro, R. L. The effects of a videotape feedback system on classroom teacher behavior. *Journal of School Psychology,* 1974, *12,* 189–198.

Wilson, S. H. & Williams, R. L. The effects of group contingencies on first graders' academic and social behaviors. *Journal of School Psychology,* 1973, *11,* 110–117.

Winett, R. A. Behavior modification and open education. *Journal of School Psychology,* 1973, *11,* 207–214.

Wolf, M. M. & Resley, T. Analysis and modification of deviant child behavior. Paper read at the American Psychological Association meeting, Washington, September, 1967.

Yussen, S. R. & Levy, V. M. Jr. Effects of warm and neutral models on the attention of observational learners. *Journal of Experimental Child Psychology,* 1975, *20,* 66–72.

Zeilberger, J., Sampen, S. E. & Sloane, H. N. Modification of a child's problem behaviors in the home with the mother as therapist. *Journal of Applied Behavior Analysis,* 1968, *1,* 47–53.

CHAPTER 9

Education

by

Appointment

VIRGINIA ROTH

DEFINITION

The alternative secondary model described in this article is basically a system of education by appointment. It is highly personal, tailored to meet the ability, interests, and future expectations of each student. It is a total system approach, although parts of the program could be implemented without abandoning the total security of an existing, more conventional method of education. The model, as conceived and practiced, is for a 9–12 high school. Again, it is easily adaptable for any age group and, in fact, able to be more quickly implemented at the elementary level where departmentalization is not the rule by reason of teacher academic preparation and requirements of accrediting agencies.

INTRODUCTION

Objectives of Education

Ideally, secondary education ought to provide two opportunities for students: 1) exploration of a wide variety of learning experiences, both academic and non-academic, and 2) discovery of methods of *how* to learn, which is more important than *what* to learn. In other words, secondary education should weave for the learner an enchantment with the discovery of learning. All the skills a student brings to high school, the ability to decode, encode, compute, give oral and written expression to thoughts and feelings, should be used as tools to unlock and understand those mental disciplines we call curriculum offerings. In the process, the student should develop a growing sense of personal self-worth, dignity, and finally, independence.

While this is happening for the student, staff should simultaneously experience the same qualities for themselves. If everyone involved in the educational process does not have a heightened sense of dignity when the learning cycle at school is over, it will have been a waste of time. The world does not need graduated automatons who can give studied answers on command. Computers can do that. The world does need graduated thinkers of all capacities who have been sensitized by an educational climate that values human respect, the right to succeed as well as the right to make mistakes, the opportunity to make educational choices and be accountable for them.

Dignity, self worth, respect are not nebulous ideas left to happenstance. They are provided, with design and effort, to everyone regardless of age or economic and ethnic origin. Human beings achieve dignity in the same way, by making choices. Choices imply options. If there is no option, there is no choice.

Teenage learners are eminently qualified to try their hand at this most human activity—making decisions. Schools are eminently qualified to provide opportunities in decision making. School is a controlled environment, the decisions are not life-death by nature, there is a mix of adult experience with youthful exuberance, and poor decisions are easily corrected.

Unfortunately, schools tend to get caught up in the external mechanisms of education instead of the human development of individuals. Most high schools organize their learning around three components which are inhuman and often inhumane: the clock, the calendar, and the schedule.

It should be clear that class schedules are never created for students; they are created for teachers. The schedule explains who will teach what, when and where. Then student requests are loaded into teacher schedules. Where there is no conflict, a student receives a schedule of teacher composites. Where there is a conflict, the student is told to choose something else that will fill time rather than meet student need or interest.

Then, the student who needs more or less time to master a given course is told to conform learning to a nine or 18 or 36 week cycle, because that is the teacher's pace.

It is not surprising that students find education an impersonal experience. It is also not surprising that James Coleman in 1975, reporting on his research in *Eqality of Educational Opportunity,* states that schools are "ageing vats" where students serve time with their peers in a lateral holding pattern.

Actually students are capable of making numerous educational decisions, and they should be encouraged to do so within the parameters of the school's goals. Students, in consultation with teachers, ought to decide what they will learn when, where, with whom (meaning both teachers and peers), and for how long a time. When these decisions are made by students, obviously a schedule becomes obsolete as well as does a school year divided into precise quarters or semesters. When students make these decisons, they force staff to redefine their roles and they open the talent bank of each teacher challenging wider varieties of information so that the teacher is forced to learn more and more also. In this way, the school becomes populated with learners—some professional and some amateur.

When decisions are made, people are accountable and dignity is subsequently enhanced. What better product to graduate into the world than the young adult who, regardless of future plans, can look back and say, "I like myself because I went to that high school."

Reasons for This System

Anyone who has been in education for at least a semester has heard or made the remark, "There ought to be a better way." When the staff at Ryan High School in Omaha, Nebraska, had said this often enough, we began to challenge what we were doing that needed improvement. This began in 1964. By 1966 we had a better way.

We refused to be manipulated any longer by the clock, the calendar, and the schedule. We began to focus on students and their needs. It was always obvious, but seldom adverted to, that the principal of a school does not follow a clock, calendar, nor schedule. And principals are kept very busy. A principal's day is shaped by the needs of the people who seek help, advice, easement of some kind, clarification, support, evaluation. If the school's leader can be productive without mechanical assistance, we wondered why not staff and, indeed, why not students.

Why not establish a system based on the principal model where each day brings different needs that are met basically by a series of appointments. The entire staff, through a two-year period of in-service, worked painstakingly together to develop a system of educating that worked with human nature instead of against it.

We had studied student body profiles and knew that student achievement over the years did not measure up to student ability. We knew that vandalism was a problem—broken windows, pennies flipped into the acoustic ceiling tiles, kicked in louvers on doors, broken mirrors and towel racks in the washrooms, broken light switches. We knew that morale was low, both student and staff. We were labelling and grouping students as bright, average, slow; and students read this device as a statement that the bright should learn together whether they like each other or not, the average should learn together in spite of everything, and the slow (students would say "dumb") should stay together and stimulate one another.

We were rewarding and punishing students with grades that were self-fulfilling prophecies of the label we had already applied to them. We kept course content a mystery to be revealed in segments 40 minutes long, five times a week, 18 or 36 weeks of the year. We were busy teaching lesson plans, not helping each student learn; and we were saying, in effect, "Eat this up. It's good for you, like spinach."

When we stepped back and looked at our discontent, we dug in. The slogan was, "If it's good for the student, we'll find a way to do it. If it isn't good for the student, why are we wasting our time thinking about it!"

The student. Each one has talent, interests, future expectations to be served by education. Each quality is variable and may change year to year, month to month, week to week. To meet these variables in all their combinations, we had to expand the curriculum offerings, vary the length of each offering according to student needs and content requirement, tie credit to mastery of course material, and leave ample room for development of new courses on demand.

In order to provide for student choices, courses needed to be adequately described with their pre-requisites, if any, and their credit yield. Graduation requirements had to be well defined, not so much in terms of specific courses, but areas of interest. Graduation requirements met would result in a diploma, any day, any month, any year.

Teachers needed choices also. They determined what they would teach within their certified area of expertise. They assigned themselves, at least two teachers per course title, so that students could have a choice of teacher on a first come first served basis. Teachers assigned their own student ratio. In the areas of English and social studies, they determined that 90–110 students would be the limits at any one time. During the course of a year, a teacher might have 500 students, but never more than 110 at any one time. As students completed courses, other students could sign up and fill the vacancy. In some math or typing, teachers might have 200–250 students at a time.

The difference in the two types of courses is simple. After all the courses were created or modified, we initially had 860 separate offerings. This grew to over 1,000 within three years. But all of the courses could be divided into two basic categories: Inter-Action and Non-Inter-Action.

An inter-action course requires discussion to learn it: most of English and social studies. Non-inter-action courses are not helped by discussion. They are basically independent study or skill mastery courses like typing, shorthand, some math, bookkeeping. These are courses that have no grey areas; there is only one right way to get the answer or perform the skill.

Inter-action courses, because they require discussion, necessitate group learning. Staff decided that a learning group should be three to six students. Fewer than three are too few minds to contact; more than six and someone won't have an opportunity to speak.

Students were then told to select their own group partners making sure that a boy and girl would be in each group because that kind of interaction is necessary also.

Once these choices were made by students (course selection, teacher selection, group selection) we were ready to educate by appointment and make learning personal, practical, likeable, and dignifying.

HISTORY

Beginnings

Innovative ideas are a long time a-borning. In the late fifteenth century and early sixteenth century Leonardo Da Vinci drew elaborate plans based on strict scientific and engineering concepts for an airplane, a parachute, and a submersible vessel or submarine. It wasn't until the twentieth century, 400 years later, that these plans were used in production. Unfortunately, world war and threat of war gave the impetus for practical applications that today are commonplace.

Three years after the American Revolution, in 1779, Thomas Jefferson proposed legislation in the Commonwealth of Virginia to offer three years of free public education to the young people of the land. His bill never passed, and it wasn't until well after his death that Horace Mann in Massachusetts in 1837 established a public schooling policy for elementary-aged children.

It took until the 1870's before the supreme court ruled in favor of a Kalamazoo, Michigan, judgement supporting a tax financed education through high school. So the high school, the last of the kinds of educational opportunity, following establishment of elementary schools and colleges, is a scant 100 years old as an accepted right of every teenager in the United States.

During the 100 years of its existence, the high school has had to define and redefine its role. It was established initially and primarily as a college preparatory school. With the increased use of technology, massive urbanization, dwindling agrarian populations, a phenomenal knowledge explosion, the immediacy of information first by radio and then by television, the high school's purposes were broadened to provide a comprehensive education for any teenager. It provides now college preparation, trade skills, clerical and business aptitudes, as well as knowledge in a variety of careers to help young adults understand the society in which they live—domestic, economic, sócial, intellectual.

The high school characteristically has reacted to rather than acted on society. Its needs have geared up a work force of teachers formidable in their training and expertise in specific curriculum offerings. It has been no small accomplishment for the secondary school to establish itself and, indeed, flourish in its first hundred years.

But innovation, an effort to act on rather than react to society, is a slow process. Probably the high school would not have developed after the 1950's if it had not been for the remarkable effect of Sputnik on this nation. Who knows.

With Sputnik's launch came an outcry of dismay from the United States citizenry. How could the products of Soviet schools put such scientific and mathematical skills to such effective use! What was the matter with education in the United States?

Federal grants became available and groups, primarily in science and math, took advantage of them. We were deluged with new programs: PSSC, SMSG, ISCS, Harvard Physics, varieties of new chemistry and biology programs. Each new program required teacher re-training and adjustments in the curriculum.

About this same time J. Lloyd Trump approached the question "What's wrong with our schools?" from a new angle. He looked not so much at curriculum offerings as at the delivery system in education. In the early 1960's the Trump Model School plan seemed like the best thing to have happened since sliced white bread and indoor plumbing.

Indeed, the Trump plan was exciting because it finally broke down the rigid lockstep pattern of education. It provided a flexible schedule to accommodate large group, small group, independent learning styles. We finally acknowledged what we always knew—that not everyone learns best in the same mode, that learners need to inquire as well as absorb knowledge from teachers, that not every course takes the same quantity of time for mastery, that students need some time space to assimilate learning.

The 1960's were a heady time to be involved in secondary education. More and more students had their focus on college and wanted that high school diploma. The campus unrest at the end of the decade really didn't make its impact felt at the secondary level until the turn of the decade. The public was supportive and made its voice heard in its clamor for quality education for all students. It was the time for bold new ventures, and those that succeeded and sank their roots in a sound philosophy of learning survived. Those that were hangers-on, band wagon advocates, change for change's sake, after a few years settled back to the pattern of the early 1950's, though with a broadened curriculum. Urban schools shifted their focus from new delivery systems for learning to an entirely unexpected delivery system of court-ordered bussing.

Current Status

The chronology of events that created a model school for a system of education by appointment are clear. They were designed in the planning process.

The actual lead time for the staff was 1964–66. This was the period to develop the original multiple curriculum offerings, prepare the staff, move from a traditional to a modular schedule, and provide options for teachers and students.

Two things must be stressed. This was a model, so there was no place else to look for a blueprint. Second, the move from a lockstep to a modular schedule was never seen as an end in itself. The modular schedule was viewed as the hallway or transit from a box schedule to an open area with no schedule. But the staff needed the security of some mechanism in the interval. It is much like a base runner reluctant to take a foot off third until there is certainty of making it home.

From 1966–73 the system was in full swing, secure, productive. The refinements were in additional course offerings, courses in the community, interdisciplinary courses, a broadened enrollment that accepted persons as young as 12 and as old as 50 or more.

All of this was accomplished with an extremely stable staff. In the transition period, there was no teacher turnover. From 1967–73 there was an average of two or three changes a year in a staff of 58 certified members.

In 1973 the principal resigned to go on to other things. In the following five-year period there was a succession of two principals, a new assistant principal, a drastic turnover in staff (upwards of 80%), and a dismal decline in enrollment.

From a model school that had spawned itself around the country and in Canada, there was some retrenching. Prior to 1973 the school was a showcase for visitors in the thousands, literally, from almost every one of the 50 States, from the Provinces, from Japan, Australia, Germany, England, Africa. Local and area universities brought their undergraduate and graduate students in education to observe the system. This no longer occurs.

Why? What can cause an eminently successful program to back pedal?

One can surmise a number of things.

Staff stability is critical. At the same time, a stable staff is not without its problems. It is a challenge to inspire the same people each year to do better what they already do so well, to take another step forward when they have already come so far. But that challenge seems far preferable to beginning each year with a number of new members who must be brought through a period of unlearning to a new learning.

Consistent and on-going in-service for the staff is critical. There must be clearly defined goals or tasks for each staff member for each year with adequate feedback and re-enforcement from the principal.

Orientation for students is critical. They must be secure in the procedure for learning if they are to be productive. They must understand clearly what the philosophy of the school is, what it means, and how they can and cannot function within its parameters.

Paraeducator help is critical. Teachers need to be freed from clerical and custodial chores if they are to meet the needs of the people they serve—the students.

Most critical of all is the role of the principal. It is the solemn obligation of that person to keep the total concept in focus. The principal must be eminently visible and available to staff and students, not behind an office door submerged in forms and paperwork that very frequently can be done by secretaries.

To keep the entire concept in mind as a whole ball of wax must be stressed. If the parts of the plan are out of focus, then it becomes easy to change parts until the whole is no longer recognizable.

When a schedule does not hold a school together dictating what will happen when and where, when there is no teacher nor student schedule except as it grows out of appointments that are made, when each day begins for virtually everyone with a blank appointment page, then what does hold the learning together? More than anything else, the human relationships within the building.

It is most essential for the principal as the instructional leader to generate a climate of respect and trust primarily for and in staff so that staff in turn can create that same climate for students.

Respect and trust have their own built-in accountability. And accountability without respect and trust leads only to degradation, dissatisfaction, and disillusionment.

It is ironic that the model for education by appointment now has only some parts of the program operational while other schools that visited the model and implemented the concept are now more complete than the parent.

The situation described here could have been greatly ameliorated if the teacher colleges had picked up the concept, not just by a show and tell visit, but by actually instructing their students about the process and using the process.

Another failure in the educating process of educators is in the area of administrator certification. It is currently easier to become a principal than to become a teacher. Principals are ex-teachers who take administrative courses at a graduate school, become certified, and then become leaders of staff. There is no required internship to test the leadership capabilities of the would-be principal. Teachers at least have student teaching experience under a qualified teacher before they are released to students. Principals have no proving ground until, unfortunately at times, it is too late.

It is one thing to be a master teacher relating well with persons younger and less experienced than oneself. It is quite another matter to be a leader of one's peers, some of whom may be more gifted in a number of ways. Until we can come up with a more selective method of certifying instructional leaders, we will continue to prove the infallibility of the Peter Principle, that human beings tend to rise to their own level of incompetence. That is a terrible risk to take in schools where the well being of so many students and their futures as well as so many staff lives are at stake.

THEORY

Learning

Of all the things that being a human being entails, learning might well be the most difficult. By the time a student gets to high school, each one has developed some system for conquering or avoiding the problem to some degree. Few have developed a real joy in the project for its own sake because they have been busy for at least eight years in developing the rudimentary skills they will need to unlock the wonders of discovery of all who have gone before.

The vast majority of incoming high school students can read, compute, and express themselves orally and in writing to some degree. The task of the high school is to take the students where they are and move them forward, in half the time the elementary teachers had, in specialized areas of concentration that ideally should prepare them to function independently in a complicated, quickly changing society. Necessarily this requires the students to do more of the work themselves than they have been accustomed to.

Students suddenly have longer periods of non-instruction time, called study time, so that they can learn. This presents problems for some of them simply because they have no experience with how to use this time. Unfortunately, many high schools do not explain this or, if they do, they depend on a group counselling session devoted to the topic of Study Skills (how to take notes, how to organize a notebook, how to read for content, how to scan a page, *etc.*); or, worse yet, a pamphlet of some kind to be read that explains the wise use of study time.

In 1974 Dr. Donald L. Rogers, Associate Professor of Secondary Education and Foundations of Eastern Illinois University, did a research project in some Omaha schools. His findings, though done independently, supported the work of David Hunt, O. J. Harvey, and others about the conditions under which adolescents can learn.

Rogers uses the term Interpersonal Orientation (I.O.) to describe kinds of learners. Once the student's I.O. is determined, the teacher should create the environment that will best assist the learner to receive, store, process, and transmit information.

Interpersonal Orientation, simply, defines the degree of dependence or independence a learner has on the teacher. There are three general groups of I.O.: low, medium, and high. Because learning is an orderly process which moves step by step, not in quantum leaps, from the known to the unknown, it requires structure.

Structure in no way should be identified with a school schedule. So often, when the public calls for more structure in schools, they are calling for discipline or timed activities that make demands on students with an implicit "Or else!" threat.

Structure is essential for all learning, but it is tied to the I.O. and should be as individual in its application as the persons involved in it. If the same structure is used for all, it must be meaningless to some. Ironically, persons who do not understand individualization in learning, or an open classroom method, think there is no structure at all when, in fact, individualization requires much more structure than a highly scheduled day. If there is no structure, the staff of the school, or at least some of the staff, has simply not understood the individualizing process and/or has not internalized the concept.

A schedule will force some physical structure. It describes who should go where, when, and for how long. But it fails dismally to provide the mental or learning structure that describes what the mind should be doing while it is there. This oversight is further complicated by the teacher who lectures consistently to a group of 25 or 30 students and requires, for the sake of the lecture, a kind of motionless attention.

Within any classroom, however, there will be all three I.O. types requiring different degrees of structure more demanding than the external imposition of a schedule. In fact, the schedule is frequently an impediment to a learning structure.

Once a teacher recognizes the I.O. of each student, the classroom environment changes drastically.

The low I.O. learner requires a high degree of structure because the low

I.O. is characterized by great dependence on the teacher—for approval, attention, re-enforcement, direction. The medium I.O. learner requires moderate structure because that student is moderately dependent on the teacher. The high I.O. learner requires little structure. That student is more independent, follows direction, has a secure self concept with regard to learning, is generally referred to as a "self-starter."

In a class in grammar, for instance, the teacher well advised about I.O. would act as follows for maximum learning. The students listen to an explanation of the material to be learned (lecture) and then receive, if they have not already been distributed, the objectives for the lesson. Now the teacher needs to isolate (not necessarily physically) the I.O. types.

For the low I.O. students, the teacher should identify in what precise place the students should sit, which precise objectives to tackle in which precise order, and how much time should elapse (10 or 15 minutes) before they check their progress with the teacher. That is much more structure than a mere schedule provides.

For the medium I.O. students, the teacher should identify the area of the room in which the students should work (not the precise seats), where to begin in their learning task (not necessarily the order to follow), and a longer period of learning time—30 minutes or until the end of the class period, whichever comes first.

For the high I.O. students, the teacher merely needs to make sure they understand the objectives. They will find their own place to learn, will attack the work in their own fashion, and will turn it in when it is completed.

Two things need to be stressed. An I.O. and an I.Q. are not identical. Some very bright students have low I.O.'s. They are often labeled "under achievers." Conversely, some average or not so average students have high I.O.'s. These students are often labeled "over achievers." It would seem fair to assume that the inappropriate achievement might well be due to inappropriate learning structures.

The second thing is that the classroom scene described above pictures a procedure in a scheduled program where classes last the same length of time for everyone. I.O. knowledge is important and useful in that situation. But how much more beneficial for the learner this application would be if education took place by appointment—shorter, more frequent appointments for the lower I.O. and longer, less frequent appointments for the higher I.O.

Then the teacher could pattern the learning devices and expectations for the lower I.O. students, working with them to bring them along to greater independence. After all, that is what learning and mastery are all about. Students who master a given piece of learning should be independent of teacher help for that small segment of their education. Unfortunately, most teachers treat all students as if they all had low I.O.'s and, as a result, learning can be diminished.

But what makes students want to learn at all? What motivates them?

For some, they are inured to schooling. Society expects them to complete high school. Fewer students resist the idea because it is the pattern of generations, and so they comply.

For others, they have goals—college or a job and the hope of advancement. They learn things they may not be truly interested in, but they are exercises that lead to a future that is seen as desirable.

A few in every school have nothing else to do and school is a place to be with their friends. There are many other motivating forces, but the one group of students who cause more alarm, anxiety, and effort on the part of parents and teachers are these last mentioned, the so-called unmotivated, the reluctant learners.

One thing must be made clear. No one is innately motivated beyond a modicum of human curiosity about the unknown. Motivation is not part of human standard equipment. Babies are not born with two eyes, two ears, and motivation. There is a normal, but not voracious, curiosity in human nature. But how do we motivate learning?

The simplest, most effective, but least worthy method to motivate students is the threat. The greater the threat, the more explicit the danger, the greater and more immediate the motivation. Put a gun to a student's temple and the student will make surprising gains in learning, especially if the gun is loaded. With schools already struggling with declining enrollment, this hardly seems a practical method, apart from all moral considerations.

Human beings (and students are just like people, only younger) succumb mightily to peer pressure, adolescent types even to a greater degree than others. In schools that permit students to work at learning with their friends or with persons of their choice, there is greater hope for motivation. When students know precisely what is expected of them in terms of a given course, when they have the objectives and know that they will be accountable (tested) on those objectives and need to prove learning with a specific degree of competency, when they are free to get help (learn) from friends as well as teachers in mastering the objectives, when they know that once the objectives are demonstrated as learned they will be rewarded and finished with the course, there is a greater allurement to get going and get finished—which is what motivation in school boils down to.

Consequences for lack of learning as well as for learning are not simple and effective enough in many schools. The ground rules for education should be quite clear:

1. The object of the process is to get the student to learn.

2. It is immoral to pose for students that they learn what they already know. We can learn only what we do not already know. We can refresh our memories by studying again what we already know.

3. The easiest way to learn anything is to teach it.

4. When a student does not know how to proceed, that student should go to a peer first for help. The teacher is the resource person, available when other students cannot be of help.

What these statements imply is that students should have a right to demonstrate what they already know and not be subject to meaningless repetition. If a school has a requirement and a student can meet that requirement prior to enrollment in the course, the school would be well advised to verify the learning, issue credit for the course, and help the student move on to something more personally challenging.

A simple example of this is in foreign language. A Chicano student may enter the high school with a fluent use of and understanding of Spanish. The student may wish to attend a college later where the equivalent of two years of a foreign language in high school is required. The wisest thing to do is let the student test out of Spanish and the school should issue credit since the subject is learned.

If the student cannot demonstrate full competency in all the areas required for credit, then the student should be directed to learn those parts of Spanish only where the deficiency occurs and request another test when the knowledge is acquired.

Schools that fail students and recycle them for a repetition of a total course 1) act contrary to the fact that no one can learn what is already known, and 2) kill motivation in the process. We defeat ourselves as we defeat students. We need to require that students learn those things they have not mastered.

The difficulty with the above theory is that it is very inconvenient for a teacher and for a highly scheduled school. But we have to keep asking: For whom does the school and its educational benefits exist? Is this a good thing to do for students?

If a school rewarded students immediately for learning, that would enhance motivation. If a student completed a course today and today received a statement of credit earned with the required degree of competency, that would spur the student on, rather than having to wait for the scheduled quarterly report card that deals with so much past and so little present.

Learning traditionally has been a slow and tedious process. But it need not be. Especially it should not be so today when there is always so much more to learn due to the extraordinary knowledge explosion.

Schools traditionally have used two methods as the major learning modes—listening and reading. Reading is slow, even speed reading. Reading is essential and has a permanent place in society's value system of educated persons. But educators must begin to act on the fact that the printing press is not a new invention and its products, printed matter, are only one source of learning.

The easiest way to learn anything is to teach it. Any instructor knows this. We all learned more our first year of teaching than during the four glorious years of getting a degree to do it. When the structure of a school permits, even insists, that students help each other, two things happen.

1. Students get immediate help, often in language and terms they can understand more readily than the teacher's direction and explanation.
2. Teachers discover that they multiplied the number of teachers by the number of students.

It must be emphasized that new instruction comes basically from teachers. Need for repetition or assistance comes from students.

Students who teach are re-enforced in their own learning by the very fact that they must process material and conceptualize it in order to explain it. No one is the loser in the process. And there is no cheating. In fact, this atmosphere of total mutual help practically obviates cheating since the students know that the teacher alone is the final evaluator to whom thay are accountable for their learning.

Other easy and immediate ways to learn are:

1. The interview. In this day of TV talk shows, students learn the interview technique through entertainment. There is a plethora of interviewees on numerous subjects students learn: many teachers, administrators, other students, persons in the community, parents, and friends outside of school. Once the student has compiled appropriate questions, learning is fast and entertaining. Again, of course, this depends on enough flexibility in scheduling that the student is free to make appointments to learn.
2. Viewing, especially when combined with listening. There are so many commercially prepared A-V materials to choose from to enrich learning. But this is a learning style that appeals in varying degrees to students at various times. Ideally, students should have a place to view when the time is right for them. If a film that is rented is in the school for only three to five days, teachers should post a time schedule of when it can be viewed (every hour on the hour, for example) and let the students select the best time for them. Again, this requires some decision making and flexibility.
3. Listening. Some students learn by listening, and listening again. Major topics of instruction should be taped so that students can replay teacher lectures for salient points.
4. Hands-on experiences. Learning is an active experience. Research indicates that the more students are actively involved in the process (talking-teaching, questioning-interviewing, viewing-taking notes, listening-taking notes, handling-examining, creating) the more they will retain.

5. Field trips. When excursions take students out of the school, and when these trips are tied to curriculum topics, students see and are helped to understand the practicality of what they learn.

Even with a great variety of learning opportunities available, intrinsic learning needs to be structured because that is the way the human mind works.

In 1967 SRA published a research project in connection with some materials on biology that they were marketing at the time. The research outlined the steps that the human mind goes through in a methodical order in its quest for knowledge. All minds work this way at all times.

1. The mind *identifies.* It points to or picks out a new object. That is why small children point so much and smile in recognition of familiar persons and things. Older persons will look around a group to identify someone or something familiar. Learning is premised on the ability to identify. That is why the alphabet and spelling, for example, stay the same even though so much of spelling defies the given sounds of the characters in the alphabet.

2. The mind *names.* Once an identity or recognition is made, the mind demands a name for it. The mind is uncomfortable, in fact, when it cannot attach names to persons, places, and things.

3. The mind *orders.* It places recognized names in some list or file of categories: animal, vegetable, mineral; light to dark; fat to thin; big to little; expensive to inexpensive. Part of the learned appreciation of a Porsche or Mercedes is the fact that either is distinctive (identifiable), has a good name, and costs a lot of money.

4. The mind *compares.* It takes the new item and automatically notes how it is like other things already stored in memory.

These first four mental processes are simple. Students do them automatically and need little if any instruction about them. The next three steps are a bit more sophisticated.

5. The mind *contrasts.* It sorts out how this new item, like some things already stored in memory, is also distinct and different from all other things. This takes greater perception and is a more difficult process. A small child will recognize dogs as dogs. Or big dogs and little dogs. It takes time to learn a beagle from a bassett or a schnauzer from a terrier.

6. The mind *constructs.* Once there is some material stored in memory, the mind will make or create something—a box, a story, a meal. To require of the mental process that it construct (a stanza, a triangle, whatever) before it has been brought through the previous five steps is to ask it to run before it can walk.

7. The mind *demonstrates.* This is show and tell time. After the mind has worked through the first six steps, it can explain it to others.

The final two steps can be quite difficult. Some people barely master them.

8. The mind *states a rule.* Given all the bits of stored information, the mind can

draw a conclusion. It can draw an inference. It can take a hint!

9. The mind *applies a rule*. A thing is mastered. Now the learning is conceptualized in such a way that the mind on its own can come up with a new idea. Once this is done, the nine steps begin all over again: What is it? What do you call it? What can it do? *Etc.*

The importance of this for learning is that the mind requires extreme respect. It is orderly by nature. It must be readied systematically for learning. To request it to do what it is not yet prepared to do (Write a poem for tomorrow before you know what poetry is or, indeed, what a verse is!) is to frustrate this delicate human ability. The horror of consistent mental frustration produces anger and a gradual erosion of self concept and human dignity.

Human nature being what it is, we work best with people with whom we are comfortable. We work even better with people whom we like. This requires, for maximum educational effort, that students select their learning partners and also their teachers. This helps to structure success for them, and nothing succeeds like success!

Teaching Theory

It is unfortunate that new teachers come directly from a college and university instructional model of lecture—assimilation—testing, because that is what they are predominantly prepared to do with their first captive audience. They must unlearn so much about what teaching is. Difficult as learning is, unlearning is even more painful.

Classrooms should not be identical within a school. Where reading is a major activity, furniture conducive to reading should be supplied: sofas, easy chairs, cushions, bean bags, tables. Adults do not read at desks, and school should prepare students for adult life.

In fact, other than where writing or like activities are required, desks are not necessary in every room. To shape the atmosphere of the space for the expected activity is part of the teaching experience. We instruct nonverbally as well as verbally.

Teaching should pose for the learner a series of educational hurdles that must be cleared. The rules should be simple, concise, and few. The expectations should be articulated and understood.

It should be stressed that the learning hurdles be challenging in content but low enough in duration of time that the learner can clear them without frustration and exhaustion. If a course has 45 objectives, they should be doled out in series of six or eight so that the students can see terminal points. No one likes to be overwhelmed with work.

The most important part of teaching is in the preparation and the interaction of the teaching staff for inspiration, experience, critique value.

Teachers involved in the same offerings should work out objectives jointly. This insures greater professional expertise for the learners and also monitors excessive repetition in future courses. More teachers will know what has already been taught and what can be expected.

Once objectives have been determined, in terms of how the mind works in learning, there should be some suggested learning activities. The best learning activity, however, generally is the one the student describes.

Teaching should include the preparation of self-tests for the student. Tests should deal with the objectives. There should be no mystery in a student's mind about what a teacher expects the student to know.

The self-test is a test students take and correct on their own. That means that the answers must be readily available and the performance criteria clearly stated. The purpose of the self-test, after all, is strictly to help the student understand what is learned and what is still to be learned. Students see no point in copying answers, since the self-test does not count as a final evaluation of learning.

When a student has mastered a segment of learning to that student's personal satisfaction, it is time to confer with the teacher. If the teacher is satisfied, the teacher has a decision to make. The self-test score may be perfect. The teacher, however, may have some insecurity about a particular student. In that case, a final test, teacher corrected, is required to give the teacher confidence that the student indeed has mastered the objectives. If a teacher who knows a given student as that kind who always learns, there is no reason why the teacher should not waive the final test on the particular objectives. What more would such an exercise prove?

When a school is organized in such a way that each student's needs are met in a personal way, the teacher's role shifts dramatically. The teacher becomes an educational consultant to the students. It is a much more professional role than that of purveyor of information. Teachers who are most successful in this system are those who refuse to slide back into the more traditional role of lecturer and giver of answers. They, in fact, exercise the law of subsidiarity which in itself confers a sense of trust and dignity both on themselves and on the students. But it is difficult because teachers are not trained to operate in this mode.

The law of subsidiarity, as it applies to education, quite simply states that persons at the top of the structure (principal) must steadfastly refuse to do those things that those at the next level (staff) can do for themselves. Persons at that level must refuse to do for those at the following level (students) what they can do for themselves. To follow this law in a school, decision-making is shared, choices are imperative, growing independence is assured, and the final result is heightened dignity.

Students learn the system readily if the teachers are consistent. Students are forced to learn how to learn. They understand that they have to use the learning skills they have acquired to find information, to work out solutions, to discover new learning. The teacher will assist by helping the student clarify a problem, by directing the student to some possible resources, by evaluating the result, and by discussing the finished product with the student.

To demonstrate this theory, let's examine two situations, one in math and one in English.

In a math area, depending upon the size of the space, there may be any number of teachers. They would be established in given areas as a base of operation, though they would walk around also to see if they can be of help. Students determine when they want to do math and for how long on any given day. When they do math, however, they will do it in the math area because that is where the resources, people and things, are.

A student, call her Mary, enters the area, looks around for a place, selects it, probably near friends. They exchange a few words of greeting and begin to compare work. It should be stressed that all math occurs in this area, pre-algebra as well as calculus. As Mary gets into the work, she finds that she is stuck and does not know how to proceed. She asks her friends. One friend tells her what she should do and Mary resumes her work until she gets stuck again. This time her friends do not know how to help her. She stands up, looks around, and recognizes a student on the other side of the room who had this same course previously. She walks over to the student.

The student helps Mary who returns to her own place again and continues to work until (1) she finishes what she set out to do, (2) has to meet an appointment that she set up with a teacher or a group of other students, or (3) gets tired of doing math. She says good-bye to her friends, gets up and leaves the math area to go somewhere else.

In all of this, a teacher never personally contacted Mary, although Mary was able to function well because of all of the teacher's preparation. Mary knew what to do and where to go for help. She knew that if a student could not help her, there were several teachers in the area and any one of them could help her. The specific teacher Mary had selected as her teacher for the course is the one Mary would have gone to for an evaluation, however.

Let's say that two days later Mary returns to the math area. During the intervening day she did not choose to do any math because she wanted to concentrate on an art project she was preparing.

When Mary returns to math she follows the same procedure: look for a place, anyplace, probably near friends. Say hello, visit briefly, get to work. Very shortly Mary completes the last of the six math objectives she had. She goes over to a file and selects the self-test for those six objectives, sits down, and takes the test. When she finishes, she goes to where the answers are kept, checks her paper and scores it. If the performance criterion was 12 of 15 correct and Mary had only 10 correct, she knows what she still needs to study.

If Mary had 13 or 14 correct, she looks around for her teacher. She takes her notebook and her test to the teacher who at that time check's Mary's work. The teacher has not had Mary turn in daily assignments. Mary has done the prescribed kinds of problems to meet her math objectives in the quantity that Mary needed to learn the material.

The teacher asks Mary if she recognizes where her error is in the item she had incorrect. Mary finds the error and explains what she should have done. Now the teacher decides if Mary needs a final, teacher corrected test or not. If the teacher determines that Mary knows the material, Mary receives the next set of objectives. If the teacher is uncertain how well Mary knows the material, the teacher will give Mary a small slip of paper to admit her to a testing room. The paper is a simple form with space for Mary's name, the teacher's name, the name of the math course Mary is taking, the title and form of the test Mary should take, and the date the test pass is issued.

Mary now can decide when she wants to take her math test. She cannot continue in math until the test is completed. She may decide to take the test later that day, some time the next day, or whenever she feels ready.

When Mary decides to take the test, she goes to the testing room, gives the pass to the paraeducator who supervises the room for all testing in the school, puts her books inside the desk, and gets the test from the proctor who has all final tests for all departments in files in the room. Mary takes the test, finishes it, returns it to the proctor who staples the test pass to it, and initials and dates the pass. Mary leaves.

The proctor at lunch time will place all the tests taken in the morning in the mailboxes of the teachers who issued test passes. At the end of the school day the proctor does the same with the afternoon tests.

_____ Department Credit Notice

Student Name:	Last	First	Initial	Date

Finished Course # _____   Named _____

Credit Earned _____   Teacher _____

Will Begin Course # _____   Named _____

                                        Teacher _____

The next day Mary goes back to her math teacher who corrects Mary's test, goes over it with Mary, and discusses the results. If the test is the final piece of work for the course Mary is taking, and if Mary met the performance criterion, the teacher will fill out a small form in duplicate that issues Mary credit for the completed course. This is Mary's receipt for learning. The duplicate copy of the form will be kept in the math department as a record of Mary's work. Then the teacher and Mary discuss the next course Mary will take in math, if indeed she intends to, and get her started in it.

Mary can take her receipt for learning and show her friends, other teachers, her folks. It's an accomplishment.

Mary in this example obviously has a high I.O. She takes precious little teacher's time. If Mary were a medium I.O. the teacher would have had her show her progress two or three times a week. If she were a low I.O., the teacher would have told her when to come to the math area, where to sit, how much work to accomplish, and to check into and out of the area each time with the teacher.

What becomes obvious is that teachers in this system give unequal amounts of time to different students. Those who need more attention can get it because those who need less make the time available. Also, teachers do not do those tasks that someone else can do equally well—like supervising tests.

In an English course example, let's follow a student named Joe. He and five friends, four boys and two girls in all, are involved in a course called Mass Media: The Mind Benders. This is a teacher created course, approved and critiqued by all members of the English Department.

Joe and his friends have been working on the course for a week. They have eight objectives to master. When they began the course the teacher had asked them to determine how they would divide the work. Joe took the first two objectives, another took two, the others each took one. They have met three times as a group during the week to share what they have learned because they are all responsible for all eight objectives, but they teach each other what each one studied.

When they feel they have a grip on things, they set up a forty minute appointment with their teacher. They know, because it is the way appointments take place, that the first 25 minutes of that appointment only they will talk. The teacher will listen, take notes, nod in encouragement, but will not speak. During the last 15 minutes the teacher will critique from notes taken during the student discussion, make corrections, comment on the value of each student's contribution, direct them to further resources to strengthen any weaknesses in what has been learned so far, and ask them when they would like to have another appointment. They may decide the work will take them a week to prepare. They make an appointment for a week later.

That is teaching. Learning takes place away from the teacher. The teacher's task is to evaluate the quality of the learning.

If Joe's group had not been prepared for the appointment, the teacher would have waited pleasantly but silently for about three clock minutes and then said, "We're wasting time. And you must have been wasting time all week as far as English goes. Some other students need me, so when do you want your next appointment?" They will be ready the next time because nothing is so unendurable as three minutes of teacher silence.

Another important aspect of the teacher role is the function of the teacher-advisor. The first fifteen minutes or so of every day begin with groups of students meeting with specific staff members. The entire professional staff—administrators, counsellors, teachers, all certified personnel—are involved in the teacher-advisor process. Because more than just the classroom teachers have this responsibility, the pupil-teacher ratio is reduced.

The purpose of the teacher-advisor concept is to insure accountability. The only option a student does not have in this system is the option not to learn. Schools exist to educate students just as hospitals exist to cure illness.

The teacher-advisor checks on progress. High I.O. students need little supervision, but they do need re-enforcement. Medium I.O. students may need to be prodded in a few areas. Low I.O. students may need to show the teacher-advisor precisely how they have scheduled themselves for the day to meet their learning responsibilities. The advisor may well tell some students, on the advice of subject area teachers, what to do on a given day or for a period of time.

As students demonstrate greater independence in their learning and a growing sense of responsibility, the advisor can give them greater latitude. The advisor for a group will be the same one until graduation when newly entering ninth graders will take their place. Each group will be a mix of ages and sex. If a student and advisor have a personality conflict, the advisor will facilitate the student's shift to another staff member. In fact, this seldom happens; but the feasibility of a move is built into the system.

When students group themselves for inter-action courses, the worry is that there will be an automatic homogeneous grouping, which is not like the real world at all. Adults do not choose bowling partners, spouses, golf foursomes, by I.Q. They choose by mutual interest, compatibility, fellowship.

Students do the same thing. They realize, and are told periodically by their advisors, that they need to earn credits to get out of high school, that, indeed, it is possible to grow old in this system if they do not complete their learning. So students usually get into groups that will help them. If a group of students form and do nothing, then the teacher can get involved and create a different mix. Because most courses need not last longer than a few weeks, there is an opportunity to work with many different students.

When a group does finish a course, their own interests and course selections most often will require that they regroup with others. If no group is available, the teacher can take the names of the one or two students (remember, a learning group requires three to six) and, as other groups finish, call the students and help them get together. If a student can't find a group to join, the teacher can insert the student in an existing group. The teacher facilitates this kind of maneuver but only if it is required.

There is no problem with the so-called loner. The shy student in a conventional classroom may never volunteer an answer because there are 25 or 30 persons listening, some of whom are unknown or even disliked. When students select their own groups, there are only five others at the most, they are interdependent for their learning, and the threat of imagined embarrassment or disaster is greatly diminished, if not eliminated. These students have a commitment to each other for the length of the course. They begin it together and end it together. Therefore they prep each other to meet the required criteria for the credit.

If a group of students at some time desires group instruction on a particular topic, it can be available without disruption of a schedule. They contact a teacher, explain their need, set up a convenient time, and have the lecture. Sometimes a teacher sees a need for group instruction. The same thing occurs: an announcement is made at least a day in advance to give students who have made other commitments an opportunity to change appointments, and the lecture is given.

Some teachers video-tape lectures that may be seen at the student's convenience and repeatedly if desired. Students may video-tape lecture topics for other students also, but under a teacher's approval.

There is a great deal of unseen structure created by teachers. Students in effect schedule themselves daily and, in doing so, schedule teachers who work from an appointment book.

Teachers need to understand and be reminded rather often that education is a business, a people business. We are in the process of selling services to people. People's needs change day to day, and that is why no two days in education can be identical if we are truly going to keep our business commitments.

One of the services teachers render is role-modelling. A simple example beyond the obvious one of adult, mature behavior, is the case of learning. Since students are expected to work at learning, they must have the opportunity to observe how it takes place. That is why teachers who need to use the school library should sit down at the tables with the students and read, take notes, do research. That is why teachers, when they are not directly involved with appointments, should work in the rooms with students, preparing objectives, creating courses, writing, reading, and solving problems. Besides, this cuts down on their homework demands. They can accomplish much of their curriculum creation responsibility on school time, just as students should accomplish their academic learning on school time.

If students work at learning six hours a day, they should leave the school at the end of the day, not to continue school at home, but to refresh themselves with other activities so that they can come back to work tomorrow.

APPLICATIONS

Curriculum, Academic

Curriculum of course is the vehicle for mastering learning. Staff must decide what students need to learn to qualify as a high school graduate, and with what degree of quality and competency. Some academic proof is required, and courses that describe that proof are mandatory. However, any student who can demonstrate possession of the performance criteria in a required course should be able to call for the test and, having met the standards, receive credit without actually going through the mechanics and time of the course itself.

It should be stressed that such courses are few in number and testing out applies to required (or basic) courses only. The elective courses should be challenging enough in terms of interest and depth that a student cannot test out of them in advance.

When education takes place by appointment, each course offering is discrete and short term. Departments list those offerings that are required and those that are elective and assign credit in terms of the content to be mastered. If the carnegie unit is used, credit is assigned in fractions; if semester hours (10 times a carnegie unit) are used, it is simpler to keep track of credits because they are issued in whole numbers.

For example, 10 semester hours (one carnegie unit) are required in high schools in American History. In terms of courses, this translates into 10 required one semester hour courses (1/10 of a carnegie unit per offering). There may be 20 or more American History course topics from which a student must select 10. This is a good case in point because by the time students get to high school, they have had two years of American History at the elementary level (which usually brings them to the twentieth century), and untold hours of it on TV in documentaries, special events, movies, *etc.* Too often in high school the conventional course starts again with the Pilgrims and the founding of the nation and the students seldom get to study in any depth the events after World War I.

Also, teachers have a wealth of preparation in their fields that they are never able to share with students in courses because the more standard curriculum as a schedule permits cannot accommodate variety. Typical is a teacher with a strong background, even a master's degree, in statistics, who is scheduled into five geometry classes each day.

It is important also that course descriptions, though brief, indicate what a course equips a student to pursue as well as what the course is about. For example, a math course called Vectors should carry this information in its description: This course is recommended for those students who want a strong background in math topics needed in physics courses. Or an offering called Linear Programming should include the information: This course is recommended for all college-bound students, business-oriented students, and students who enjoy graphing.

Besides the course description and credit yield, there should also be a pre-requisite: Required, None, a previous course, or Department Consent. The last notation is especially important to offset the possibility that more talented students may choose less challenging courses just to acquire easy credits. For example, a talented science student may decide to loaf through Household Electricity, but that likelihood becomes dim when the pre-requisite is Department Consent.

One thing must be stressed. When a department decides how many credits are required for a diploma, the teachers in that department must offer sufficient courses of varying degrees of demand, depth, and interest so that every talent level of the students can meet the requirement.

Typical courses in Language Arts might include: A Library Is . . . (required); Shakespeare: A Taste; Lyric Poetry: Then and Now; Introduction to the Art of the Film; Write You Must: Composition I (required); Write You Must Again: Composition II (required); History of the English Language; I-Spy Literature; The Development of the Short Story; Children's Literature; The Evolution of a Hero, *etc.*

Typical courses in science include: Environmental Science, Man and the Sea, Scientific Research, Man in Space, as well as biology, chemistry, and physics topics.

Art offerings include the Natural Way To Draw: Contour; The Natural Way To Draw: Form; Forms in Space; Creative Batik and Tie-Dying; Creative Mosaics; Creative Enameling; Creative Cloisonne: Jewelry; Camera and Darkroom; Photography As an Art.

Business Department offerings include, besides shorthand and various typing courses, Job Application, The Receptionist, Filing, Taxes, Investing, Salesmanship, Buying and Pricing, Product Planning, Management, Cashiering.

There are also various interdisciplinary courses. These require a series of appointments with a teacher from each discipline involved in the course. Students who select these courses may have the credit earned applied to that academic area they may need to fulfill a graduation requirement. This is done because State Departments of Education and College Admissions personnel like to have credits defined in academic categories.

Examples of interdisciplinary courses are Entertainment Today (offered for credit in Communications, Music, Art); French for the Sciences (French or Science); Science Math (Science or Math); The Metric System (Science or Math); Applied Statistics (Math, Science, Social Studies, P.E.); Sit-In on Protest (Art, Music, Social Studies, Communications); Macrame (Home Ec. or Art).

As students learn and earn credit, they receive credit slips (the receipts for learning); and the specific course with the name of the department as well as the teacher who issued the credit is typed onto the transcript for each student. The transcript resembles a college transcript, then, with department, course title, instructor's name, and credit for each course.

At any one time, students may be involved in four to seven courses. As a student completes one course, another takes its place. During the school year, a student will conceivably complete 25 different courses, but only have a few at any one time.

Students are most adroit in pacing themselves. Very few end the year in the midst of a course. But those who do simply pick up where they left off when fall comes around.

Obviously, students do not fail. The school is in the business of trading credit for learning. When a course is completed (objectives and performance criteria met), credit is issued. Until the course is completed, credit is withheld.

Because of the nature of the system, all teachers deal with the handicapped students, who are mainstreamed and supported by advisors, teachers, other students, counselors. They are not isolated. They know that if it will take five years to complete high school, they have the time with no stigma, especially since the usual classification of Freshman, Sophomore, Junior, Senior is gone. They are all students spending different lengths of time in courses, and most courses will be a mix of ages.

Curriculum, Non-Academic

Not everything can be individualized. Students who take Chorus or Band must be together at the same time following the same music. This necessitates that there be specific times each week when the band, for example, will have a total rehearsal time.

The Band Director can set aside two or three times a week when students will meet as an ensemble. All other appointments and activities must be plotted around those times. However, at general rehearsal time, the Director may well discover the need for the woodwind section to practice separately. The students and Director decide a common time and a separate practice period can be handled without disruption of a schedule. The students merely arrange their personal schedules to accommodate this session.

The same thing applies to Chorus groups. If, at general rehearsal time, the Choral Director hears that the tenors are consistently flat or do not know the music, a sectional practice time is arranged. A fringe benefit of this procedure is that the other students do not get restless or disruptive waiting for the Director to finish practicing with the tenors.

Even in P.E. with its emphasis on life-long sports and activities, appointments can be made. Students select their teams for a course in volley ball, for example, and sign up to practice in the gym with another team twice a week, one hour each practice time. They know that as a team, each member must know how to play the game, score the game, and referee the game. The P.E. instructor is in the gym anyway, so when the teams come (on a first come, first served sign-up basis), the instructor is available to teach, observe, evaluate. While two teams are practicing volley ball, other students may be practicing shuffle-board or tumbling or badminton at the same time and the instructor moves from group to group as advice or help is needed.

Varsity athletics, on the other hand, take place after school hours with the specific coaches for the seasonal events.

This system, with student-created schedules, can accommodate a wide variety of community-based course offerings. Students who may wish to be involved with some social agencies can have a teacher make the contact, describe the objectives to be mastered, arrange time to work at the agency under the agency personnel, report their work to the instructor at the school, and receive credit for the course. Students get involved in Head Start projects, City Planning councils, Child Abuse centers, Nursing Homes. The only limitation is the boundary of imagination when it comes to learning, being responsible, and getting involved.

Where the system is really an evident plus is in the area of practical arts and industrial arts. Students who take a course in Clothing Construction can actually block out a half day or an entire day to cut a pattern, pin and baste the fabric, sew it, finish it, get it approved, and take it home to wear. Conventional systems do this same task but in such fragmented periods of time over many days that the finished product is old before it is ever worn.

There is a need for times when the entire student body can come to- gether. For this reason, approximately 40 minutes are reserved by the school each week, same time, for assemblies or sectional meetings. Students do not make appointments for those 40 minutes. If no assembly or meeting occurs, the time is available to study or fit in an appointment. But the school has the prior right to that time each week.

Many clubs and activities can meet on school time, especially if the club has a reasonably small membership like French Club, Chess Club, Science Club, Future Teachers of America, *etc.* The staff moderator and club membership set a meeting time once a month and work appointments around it. Large clubs, like Pep Club, need to meet after school because otherwise nothing else could occur.

Student Evaluation

The evaluation process is constant because teachers are working with small groups (maximum of six) or one-on-one at all times. As students complete work, they receive credit slips as described and their transcripts are updated. There is a great deal of testing in each course: self tests which are student self administered and corrected as often as a student desires and formal teacher-corrected final tests.

Besides these in-house testing programs, there are batteries of standardized tests for different age groups scheduled weeks in advance so that students can free a day or a portion of it for the time required. The regular testing program includes the DAT or a comparable aptitude test, the Strong Vocational batteries, the PSAT, SAT, ACT, individual State and National tests in specific disciplines (math, foreign language, science), *etc.* There is little if any emphasis on I.Q. tests.

The standardized test scores are generally issued in triplicate, one copy each for the student, the counsellors, the transcript. The scores are affixed to the student transcript for the help of college admissions officers and future employers as requested.

Four times a year the staff sends a progress report home to the parents or guardians. The progress report forms are simple and there is one copy sent for each course in which the student is currently involved.

The form states the student's name, the name of the course, the amount of credit the course will yield, when the course was begun, how far the student is in the course, and whether the work so far is satisfactory or not. If a course has 24 objectives, the teacher will state how many have been achieved (like six of 24). At the bottom of the form the teacher will check whether the work indicates a conference with the parents or not.

If a conference is indicated, the teacher will list the school or home phone number at which the teacher prefers to be contacted with some suggested times for the phone call.

If a conference is not indicated, the teacher will indicate that by check-

_____   _____   _____
Name of School   Address   Phone

                                    Date _____

The parents of _____

     The above student is enrolled in course # _____ in the _____
Department. There are _____ objectives to the entire course. The student at
this time has completed _____ objectives. This course yields _____ semester
hours of credit.

     The work is _____ satisfactory   _____ unsatisfactory.

_____ I would appreciate it if you would phone me at _____
          Preferred time _____.

_____ At this time it will not be necessary to contact me unless there is
          some information you desire.

                        Sincerely,

                        Instructor

ing the appropriate area which says that a conference is not necessary
unless the parents wish to speak to the teacher.

The progress reports deal with courses currently studied, not courses
completed. The credit slip (receipt for learning) indicates completion.
Therefore when the first progress reports are issued around Thanksgiving
time, each student will have five or so reports sent home. By the time the
end of the year reports go home, 90% of the students will not have any
because all the courses are completed. The other 10% may have one or two
reports sent home.

Parents at any time may set up appointments on school time to talk to
teachers. Such an appointment is only one more in a system that functions
in that style. In fact, not many parents set up such appointments. They
may, however, drop in at any time simply to observe the school process.

By now it should be obvious that grades are not issued. Grades at best
are subjective, depending often on a teacher's metabolism on a given day.
Before grades are discontinued, it is important to check with colleges and
universities to explain the system and the transcript so that the graduates
will be accepted.

Athletic scholarships are issued nationally at this time only on grades.
Therefore a simple thing to do is to take the percentile from the most

recent DAT or other similar test and create a grade, grade point average, and approximate rank in class since the school, by policy, does not compute these data for all students.

Counseling

In most high schools, counsellors are responsible for the master schedule, for dropping students out of and into classes during the year, for listening to complaints about teachers to whom students were assigned, and for various other chores related mostly to the schedule. This often makes the counsellors *personnae non gratae* with the rest of the staff.

When the schedule is eliminated, a big piece of the counsellor's time is freed. (It should be noted that no part of the university preparation for counseling includes schedule building.) When students select their courses, which are short term and tailored to fit each student's needs, they don't drop out of them.

When students select their own teachers, they don't complain about them. This matter of students selecting teachers at first strikes fear into the hearts of some staff members. The fear is proved to be unfounded. They all get enrollments because some kinds of teachers appeal to some kinds of students. Also, some courses are required and a choice of teachers that may be limited to two on a first come, first served basis will quickly fill a teacher's load. Lastly, when teachers find that they are on the open market in terms of the students, it is amazing how the most cantankerous and dour types become more caring, gentle, concerned about student welfare.

Counsellors in an appointment system can assume the role for which they were trained. The vast majority of their time is devoted to personal counseling. This may be individual or group counseling. They also arrange for visits with college admissions officers, visits to business and industry, job placement, college placement, college scholarships. This means that they must know requirements for colleges to which students apply and keep the information available and updated. They must also keep on top of national trends in career possibilities as well as the status of the local job market.

In addition to this, the counsellors interpret all standardized test results for the students in small groups by appointment and indicate areas of weakness that could be strengthened by additional course work in specific disciplines.

The actual academic counseling, however, is done by the teachers. As a student finishes a math course, the student gets a credit slip and at that time the math teacher will ask, "Are you going to take another math course now? Which one?" The teachers are eminently qualified to know the math ability of the students they have had, and they know if a selected new course is appropriate for what the student may need for a chosen career or for college preparation.

Another important function of the counsellors is orientation for new students at the beginning of each year. The counsellors help them understand the procedure, meet with the students both singly and in groups, help them identify places, persons, and things. During September each year the counsellors make specific appointments for orientation purposes.

Teachers may make referrals of students who seem to need counseling services. Most of the time these referrals come from the teacher-advisor role, since the teacher in an academic area can usually counsel a student adequately about any course difficulty or problem.

Because counsellors are also teacher-advisors, they develop an identity and empathy with the teachers while, at the same time, they are different in terms of specific academic responsibility. They are seen as important and helpful members of the staff by the teachers, particularly in terms of their services in the area of orientation.

Discipline

The more rules a school has, the more risk there is in turning teachers into patrol squads. Schools should not have rules that cannot be enforced. They should be few, simple, and clearly understood, with their sanctions, by staff, students, and parents.

Education by appointment places a high degree of value on personal dignity with concomitant responsibility. Rules, therefore, deal with those aspects of behavior.

Since students always have something prescribed to learn, they have no need to wonder what to do. They move about freely; but there is a requirement that when they are in the halls, they be in motion toward someplace, not congregating and clotting up traffic. When they need to, without any pass and clerical red tape, they may go to the office, a locker, the media center, a counsellor, the washroom, any area of study.

If they loiter in the halls, any teacher who may also be moving about will simply say, "Please move along." Teachers are told never to raise their voices at students, not to be obstreperous. When teachers yell at students, they encourage students to yell back; and then the student is wrong even though the teacher incited the incident.

Because appointments are the rule of each day, it is important that they be kept punctually. If a student who has set up an appointment with a teacher fails to show up, has not arranged in advance to be late or to transfer the time to another hour or another day, the student is wrong. A teacher's time has been reserved uselessly when the teacher could have made an appointment with someone else. The result is an automatic detention of 40 minutes after school. This is well defined and clear to all.

If a student has a doctor's appointment or some other legitimate reason for postponing the detention, that can be arranged. If a student wishes to postpone the detention for less than a serious reason, the assistant principal, who is the recourse for this kind of transaction, simply says, "Fine. On what two nights do you want to do this?" It's a case of double time. Few detentions are postponed unnecessarily.

After school the 10 or 12 students on any given day who must serve detention, report to a specified room where they may study silently under the supervision of a paraeducator.

Obvious regulations, not untypical of other schools, exist for absence from school, release of students at parental request or for jobs, and for truancy. The system apparently does not make truancy attractive, for very few try it each year. When it occurs, there is a conference with the student and parents, and an appropriate number of detention periods are prescribed.

Drugs and alcohol can be a problem with some students. They are told, and the parents are informed in advance, that it violates the school environment for a student to be under the influence of chemicals, to be in possession of them, or to be trafficking in them. Since society does not view this activity as appropriate in anyone, an offender will be ostracized from school society for a specified length of time. The offender may come to school in the morning early or after school hours to get help from a teacher, turn in work, *etc.* Students are not restricted from learning, but they are restricted from peer society for awhile until their behavior is modified. In some cases, where no one is at home during the day, the student may be restricted to a small office-type room in which to study in isolation from friends.

There really is no need for further imposition of regulations. Furthermore, teachers would not be able to enforce more nor to enforce them equally. As it is, because discipline problems are greatly minimized with this system, teachers tend to view minor problems out of proportion. Examples are the teacher who might get excited because six students are standing in a hallway. The best response is: "Good! That means that 994 are in learning areas!"

ROLES

Administration

It goes without saying that the School Board and Superintendent need to understand the system, support it, and commit the necessary resources to it. Since it does not cost more than a conventional system, the commitment of resources means basically a commitment to employ quality staff members with strong academic preparation in their disciplines.

Of greater concern to the day to day operation of the school is the principal. This person has to be highly visible and available to the staff, modeling for staff the kind of behavior staff should model for students. This means that the principal must be in and out of learning areas, not policing them, but drawing up a chair to listen to discussions in an appointment, to sit down with a student and ask how things are going, to sit down with a teacher in a learning area to encourage or advise, to demonstrate sincere interest in the process of learning.

The principal also needs to meet at stated times with department heads about curriculum revision, additions and deletions, assignment of credit and prerequisites. On request, the principal should attend departmental meetings.

Once a month department heads need to give a formal, brief, written report in duplicate to the principal. The report cites the observed departmental strengths in the last month, the weaknesses, and any recommendations. The principal then can comment on the report, return one copy and keep one for reference. A quick glance at these reports will help with questions posed by Board members, parents, or the public.

It is primarily the principal's task to keep the whole ideal, the philosophy of the school, always in mind so that events are viewed in perspective. It is the principal's task to ask constantly when ideas are aired, "Is it good for the students? If it is, let's find a way to do it!"

In terms of curriculum, the principal's chief role is that of devil's advocate asking questions like, "Why do you think that course is better than this one? Have you considered offering this kind of course? What sort of student talent are you creating this course for?"

There is a need for the principal to be sensitive to the frustrations of teachers, supplying clerical help for them, seeing that their space is clean and attractive, understanding their problems, and mostly re-enforcing their good, hard work. The principal needs to depend on the staff in the exercise of the law of subsidiarity, letting them make their own decisions, settle their own misunderstandings among themselves and holding them accountable for those decisions and behaviors.

In other words, the principal needs to be a good listener with some human relations skills.

No matter how effective everyone else in the school is, no matter if the school system has a public relations person or not, the face of the school to the public is the principal. It is the principal who gets the phone calls from parents, the media, the community. It behooves the principal to know every aspect of the school's operation.

There should be specific times when the principal speaks to the student body, to student groups, to be seen and to share ideals and future plans. There should be specific times when groups of students, particularly student government members, speak with the principal so that they can be collaborators in the school.

There are numerous small things a principal can do to help create the appropriate school climate: keep the office door open except in very private and confidential discussions or at the request of those who come to the office; arrange the office furniture in such a way that a passer-by will not recognize who is in the principal's office; eat lunch frequently with the staff; drop into the coffee room and visit with whoever is there about what that person wants to speak of—a game, family, a course, vacation.

The principal needs to inspire. The inspiration has to be for excellence, creativity, hard work, accountability. When a principal says yes, it must mean yes; no must mean no; there is not room for firm maybes.

School should not be static. One important role for the principal is to create brain-storming sessions with varieties of staff groups. In this way, ideas are heard, sifted, refined, and eventually implemented.

Faculty

There are numerous decisions staff can make. Annually, they can elect their own department heads. In schools, the position of department head carries with it some monetary compensation. When teachers elect one of their peers for an increase in salary, they will see to it that the person earns it.

The department head calls monthly meetings. This can be arranged on school time for the most part by simply clearing appointments for 40 minutes. If a department does this, it should post the time so that not more than one department at a time is unavailable to students.

At department meetings, work may be assigned (course objectives, learning activities, test production), courses may be critiqued, credit assignments may be discussed, performance criteria may be clarified.

When education by appointment takes place, staff is always working on next year. Once the courses are agreed upon, they are given to the students for registration in very early spring. When the students have selected their courses for the next year, the staff makes their own teaching assignments.

All of them will get to teach something they like, trading off on one another's strengths and weaknesses. Most of them also will select something with less than great enthusiasm. But it is their choice, not a programmer's decision, and therefore the chances of success of an unpopular assignment are greatly enhanced. If a teacher came to school in the fall and discovered the assignment of a course that was unwanted, the teacher could fail in the effort because of "someone else's fault." When the teachers select their own courses, they tend to make the course successful.

After the courses are divided among the staff, they can decide their teaching load to meet the requests of the students. And they can enforce that load among themselves so that some teacher with misplaced sympathy will not assume such an overload that students indeed are not helped, but rather hindered in learning.

Staff, by student request, can create new courses at any time as long as each new course is critiqued and approved by department members. Staff also might direct students to create some courses, for credit, that can be used by other students.

Staff members badly need to laugh together at times. They plan several parties each year, spouses invited, to enjoy each other socially. These events include everyone on the payroll—custodians, food service personnel, paraeducators, teachers, administrators.

The strength of the system really depends on how well each teacher has internalized the concept and how consistent each teacher is in implementing all phases of it. The major orientation and inservice is in the fall of the year at the pre-opening workshop. But each month at a faculty meeting some aspect of the system can be explored.

Once a month for faculty meetings school will dismiss 45 minutes early. It is always on that day of the week when the school has time reserved for assemblies and no appointments take place. In lieu of an assembly or other meeting, school dismisses and the faculty meeting takes place during regular school time so that coaches as well as other teachers can attend. Speakers may be brought in or departments may meet or report on previous meetings. The more staff shares with each other, the more they stimulate ideas and workable methods for each other.

Students

If it takes a year or two of lead time for staff to get ready for a new design in a school's operation, it takes students a week or two. For many of them, it takes only a day or two, depending on how well the total staff has internalized the concept.

Students are collaborators in the educational process. When they learn by appointment, they share the teaching role, as has been pointed out. The work, by the very nature of the course content, helps them pace themselves at a rather steady rate, some faster, some slower.

The thing educators often fail to recognize is that when students can learn at their own rate, there is a rate. No student should be permitted to do nothing over a protracted length of time. Schools exist to educate, not to help students become cauliflowers. But the rate should accommodate the learner. We don't expect a row boat to tow water skiers, and it's a waste of time to trout fish in a speed boat.

Most students will tend to establish a pattern for themselves. But it is their pattern, not a schedule imposed on them. Though they can move freely, they tend to find a place and stay there for an hour or so. In fact, there is surprisingly little traffic in the hallways at most times.

Because students are actively involved in learning, sharing ideas with each other, talking about what they are studying, keeping appointments, comparing their work, the hallways are remarkably quiet. It is almost as if the students don't have to talk there and it is a chance not to have to speak.

Those students who need periods of quiet in which to read or solve a knotty problem have the library and also the cafeteria. The cafeteria is a total silence area, except during lunch time, where students are guaranteed quiet. The room is monitored to keep the peace by a paraeducator.

Though high school is basically a four year learning process, more than half the students complete the diploma requirements in three to three and a half years. They may finish school when their work is over, diploma in hand, and go on to a university or into a job. Those who plan to go on to college generally work things out to coincide with the college semester entrances. Those who go on to work generally have a job lined up and a starting date established. The students are masterful at implementing Parkinson's law: Work expands or decreases to fill the time available.

Of those students who complete diploma requirements in less than four years, about half of them stay on and take more courses. It is impossible to exhaust the curriculum offerings.

One of the major reasons why the students handle this unscheduled routine so well is because the first week of school is devoted annually to orientation in general and by course offerings in particular. It is then when students form their learning groups, select their teachers, get the initial objectives and directions for each course. That is the week when teachers do most of the talking. The rest of the weeks, the teachers do most of the listening.

It may seem irresponsible to the conventional minded educator to "waste" a week of school in orientation. It is not wasted; it is grist for the mill. Once the students are organized, they make up for lost time.

About two to five per cent of the students require more than four years to get a diploma. There is no problem with this and the students invo'ved do not seem to mind. It is better than the alternative, which is forced summer school for two or three years for students who already find learning difficult and need a vacation from it. What is the difference in terms of time if they take four and a half t. five years in succession or the same amount of time by absorbing summer breaks. No one has ever taken more than five years to graduate.

Sometimes older students enroll in the school, persons who dropped out of a high school around sophomore year, worked five years or so, and discovered that a high school diploma would enhance their opportunities for advancement. They can work in a few courses around their job schedule, and get a diploma.

Sometimes parents, particularly mothers who are unemployed out of their homes, decide to take some courses. They can do this and arrange the time most suitable for them. The courses that attract such women are art, home economics, and business. They work in the rooms along with the students and everyone accepts everyone. The students tend to encourage the adult learners and take an interest in their projects.

Parents

Educators so often forget, like other professionals, that while they are creating plans, preparing to implement them, they dress the ideas in a jargon incomprehensible to the lay person.

It is vitally important that parents understand what is happening, why there is a change, what the expected results are, how they will be informed and kept updated, and what they can do to help. As this decade, indeed this century, winds down, it is more difficult to get parent committees together, enthusiastic and wide attendance at meetings, and commitment of family time to school projects. But the staff must make the effort anyway. If something occurs that is offensive to the parents, usually due to their lack of understanding of purpose, they will band together and find time to put the school back in its place.

Education by appointment is a new experience for parents. When the staff is committed to the concept, early in the planning stages, parent meetings must occur to explain what, why, how, and when. There should be ample time for questions, patience in answering, and a climate of collaboration.

An ideal, practical format in the education of parents to educational evolution is difficult to come by, but the following has met with varying degrees of success, depending on the time of the year and the topic of the meeting.

Once a month, except during the summer holiday, the school schedules its Parent Night. It's the same night of the same week each month so that the routine is easy for the parents to calendar. It is never on Monday because of competition with televised sports events, and never on Friday so that it does not interfere with family weekend plans.

The night begins at 6:30 when the entire staff reports to their usual learning-teaching area in the school. They will be there until 7:30 so that any parent who wishes to speak to any teacher can do so. These are the "official" conference times. If many parents arrive on a given evening, some may have to make other appointments at other times, but this seldom happens because parents want to see different teachers and all can usually be accommodated in an hour.

At 7:30 the teachers may leave, though they often stay either because some of them are involved in the next event or they are interested or curious. The next hour is time to explain aspects of the program. Teachers may demonstrate its application with some students who have been asked to come and help. Charts of progress or test results will be explained. Outside speakers may be engaged on pertinent topics. Sessions in parenting will be offered.

The primary purpose, of course, is to update parents. The education they had was not like the education their children are receiving, and the parent frame of reference creates problems in understanding. It is as if everyone is an expert in education because everyone has had some. The school has to help the parents broaden their frame of reference.

From 8:30 to 9:00 there is open forum time, unless the format of the evening has been small discussion groups and forum time already. During that time questions get answered and, hopefully, fears are allayed. The effort is made not to keep anything about the school's operation a secret.

This session is followed by refreshments prepared by different parent committees.

Out of Parent Night come the working committees that involve shared decision-making, staff and parents. Ideas for courses arise, materials are examined, parent talent is tapped to work with groups of students in particular disciplines.

In the late 60's, however, it was much easier to get great parental involvement than it is now. Some come for a conference and leave. But the school makes the effort and that in itself is welcomed by the parents even if they cannot participate each month.

SYSTEM IN ACTION

As with most schools, the bus schedule determines the length of the school day.

About 30 minutes before the last bus arrives, all the teachers report to take care of last minute details before their clients come. A few minutes after the last bus, a bell rings to mark the official beginning of the work day. All students report to the rooms of their teacher-advisors. The first business is to take attendance and send the names of the absentees to the office.

Immediately, announcements are made over the P.A. These are details that may affect the day of the students. Example: "Mrs. Miller will not be here today. Those students who have appointments with her should see her tomorrow morning to arrange new times." In this system, there is never a need for a substitute teacher because the students always have other things to do.

Another example: "This morning at 11:00 o'clock a representative from the University of Nebraska will be here to talk to interested students about the university's admissions policies and costs. Those who wish to hear the representative, go to room 120. It will take 45 minutes. Students who have appointments scheduled at that time should see their teachers in advance to reschedule their time." In this system, classes are not interrupted for this kind of event, because there are no conventional classes. For the same reason, students can never cut classes.

For the next 10 or 15 minutes, the advisors check on the progress of their students, help some to plan their day, encourage them, and, in general, serve their needs. At the end of this session, a bell will ring to mark the beginning of the learning activities. That is the last bell until the end of the day. There are wall clocks in the rooms, most of the students wear watches, and everyone can tell time. They learned that skill years ago.

We will look first at a typical teacher's day, and then at a student's day. Call the teacher Bob. He teaches in the English department.

Each classroom is devoted to a subject area. Bob's room has English course resources in it. He has some bean bags, desks, and tables in it. Because there are not as many classrooms as there are teachers, some rooms have two teachers of the same subject area in them. They share space, things, students. Because some teachers work in two subject areas, like English and French, they make a distinct separation of roles for their students: English only in the morning; French only in the afternoon.

After Bob's advisees leave to go about their business, Bob checks his appointment sheet for the day. He begins with a 40 minute appointment with six students at 8:30. Meanwhile about 30 other students come into his room to study. They sort themselves out to read in bean bags or work together in groups of three to six.

When Bob's appointment group arrives, they sit around a table and make room for Bob. There are Hello's and How are you doing? The students get their notes out and Bob gets his note paper and pen. The students discuss for 25 minutes and Bob does not interrupt them.

After 25 minutes Bob calls time and critiques the group's learning. He re-enforces the good, corrects the wrong (including "Joe, don't use a double negative. If your idea is valuable, then you must value correct expression, too.") and he directs them to further resources and learning. Bob might also say, "Sally, you hardly contributed during this session. Now at the next appointment, you carry the first five minutes and the rest of you get her ready to do that. I'll make a note of it here among my comments about this appointment."

There may be an exchange of questions and answers, a call for clarification, and at the end they will agree on the time of their next appointment, in about a week. It is now 9:10.

Bob checks his appointment sheet and sees that he has no appointment for 20 minutes. He moves about the room to see if anyone needs his help. If no one needs him, he will sit down and read or create some objectives for a course or correct some papers.

At 9:30 a group of three comes in for a 20 minute appointment. Bob listens for 15 minutes and critiques for five. During all of this time students have been coming in to study or leaving to go someplace else to study. This process continues until 12:30 when Bob goes to lunch.

After lunch Bob had planned to meet with two other English teachers in his room to talk about common problems they have with a new course they are all teaching. They meet in part of the room while students meet in the rest of the room.

The rest of the day is filled with appointments, helping individual students, reading, writing, or correcting papers. At 3:10 a bell rings and all advisees return to the advisor rooms for attendance check, announcements about after-school activities, and dismissal to catch buses at 3:15.

It should be stressed that an English room becomes an English lab just as science labs and art rooms have always been special places. When students want to study English, they go to any English lab; when they study social studies or math they go to any social studies or math lab. It is in those labs that the resources, materials and people, are available.

Students, however, get comfortable eventually with certain places and settle down to a pattern of a few rooms. There will be an age mix, a variety of courses being learned in each room, but always within the same discipline.

Let's follow a student named Peg. During teacher advisor time she states that her day will involve three major topics. At 8:30 she will go to a math lab and complete a course she is working on. She figures it will take her an hour and a half. She knows from experience that after that she will want to go to a room with a bean bag, maybe Bob's, and sit down for awhile and stare into the middle distance.

At 10:00 she will meet four other students in a social studies lab and go over the course they are in together called Native Americans. They will firm up an appointment they have at 11:00 with a social studies teacher.

At 11:40 the appointment is over and Peg goes to lunch which is served between 11:30 and 1:00. At 12:15 Peg goes back to the math lab to check her notes. She wants to go to the testing room at 1:30 to take her final test in the course she completed that morning. At 2:15, with 45 minutes left, she goes off to keep a group English appointment with Bob. There are a few minutes after that before the final bell rings, too little time to do much of anything, so she chats with some friends before she must report to her teacher advisor for attendance check, last minute announcements, and dismissal.

Peg actually was involved in only three of the six courses she is carrying: math, social studies, and English. This is typical. Tomorrow she can do science, art, and P.E.

The students tend to spend longer periods of time at one time on a course than the conventional schedule allows. In this way, they accomplish more because they don't have to stop and start every 40 minutes and shift mental gears six times a day. In other words, they work in a much more adult fashion.

The classrooms are not closed to the students, even when a teacher takes a 15 minute coffee break, goes to the washroom, or goes to the library to do some work. The only exception is the science labs or similar areas (shop, art) where there is material or equipment that could harm a student. Then, either another teacher has to come in or the room will be very temporarily locked. All the non-accident prone rooms are like honor study halls in the more conventional system whenever a teacher leaves.

The system is complex in initial organization, demanding in teacher consistency; but it is transparently simple in operation.

It would be ideal if learning areas could all be enlarged from the typical classroom size, but it isn't essential. Where a few walls can be removed in the structure, they should be to allow space for two or three teachers in an area. If there is carpet, so much the better, especially in areas with heavy reading requirements so that students can sit on the floor if they wish to.

There is a required accommodation to sound. The rooms are not silent. But there is a difference between sound and noise. Noise is sound out of place.

Students are used to sound while they study. Parents often call that sound noise—loud stereos in their children's bedrooms. But students in this system of learning, when asked if the sound level bothers them in a room, look perplexed and ask, "What sound?"

PROSPECT

There are schools around the country that have adapted this system, from The Bronx to Long Beach, from San Antonio to Estacada, Oregon. Canadians, too, have implemented it, particularly in the Toronto and Vancouver areas.

What is its future? Fragile.

There are so many forces that interfere with this kind of change. A new principal who has not thoroughly internalized the concept can kill the program rather quickly. So can a new principal with a weak personal self-concept who will be threatened by ideas of teachers.

Sizeable turnover in staff without sufficient preparation or inservice can do the system damage.

Current and forseeable tension over high school declining enrollment with subsequent RIF policies can make teachers more receptive to the *status quo* than to change.

Teacher training colleges for the most part have not and are not preparing teachers for this kind, or any kind, of innovation. Even worse is the college curriculum for administrator candidates. Courses are designed to explain recent educational legislation, school financing, general school law—courses that will help the new administrator be a good manager. But where are the courses to help the would-be superintendent or principal understand how to help staff be creative and implement new methods.

As a result, schools using the system described here must be self reenforcing, self encouraging, self critical. An external support system does not exist.

That the system works is proved. That it is good for students and staff is proved. Both learn and both are happy in the process. Students who have gone on to college over the years have attested to the system with words like: "I didn't have any adjustment problem. I knew how to use my time." "If anything, I was over-prepared because I had to wait for the professor to explain how to do things I already knew how to do."

Personnel directors in various businesses have commented about graduates of the system: "They know how to keep themselves busy and don't wait to be told what to do." That in itself is a highly marketable skill.

All change takes place after three qualities are present; organized change, that is, not chaotic change. The required qualities are dissatisfaction, creativity, and intestinal fortitude, which is a nice way of saying guts. When these qualities are present, this system can flourish. If any one of the qualities is absent, the *status quo* will endure.

But this system is good for students. Educators ought to find a way to do it.

REFERENCES

Coleman, James S., et al. *Equality of educational opportunity*. Washington, D.C.: U.S. Government Printing Office, 1966.

Fantini, Mario. *Making urban schools work*. New York: Holt, Rinehart & Winston, 1968.

Glasser, William. *Schools without failure.* New York: Harper and Row, 1969.

Glines, Don E. *Creating humane schools.* Mankato, Minnesota: Campus Publishers, Expanded Supplementary Edition, 1973.

Harvey, O. J., et al. *Conceptual systems and personality organization.* New York: John Wiley and Sons, 1961.

Holt, John. *How children fail.* New York: Pitman, 1964.

Holt, John. *How children learn.* New York: Pitman, 1967.

Holt, John. *Summerhill: for and against.* New York: Harold Hart Publishers, 1970.

Holt, John. *The underachieving school.* New York: Pitman, 1969.

Holt, John. *What do I do Monday?* New York: E. P. Dutton Co., 1970.

Hunt, David E. *Assessment of conceptual level: paragraph completion method (PCM).* Unpublished paper, Ontario Institute for Studies in Education, 1973.

Mager, Robert. *Analyzing performance problems or "you really oughta wanna."* Belmont, California: Fearon Publishers, 1972.

Mager, Robert. *Goal analysis.* Belmont, California: Fearon Publishers, 1972.

Maslow, Abraham H. *Motivation and personality.* New York: Harper & Row, 1954.

Piaget, Jean. *Structuralism.* New York: Basic, 1970.

Rogers, Donald L. *Determination of effect on students of different interpersonal orientation in BSCS biology classes having similar classroom climate.* Unpublished doctoral dissertation, University of Nebraska, 1970.

Roth, Virginia. *A model for an alternate high school* (monograph). Wyandotte, Michigan: Downriver Learning Disabilities Center, 1973.

Silberman, Charles. *Crisis in the classroom.* New York: Random House, 1970.

Townsend, Robert. *Up the organization.* New York: Knopf Co., 1970.

Trump, J. Lloyd. *Flexible scheduling: fad or fundamental.* Mimeographed. Washington, D.C.: NASSP, NEA, 1963.

Trump, J. Lloyd. *Focus on change.* Chicago: Rand McNally, 1961.

Trump, J. Lloyd. *Problems faced in organizing schools differently.* Mimeographed. Washington, D.C.: NASSP, NEA, 1966.

CHAPTER 10

Education

in and for

the Future

HAROLD G. SHANE

"All education springs from some image of the future." Alvin Toffler[1]

INTRODUCTION

This chapter departs from the format of the earlier chapters, because while other chapters have dealt with the past and with the present, this one focuses on the significance of the future for education.[2] The pages which follow are concerned with what schools can become and with tomorrow's possible worlds in which children and youth, hopefully, will be prepared, intellectually and psychologically, for life in a new millennium different from any that prophets might have predicted.

Futures Studies Defined

In THE EDUCATIONAL SIGNIFICANCE OF THE FUTURE (Shane, 1973), *futures studies* is defined as "a new discipline concerned with sharpening the data and improving the processes on the basis of which policy decisions are made in the various fields of human endeavor, such as business, government or education."[3] In particular, the purpose of futures research is to help policy makers clarify their goals and values and choose wisely from among the alternative courses of action available to them. While wise and prudent education leaders long have gathered data to improve their decision making, futures studies is a more specific process —one that is much more methodical in its conception and operations— than was true of procedures used prior to systems approaches devised after 1940.

Edward Cornish (1974) uses a somewhat different approach when he defines the term *futuristics* as "A field of activity that seeks to identify, analyze, and evaluate possible future changes in human life and the world. The word implies a rational rather than mystical approach to the future, but also accepts artistic, imaginative and experiential approaches as offering contributions that can be useful and valid."[4]

As far as teachers and other educators are concerned, futures studies can be described as a methodical process of sensitizing educational leaders to possible alternative futures and their consequences, in order to reach policy decisions regarding development of curriculum, improving educational administration, and various other factors involved in schooling.

Futures research differs from conventional educational research and planning in several ways. *First,* it concentrates on a broader range of alternative courses of action than traditional educational research has done. *Second,* futures research tends to emphasize multiple, alternative avenues along which one may move, rather than strictly linear projections or linear types of research. A *third* characteristic is that futures research relies more heavily on rational analysis of possible future developments and their consequences, and places less emphasis on statistical analysis or projections. *Finally,* traditional planning tends to be Utopian—in the sense it sees tomorrow's schools as evolved from today's schools, but with their problems removed. In contrast, futures concepts of education tend to seek both improved and different models for the decades ahead.

That is to say, educational futurism seeks not merely to reform the past but to create new and better environments. In this sense, it is in the liberal tradition associated with such educational figures as John Dewey, William H. Kilpatrick, Harold Rugg, and Theodore Brameld.

THE IMPORTANCE OF FUTURES STUDIES FOR EDUCATION

There are many reasons why the future is a matter of great importance for education. As responsible members of the human community, we are concerned that the youth of tomorrow have an effective world in which to live. Also, a careful study of values for the future may help to improve the present psychological climate in public education, which has been sometimes dreary and occasionally dangerous. Many fundamental social problems—problems of a society in transition—can be attacked through education once we have rediscovered our sense of purpose and examined alternatives before us.

It also is important to recognize that, potentially, education is an important way of *creating* the future. Schools and various other educational media serve as laboratories in which to test ways of meeting the needs of a changing society. School is a place for giving substance to those values which will insure a better future. While schools at present do not so much create the culture as reflect it, they nevertheless can play an important part in shaping the various social decisions which educated humans will make in coming decades.

TOOLS FOR EXPLORING THE FUTURE

Both the present and the past are important resources for viewing or anticipating what the future will be like. Since knowledge can only come from the past, we must utilize the history of the race for purposes of discerning—as far as we are able—the nature of alternative probable futures which will, in time, become history. A number of tools have been devised by students of the future to help us do this.

Linear Projection

One of the most common tools is the so-called linear projection. A well-established means of extrapolating trends, the linear projection is used when we assume that the future will, in many ways, resemble the past.

Dialectical Extrapolation

A variation on the linear projection is dialectical extrapolation. This is an "if-then" statement that allows us to move from given data to certain reasoned judgments. For example, *if* between 4,000 and 5,000 persons become 65 years of age each day, and *if* this constitutes an increase in our population of senior citizens from roughly twenty million to thirty million over the next decade or two, *then* we can expect certain outcomes to follow. To illustrate, it seems likely that there will be an increase in political conservatism. Certainly, health care will more explicitly emphasize gerontology. Furthermore, young couples may well be challenged by the question of *parent* care just as they are now concerned with problems of *child* care! A development already happening before our eyes is the increasing number of T.V. commercials which feature the needs of older people and which stress products consumed by the elderly.

The Concept of Alternative Futures

By the mid 1960's, futures research theory, while continuing to make limited use of linear projections, also shifted to exploring the concept of alternative futures. It began to be recognized that the concept of a single, inevitable future is less tenable than the idea that there may exist an infinite number of alternative futures. In short, human adaptability reflected in the choices made by individuals and groups regarding their use of resources, futurists began to see, actually creates or at least influences whatever future eventually materializes. Hence, rather than focusing on a passive acceptance of an inescapable projection, futures research is concerned with the multiplicity of possibilities and the element of human choice which may dynamically shape the future. As David Rockefeller commented to the writer in the mid-70's, "A Club-of-Rome type of report can't really probe the limits to growth because there is no way for their projections to allow for the adaptability of humans. The validity of projections depends on the [validity of the] data that were used in the first place."

Cross-Impact Analysis

Inevitably, the consideration of alternative futures in education and other fields led to the development of the "cross-impact" concept, which is used in both education and other fields. This involves examining not only the alternative futures that may unroll for education but also certain developments that are occurring in other disciplines such as physics and biochemistry as they have an impact on education. For example, if major breakthroughs are made in the use of holography, which is the projection of three-dimensional images through the use of laser beams, it may be possible to reproduce in the classroom nearly perfect images of various complicated objects which normally could not be physically brought into a room. Conceivably, holography might turn an entire classroom into a fantastic teaching aid, reproducing, for example, in the most faithful detail, the sounds and sights that one might see in contemporary center-city London. Patently, the development of such a formidable teaching aid— already in an advanced experimental stage—would have an enormous bearing upon educational methods for making education more realistic. If field trips must be curtailed in the future because of diminished energy reserves for transportation, for instance, holography could go a long way towards filling the gap, since many of the sights and sounds of distant places almost inevitably will be recreated in the classroom during coming decades.

Simulation Models

Various other simulated approaches to learning, such as models and games, are another means of studying the future. A variety of models of a highly complex nature are used, for example, in training airlines pilots and persons engaged in the space program. Computer assisted games and mathematical models are now commonly used, as are experiential exercises, such as the "experience compression" technique. The latter, sometimes used among business and educational leaders, is usually a one or two-week intensive workshop in which participants are given probabilistic developments to consider and must reach decisions regarding action to take within a few hours or days, thus simulating decision making that would normally be undertaken over a much longer interval.

SOME PROBLEMS OF FORECASTING AN UNKNOWN FUTURE

The Future as Terra Incognita

Any attempt to examine educational futures must be undertaken with a clear understanding that often prophecies and assumptions prove to be mistaken. History is full of forecasting blunders. Advisors to the King and Queen of Spain, for example, contended that it was impossible for Columbus to make his voyage. In the fourteenth century a high official in the British army derided the idea that bows and arrows would ever be replaced by gun powder. A century and half ago, a British railroad designer concluded that a speed of more than 10 or 15 miles an hour was a physical impossibility. Vannevar Bush commented to President Truman that a nuclear device would never go off just shortly before the "impossible" happened.

Such mistakes in judgment notwithstanding, persons contemplating education futures must attempt to forecast some of the ways that the world may be changing during the next several decades because their work and responsibilities require it. They must do so, however, taking care to distinguish between "predicting" and "forecasting." Prediction smacks of prophecy or fortune telling—processes not necessarily based on reasoned data. Forecasting, on the other hand, is concerned with developments that appear probable on the basis of reliable data at hand. It may not always be possible to foretell the exact form a development will take, but its occurrence may be forecast with some confidence. This is especially true when one considers the power of human agencies to set goals and direct actions toward achieving desired outcomes. Likewise, the self-fulfilling prophecy is a force to be considered in the forecasting of future developments.

Some Elements Influencing Educational Forecasts

While the exact details of the future cannot be known, many broad strokes on the canvas of the future can already be discerned. For example, scholars and laymen alike agree that we are presently moving through an enormous contemporary system break in which the old ways that have governed our lives are irreversibly changing. We are engaged in change processes of far greater world scope and consequence than the gradual decline and fall of the Roman Empire's hegemony over the peoples of antiquity.

There are a number of signs which indicate the magnitude and speed with which changes occur around us. These signs include a variety of pressures for a better economic deal from third world countries; the growth of environmentalism; widespread disenchantment with material things; discontent with sleazy products and misleading ads; and uneasiness about institutions—governmental, business, military and labor, not to mention religious and educational institutions—and the breakdown of old guidelines which once were the basis for codes of conduct in U.S. culture.

The various liberation movements striving to improve the lot of the old, the young, women, children and various minorities as well as rampant job alienation and workers' demands for greater participation in the governance of companies—these are but a few signs of the tensions generated by rapidly changing times.

In this period of transition, what are some of the developments which it seems likely we can anticipate?

SOME CHARACTERISTICS OF PROBABLE FUTURES WITH A BEARING ON SCHOOLING

Events in the world around us give evidence that tremendous changes will occur both socially and technologically. Looking at the smallest social unit, the family, there are signs that alternative family structures will continue to spring up. Although the basic human need for a primary affinity group or family remains, the number of new forms, whether created by choice or by necessity, can be expected to continue to expand.

On another level, the larger social communities, cities, nations and supra-national groupings will contend with continued population growth, lingering poverty and hunger, and the challenge of living humanely in the ever-spreading megalopolis. Societies will be forced ever more vigorously to face the need to control waste and to limit irresponsible and needless consumption of resources. These conditions promise to lead to the development of more and more remedial legislation and to the growth of bureaucracy in the years ahead. The result promises to be a more disciplined way of life for all. Efforts to improve the human condition are trending toward a variety of welfare programs, minimum income guarantees, and the like, which imply a greater degree of regimentation than we have as yet been required to have in our efforts to insure equity and to reduce welfare cheating.

The continuing economic discomfort caused by inflation and unemployment may lead—and probably *will* lead to more thoughtful conclusions than humans have made in the past about the limits of growth and the limits of abundance, especially in the U.S. It is possible, too, that in the future our emphasis on the GNP (Gross National Product) will be reduced, although not replaced by an emphasis on the GNW (Gross National Welfare)—a term coined by economist Walter W. Heller."GNW" refers to the ways in coming decades that we may measure the success of our society not by how many *goods* we produce but by the kinds of *services* that are provided and by the kinds of equitable conditions that prevail. The "conditions" to which the writer refers are such things as how many people participate periodically in continuing lifelong education programs; what provisions are made for the care of the "frail old" and the very young; the quality of human relationships in our society; and how wisely we are conserving our environment and recycling or carefully investing global natural resources.

All of these questions imply a drastic shift in emphasis from the present production-oriented view of our economy to a view that emphasizes quality of life with consequent implications for schooling. Educators will have to take into account the high cost of accomplishing all of these things. Educators themselves are going to have to help to pay the bill! Many persons in the field of education at present consider $15,000 to $16,000 a year a moderate income for the experienced teacher. If, in the late 70's, one earned $15,898, or more, they were in the group paying 72% of all federal income taxes. At the same time, persons in the bottom 10% income bracket paid .01% of the taxes.

How is this relevant to education? It is simply a fact of life that the price of education is constantly rising as inflation continues and as the scope of the responsibilities assigned to educational agencies increases. For example, under recently enacted legislation several long-delayed programs have been begun to provide for the welfare of handicapped Americans. In general, educators have long supported such efforts. However, very few of us realize that in the 1970 census, forty million Americans were listed as handicapped, and if one were to include drug addicts, alcoholics and persons temporarily injured in ski accidents, automobile collisions, or the like, at any given time there are perhaps as many as seventy million persons who fall into the category of the handicapped, *eight million of whom are children!* The cost of educational provisions for just the school-age children alone is astronomical.

Our ability to cope with domestic economic problems likewise will be influenced by the rapidly increasing interdependence among nations. As nations become more and more aware of their mutual need for one another's goods and services, hopefully they will be adopting a mode of behavior which may be described as one of "dynamic reciprocity."

Our global interdependence will be accompanied by ever greater complexity of life; by increased tension as the countries of the world seek greater stability. The impact of technology will continue to accelerate, too, and we can expect that life also will be made increasingly complex as technological breakthroughs such as cloning, extrauterine pregnancies, and improved communication satellites constantly occur.

THE RECENT "HISTORY OF THE FUTURE" BECOMING THE PRESENT

Various planning techniques pioneered during World War II laid the foundation for contemporary futurism and have had a bearing upon the study of the future in education. Presently, a wide variety of agencies, industrial, military and governmental, are making use of futures research. Among these are companies such as the RAND Corporation and the Education Group of the Singer Company; non-profit organizations such as the Futures Group and the Institute for the Future respectively located in Middletown, Connecticut, and Menlo Park, California; as well as a variety of public and private commissions, survey groups and academic projects.

The NEA Study of Educational Change

One of the most important recent efforts in education future studies began in 1975 when a twenty-two member pre-planning committee of the National Education Association, along with four NEA staff members began the task of reassessing and reformulating the seven cardinal principles of education. By 1977 nearly 50 competent teachers and many well known figures had served as interviewees in the study.[5]

These seven principles had been first published in a 1918 report of the Commission on the Reorganization of Secondary Education, sponsored by NEA. The decision of NEA to study, revise and reissue these principles in 1976 is eloquent testimony to their essential adaptability as reflected in their longevity. While the 1976 study often expanded the scope of the principles, it emphatically reaffirmed their validity as a statement of objectives or goals for U.S. education. As originally stated, the seven cardinal principles identified seven objectives as necessary in the education of every American girl or boy: These seven were: (1) health, (2) command of fundamental processes, (3) worthy home membership, (4) vocation, (5) civic education, (6) worthy use of leisure, and (7) ethical character.

Nearly 60 years later, the NEA study of the seven cardinal principles found them not only still valid in the 1970's, but also worthy of the kind of expansion that would seem needed for their continued application in the future. However, many of the meanings originally associated with the cardinal principles, according to the panelists, were considerably too narrow for learning and living in an interdependent human community. The committee also noted that the seven cardinal principles as originally interpreted seemed to place a much heavier burden on the school than that institution could reasonably be expected to bear, while the roles of church, community, and family were not emphasized sufficiently. The principles also did not acknowledge the increasing need for lifelong adult education, for "learning how to learn," which has since come to be recognized. Because of these and other considerations, the seven cardinal principles need to be redefined and reinterpreted.

The Seven Cardinal Principles Reinterpreted for 21st Century Education

The reinterpretation of these principles has taken place in two steps: First, in 1927, the National Congress of Parents and Teachers incorporated the seven cardinal principles into their permanent platform, while commenting and expanding on many of their original meanings. Secondly, in 1976, the National Education Association panelists again reinterpreted the principles, making them much more sophisticated and showing their applications to current problems.[6] The high points of their commentary on each principle may be summarized as follows:

1. *Health.* By 1927, health had been expanded from the original meaning of health instruction and the promotion of good health habits and physical activities. Added were mental and emotional fitness and safety habits. The role of the home was mentioned along with that of the community in being responsible for such things as sanitation, control of disease, pure air, and the provision of playgrounds and parks. Teachers were told to teach children health habits and to arrange for physical examinations for them.

In 1976, the National Education Association panelists directed attention to the need for mental health in interpersonal and intercultural relations. They went on to point out the responsibility of schools and other educational agencies for raising the consciousness of students with regard to the unhealthy aspects of U.S. lifestyles. They also stressed that children and youth need to be made aware that overconsumption can be as damaging as under-consumption and that both can have an adverse effect on one's behavior. "Health education" was also seen to include creating an awareness of environmental dangers such as air pollution. The panelists recognized stress as an important source of modern health problems, and they encouraged attention to nutritional and dietary education. Health education was now considered to include topics such as drug education and—at appropriate age levels—an insight into healthful family living, including such topics as sexuality, marriage, divorce, and understanding human needs for love and acceptance.

Panelists also pointed out the special challenge of world-wide health issues, in a world in which a few privileged people have access to heart transplants while the masses in the rest of the world may live an entire lifetime without ever even seeing a doctor. A cross-cultural consciousness was also evident in the recommendation that the lot of women in developing countries must be appreciably improved before significant improvements will be made in world health problems.

One can conclude from the NEA panelists' recommendations that the major goal of health education is the total mental, physical, and emotional health of the person. But this individual goal is seen in relationship to environmental problems and to conditions in other countries on an interdependent planet.

2. *Command of Fundamental Processes.* In keeping with the concern of the early 70's that education go back to the basics, the NEA panel confirmed the fact that mastery of the three R's remains an imperative for living in our times. However, there are additional skills that should be included among the fundamental process of education. Among these are skills in humanistic processes such as the knowledge of human relations, group processes and skills based on cross-cultural and multi-ethnic insights. Also, young people seem to need education that will help them to live with a great deal of uncertainty, change, and complexity. In addition, they need to develop the ability to anticipate what is likely to happen. Typical "anticipatory skills" would include the ability to see relationships and to make correlations; plus the skills of *sorting, weighing,* and then *acting* on data; the ability to evaluate choices and make wise decisions; and finally, understanding *the functions of power* at all levels of society ranging from the home and neighborhood, to national and international levels.

Other "basic" skills for living in the complex future include learning how to adapt to new structures in society, since the young people of today will encounter countless new situations both domestically and internationally throughout their lives. To acquire these kinds of basics, as noted above, one must learn how to learn. That is, young people need to learn how to make life-long use of the various in-school and out-of-school resources that are becoming increasingly available. They also need to have an understanding of computer languages. Continuing learning requires the improved ability to cope with increasing specialization through a command of cross-disciplinary understandings.

3. *Worthy Home Membership.* It was clear to the NEA panelists when they considered worthy home membership, first, that the nature of the family is changing constantly; secondly, that the family remains an element of great importance—one that is greatly needed in our culture. Lastly, it was noted that the schools are obliged to adapt themselves to emerging home and family changes and in the process must rethink the meaning of the

term "worthy."

Some of the factors which have brought about sweeping changes in home life number among them the new opportunities and roles which are developing for women, the impact of television, the decrease of the home's influence on the individual as other influences increase, and the proliferation of a number of different kinds of "affinity groups" that gather people together in a home relationship often quite different from the traditional family unit. Interpreting this principle of education, all panelists agreed that whatever the living arrangement and however experimental and novel it might be, some form of family membership— some form of associated living in a warm human ecosystem—is still very important to an individual.

In view of the many problems besieging family life in our times, recommendations for the future include the following: *First,* schools must take into account that very often less education is going on at home than in prior decades and therefore the school must endeavor to make up for some of these deficiencies. *Second,* in many countries, including the United States to some extent, it is necessary for the status of women to be improved further if family life is to flourish. *Third,* as far as possible, it seems appropriate for schools to make a carefully planned effort to help society appreciate the values of family living. *Fourth,* parents, because they are so often outside the home, should be encouraged by teachers to use the time they have with their children as high quality time, and plan activities to maximize the development of their relationships with their children during these contacts. And finally, in school, children might be given experiences that help them to appreciate what good home living involves and to understand the nature of family responsibilities and duties as well as privileges and opportunities.

4. *Vocation.* The value of vocational education remains unquestioned but in reinterpreting this principle, there was considerable disagreement among NEA panelists. Some members felt that specific vocational training or preparation for the future should be carried on in the secondary and post-secondary schools. Others took the stance that a general education is the best preparation for vocational success or they argued that perhaps most vocational preparation should occur outside the school. The original interpretation of the word, *vocation,* nevertheless, seems to hold up, for it includes equipping the student to earn a living, to serve society through his work, to maintain right relationships toward fellow workers and society, and, as far as possible, to find personal satisfaction and development through work.

In view of the fact that society is changing so rapidly, no one really knows what vocations are going to be required 10 or 15 years from now. However, certain general applications of this cardinal goal can be enumerated. *First,* students need to be taught the habit of lifelong learning as an actual vocational skill; *secondly,* competence in problem-solving seems to have become a basic requisite for vocational efficiency. *Third,* a good general education should be acquired by our youth before the teaching of specific skills is undertaken regardless of whether this occurs within or without the school. School itself should focus on general requirements for all vocations and on preparing the person for periodical retraining for specific jobs. Vocational education, furthermore, should help future policy makers and workers in all fields to become aware of the necessity for combating pollution and for maintaining an awareness of ecological problems that might be involved in various jobs and professions.

A future-focused vocational education should reflect awareness of special problems such as the unemployment rate among unskilled workers and the "overprepared" college graduate. As much as possible, at all levels of skill and vocational expertise, the schools need to help students cultivate the power of reason, increase personal-occupational knowledge, and to facilitate the satisfactions of self realization, without which work has little meaning.

The need for vocational training was recognized by the NEA study as especially severe in developing nations where less and less work is available to untrained and often rapidly growing populations. One more important point is that vocational education ought more fully to recognize the individual's need for economic independence and a feeling of self respect, both of which derive from an opportunity to exercise one's abilities and to strive for some form of excellence.

5. *Civic Education.* In the original 1918 statement, and again in the 1976-77 revision, civic education was recognized as a vastly important part of the educational process. The ideal of "civic righteousness" was considered to be just as valid now as ever it had been. To achieve the ideal, however, citizens must acquire a greater familiarity with their social agencies and institutions. They must know the *means* and *methods* that will promote the attainment of worthy social ends, and develop skills in implementing changes. Habits of cordial cooperation and willingness to be responsible through personal participation in social undertakings were included among the essentials of good citizenship.

Citizenship was considered the primary goal of instruction in geography, history, civics, and economics at the secondary school level. In our times, judging from the panelists' comments, it would seem impossible to over-estimate the importance of understanding what it means to live in a world—one endangered by sophisticated weapons—in which multi-ethnic and polycultural perceptions promise increasingly to determine the course of world events for the foreseeable future. Learners presumably must understand how persons in different cultures feel and learn to empathize and identify with them. An understanding of functions of power and a dedication to human equity are increasingly vital. A major challenge we face here in the United States is the creation of a nation in which minorities are not forced to seek Balkanized power in order to achieve greater equity. The best solution to the growth of self-interest groups apparently is to be found in recognizing that genuine equals have no power over equals nor any need to lobby for or exercise it. Obviously much remains to be done in American society to move toward breaking down barriers inherited from U.S. history in which the disadvantaged, including minorities, have long struggled for their rights.

The key element in civic-mindedness of the future will be world-mindedness, or so the ideas of panelists suggest. Recurring phrases such as "loyalty to the planet as well as to the nation," "the need for a world view," and "membership in a larger society" all indicate that the 1977 report agreed on this point. Some NEA panelists emphasized that civic education should make clear the need to narrow the gap between the industrially developed nations and those less developed. They also pointed out that a liberal education should give as much heed to national and international problems as to foreign language, and that instruction should point out both the difficulties and the challenges that exist in both laissez faire and planned societies.

Although the ideal of democracy must be presented according to the NEA report, it is also necessary to encourage a respect for the achievements, possibilities and limitations of other nations. "The study of dissimilar contributions in the light of the ideal of human brotherhood should help to establish a genuine internationalism free from sentimentality, founded on fact, and actually operative in the affairs of nations."[7] Special attention must be paid to the need for the United States to improve its moral posture and leadership in the world by improving the ethics of its own politicians. Efforts must also be made to keep special interest groups from putting pressure on government leaders in order to obtain special favors of preferential treatment at the cost of minority groups.

The panel went on to state that particular heed must be paid to the possibility of nuclear war and to the increasing interdependence of all nations as they meet on their international frontiers and need to recognize the danger to all of aggression. Process skills—the ability to work well with others, compromise, cooperation, cooperative decision making, and the management of conflicts—are all critical needs of future world citizens. By providing these transferable skills, education can contribute to the needs of the future in this area.

Finally, one of the chief means by which schools can encourage civic education is for the schools themselves to function in a more democratic way and to provide an environment in which teachers and students can interact with each other as equals even though their roles differ. One of the ways in which this might be carried out is to replace the traditional *student* council with a *school* council to which both *pupils and teachers* are elected. Such a body should have merited prestige, responsibility, power to legislate, all within reasonable, prescribed limits, for the general welfare of the human community within the school. Whether it deals with issues such as running in the halls in an elementary school or allowing the use of alcohol in a college campus dormitory, such a school council could deal with real problems particularly those with ethical implications. Students thus would gain experience in grappling with moral issues appropriate to their ages and maturity.

6. *The Worthy Use of Leisure.* In the original 60-year-old statement of this goal, one senses that leisure was thought of as a break from intense physical labor and often was something pursued either on a religious holiday or other brief holidays, rather than at intervals spread throughout the work week and work year. Leisure, in fine, was understood in 1918 as a means of renewal in order to allow workers to return to tasks refreshed.

In reinterpreting this principle for life in a new century where today's youth will spend most of their lives, several changes must be taken into account. First, the dividing line between leisure and work is becoming less and less clear. This is occurring partly because people today have more time for relaxation, and partly because more are involved in work that is energy intensive rather than physically labor intensive, and this kind of work leaves people less physically fatigued. What is more, the traditional dichotomy between work and leisure will probably continue to blur even further as men and women freely engage in types of work and leisure activities which were formerly more rigidly restricted by sex roles.

The purposes of leisure time in a transitional society are still basically recreation and self-fulfillment, but many new factors are shaping the uses of leisure in our day. Because of economic pressures many people are obliged to expend great portions of their leisure time on a second job or in working overtime. In addition, many of our youth are, or plan to be, two-career couples, a phenomenon which by 1980 will account for about two-thirds of all consumer demand.[8] Schools and other educating agencies must rise to the challenge of helping an entirely new spectrum of workers to develop new skills—women in particular—and enable them to become more productive so that they will achieve an economic level at which leisure time will become available to them.

The increasing complexity of our American lifestyle often gives us time and labor saving devices on the one hand, and imposes on us a whole new set of time-consuming tasks to be performed on the other hands, tasks such as driving the children to school or to outside school activities, entertaining the spouse's clients or boss, handling financial matters, coping with bureaucracies, paying bills, doing taxes, and so forth. It should also be noted that in the mid 1970's over half of the mothers of school-age children were working either full or part-time in addition to carrying out their home responsibilities. This change, along with readjustments in sex roles and new economic conditions, presents education with the substantial challenge of helping young and old people alike to cope with all complexities of modern life and find ways of preserving leisure in spite of innumerable demands.

7. *Ethical Character.* This principle was originally considered of paramount importance by the authors of the seven principles. In 1976, NEA panelists ranked it, if anything, as even more important. Building ethical character begins with an understanding of the need for ethical models among both young and old. Such models might be found among government leaders, leaders in labor and industry, the church, education or entertainment. But to have ethical leadership there must be a society that honors and supports or chooses worthwhile models as their leaders. The ethical development of the individual and that of the society are both evolutionary and interactive. Helping learners to build an ethical character includes providing them with a sense of respect for the institutions that give democracy meaning, respect for the human conscience, and respect for the individual human life.

This is a kind of learning which takes place not so much through teaching facts or concepts but through the process of education itself—processes in which the policies and practices of school itself exemplify the principles to be absorbed. It is primarily the present and future task of the family or other affinity group, and of the school, to provide young persons with experiences that help to create an ethical character. These two settings, the family and the school, are the milieux which do the most to strengthen or to diminish a person's ability to resist manipulation. They either nurture or undercut the ability to make decisions without confusion, and the ability to triumph over inner and outer turmoil. It is at school and at home that one either develops the talent for self direction or one learns to accept the dictates of tyranny whether it be mechanical or authoritative or the "expert" with all the answers.

As home and school guide young people in acquiring ethical character, parents and teachers need to reassess the importance of both reasoned discipline and of rules that are firm and fair, rather than harsh and arbitrary. In this process they must remember that ethical character grows from within and cannot be imposed. The success of love and guidance and discipline is demonstrated as children eventually outgrow their need for external parent-teacher control and gradually assume control over themselves.

In addition to embodying the process of respect for human values in the process of education, schools must help students actively learn how to place value on the elements of their lives. As Alvin Toffler points out in his classic FUTURE SHOCK, "Millions of people pass through the educational system without once having been forced to search out the contradictions in their own value systems or even to discuss these matters candidly with adults and peers."[9] Learning to value what is worthwhile, to examine one's lifework and lifestyle and in this context, to see relationships, to sort them out, to weigh them, and to make decisions,—all of these are necessary skills if we are to move toward an era of dynamic equilibrium in which humankind is increasingly in balance with itself and then completely in balance with the entire ecosystem.

These seven principles of education, then, as originally stated in 1918 and as reemphasized and reinterpreted in the late 70's, provide an example of how future studies builds upon our present and past in order to project the needs and alternatives of our educational future.

EXPANDED FORMS OF EDUCATION IN TOMORROW'S WORLD

The articulation of the seven cardinal principles as goals relevant to education today clearly poses a mighty challenge to us all. Certainly, the school alone cannot supply all of the educational input that the future requires.

Educators have, for years, made a distinction between *education* and *schooling.* There are some important differences between what a school can accomplish and what must be done by the schools in cooperation with a wider range of other social agencies. Unquestionably, education will be of consummate importance between now and the year 2000, but the role of the conventional school is less certain. There are two reasons for emphasizing education and examining closely the role of schools.

First, lifelong education is important because many of the social decisions with regard to worldwide problems, decisions which must be made in the next twenty years, will, perforce, be made by persons *who have already completed their schooling.* Even the oldest students who are now in high school and college are not as likely to be in positions of power in political, economic, military, industrial, and labor circles as are their adult seniors who are already out of school. These post-school age leaders and millions of other Americans and persons all over the world will have an increasing need to keep informed about a rapidly growing mass of data. This means that media other than schools, such as the press, and educational and commercial television, will be required to carry a substantial amount of responsibility for providing these people with the kind of information and insights they will need for clear thinking and sound judgments based on enlightened self-interests and an understanding of the general welfare.

There are probably tens of thousands of Americans who could talk from anywhere from an hour to a semester about the problems of the population explosion, resource depletion, world hunger and international tensions and the like. Virtually none of the information which they might provide to listeners is information that they acquired as part of their formal schooling. Rather, it has been acquired in the processes of lifelong learning. They have somehow *informed themselves* about these issues.

Furthermore, there are numerous scientific and technological developments which occur throughout life and which one has no opportunity to learn about in school. Consider, for example, that about 70% of the drugs dispensed by American pharmacists didn't even exist thirty years ago. Obviously, pharmacologists and physicians need to keep up with such changes. In different ways, each of us, regardless of profession, needs to know something about learning throughout life.

This is what we mean when we stress the importance of education as distinct from schooling per se. We are not demanding or reducing the importance of schooling; we are simply emphasizing the need for extending throughout one's lifetime (1) the learning process and (2) the individual's ability to acquire needed information.

GENERAL PREMISES FOR EDUCATIONAL CHANGE

Given the challenge as we have outlined it above, what will the educational system of the future be like? Although the details cannot be foretold precisely, the broad outlines begin to emerge when we examine the premises that will serve as the basis for change. Our premises fall into four groupings: those concerned with *goals*, with *structure*, with *process*, and with *curricular content*.

Goals

Rather than lacking goals and objectives in the past, educators have been contending with a glut of vague and conflicting goals, which sometimes has caused more energy to be spent in arguing over objectives than in achieving them. As long as a social consensus is lacking regarding what it should really accomplish, U.S. education will continue to flounder. Formulation of clearer, simplified and relevant goals will require taking into account the rapid increase in our affluence and the even greater increase in our appetites for material gains. The time has come to reassess our social, material, and educational aspirations, to determine what lifestyle our biosphere is capable of sustaining globally, and to create new, equitable, and humane aspirations towards which we can make realistic progress.

Stru‹ ture

Planning future educational structures must allow for the opportunity for universal, *earlier* childhood education. Testing, we believe, will take place from before birth to assess physical condition and, after birth, of mental development as well. Experiences may be planned for the child, beginning with birth itself, that will provide desirable cognitive and affective input. Methodical schooling should probably begin thereafter by age three. As educational agencies become increasingly aware of special problems such as child abuse and child neglect, they will offer special social services to children as young as age two. Parent education must be a major ingredient in any early childhood program to ensure good "parenting" and coordination of school-family relations.

Emphasis throughout the child's schooling should be on a "personlized" program, as discussed above. Structurally, this will mean the gradual demise of the K-6 model of school organization or others using arbitrary, age-based grade levels. Rather, ability, motivation and readiness will determine where each learner will function best, and when and where teaching and learning should take place. How these experiences are structured should not be bound by either the school's walls or by our preconceived ideas of what should be learned at a given age.

These principles apply not only in early childhood education but throughout the elementary, middle and secondary school years, and on into adult life, including both the "young old" between 65 and 75 and the "frail old" of 75+ years. Lockstep movement up the steps of a regimented curriculum will give way to unbroken progress through a continuum of the seamless curriculum. At the secondary and post-secondary levels, this would involve abandonment of many rigid requirements for admission, graduation, and the like, along with careful guidance of the individual student, and in-service programs to help teachers rethink their functions independently of semester time-frames and strict subject matter parameters.

On the international level, instructional programs will begin more widely to be developed in all nations to address the need not only for universal literacy and basic skills but for ongoing adult education, particularly vocational preparation and membership in a global community. Widespread unemployment among the unskilled in the U.S. and overseas will add to the urgency of such programs. Even where unemployment is less severe, adults of all ages will face the necessity of keeping well informed, of often holding a sequence of different jobs that require learning new skills, of adjusting to post-retirement careers, and of having more leisure time for learning throughout their adult years, even into old age.

Process

The new structures suggested above will result not only from changing needs of the population, but also from a growing recognition on the part of educators that *how* we teach may be of coordinate importance with *what* we teach. The trend to stress the *process* of learning along with the *content* of the curriculum will grow stronger as schools provide students with carefully planned opportunities to experience processes that will prepare them for living. Teachers will recognize that students learn best when their experiences are at least partly self-directed rather than imposed by someone else. Learning situations obviously can be designed to allow students to work closely with others on matters of common concern, to clarify and refine their interpersonal relationships; to deepen their understanding of what is involved in a collaborative project, and to gain satisfaction from contributing to group activities.

Schools for living in the 21st century will no longer be considered merely dispensaries of truth, and education will not be construed merely as knowing a body of "answers." Rather, students will be encouraged to ask appropriate questions, and to engage in the process of exploring an issue creatively and in the context of carefully acquired, accurate information or data. True learning will focus less on knowing facts and more on the ability to interpret, judge, and place value upon them. Teachers can aid tremendously in this kind of learning by realizing the extent to which their own body language and expressions communicate their feelings and values. Phrased in another way, teachers will be able to reduce the amount of *manipulative* interaction in the school as they clarify their own values, attitudes and hidden agendas, and allow students objectively to assess and accept or reject them.

It is also becoming necessary for the teaching profession of the future to recognize and to respect the uniqueness of each learner and to allow for a wide range of performance from all. Success and failure need to be defined in terms of individual achievement, not by comparison with others. Good instruction thus becomes personal rather than individual. Classical *individualized* instruction was designed to emphasize speedy learning and high performance on standardized or norm-referenced tests, but *personalized* instruction recognizes the individual uniqueness of each learner and is designed to allow each one to attain whatever competency level is possible without premature or unreasonable pressures. Personalized teaching, by the way, does not imply a lack of standards, but it does recognize that all learners follow unique physical, social, and academic developmental patterns.

Curriculum

Basic communication skills such as the ability to handle the written and spoken word and to deal with number concepts will remain not an essential part of the curriculum but matters of increasing importance. Interdisciplinary learning, it seems likely, will be stressed as will the art of comprehending and anticipating complex relationships. As fields of knowledge expand rapidly and become more closely interassociated, multi-disciplinary solutions to problems will become increasingly necessary. Traditional instructional methods seem certain to expand to include greater stress on problem-solving and decision-making skills. These skills flow naturally from the process of giving children a fuller picture of world realities not only in their immediate communities but on a worldwide basis. As children become acquainted with these realities, they must begin to sense that there are alternatives open to them, in the classroom, in the careers they are planning, and in a broader setting for all human kind. Education needs to provide children with the ability to identify needs and alternative solutions, and then to analyze each alternative in the light of its consequences.

Each choice one makes with respect to alternatives has both desirable and undesirable consequences, which must be weighed and balanced. One of the factors which will determine the way we assess future alternatives available to us is our value system. Education for valuing, therefore, is an important part of teaching students the decision-making process. Once alternatives have been identified and assessed, it becomes timely to choose and to implement the more promising, socially desirable choices. Part of being an educated person, then, means learning to understand, both (1) how one structures one's decisions and (2) what kind of information one must acquire in order to make reasoned, responsible choices and then act upon them.

The need for additional vocational education, as mentioned earlier, provides a good example of how decision-making skills actually can be taught in the context of vocational guidance. Young men and women can be helped to see not only what they possess as personal qualities, their own skills and aptitudes, but also the alternative occupations available to them in society. They are able thereafter to generate alternatives and to predict consequences of each occupation choice available to them. It is possible for them to make a final choice and pursue it as a concrete means of learning the decision-making process. This is a process which is repeated over and over again, both individually and culturally and on a worldwide scale as we go about the tasks of conceiving and then building the future.

The kind of future-oriented education of which we speak is one that *helps to build creativity* in the best sense of the word. Creativity enables us to lead a life that readily adapts itself to changing times and to express ourselves through esthetic impulses. This is the power that will help to shape the world in creative ways, many as yet unthought of, rather than simply having recourse to the past by merely projecting present methods into the future.

With regard to specific subject areas of the curriculum, it should be recognized that a sound liberal education will also be inherently vocational in the years ahead. Conversely, good vocational or occupational education should be more thoroughly permeated by the content of a general or liberalizing curriculum. In approaching other specific subject areas, students must be taught the concept of alternative futures, so that looking at each discipline separately and in conjunction with one another, students may be able to contemplate what emerges as the more desirable images of tomorrow's possible world. It is from this image that they repeatedly gain a sense of changing goals and of the motivating spirit of "human community" that are needed to serve as guides to action.

An interdisciplinary approach is necessary in the subject matter fields also so that education better can serve to provide students with a deeper understanding of contemporary threats to the biosphere. Youth must be taught to value useful service to society as we seek to restore and to maintain the environment. And they must understand the necessity for restoring a dynamic equilibrium between human beings and the environment. Work in the social studies, then, should be redesigned in order to promote a grasp of human geography and of planetary cultures as they exist today and as they may promote desirable alternative futures.

In studying possible futures, the natural and physical sciences, both in content and methodology, should serve as illustrations of truth-validating inquiry. Not all students need to master the sciences as systematized knowledge, because not all will be professional scientists and such scientific knowledge now becomes obsolete quickly. However, all young learners *do* need to acquire lifelong habits of thinking, inquiring, and acting that reflects the methodology of prudent scientific thought. In teaching the symbolic sciences, such as foreign language, language arts, linguistics and mathematics, future stress must be placed not only upon basic communication skills; learners also need to acquire the ability to recognize propaganda, shoddy advertising, and the dangers in political double talk. Education, we stress, needs to emphasize the art of communicating ideas clearly and the ability to analyze and enjoy what is seen, heard, and read in a world rich in the symbols of language.

BY WAY OF SUMMARY: SOME PROBLEMS AND DILEMMAS OF THE FUTURE

Among the many complex problems discussed and implied in this chapter already, three deserve a final comment which also serves as a broad summary of the ideas presented in the final chapter. These are the challenge of motivating youth today and in coming years, the challenge of equity, and the concept of neoculturation.

Finding New Motivation for Youth

If we are to prepare persons to live in a changing world, it will be necessary to recognize and to counterbalance some of the aimlessness and negative attitudes common in many of today's youth. Motivating young people has become an increasingly fascinating challenge to persons on the elementary level and particularly at the secondary and post-secondary levels. One hundred years ago, young people often had to look after themselves. They worked in mines and factories for up to 14 hours and sometimes beginning as early as eight years of age. Today, however, U.S. child labor laws, aid to dependent children, and a variety of social innovations have mitigated for both youths and adults, some of the dangers, fears, and challenges which existed during those years of fading memory. Society now tends to assume greater responsibility for many of its needy, even when they do not contribute directly or indirectly to society. Laudable as many of the social measures may be, one of their results is that many of our less gifted or less motivated youth are apt to be tempted to dawdle along life's roads, enjoying themselves but without engaging in fully productive activities.

There are other youths, however, who are bright and have considerable drive but who—in one sense—unfortunately are clever enough to look ahead over the next twenty years and recognize that there may not be enough affluence to go around. They are aware that we may have reached the socially acceptable limits of material growth and this insight is understandably discouraging to them.

To use a simple old analogy, it is possible that youth in the next twenty years will be motivated by neither the club nor the carrot. The club of fear of survival has been removed by humane policies and at the same time, the carrot of self aggrandizement, of achieving "equality with the upper ten percent," has been diminished. Therefore, as we contemplate learning at the end of the twentieth century, a primary challenge of education is to find new sources of motivation, and to aid young people in discovering sound, future-focused role images which they can create for themselves or observe and emulate.

The Challenge of Equity

As John Rawls,[10] has pointed out, there are two basic principles of justice. Persons (1) have equal citizenship rights in a democracy and presumably (2) should have equality of opportunity. According to Rawls, all social values such as liberty and opportunity are to be distributed equally *unless an unequal distribution* with respect to these values is to everyone's advantage.[11] An *equitable* education, therefore, may not be a merely *equal* one. Justice may best be served by providing different treatment for the gifted, the handicapped, the culturally different.

On the other hand, one must ask whether special provisions for people with special needs discriminates against the "average" or "normal" persons, who do not receive any extra attention. (This basic issue was involved in the Bakke case on which an opinion was handed down by the Supreme court during 1978). Education in the future will require a very careful study of the real meaning of equity and equality and of what can be attained in a transitional society with finite resources—for example in providing education for all handicapped children as noted earlier in the chapter.

Toward Neoculturation

Shirley Engle and Wilma Longstreet in the 1978 ASCD YEARBOOK[12] present a thoughtful and provocative chapter on Education for a Changing Society. They point out that traditionally the function of education has been "enculturation," that is, a process by means of which an individual learns the traditional content of the society or culture of which he is a part. Through education, the student absorbs the values and lifestyles of his culture.

However, Engle and Longstreet[13] go on to question whether or not our transitional society has the right to formulate lifestyles for generations yet to come. This view brings to mind the thought that perhaps we should begin to think of the function of education not as providing continued *en*culturation, but an approach involving *neo*culturation. This concept suggests opening the curriculum so that the student, rather than being locked into the past, is urged to explore more and new ways to move with confidence into the future. Unquestionably, these doorways to tomorrow would lead to the acquisition of substantive knowledge, but neoculturation would be a less haphazard kind of education than that associated, since the turn of the present century, with various elective systems. Neoculturation tends to unify learning as a process of exploration in which the young acquire ideas and concepts and at the same time gain awareness of the strategies required to carry them out in the period of social change. The challenging task is finding ways to do so while time remains to brighten the human prospect for life not just in a new century but in a new millennium.

NOTES

1. Alvin Toffler (ed.), LEARNING FOR TOMORROW. New York: Random House, 1974, p. 3.
2. Much of the information in this chapter is based upon 15 years of future studies by the author. These include in-depth study of futurism for the United States Office of Education in 1973; funded research by the Danforth Foundation during 1974 and 1975; and a study of the future and its educational implications sponsored by the National Education Association and published in 1977.
3. See Harold G. Shane, THE EDUCATIONAL SIGNIFICANCE OF THE FU-TURE, Bloomington, Indiana: Phi Delta Kappa Foundation, 1973, p. 1.
4. Edward Cornish and Associates, THE STUDY OF THE FUTURE. Washington, D.C.: The World Future Society, 1977, p. 258.
5. For details, see the NEA report, CURRICULUM CHANGE TOWARD THE 21st CENTURY. Washington, D.C.: The NEA, 1977. Among the panelists: Ben Bloom, Lawrence Cremin, David Rockefeller, Jonas Salk, Theodore Hesburgh, Norman Cousins, Elise Boulding, Helvi Sipila, Robert Havighurst, Studs Terkel, Ralph Tyler.
6. The actual report appeared in 1977 as CURRICULUM CHANGE TOWARD THE 21st CENTURY. See bibliography.
7. *Ibid.*, p. 50.
8. Estimate by research specialist Fabian Linden, cited in TIME, 112:57, August, 1978.
9. Toffler, *ibid.*, p. 417.
10. John Rawls, A THEORY OF JUSTICE. Cambridge, Mass.: The Belknap Press of Harvard University Press, 1971. Pp. 60–61.
11. *Ibid.*, p. 62.
12. Shirley H. Engle and Wilma S. Longstreet, "Education for a Changing Society," in J. J. Jelinek (ed.), IMPROVING THE HUMAN CONDITION. Washington, D.C.: The Ass'n for Curriculum Development, 1978. Pp. 226–259.
13. *Ibid.*, p. 238.

REFERENCES

The books by Brown, Cornish, and Dickson were chosen to provide the reader with an overview of the field of futures study. The other five volumes present the futurist style of conceptualizing the curriculum.

Brown, Lester, R., *The twenty-ninth day.* New York: W. W. Norton & Company, Inc., 1978.
Cornish, Edward, *The study of the future.* Washington, D.C.: World Future Society, 1977.
Dickson, Paul, *The future file.* New York: Rawson Associates, Publishers, Inc., 1977.
Kauffman, Draper, L., Jr., *Teaching the future.* Palm Springs, California: ETC Publica-

tions, 1976.

Orlosky, Donald E., and B. Othanel Smith, *Curriculum development: Issues and insights.* Chicago: Rand McNally College Publishing Company, 1978.

Shane, Harold G., *The educational significance of the future.* Bloomington, Indiana: Phi Delta Kappa Educational Foundation, 1973.

Shane, Harold Gray, *Curriculum change toward the 21st century.* Washington, D.C.: The National Education Association, 1977.

Toffler, Alvin, and others, *Learning for tomorrow.* New York: Vintage Books, 1974.

Name Index

Thomas, S., 132, 139
Thoresen, C. E., 326, 329
Thorndike, E. L., 304, 305
Toffler, Alvin, 387, 402
Trump, J. Lloyd, 350
Tucker, R. D., 338

Valett, R., 268

Walberg, H., 132, 139
Walker, H. M., 319
Wallechinsky, D., 47
Walton, Frank, 208
Washbourne, Carleton, 3
Wasik, B. H., 322
Watson, John B., 305, 307
Weber, Lillian, 111, 135
Webster, W. J., 307
Weinstein, G., 257
Wessler, R., 273

Wheelis, Allen, 286
White, M. A., 323
Whitehead, A. N., 103
Whittington, Richard, 207
Williams, J. E., 340
Williams, K. P., 333
Williams, R. L., 339
Wilson, Margaret, 159
Wilson, S. H., 339
Winne, P. H., 318
Wirt, William A., 3, 110
Wolf, M., 306, 316
Wolfe, J., 273
Wood, Fred W., 65
Woodring, Paul, 22

Yussen, S. R., 335

Zami, L. P., 329
Zunin, L. M., 286

Subject Index

419

THE BOOK MANUFACTURE

Alternative Educational Systems was typeset at Auto-Graphics, Inc., Monterey Park, California, and was printed and bound at George Banta Company, Inc., Menasha, Wisconsin. The cover design was by Jane Rae Brown, Chicago, Illinois. The type is Palatino.